THE AGE OF DIGNITY

Human dignity is one of the most challenging and exciting ideas for lawyers and political philosophers in the twenty-first century. Even though it is rapidly emerging as a core concept across legal systems, and is the first foundational value of the European Union and its overarching human rights commitment under the Lisbon Treaty, human dignity is still little understood and often mistrusted. Based on extensive comparative and cross-disciplinary research, this path-breaking monograph provides an innovative and critical investigation of human dignity's origins, development and above all its potential at the heart of European constitutionalism today. Grounding its analysis in the connections among human dignity, human rights, constitutional law and democracy, this book argues that human dignity's varied and increasing uses point to a deep transformation of European constitutionalism. At its heart are the construction and protection of constitutional time, and the multi-dimensional definition of humanity as human beings, citizens and workers. Anchored in a detailed comparative study of case law, including the two European supranational courts and domestic constitutional courts, especially those of Germany, the United Kingdom, France and Hungary, this monograph argues for a new understanding of European constitutionalism as a form of humanism.

The Age of Dignity

Human Rights and Constitutionalism in Europe

Catherine Dupré

•HART•
PUBLISHING
OXFORD AND PORTLAND, OREGON
2018

Hart Publishing
An imprint of Bloomsbury Publishing Plc

Hart Publishing Ltd
Kemp House
Chawley Park
Cumnor Hill
Oxford OX2 9PH
UK

Bloomsbury Publishing Plc
50 Bedford Square
London
WC1B 3DP
UK

www.hartpub.co.uk
www.bloomsbury.com

Published in North America (US and Canada) by
Hart Publishing
c/o International Specialized Book Services
920 NE 58th Avenue, Suite 300
Portland, OR 97213-3786
USA

www.isbs.com

First published in hardback, 2015
Paperback edition, 2018

British Library Cataloguing-in-Publication Data
A catalogue record for this book is available from the British Library.

ISBN: PB: 978-1-50992-001-3
HB: 978-1-84946-103-0

Typeset by Compuscript Ltd, Shannon
Printed and bound in Great Britain by
Lightning Source UK Ltd

To Stephen

Acknowledgements

Another book, another decade gone by.[1] Although this book was not written as a sequel to the first one, the developments in constitutional practice have confirmed both the significance of human dignity for European constitutionalism and the necessity of understanding and constructing this concept in an explicit and transparent manner. The reflection and work leading to this book have stretched over many years, during which I benefitted from the invaluable support of a number of institutions, which I gratefully acknowledge here. At the very start of this project, the European University Institute awarded me a Jean Monnet Research Fellowship (2002–03); in 2009 the British Academy funded a visit to the Max Planck Institute for Comparative Public Law and International Law in Heidelberg;[2] and the Leverhulme Trust awarded me a 10-month Research Fellowship (2010–11),[3] without which this book would not have come to light.

I further benefitted from the kindness and perceptive comments of colleagues who read draft chapters. In a rough chapter order, they are Otto Pfersmann, Matthias Mahlmann, John Williams, Antoine Lyon-Caen, Garrett Barden, Günter Frankenberg, Cesare Pinelli and Mark Tushnet. In addition, I am also grateful to Lee Swepston (formerly of the International Labour Organization), who brought the ILO into my field of vision, and to Robert Estier for sharing his expertise in French political history. My reflection on human dignity and the development of this project have been tested by two sets of events taking place when I was writing this book: the constitutional reform in Iceland and the adoption of the Fundamental Law in Hungary. My thanks go to Ágúst Thór Árnason (University of Akureyri, Member of the Constitutional Committee) for discussing the constitutional drafting process with me and inviting me to talk about dignity in Iceland at the time, and to Kriszta Kovács and Gábor Attila Tóth for involving me in the Hungarian discussions. Last but definitely not least, Richard Hart's support went far beyond the publication contract that he offered me in 2010; his initial enthusiasm and his encouragement towards the end gave me the sense of home I needed to undertake and complete this project.

[1] C Dupré, *Importing the Law in Post-communist Transitions: The Hungarian Constitutional Court and the Right to Human Dignity* (Oxford, Hart Publishing, 2003).

[2] BA Small Grant SG54219.

[3] RF/8/RFG/2010/0228.

One of the difficulties of this work has been to gather relevant materials documenting legal developments and discussions stretching across the whole of the European Union, its (selected) Member States and ECHR case law, together with scholarly analysis. Another difficulty has been to keep track of the fast pace of human dignity developments in case law, constitutional codification and academic literature. It is therefore with a cautious sense of achievement that I am happy to state that this book reflects the legal developments and academic discussion of human dignity and European constitutionalism at the time of writing these lines, with the latest and last addition being Aharon Barak's book that he very kindly sent to me.[4]

This book is dedicated to the first of my readers, Stephen Skinner, who helped me make it through to the end.

Truro, 27 January 2015

[4] A Barak, *Human Dignity: The Constitutional Value, The Constitutional Right* (Cambridge, Cambridge University Press, 2015).

Short Table of Contents

Full Table of Contents

Table of Cases

Chronological Order

European Court of Human Rights

ECJ/CJEU

German Federal Constitutional Court

France

UK

Ireland—High Court

1

Introduction

I. THE RISE OF DIGNITY

IF THE TWENTIETH century marked for some the end of history and of human rights, the twenty-first century definitely seems to be the century of human dignity, a concept that has become ubiquitous, attracting a significant amount of scholarly attention across a range of disciplines. Heralding the beginning of a new era in international human rights protection in 1948[1] and long the distinctive hallmark of West German post-war constitutionalism,[2] dignity now appears to have become a global concept, taking root in codified constitutions and blossoming in the fertile soil of human rights adjudication.[3] This expansion is arguably related to two tectonic shifts that have affected constitutionalism and human rights at the turn of the century. One is the profound questioning of the familiar and established boundaries of human life and death that were triggered by new biotechnologies, such as medically assisted procreation, pre-implantation diagnosis in order to screen 'defective' human embryos, the possibility of keeping death

[1] Article 1 of the UN Universal Declaration of Human Rights was the first codification of human dignity in such explicit connection with human rights; it reads: 'all human beings are born free and equal in dignity and rights. They are endowed with reason and conscience and should act towards one another in a spirit of brotherhood'. The influence of this Article in the subsequent spread of human dignity world-wide should not be underestimated; however, it is not the only, nor perhaps the main, reason for the rise of dignity in the field of constitutionalism and human rights. Generally see P Capps, *Human Dignity and the Foundation of International Law* (Oxford, Hart Publishing, 2009).

[2] The literature on dignity in German law is vast and will be referred to as relevant in this book. Key introductory references include: Horst Dreier, 'Human Dignity in German Law' in M Düwell, J Braarvig, R Brownsword and D Mieth (eds), *The Cambridge Handbook of Human Dignity* (Cambridge, Cambridge University Press, 2014) 375–85; M Mahlmann,'The Basic Law at 60: Human Dignity and the Culture of Republicanism' (2010) 11 *German Law Journal* 9; and DP Kommers, *The Constitutional Jurisprudence of the Federal Republic of Germany* (Durham, NC, Duke University Press, 1997).

[3] C McCrudden, 'Human Dignity and Judicial Interpretation of Human Rights' (2008) 19 *European Journal of International Law* 655; LR Barroso, 'Here, There and Everywhere: Human Dignity in Contemporary Law and in the Transnational Discourse' (2012) 35 *Boston College International and Comparative Law Review* 332; E Daly, *Dignity Rights: Courts, Constitutions and the Worth of the Human Person* (Philadelphia, PA, University of Pennsylvania Press, 2013); and D Shultziner and GE Carmi, 'Human Dignity in National Constitutions: Functions, Promises and Dangers' (2014) 62 *American Journal of Comparative Law* 461.

artificially at bay with so-called life support machines, and the (near) possibility of producing human clones. In response to these disquieting and exciting possibilities, human dignity soon seemed a self-evident tool that could be used by scholars and scientists alike in an attempt to chart a course through these new territories in order to distinguish right from wrong.[4] The second tectonic shift that has triggered the rise of human dignity is arguably the process of democratisation, particularly after decades of Communism in Central and Eastern Europe and of Apartheid in South Africa. The latter's impact on human dignity has been extremely far-reaching, affecting both human rights adjudication and constitutional justice in South Africa,[5] as well as propelling onto the world stage of the English-speaking academe, a concept that had until then largely been discussed within the fairly closed boundaries of German law. As these boundaries have become increasingly porous,[6] so has the awareness of human dignity and its potential in human rights adjudication grown. Despite evidence of human dignity's crucial role in laying liberal foundations for democracy after dictatorship,[7] codification of human dignity in post-communist constitutions at first attracted little attention among Anglophone academics, but has now become a regular feature of dignity studies, being relied on as further evidence of the concept's inflationary use in constitutional case law, with its specific contextual significance often being largely missed.[8]

The codification of human dignity under Article 1 of the European Union Charter of Fundamental Rights ('EU Charter') in 2000 at the Nice summit ('Human dignity is inviolable, it must be respected and protected') marked both the end of the 1990s and the beginning of the new century, as well as arguably of a new stage in human dignity's uses and development. As one of the first visible manifestations of the linkage among human rights, human dignity and constitutionalism at the European supranational level, Article 1 clearly signalled that human dignity had left the realm of post-dictatorial transitions and the narrow and more technical field of bioethics.

[4] For the United Kingdom, see D Beyleveld and R Brownsword, 'Human Dignity, Human Rights and Human Genetics' (1998) 61 *Modern Law Review* 661. Generally see R Andorno, 'Human Dignity and Human Rights as Common Ground for a Global Ethics' (2009) *Journal of Medicine and Philosophy* 1; and G Frankenberg, *Autorität und Integration, Zur Grammatik von Recht und Verfassung* (Frankfurt am Main, Suhrkamp, 2003) 283–95.

[5] L Ackermann, *Human Dignity: Lodestar for Equality in South Africa* (Cape Town, Juta & Co, 2012); and D Cornell *et al* (eds), *The Dignity Jurisprudence of the Constitutional Court of South Africa: Cases and Materials* (New York, Fordham University Press, 2013).

[6] In this respect the publication in English of German studies on human dignity certainly has contributed to raising awareness of this concept in English-speaking academia. See references above for examples.

[7] C Dupré, *Importing the Law in Post-communist Transitions: The Hungarian Constitutional Court and the Right to Human Dignity* (Oxford, Hart Publishing, 2003).

[8] Christopher McCrudden first raised this with reference to my work in his seminal paper of 2008, above n 3. Subsequent references were made in the work of Barroso and of Daly, above n 3.

The subsequent discussions about the positioning of the EU Charter within the Treaty Establishing a Constitution for Europe were perhaps the second visible manifestation of the importance of the dignity and human rights commitment for the overall constitutional and political identity of the European Union.[9] Yet this was only the tip of the dignity iceberg and a closer look quickly reveals the pervasive codification of human dignity at all normative levels in Europe, particularly in Member States' constitutions, in the Conventions of the Council of Europe and its prolific use in case law, both at national and supranational levels, notably by the European Court of Human Rights (ECtHR), according to whom protecting human dignity and human freedom is the essence of the European Convention on Human Rights (ECHR).[10]

With the coming into force of the Lisbon Treaty (TEU) in December 2009, human dignity has not only become the first right and principle under Article 1 EU Charter, it is also the very first foundational value of the EU under Article 2 TEU.[11] This prominent position acknowledges the EU's renewed interest in human rights and, according to the EU Charter Preamble, its commitment 'to place the individual at the heart of its activities'. Such codification at the EU's highest normative level is all the more significant in that it echoes, and arguably endorses, a similarly strong dignity commitment that has gradually been enshrined in almost all Member States since the end of the Second World War. Despite this normative prominence, however, the precise meaning of human dignity and its full significance for European constitutionalism remain to be clarified. Constitutional texts, including the TEU, offer no elaboration beyond asserting dignity's inviolability and its foundational role in relation to human rights and democracy. While turning to constitutional case law in search of a meaning may at first seem a suitable way of seeking to understand human dignity, re-constructing a clear meaning for the concept only out of its case law soon proves to be not only a difficult, but also an elusive task.

2009 can therefore be seen as a paradoxical stage in dignity's development, whereby its normative status has never been so strong while its semantic status has never been less clear, due to the lack of sufficient case

[9] C Dupré, 'Dignité dans l'Europe constitutionnelle: entre inflation et contradictions' in J Ziller (ed), *L'Européanisation des droits constitutionnels à la lumière de la Constitution pour l'Europe* (Paris, L'Harmattan, 2003) 121–35.

[10] *SW v United Kingdom*, Application no 20166/92, ECtHR, 22 November 1995. See also the PhD thesis of B Maurer, *Le principe du respect de la dignité humaine dans la Convention Européenne des Droits de l'Homme* (Paris, La Documentation Française, 1999).

[11] Article 2 TEU reads: 'The Union is founded on the values of respect for human dignity, freedom, democracy, equality, the rule of law and respect for human rights, including the rights of persons belonging to minorities. These values are common to the Member States in a society in which pluralism, non-discrimination, tolerance, justice, solidarity, and equality between women and men prevail'.

law at the EU level and the limited amount of scholarly studies of human dignity as a European concept.[12] In English, studies of dignity's significance in the EU can still be counted on the fingers of one hand.[13] This book therefore aims to fill this gap by addressing the mystery of the foundation of European constitutionalism and its human rights in a concept characterised by an exceptional normative strength, namely, its inviolability.

II. POSITIONING HUMAN DIGNITY AT THE HEART OF EUROPEAN CONSTITUTIONALISM

The scarcity of scholarly studies of human dignity in a European perspective may not be due entirely to the apparent novelty of a concept only brought to the fore of EU law since 2009, to take the coming into force of the Lisbon Treaty as giving it greatest visibility. Human dignity is a notoriously difficult concept to grasp and to define, indeed understanding it is arguably such a scholarly challenge that the best we can hope for might be a fragmented and partial picture. At a complex crossroads of many disciplines, including history of ideas, philosophy, theology, sociology, political theory and law, we might have to contend with the kaleidoscopic picture typically constructed by edited collections of essays.[14] The global appeal and uses of human dignity

[12] See, eg and primarily in German: M Borowsky, 'Würde des Menschen' in MJ Meyer (ed), *Kommentar zur Charta der Grundrechte der europäischen* Union, 4th edn (Baden-Baden, Nomos Verlag, 2014) 1–124. See also the thesis of Katrin Schwarzburg, *Die Menschenwürde im Recht der europäischen Union* (Baden-Baden, Nomos, 2012). Studies of dignity with a limited comparative scope include G Bognetti, 'The Concept of Human Dignity in European and US Constitutionalism' in G Nolte (ed), *European and US Constitutionalism* (Cambridge, Cambridge University Press, 2005) 85–107; I Gutiérrez-Gutiérrez, 'Die Menschenwürde als europäischer Verfassungsbegriff—Rechtsvergleichender und verfassungsrechtlicher Beitrag zur deutschen Debatte um die Menschenwürde' (2006) 89 *Kritische Vierteljahreschrift für Gesetzgebung und Gesellschaft* 384; M Di Ciommo, *Dignità Umana e Stato Costituzionale* (Florence, Passigli Editori, 2010). In his book, Aharon Barak surveys the uses of dignity in US, Canadian, German, South African and Israeli constitutional law, dedicating a separate chapter to each country: *Human Dignity: The Constitutional Value and the Constitutional Right* (Cambridge, Cambridge University Press, 2015).

[13] J Jones, '"Common Constitutional Traditions": Can the Meaning of Human Dignity under German Law Guide the European Court of Justice?' (2004) *Public Law* 167; and 'Human Dignity in the EU Charter of Fundamental Rights and before the European Court of Justice' (2012) 33 *Liverpool Law Review* 281. See also C Dupré, 'Article 1: Human Dignity' in S Peers, T Hervey, J Kenner and A Ward (eds), *The EU Charter of Fundamental Rights: A Commentary* (Oxford, CH Beck/Hart Publishing/Nomos, 2014) 3–24.

[14] See, eg S Marcus Helmons (ed), *Dignité humaine et hiérarchie des valeurs: les limites irréductibles* (Brussels, Bruylant, 1999); D Kretzmer and E Klein (eds), *The Concept of Human Dignity in Human Rights Discourse* (The Hague, Kluwer Law International, 2002); RP Kraynak and G Tinder (eds), *In Defense of Human Dignity: Essays for Our Times* (Notre Dame, University of Notre Dame Press, 2003); EJ Eberle (ed), *Dignity and Liberty: Constitutional Visions in Germany and the United States* (Westport, CT, Praeger, 2002). More recently see C McCrudden (ed), *Understanding Human Dignity* (Oxford, Oxford University Press, 2013); and M Düwell, J Braarvig, R Brownsword and D Mieth (eds), *The Cambridge Handbook of Human Dignity* (Cambridge, Cambridge University Press, 2014).

call for a global perspective, and a number of studies have confirmed its abundant uses, without always succeeding in fully illuminating its development. If human dignity's universalism is one of its key features, its eminently local and cultural specificity point to single-system studies as perhaps the best way to understand the concept's mysteries.[15] Finally, it may well be that human dignity's incursions into the legal field cannot be understood without first clarifying its philosophical[16] and theological[17] dimensions.

A. European Constitutionalism: An Equilibrium of Sovereignty

The approach chosen for this study is both more modest and more ambitious. First, if we want to understand human dignity in its European dimension we arguably have to study it from a European perspective; at the same time the European scope of this study, as an intermediate level of engagement between the local and global levels, is a realistic way of making sense of this concept. This study's methodological starting point is therefore to position human dignity squarely at the heart of European constitutionalism, which includes, but is not limited to, the EU order. Following the path opened by German scholars and notably by Peter Häberle,[18] European constitutionalism is understood as including the EU and its Member States considered together.[19] The multi-layered normativity arising out of this imbrication of

[15] See, eg on France: ML Pavia and T Revet (eds), *La dignité de la personne humaine* (Paris, Economica, 1999); X Bioy, *Le concept de personne humaine en droit public* (Paris, Dalloz, 2003); C Girard and S Hennette-Vauchez (eds), *La dignité de la personne humaine: recherche sur un processus de juridicisation* (Paris, Presses Universitaires de France, 2004); on Italy: E Ceccherini (ed), *La Tutela della Dignità dell'Uomo* (Naples, Editoriale Scientifica, 2008); on the United Kingdom: D Feldman, 'Human Dignity as a Legal Value, Part I' (1999) *Public Law* 682, and 'Human Dignity as a Legal Value, Part II' (2000) *Public Law* 61. For a recent study in the German context, see C Goos, *Innere Freiheit, Eine Rekonstruktion des grundgesetzlichen Würdebegriffs* (Bonn, Bonn University Press, 2011).

[16] See, eg A Kolnai, 'Dignity' (1976) 51 *Philosophy* 251; TE Hill, *Dignity and Practical Reason in Kant's Moral Theory* (Ithaca, NY, Cornell University Press, 1992); P Tiedemann, *Menschenwürde als Rechtsbegriff: eine philosophische Klärung* (Berlin, Berliner Wissenschafts-Verlag, 2007); HJ Sandkühler (ed), *Menschenwürde: Philosophische, theologische und juristische Analysen* (Frankfurt am Main, Peter Lang, 2007); J Habermas, 'The Concept of Dignity and the Realistic Utopia of Human Rights' (2010) 41 *Metaphilosophy* 464; R Dworkin, *Justice for Hedgehogs* (Cambridge, MA, Belknap Press, 2011), ch 9; O Sensen, *Kant on Human Dignity* (Berlin, De Gruyter, 2011); and M Rosen, *Dignity: Its History and Meaning* (Cambridge, MA, Harvard University Press, 2012).

[17] See, eg J Soskice, 'Human Dignity and the Image of God' in C McCrudden (ed), *Understanding Human Dignity* (Oxford, Oxford University Press, 2013) 229–43.

[18] M Kotzur, 'Peter Häberle zum 80. Geburtstag' (2014) 139 *Archiv des öffentlichen Rechts* 287.

[19] P Häberle, *Europäische Verfassungslehre*, 6th edn (Baden-Baden, Nomos, 2009) and P Häberle, *L'État constitutionnel* (M Roffi (trans), C Grewe (ed), Aix-en-Provence, Presses Universitaires d'Aix-Marseille, 2004); see also I Pernice, 'Multilevel Constitutionalism in the European Union' (2002) 27 *European Law Review* 511 and I Pernice *et al* (eds),

constitutional orders is no doubt a significant characteristic of European constitutionalism.[20] This study, however, focuses on the dynamic interaction among constitutional orders that make up European constitutionalism,[21] as this arguably brings to the fore the role of key actors in this process who are also key actors in the construction of human dignity, namely, constitutional courts and the EU supranational court.

To this definition of European constitutionalism, this study adds another dimension, namely, the ECHR and its case law. Regardless of EU accession to the ECHR grinding to a halt due to the CJEU Opinion 2/13,[22] it is argued that European constitutionalism can only be fully understood by considering together the constitutional orders of the EU, of the ECHR and of their common Member States.[23] Historically, the Council of Europe and the European Economic Community (EEC) were arguably two sides of the same coin of democracy. The EEC was meant to help reconstruct peace and democracy after war and dictatorship through the creation of a common market; the Council of Europe was designed to promote a number of civil and political rights seen as the core of democracy through its main convention, the ECHR.

Over the years, the two supranational orders have become increasingly imbricated and are now brought closer together in a rich web of interconnections, that are beginning to attract scholarly attention.[24] The so-called Copenhagen criteria set in 1993 were perhaps the first significant sign of this increasing dynamic of integration, as the de jure requirement that candidate countries meet certain human rights standards for EU accession de facto meant that accession to the ECHR became a preliminary step toward EU membership.[25] Expectation of human rights compliance was soon to be extended to the EU itself and to its existing Member States, leading

Konstitutionalisierung jenseits des Staates: Zur Verfassung der Weltgemeinschaft und den Gründungsverträgen internationaler Organisationen (Baden-Baden, Nomos Verlag, 2002). Following in these footsteps is the more recent work of M Di Ciommo, *Dignità Umana e Stato Costituzionale* (Florence, Passigli Editori, 2010).

[20] N Walker, 'The Idea of Constitutional Pluralism in the European Union' (2002) 65 *Modern Law Review* 365; JHH Weiler and M Wind (eds), *European Constitutionalism Beyond the State* (Cambridge, Cambridge University Press, 2003).

[21] A von Bogdandy and J Bast (eds), *Principles of European Constitutional Law*, 2nd edn (Oxford, Hart Publishing, 2010) 38–39.

[22] Opinion 2/13, see S Peers, 'The EU's Accession to the ECHR: The Dream Becomes a Nightmare' (2015) 16 *German Law Journal* 214.

[23] C Dupré, 'Unconstitutional Constitutions: A Timely Concept' in A v Bogdandy and P Sonnevend (eds), *Constitutional Crisis in the European Constitutional Area: Theory, Law, Politics in Hungary and Romania* (Oxford, Hart Publishing, 2015) 351–70.

[24] K Dzehtsiarou, T Konstadinides, T Lock and N O'Meara (eds), *Human Rights Law in Europe: The Influence, Overlaps and Contradictions of the EU and ECHR* (London, Routledge, 2014).

[25] W Sadurski, *Constitutionalism and the Enlargement of Europe* (Oxford, Oxford University Press, 2012).

to the adoption of an EU-specific bill of rights, the EU Charter, in 2000, which endorsed most if not all the ECHR rights, particularly the absolute prohibitions under its Title I on Human Dignity. In the meantime, the two supranational courts gradually developed their respective case law mindful of the other's judgments.[26] What started as an informal relationship based on mutual trust has now become a formal requirement that the CJEU read the EU Charter rights corresponding to the rights guaranteed by the ECHR as having the same scope and meaning as those laid down in the Convention (under Article 52.3 EU Charter). From a political theory perspective, bringing together the two supranational orders in the construction of European constitutionalism is crucial if we consider constitutionalism as a doctrine promoting constitutional means to foster democracy and to prevent abuses of sovereignty, at whichever level it may be exercised. This, it is argued, has been a key rationale driving the post-war European construction, the aim of which is not to supersede national sovereignty by supranational sovereignty, but arguably to develop a new level of sovereignty, so that the exercise of sovereignty at one level can always be held in check by another. This can be seen in the way in which (some) constitutional courts and the European Court of Justice/Court of Justice of the European Union (ECJ/CJEU) have developed a sort of judicial dialogue through which the scope of human rights and the boundaries of sovereignty may be determined.[27] It is suggested that adding the ECHR (and its case law) complements (and perhaps completes) the construction of European constitutionalism. By joining the dots among its three normative orders, the EU, the ECHR and their common Member States, this perspective renders more visible the existing channels of communication among them, thus creating a fuller picture of European constitutionalism, and making it possible to engage in more meaningful critical discussion. Moreover, from a perspective of minimising possible abuses of sovereignty (at whichever level), balancing three levels and types of sovereignty is a more effective way of safeguarding democracy and human rights, because seeking an equilibrium among three types of sovereignty arguably promotes a more effective system of checks and balances, by avoiding possible alliances of sovereignty, without counterweight.[28] In this respect, the

[26] S Douglas-Scott, 'A Tale of Two Courts: Luxembourg, Strasbourg and the Growing European Human Rights Acquis' (2006) 43 *Common Market Law Review* 629.

[27] M Kumm, 'Who is the Final Arbiter of Constitutionality in Europe?: Three Conceptions of the Relationship between the German Federal Constitutional Court and the European Court of Justice' (1999) 36 *Common Market Law Review* 351; see also A v Bogdandy *et al*, 'Reverse So Lange: Protecting the Essence of Fundamental Rights Against EU Member States' (2012) 49 *Common Market Law Review* 489 and A Torres Perez, 'Melloni in Three Acts: From Dialogue to Monologue' (2014) *European Constitutional Law Review* 308.

[28] We have seen these alliances of sovereignty at work in the management of the Euro-crisis: C Joerges, 'Europe's Economic Constitution in Crisis and the Emergence of a New Constitutional Constellation' (2014) 15 *German Law Journal* 985.

ECHR's exclusive focus on human rights protection and its unique expertise in this field makes it an (almost) ideal third actor in the process of checks and balances of sovereignty within European constitutionalism.

Seen in this light, the codification of human dignity in foundational texts (such as the TEU and domestic constitutions) and the acknowledgment of its essential importance by the ECtHR and domestic constitutional courts alike takes its full significance. Namely, human dignity is not only the foundation of human rights and democracy in each constitutional order considered separately, it is what brings all the constitutional (at national and supranational levels) orders together, giving European constitutionalism its unique identity and dynamic. In methodological terms, studying human dignity in European constitutionalism therefore requires a critical comparative analysis of these orders considered in their dynamic interaction, by adding to the text of constitutional (or primary law) provisions their construction by judges.

B. Comparison: Mapping the Dignity Archipelago[29]

Considering the pioneering nature of this study and the almost complete absence of academic literature of a similar scope, and considering as well that doctrines or theories of European constitutionalism have so far focused mainly on the European Union, the first step in this study was to map the constitutional uses of human dignity across Europe, understood as specified above, as meaning the EU, the ECHR and their common Member States.

As the difficulties of an in-depth comparative study of 28 national systems together with two supranational systems were enough to discourage any well-seasoned comparatist, the first methodological issue that arose was therefore that of selecting a smaller range of constitutional orders, a key condition for the feasibility of this study. However, when it comes to comparison, small is not always necessarily beautiful, and in order to be meaningful, a key condition of scientific credibility was the representative quality of the selected sample of constitutional orders. The two supranational legal systems had to be included because of their essential European scope as well as, in the case of the EU, the supremacy of their norms over domestic law. Moreover, it seemed obvious that any study of human dignity in relation to European constitutionalism must include (West) Germany's construction of this concept, considering its historical role in re-building democracy and providing a basis for human rights, as well as its substantial influence on the development of human dignity at both European supranational levels.

[29] With René Char's poetry on my mind: M-C Char *et al* (eds), *Poèmes en Archipel: Anthologie de Textes de René Char* (Paris, Gallimard, 2007).

It nevertheless seemed equally clear that constructing a European meaning for human dignity could (and should) not be reduced to its German incarnations and influences alone.

The additional national systems considered here were selected on a combination of three criteria. First, the study had to consider both civil law and common law constitutional orders, so the United Kingdom had to be included so as to avoid any misconstruction of human dignity as an exclusively civil law concept. The second selection criterion proceeds from a similar spirit of inclusion and is meant to reflect the key stage in the development of European constitutionalism that post-communist transitions represented. Quantitatively, it is important to acknowledge that over one-third of the current EU Member States are former communist dictatorships; qualitatively, it is suggested that the EU enlargement to post-communist states has substantially transformed the EU. If the Treaty Establishing a Constitution for Europe was ultimately not adopted, the Lisbon Treaty retained many of its features, including the EU Charter, which has the same normative ranking as the Treaties, albeit in a separate document. From this perspective, Hungary seemed to be a good choice as it played a leading role in the post-communist transition in the region and its constitutional court developed a rich and sophisticated dignity case law in the foundational years of the transition towards democracy.[30] As it happened, and this is not a development I could have predicted when I embarked on this project, Hungary has proved to be a particularly valuable example for the study of human dignity in European constitutionalism, as it was the first EU Member State to adopt a new constitution in the twenty-first century. Its Fundamental Law, in force since 2011,[31] gives human dignity a prominent, yet disquieting, constitutional position, and could be seen as the exception confirming the general pattern constructed in this book, or (as may be the case) the beginning of a new dignity trend in European constitutionalism.[32] The third selection criterion adopted for the selection of Member States was guided by the need to include in this study constitutional orders which, despite not having codified human dignity in their constitution, have discovered and constructed this concept in relation to human rights through constitutional adjudication, an

[30] C Dupré, *Importing the Law in Post-communist Transitions: The Hungarian Constitutional Court and the Right to Human Dignity* (Oxford, Hart Publishing, 2003).

[31] GA Tóth (ed), *Constitution for a Disunited Nation: Hungary's New Fundamental Law* (Budapest, Central European University Press, 2012); I Pogany, 'The Crisis of Democracy in East Central Europe: The "New Constitutionalism" in Hungary' (2013) 19 *European Public Law* 341; and L Sólyom, 'Normenhierarchie in der Verfassung und verfassungswidrige Vefassungsänderungen' (2014) 55 *Jahrbuch für Ostrecht* 11. Generally see J Stolz, *Hongrie: apprentie sorcière du nationalisme* (Paris, Éditions du Cygne, 2012) and P Lendvai, *Hungary Between Democracy and Authoritarianism* (London, Hurst & Company, 2012).

[32] C Dupré, 'Human Dignity: Rhetoric, Protection, and Instrumentalisation' in GA Tóth (ed), *Constitution for a Disunited Nation: On Hungary's 2011 Fundamental Law* (Budapest, Central European University Press, 2012) 143–70.

alternative to formal constitutional codification. France seemed to be a suitable example of this approach for the purpose of this study:[33] an exception to the otherwise general post-war and post-dictatorship approach to human dignity, France chose to enshrine human dignity neither in its 1946 Constitution, nor in the 1958 Constitution. Thus, it provides a valuable example of human dignity as a purely judge-made constitutional concept in the context of a civil law legal system. This study is therefore primarily anchored in a close analysis of German, UK, Hungarian and French constitutional constructions of human dignity (for the domestic constitutional orders), combined with the EU and the ECHR, together with their respective case law. This study is not, however, limited to these constitutional orders and I have tried as much as possible to consider other Member States, including Italy, Belgium, Spain, Portugal, Greece and Finland.

Finally, intellectual honesty requires me to make it clear that if most constitutions in Europe enshrine human dignity, not all do so: Cyprus, Malta, the Netherlands, Denmark, Ireland (apart from the Preamble)[34] do not contain any textual reference to human dignity (at least as far as the English translation is concerned). This empirical observation would, of course, need to be checked further by a careful examination of the case law of these systems, which have fallen outside the scope of this book. For now, it is argued that this does not undermine this study's methodological soundness, nor does it undermine its overall argument. In fact, these apparently dignity-free codified constitutions might point to key features of dignity constitutionalism as discussed in this book. In particular, they may point towards the connection between dignity and republicanism; *a contrario*, constitutional monarchies, such as Denmark and the Netherlands, have not codified dignity, nor has the United Kingdom, another constitutional monarchy albeit without a codified constitution. Spain did enshrine dignity, but in that case it may be thought that the post-dictatorship context of codification was the decisive factor in choosing to do so. Moreover, dignity codification might be connected to a particular constitutional culture, as can be illustrated by some of the Nordic states, which did not codify dignity, characterised (among other factors) by limited judicial review on the grounds of human rights and a (traditionally) strong welfare state.[35] The Nordic distinction, while being important, might however not be so clear-cut. The constitutional developments in Sweden[36] and more particularly perhaps in Finland, with the codification

[33] Austria too appears to have followed the path of case law construction rather than constitutional codification: K Burger, *Das Verfassungsprinzip der Menschenwürde in Österreich* (Frankfurt am Main, Peter Lang, 2002).

[34] T Iglesias, 'The Dignity of the Individual in the Irish Constitution: The Importance of the Preamble' (2000) 89 *Studies* 19.

[35] M Scheinin (ed), *The Welfare State and Constitutionalism: Nordic Perspectives* (Århus, Phønix-Trykkeriet A/S, 2001).

[36] Sweden enshrined dignity in 1974 under Art 2 of its Instrument of Government.

of human dignity under Article 1 in 1995 and 2000, could well indicate a possible change in this approach,[37] a change that might be encouraged by the increasing normative force and scope of the EU Charter.

Overall, these dignity-free constitutions form part of this study in the sense that their existence and their different approaches to human dignity have given me food for thought, hopefully avoiding thereby an overly smooth and oversimplified construction of this concept's role in European constitutionalism. In any event, as human dignity is enshrined and developed at both supranational levels, it is argued that this concept remains valid and relevant in the context of European constitutionalism, even if it is not enshrined in every one of the Member States' constitutions.

The process of mapping human dignity in European constitutionalism started with an inventory of all such constitutional and treaty (to include the TEU and the Charter) provisions. For this purpose, I have selected only those provisions which explicitly refer to 'human dignity', rather than to some kind of functional equivalent or paraphrase for human dignity.[38] Confirming the relationship between human dignity and European constitutionalism, this gave the contours of the dignity archipelago and its main islands. Considering that textual provisions on human dignity tend to provide no elaboration on what the concept is intended to mean, including case law was the necessary second step in the process of mapping human dignity across Europe. As this study's focus was on constitutionalism, I selected constitutional case law, understood here as the case law delivered by (formal) constitutional courts, namely, the German and Hungarian constitutional courts, the UK Supreme Court (and when relevant its High Court and Court of Appeal), the French constitutional council and the supranational courts, the ECtHR, and the Court of Justice in its ECJ and CJEU incarnations.[39]

[37] The Icelandic attempt to codify human dignity in the process of constitutional revision that followed the financial collapse of its economy in 2008 might perhaps be seen from this perspective, despite the fact that the constitutional proposal was eventually dropped after the election of a new Parliament in 2011.

[38] I have used for this purpose English translations provided in the volume *Constitutions of the Countries of the World* and 'human dignity' as a key word for my search, cross-referencing my results with references I could find in scholarly commentaries. As far as I could, I have also checked the original word or phrase (in French, Italian, German, Hungarian, Spanish, Polish, Portuguese, Romanian and Greek); but where I could not do so, I have had to rely on the translation's quality and to assume that the translated phrase 'human dignity' does correspond to 'human dignity' in the original text. See more generally M Mahlmann, 'Six Antidotes to Dignity Fatigue in Ethics and Law' in C McCrudden (ed), *Understanding Dignity* (Oxford, Oxford University Press, 2013) 593, 594–96.

[39] I am not entering into discussions about the 'constitutional court' nature of the ECJ/CJEU, nor am I discussing whether it is a supreme court or a human rights court. It is chosen here as the highest court of the EU judicial order and the court which ultimately can decide on the interpretation of primary EU law, including dignity provisions, in an authoritative manner. At the time of writing and with no foreseeable prospect of EU accession to the ECHR, it

While I explain my methodology in relation to case law in more detail in Chapter 4, it is important to note three points at this introductory stage. First, I have deliberately sought to avoid two opposite approaches to studying human dignity case law that are often to be found in this concept's scholarly studies. One consists in a systematic cataloguing of all human dignity uses in case law (perhaps most clearly illustrated by German scholarship on German constitutional law), and the other consists in (in my view) a rather impressionistic survey of dignity case law, which tends to present specific human dignity rulings out of context and is perhaps most clearly illustrated in sweeping comparative surveys of human dignity considered as a global concept. Instead, and this is my second point, wherever possible I have opted for a contextual analysis of dignity case law, taking its wider setting into account, such as the positioning of a given ruling as part of a body of case law, the wider social and political context, as well as the general cultural context in which judges operate. In this respect, while the selection of constitutional orders had to be representative of what are arguably wider trends in human dignity usage across Europe, it made sense to include orders with which I had a sound degree of familiarity, due to having studied, taught about and researched them in great detail over (for some of them) more than two decades. The third and last methodological point to note in relation to case law is that I have sought to consider and present judicial construction of human dignity in the cross-European integrated dynamic that (as discussed above) is one of the key features of European constitutionalism. Readers will therefore not find a presentation and discussion of human dignity case law according to compartmentalised studies of each constitutional order considered here. Instead, I have sought to approach individual human dignity cases as forming part of a whole, assuming the interconnection of rulings—sometimes made explicit by judges' reliance on comparative law—rather than their disconnection.

Overall, this particular methodology, namely, the unique range and type of constitutional orders considered here and their contextual critical analysis, has brought to light a new picture of human dignity, confirming and illuminating its connections with European constitutionalism.[40] Mapping

seems clear that human rights adjudication is going to be a growing part of its case law and wider 'constitutional' role. Generally, see O Gerstenberg, 'Expanding the Constitution Beyond the Court: The Case of Euro-Constitutionalism' (2002) 8 *European Law Journal* 172; and J Komárek, 'National Constitutional Courts in the European Constitutional Democracy' (2014) 12 *International Journal of Constitutional Law* 525.

[40] WG Sebald, 'Conversation with Joseph Cuomo' in LS Schwarz (ed), *The Emergence of Memory: Conversations with WG Sebald* (New York, Seven Stories Press, 2007) 95: 'If you look for things that are like the things that you have looked up before, then, obviously, they'll connect up. But they'll only connect up in an obvious sort of way, which actually isn't, in terms of writing something new, very productive. So you have to take heterogeneous materials in order to get your mind to do something that it hasn't done before. That's how I thought about it. Then, of course, curiosity gets the better of you'.

the contours of an archipelago, identifying its key islands, measuring the height of its summits, the depths of its waters and charting its currents were only one part of the study of human dignity undertaken here; and as 'curiosity got the better of me',[41] making sense of their connections over time was another.

C. Constructing a Narrative

The mapping of human dignity across European constitutionalism revealed that there is much more to human dignity than its apparent 'big bang' emergence in the immediate post-war period. Therefore, central to the construction of human dignity as a constitutional concept undertaken in this study has been its positioning in a longer-term perspective in order to understand the key stages of its development. While this study draws on a number of valuable historical accounts of human dignity,[42] it does not propose a mere sequence of human dignity-relevant dates and events. Rather, what is attempted here is a narrative for human dignity in the context of European constitutionalism, namely, to reconstruct the connections among these events and to bring to light their deeper and more complex significance, and ultimately to make sense of human dignity by telling a fuller story from its origin to its current uses.[43] The narrative presented here is therefore not purely factual or historical, but is also driven by a spirit of theoretical and critical investigation into human dignity and European constitutionalism. In plain terms and above all, it is based on the methodological assumption that in order to answer the question 'what is human dignity in European constitutionalism?', one has first to address the questions of 'when?', 'where?' and 'why?'.[44] The question 'where?' is perhaps the easiest to address as it is largely answered by the normative and geographical focus on European constitutionalism, made of the components identified above in terms of constitutional orders, together with the focus on constitutional (and treaty) provisions and relevant case law as explained above. The answer to the question 'when?' is partly to be derived from the answer to the question 'where?' as far as dates are concerned, because, when it comes

[41] See Sebald, above n 40.

[42] Notably: B Giese, *Das Würde-Konzept, Eine normfunktionale Explikation des Begriffes Würde in Art.1 Abs 1 GG* (Berlin, Duncker und Humblot, 1975); and P Kondylis, 'Würde' in O Brunner, W Conze and R Koselleck (eds), *Geschichtliche Grundbegriffe, Historisches Lexikon zur politisch-sozialen Sprache in Deutschland* (Stuttgart, Klett-Cotta, 1992) vol 7, 645–77.

[43] This approach to narrative follows T Honderich, *The Oxford Companion to Philosophy*, 2nd edn (Oxford, Oxford University Press, 2005) 638.

[44] C Dupré, 'Constructing the Meaning of Human Dignity: Four Questions' in C McCrudden (ed), *Understanding Human Dignity* (Oxford, Oxford University Press, 2013) 113–22.

to constitutional codification, the two can easily be matched: 1947 (Italy); 1949 (West Germany); 1974 (Sweden); 1975 (Greece); 1976 (Portugal); 1978 (Spain); 1989 (Hungary); 1991 (Croatia, Bulgaria, Romania and Slovenia); 1992 (Estonia, Slovakia, Lithuania and Czech Republic); 1993 (Latvia); 1994 (Belgium); 1997 (Poland); 2000 (Finland);[45] 2009 (EU); and 2011 (Hungary). When it comes to case law, however, identifying relevant dates can be a less straightforward process and, as discussed in Chapter 4 in detail, some degree of intuition and intellectual re-construction may be required. What matters, however, is not just a date or chronological sequence, but dates' wider significance in political and constitutional terms. Addressing the question 'why?' then partly depends on the answer to the questions 'where?' and 'when?'. Moreover, it requires considering the question 'who?'. First are the constitution-drafters, whose individual identities are often dissolved in their group or institutional identity, to the extent that answering the question 'why?' by the question 'who?' is rarely attempted, as it often brings a partial answer.[46] The second focus is therefore on judges, whose contribution to the construction of human dignity has been decisive, and can be closely studied on the basis of their judgments, whether judicial style and culture allow for separate opinions or not. This study's third focus flows from the second in the sense that a judgment's prerequisite is a dispute involving an alleged victim of a human dignity breach. While a detailed engagement with applicants' constructions of this concept falls outside this study, it must be borne in mind that what can be called their individual dignity stories have formed an essential part in the construction of the wider narrative of human dignity as a constitutional concept.

Finally, I have sought, as much as possible, to position specific developments of European constitutionalism and of dignity case law in their wider political, social and cultural contexts, using the date of the adoption of a given constitution or of a given judgment as the first contextual indicator. The dates of constitutions pointed to contexts that were easy to identify, such as the end of the Second World War, of civil war and military dictatorship

[45] Strictly speaking, human dignity was first codified in Finland in 1995. Finland subsequently decided to streamline its constitutional norms leading to the adoption of a revised Constitution in 2000, which endorsed the dignity provisions. The date of 2000 is therefore adopted here to refer to the (latest) codification of dignity. Generally see J Husa, *The Constitution of Finland: A Contextual Analysis* (Oxford, Hart Publishing, 2011) 174–77.

[46] Beyond the *travaux préparatoires* of constitutions, this type of information tends to have been rarely recorded and even more rarely investigated, with one exception being the influence of Jacques Maritain on the drafting of the UN Universal Declaration of Human Rights. See, eg P Valadier, 'Jacques Maritain's Personalist Conception of Human Dignity' in M Düwell, J Braarvig, R Brownsword and D Mieth (eds), *The Cambridge Handbook of Human Dignity* (Cambridge, Cambridge University Press, 2014) 260–68. On the discussions leading to the German Basic Law, see for instance C Goos, *Innere Freiheit: Eine Rekonstruktion des grundgesetzlichen Würdebegriffs* (Bonn, Bonn University Press, 2011); on the adoption of the EU Charter, see M Borowsky, 'Würde des Menschen' in J Meyer (ed), *Kommentar zur Charta der Grundrechte der Europaischen Union*, 4th edn (Baden-Baden, Nomos, 2014) 1–124.

or of communist dictatorship. The inventory of constitutional provisions and case law shed new light on the two key human dignity dates, namely, 1949 as the adoption of the West German Constitution and 2009 as the coming into force of the Lisbon Treaty, showing them not to be old or recent isolated events, but as part of a complex chain of events, and indeed of a wider process constructing both dignity and European constitutionalism, thus arguably bringing to light key stages in the construction of European constitutionalism, which have also significantly shaped the development of human dignity positioned at its heart.

While this study's original aim was to reflect on this process of change and construction, it is fair to state that I could not anticipate the number of changes that have arguably shaken this apparently steady rhythm of construction, affecting most (if not all) elements included in it. Nor could I anticipate the magnitude of some of these changes, which, as it increasingly appears, are questioning some of the core assumptions at the heart of European constitutionalism, such as respect for the rule of law, democracy, human rights, as well as social peace.[47] This study of human dignity and European constitutionalism must not, however, be read as a response drafted in the heat of the moment. Rather, the whole project has been envisaged with the normal functioning of democracy and constitutionalism in mind. However, I could not ignore the growing number of crises unfolding over the duration of this project, perhaps most notably the Euro crisis, the adoption of the Hungarian Fundamental Law in 2010, and the Icelandic experience of constitutional revision which ultimately did not lead to a new constitution, but might nevertheless be seen as an emblematic development in the age of dignity.[48] It is fair to say that these crises have affected my thinking on human dignity and European constitutionalism, leading me to work these new developments into my reflection and analysis, and putting my underlying hypotheses to the test of reality, and (so far) confirming them.

III. HUMAN DIGNITY AS A CONSTITUTIONAL CONCEPT

The rise of human dignity in the field of human rights and constitutionalism has been received with a fair amount of scholarly scepticism and criticism, perhaps particularly so among Anglophone academics. Much ink has been used in discussing the precise legal nature of human dignity, namely,

[47] See, eg AJ Menéndez, 'The Existential Crisis of the European Union' (2013) 14 *German Law Journal* 454; and C Offe, 'Europe Entrapped: Does the EU have the Political Capacity to Overcome its Current Crisis?' (2013) 19 *European Law Journal* 595.

[48] ÁT Árnason, 'A Review of the Icelandic Constitution: Popular Sovereignty or Political Confusion' (2011) *Bij de Buren* 342; and H Landemore, 'Inclusive Constitution-Making: The Icelandic Experiment' (2014) *Journal of Political Philosophy* 1.

whether it is a value or a right, or perhaps both.[49] Additionally, struggling to assign to it a particular normative substance, some critics have been prompt to denounce human dignity as a useless[50] or empty[51] concept. However, little attention appears to have been paid to its 'simpler' nature as a concept, that is as a problem-solving tool of European constitutionalism. This section sets out the core methodological assumptions that have guided the construction of dignity as a constitutional concept for the purpose of this study.

A. A Heuristic Concept

The contextual and comparative approach adopted in this study has highlighted the relative novelty of the concept of human dignity, which mainly entered the field of constitutionalism in 1946–49, subsequently acquiring greater visibility due to increased constitutional codification and judicial use in the 1990s, and which was to be codified at the highest supranational level very recently, in 2009 (to take the date of entry into force of the Lisbon Treaty). Therefore, to a large extent the critique referred to above arguably reflects human dignity's novelty as a constitutional concept rather than its intrinsic uselessness or emptiness. Admittedly, the gap between constitutional codification of a phrase like 'human dignity', its development by judges on a case by case basis, and the construction of a theoretical meaning for it is wide. This study, however, is based on the methodological assumption that trying to fill this gap to the brim, that is to proceed on the expectation that human dignity can only be a useful concept if and when normatively full, is misguided. On the contrary, this study rests on the methodological assumption that human dignity is a heuristic concept,[52] the meaning of which can never be complete nor fully known. With reference

[49] GP Fletcher, 'Human Dignity as a Constitutional Value' (1984) 22 *University of Western Ontario Law Review* 171; C O'Mahony, 'There is No Such Thing as a Right to Human Dignity' (2012) 10 *International Journal of Constitutional Law* 551; and A Barak, *Human Dignity: The Constitutional Value and the Constitutional Right* (Cambridge, Cambridge University Press, 2015).

[50] R Macklin, 'Human Dignity is a Useless Concept' (2003) 327 *British Medical Journal* 1419; see also C Foster, *Human Dignity in Bioethics and Law* (Oxford, Hart Publishing, 2011), ch 4 'Dignity is Useless', 58–67.

[51] M Bagaric and J Allan, 'The Vacuous Concept of Dignity' (2006) 5 *Journal of Human Rights* 257, with a response by S Grover, 'A Response to Bagaric and Allan's "Vacuous Concept of Dignity"' (2009) 13 *International Journal of Human Rights* 615. C McCrudden also found the concept to be empty: C McCrudden, 'Human Dignity and Judicial Interpretation of Human Rights' (2008) 19 *European Journal of International Law* 655, 698; followed by PG Carozza, 'Human Dignity and Judicial Interpretation of Human Rights: A Reply' (2008) 19 *European Journal of International Law* 931.

[52] With thanks to Garrett Barden for offering me this word in the first place.

to the 1948 United Nations Universal Declaration of Human Rights, Glenn Hughes elaborates on this in the following terms:

> Something has a 'heuristic' character when it invites, and serves in, the effort of discovery. The x in an algebraic equation is a heuristic symbol, standing for a mathematical content which we do not yet know but aim to discover. Any word can be said to have heuristic meaning for us as soon as it piques our curiosity due to our awareness that, while we have some understanding of its meaning, our knowledge of that meaning is unclear or incomplete ... But some words denote concepts that are intrinsically heuristic in nature. These are concepts whose meaning-content can be increasingly grasped with successive acts of knowing, but where further significant discovery always remains possible, because the concept's meaning can never be fully understood by an existing human being.[53]

Human dignity is such 'an intrinsically heuristic' concept, and this is why in order to understand it, it is important to position it in a wider context, such as that of European constitutionalism, and to consider it in its evolution, that is as a product of successive uses in an attempt to address a number of issues and solve a number of problems. Seen from this perspective, raising the question 'why?' as suggested above becomes particularly pertinent in seeking to define human dignity as a constitutional concept. Moreover, a certain semantic malleability becomes a sign of the concept's vitality rather than of its inherent weakness. In fact, as will be discussed in this book, human dignity has only gradually acquired its current constitutional substance and significance as a result of a number of stages of transformation, each of them associated with a key question of how best to protect and promote humanity and democracy.

Accepting a certain conceptual malleability and openness is not to say, however, that human dignity has no legal definition, or that its definition is so vague or uncertain as to render it useless. Quite on the contrary, as demonstrated in this book, European constitutionalism arguably offers a very strong normative definition (human dignity is inviolable), a very precise definition (as a constellation of absolute prohibitions well established in case law since the post-war years), and a very rich definition (as developed in the case law of Member States, of the ECHR, and increasingly of the CJEU). As a result, human dignity has now acquired a distinctive constitutional meaning drawing from, but not exhausted by, its ordinary meanings or uses, such as decency and (self)-respect. For these reasons, human dignity is understood as a first order principle of European constitutionalism, akin to the rule of law and separation of powers,[54] providing both the foundation and the mechanisms to ensure its continuous development. Finally and for the sake of completeness, it is perhaps informative to note that in some

[53] G Hughes, 'The Concept of Dignity in the Universal Declaration of Human Rights' (2011) 39 *Journal of Religious Ethics* 1, 8.

[54] C Dupré, 'Human Dignity in Europe: A Foundational Constitutional Principle' (2013) 19 *European Public Law* 319.

languages and constitutions the idea of dignity has been expressed by a word that can (also) literally be translated in English by 'worth' rather than 'dignity'. This is the case notably in Sweden (Article 2)[55] and in Greece (Article 2). In relation to Greece, this ambiguity has been lifted by pointing to further textual clues in the Constitution, arguably confirming the drafters' intention to enshrine 'dignity' rather than 'value/worth'.[56]

B. A Secular Concept

The second methodological assumption underlying this study has been to consider human dignity as a secular concept. To be sure, it is a concept with deep and complex roots both in religion and in theology,[57] but for the purpose of European constitutionalism, it is argued that these religious dimensions have to be left out of the construction of human dignity as a constitutional concept. The argument for secularity has been persuasively and recently made by George Kateb in the following terms:

> Christianity teaches us that being human is a good enough (though temporary) condition for God. But we should try to do without such props; they can always give way to enlightenment. Furthermore, given the extent of suffering in human history, much of it owing to human wickedness, *God the creator has endured a perpetual legitimation crisis all through the history of theological reflection. Secularism relieves us of his burden.*[58] (emphasis added)

This argument goes further than God's legitimation crisis highlighted above;[59] a constitutional definition of human dignity, it is argued here, is

[55] Sweden has adopted both concepts of 'worth' and 'dignity' in its 1974 Constitution, which reads: 'Public power shall be exercised with respect for the equal worth (*värde*) of all and the liberty and dignity (*värdighet*) of the private person'. This choice of terms remains a little ambiguous bearing in mind that the official translation for 'dignity' under Article 1 UN Universal Declaration of Human Rights is '*värde*'. With thanks to Mattias Falk, international secretary of the Equality Ombudsman, for bringing this to my attention.

[56] See, eg Peter Häberle's observation in relation to the Greek Constitution: 'Les art. 1 et 2 de la Constitution grecque (1975) dessinent déjà un parallélisme entre la dignité humaine et la souveraineté populaire. Si l'art. 1 al. 2 dispose "La souveraineté populaire constitue le fondement du régime politique", l'al. 3 poursuit "Tous les pouvoirs émanent du peuple, existent pour lui ..." Lorsqu' ensuite l'art.2 al. 1 proclame "l'engagement fondamental" de l'État envers le respect et la protection de la dignité humaine, la souveraineté populaire et le concept de dignité humaine sont reliés entre eux dès le départ'. *L'État constitutionnel* (Aix en Provence, Presses Universitaires Aix Marseille, 2004) 145.

[57] See, eg MJ Perry, *Toward a Theory of Human Rights: Religion, Law, Courts* (Cambridge, Cambridge University Press, 2007); or J Coughlin, 'Pope John Paul II and the Dignity of the Human Being' (2003) 27 *Harvard Journal of Law and Public Policy* 65.

[58] G Kateb, *Human Dignity* (Cambridge, Belknap Press of Harvard University Press, 2011) 25. See also M Mahlmann, 'Six Antidotes to Dignity Fatigue in Ethics and Law' in C McCrudden (ed), *Understanding Dignity* (Oxford, Oxford University Press, 2013) 593, 607–8 and D Carusi, 'Laicità del Diritto e Pari Dignità delle Persone' (2009) 1 *Politica del Diritto* 93.

[59] Generally see C Taylor, *A Secular Age* (Cambridge, MA, Belknap Press of Harvard University, 2007); P Bahr and HM Heinig (eds), *Menschenwürde in der säkulären Verfassungsordnung: Rechtswissenschaftliche und theologische Perspektiven* (Tübingen, Mohr Siebeck,

ontologically incompatible with a religious definition. This incompatibility goes to the heart of European constitutionalism, which is based on the paradigm that democracy is about taking the ultimate political power away from God and his or her representative on earth to give it to human beings.[60] It is the rejection of God from the political equation that historically made it possible to turn human beings into citizens and actors in their political destiny, as opposed to subjects of a ruler whose sovereignty (and wisdom) was presented at the time as being as absolute and unquestionable as that of God. This move away from religion as the defining factor in constructing human dignity has been a gradual one that started as far back as the Renaissance, with the work of Pico della Mirandola (discussed in Chapter 2) taking its full significance, and the Enlightenment, with the French Revolution and the work of Immanuel Kant in particular, who made it possible for lawyers to think about human rights and constitution-making without making reference to God.

Historically, the rise of human dignity as a constitutional concept has paralleled the gradual fading away of God and (Christian) religion both as a legitimate source of political power and a judicial argument in human rights adjudication. In this sense, the 1948 Universal Declaration of Human Rights very deliberately broke the last ties with God or divine authority in placing the source of rights in men themselves, namely, in their dignity from birth.[61] A year later, these issues were discussed again by the drafters of the German Basic Law, who clearly opted against establishing connections between dignity and God, and chose to promote a deliberately secular concept instead.[62] More recently and at the supranational level, this approach was followed by the EU Treaty establishing a Constitution for Europe, and eventually by the Lisbon Treaty.[63]

2006); and H Hofmann, 'Die versprochene Menschenwürde' (1993) 118 *Archiv für öffentliches Recht* 357, 362.

[60] G Kateb, *Human Dignity* (Cambridge, MA, Belknap Press of Harvard University Press, 2011) 27: 'Humanity must be the judge in its own case, with all the strains and perplexities such a condition engenders. It is also the only audience or interlocutor for the discussion. There is no arbiter or sponsor. Humanity talks to itself about itself, it judges itself, it invents the questions and answers, it alone worries about human dignity. There is no appeal beyond itself. But the discussion must go on because there are certain questions that must be answered, and can only be answered by reference to the idea of human dignity. Or we can say more modestly that human dignity supplies the least unbelievable answers'.

[61] J Morsink, *The Universal Declaration of Human Rights: Origins, Drafting and Intent* (Philadelphia, PA, University of Pennsylvania Press, 1999); G Hughes, 'The Concept of Dignity in the Universal Declaration of Human Rights' (2011) 39 *Journal of Religious Ethics* 1.

[62] C Goos, *Innere Freiheit: Eine Rekonstruktion des grundgesetzlichen Würdebegriffs* (Bonn, Bonn University Press, 2011) 75–93, 88.

[63] See, eg J Weiler, *Un'Europa Cristiana* (Milan, Rizzoli, 2003) discussed by AJ Menéndez, 'A Pious Europe? Why Europe Should Not Define Itself as Christian' (2005) 30 *European Law Review* 133. To be clear and to avoid any possible misunderstanding, constructing human dignity as a secular concept does not exclude religion and religious freedom from European constitutionalism, as it is guaranteed under the ECHR and domestic constitutions.

Two exceptions can be noted to this trend, namely, the Irish Constitution of 1937 and the 2011 Hungarian Fundamental Law. The first one may be explained by its pre-war date of adoption, in addition to the strength of the Catholic religion in Ireland.[64] With regard to the second, it may be seen as the exception confirming the rule, or rather principle, of secularity in European constitutionalism; namely, by the admission of the Hungarian Prime Minister during the summer of 2014, that Hungary is becoming (and deliberately so) an 'illiberal democracy', drawing its inspiration from China and Russia rather than from the democratic heritage of European constitutionalism.[65] The Hungarian constitutional Preamble of 2011, which brought religion (mainly Catholicism in that case) back into constitutionalism[66] is a powerful reminder of the wider religious undercurrents in human rights discourse,[67] and of the temptation to turn to religion, particularly perhaps to Catholicism, in order to define human dignity in constitutional terms. The strength of academic feelings and exchange of arguments in this debate point to the difficulty of defining human dignity in purely secular terms.[68] This raises wider issues about the ability of human rights theories and of constitutionalism to provide convincing answers to the ultimate foundation of human rights and democracy, that do not rely on the argument of God or of 'Nature'.[69]

It is true that some of human dignity's more recent uses in case law have reflected instances where human beings have tried to 'play God', particularly

[64] S Moyn, 'The Secret History of Constitutional Dignity' in C McCrudden (ed), *Understanding Human Dignity* (Oxford, Oxford University Press, 2013) 95–113. In addition, it has to be noted that the English translation 'dignity' is not deprived of ambiguity as the original term in Gaelic (the authentic language of the Irish Constitution) '*uaisleacht*', might be more accurately understood as 'nobility', 'generosity', 'rank' than 'dignity'. With thanks to Garret Barden for explaining this to me.

[65] Speech by V Orbán in July 2014 on his intentions to promote 'illiberal democracy' in Hungary: available at www.miniszterelnok.hu/beszed/a-munkaalapu-allam-korszaka-kovetkezik, with a translation in in English available at http://budapestbeacon.com/public-policy/full-text-of-viktor-orbans-speech-at-baile-tusnad-tusnadfurdo-of-26-july-2014.

[66] The National Avowal declares: 'We are proud that our king Saint Stephen built the Hungarian State on solid ground and made our country a part of Christian Europe one thousand years ago … We recognise the role of Christianity in preserving nationhood. We value the various religious traditions of our country'. See S Radnóti, 'A Sacred Symbol in a Secular Country: The Holy Crown' in GA Tóth (ed), *Constitution for a Disunited Nation: On Hungary's 2011 Fundamental Law* (Budapest, Central European University Press, 2012) 85–110.

[67] R Hirschl, *Constitutional Theocracy* (Cambridge, MA, Harvard University Press, 2010) and MJ Perry, *Toward a Theory of Human Rights: Religion, Law, Courts* (Cambridge, Cambridge University Press, 2007). For a more critical take, see N Ghanea, A Stephens and R Walden (eds), *Does God Believe in Human Rights? Essays on Religion and Human Rights* (Leiden, Martinus Nijhoff Publishers, 2007).

[68] Generally see I Leigh and R Ahdhar, 'Post-Secularism and the European Court of Human Rights: or How God Never Really Went Away' (2012) 75 *Modern Law Review* 1064.

[69] See, eg P Häberle, '"Gott" im Verfassungsstaat?' in P Häberle (ed), *Rechtsvergleichung im Kraftfeld des Verfassungsstaates: Methoden und Inhalte, Kleinstaaten und Entwicklungsländer* (Berlin, Duncker und Humblot, 1992) 212–25. See also A Kohen, *In Defense of Human Rights: A Non-religious Grounding in a Pluralistic World* (Oxford, Routledge, 2007).

with regard to issues such as human procreation, sexuality and dying, in which (Catholic) religion might have claimed at one time a privileged role in shaping social expectations and practices, as well as the law and human rights interpretation.[70] In relation to these issues, dignity-based claims have tended to focus on a greater degree of self-determination, going at times against (Catholic) religious teaching, particularly perhaps with regard to women's place in society, abortion, or sexuality, so that the territory once primarily occupied by religious reasoning is being increasingly shaped by the secular rationality of human rights.

Advocates of human dignity must, however, be cautious not to turn this concept into the core of a secular religion for twenty-first century Europe,[71] nor must they attempt to deify it. If human dignity can be about hope, a greater sense of justice and the belief in a better world or future, it must arguably not be turned into a messianic concept.[72] It is suggested that the best way to avoid this risk is arguably to construct human dignity as a *res publica* positioned at the heart of constitutionalism, namely, a good belonging to all and determined by all at the core of democracy.

C. Human Dignity as *Res Publica*

In order for human dignity to be an effective problem-solving tool of constitutionalism, it has to be considered as a good belonging to all, shaped by all, and for all. This is not to deny the other dimensions of human dignity, namely, in the context of religion, theology, philosophy or ethics. However, as George Kateb so sharply saw, human dignity has nothing to do with morality, it is about human existence;[73] and human rights are one of the best legal devices invented to protect it.[74]

Human dignity can be understood and constructed as *res publica* in a substantive perspective. As such, it is a powerful reminder of the principle of indivisibility which has been the bedrock of all human rights since 1948.[75]

[70] See, eg the discussion on abortion: R Siegel, 'Dignity and Sexuality: Claims on Dignity in Transnational Debates over Abortion and Same-sex Marriage' (2012) 10 *International Journal of Constitutional Law* 355.

[71] J Isensee, 'Menschenwürde: die säkulare Gesellschaft auf der Suche nach dem Absoluten' (2006) 131 *Archiv des öffentlichen Rechts* 173.

[72] J Moltmann, *On Human Dignity: Political Theology and Ethics* (Minneapolis, MN, Fortress Press, 2007) 173–87; generally see M Freeman, 'The Problem of Secularism in Human Rights Theory' (2004) 26 *Human Rights Quarterly* 475.

[73] G Kateb, *Human Dignity* (Cambridge, MA, Belknap Press of Harvard University Press, 2011) 10–17.

[74] L Hunt, *Inventing Human Rights: A History* (New York/London, WW Norton & Company, 2008).

[75] See, eg B Klein Goldewijk, A Contreras Baspineiro and PC Carbonari (eds), *Dignity and Human Rights: The Implementation of Economic, Social and Cultural Rights* (Antwerp, Intersentia, 2002).

While their application might differ in practice, with discussions on horizontality and on justiciability for some rights, it is only due to their principled indivisibility that new rights can be protected, and that human rights protection might be extended from the current generation to future generations. Furthermore, considering dignity as *res publica* means including all human beings within its protective scope, regardless of the degree of self-awareness of their humanity or their ability to take rational decisions affecting their life and death. As a result, in the dignity paradigm human beings deprived of autonomy, because they are, for instance, too young or too old, severely disabled or in a persistent vegetative state, are not treated as an exception when it comes to determining the scope of their human rights and to protecting them.[76] As *res publica*, human dignity is not designed just for the strong, healthy, assertive and competent, it is designed to bring into the centre of constitutionalism those who are on the margins of human rights, and whose protection (particularly perhaps in adjudication) often depends largely on a judge's sensitivity and humanity, rather than on a known and transparent set of rules. Similarly, as *res publica*, human dignity is not meant only to protect citizens, leaving the level of human rights protection of the non-citizens, such as refugees and asylum-seekers, to be decided by distinction and exception.[77] Above all, as *res publica*, human dignity protects humanity, understood as the humanity that we equally share as human beings; it is also increasingly used to acknowledge through the prism of human rights the importance of mankind and of future generations, the protection of which can be addressed, and hopefully achieved, with the tools and in the framework of European constitutionalism.

Admittedly, it is not always easy to protect a good with a contested definition, or that does not exist yet (such as future generations), or to decide whether a group of cells forms part of humanity. Human dignity as *res publica* therefore requires that the determination of the boundaries of humanity and the normative scope of dignity have to be determined in a public and transparent manner. Positioning human dignity at the heart of European constitutionalism is therefore essential, as, at least in theory, this is arguably the only framework open to all and in which all can be involved, one way or another, in making decisions that contribute to shaping it as a concept, thus defining and protecting humanity. Unlike religion or bioethics (to name

[76] C Dupré, 'Human Dignity and the Withdrawal of Medical Treatment: A Missed Opportunity?' (2006) 6 *European Human Rights Law Review* 687; see also M Neal, '"Not Gods but Animals": Human Dignity and Vulnerable Subjecthood' (2012) 33 *Liverpool Law Review* 177.

[77] Historically, this is one of the philosophical sources of human dignity: H Arendt, *The Origins of Totalitarianism* (New York, Harcourt, Brace, 1973) and A Kesby, *The Right to Have Rights: Citizenship, Humanity and International Law* (Oxford, Oxford Scholarship Online, 2012).

two frequent dignity domains), constitutionalism is by definition inclusive, transparent and accessible to all, with discussions taking place in public fora such as parliaments and courts.[78] In this respect, while not being faultless, European constitutionalism offers a uniquely sophisticated framework of public discussion, including a range of directly and indirectly elected decision-making bodies, which are connected to each other in a number of ways. Importantly, European constitutionalism further offers the possibility of a uniquely sophisticated system of human rights and of constitutional adjudication brought together by formal procedures, such as judicial remedies and request for interpretation; and informal connections, such as reliance on comparative law or on the constitutional traditions common to Member States. Above all perhaps, what makes the discussion and determination of human dignity as *res publica* possible is the shared language of human rights, spoken by all, either in a professional or lay capacity, and the overarching commitment to making human dignity an inviolable good of European constitutionalism, a powerful political commitment that was first formulated in Member States and more recently enshrined in the strongest possible way, namely, at the EU supranational level, thus binding the European Union, its institutions, bodies, offices and agencies, as well as its Member States.

IV. THE AGE OF DIGNITY

Capturing all the facets of a complex concept such as human dignity is no easy task and doing so in a limited number of years and words does not necessarily make things easier. Understanding human dignity cannot be left to intuition alone, nor to its apparently circular connection to humanity. Moreover, while it is presented as inherent in human beings, who are assumed to be born with dignity according to the post-war human rights paradigm, it is argued here that human dignity has arisen out of a number of struggles that have paved the way in the development of European constitutionalism. This book therefore involves a dual process of looking backwards in order to look forwards, in an attempt to bring to light connections that are not quite yet visible, but that are revealed by the critical and comparative analysis of human dignity considered in its integrated European dynamic, as it is presented here.

[78] As well as through street movements, such as the Spanish 'Indignados' at the origin of the new Podemos party. Generally see S Hessel, *Indignez vous!* (Montpellier, Indigène éditions, 2010).

A. Origins, Contexts and Complexities (1789–2009)

At the beginning of a study of human dignity's connections to constitutionalism and democracy in the twenty-first century, it is important to reflect on how this concept has emerged in the field of human rights law. The next three chapters therefore consider more closely the various stages of its construction as a legal concept and the historical forces that have propelled it into the field of constitutionalism in Europe. For it is argued that we are not born in dignity. The history of human dignity is that of an ideal shaped by hopes and fears, which gradually became an idea, before being crystallised as a legal concept in an attempt to prevent mass extermination of human beings from recurring and to protect our fragile humanity. The overall purpose of these chapters is therefore to look behind and beyond the post-war foundations of human rights, which present dignity as a special quality with which we are born, and to pay closer attention to the concept's history, which while somehow never being fully scrutinised, has already developed into a routine account, starting around 1785, with the publication of Kant's *Groundwork of the Metaphysics of Morals*, and ending in 1949 with the adoption of the West German Basic Law. Such a potted history of dignity is incomplete and, perhaps more importantly, does little to improve our understanding of a concept, which is today at the heart of our human rights system.

Chapter 2, entitled 'We Are Not Born in Dignity', addresses the issue of commencement, often reduced to a question of finding the right date from which the dignity story can start. A different approach is chosen here, which is to focus not on dates but on substance, and the chapter rests on the assumption that the commencement of a legal concept is an ideal. Human dignity, it is suggested, was imagined as a powerful philosophical and political ideal, both expressing and promoting dreams of freedom, equality and political empowerment, before it could be turned into a constitutional concept at a much later stage. The dignity ideal is arguably so powerful that formulating and realising it (or at least endeavouring to do so) were made possible in moments of deep social and political change. In this sense and context, dignity is tightly connected to revolutions, both as the ideal inspiring changes and as a tool making it possible to establish a new and more just political and legal order. What those changes have ultimately sought to establish is an always fuller definition and protection of humanity, as man, citizen and worker, which lie at human dignity's conceptual core.

Chapter 3, entitled 'The Foundations of European Constitutionalism: 1949, 1989, 2009', focuses on the transformation of human dignity into a legal concept through its codification in European constitutions adopted after the Second World War, which is perhaps the more often rehearsed account of human dignity's rise as a constitutional concept, largely (if not exclusively) centred on the emblematic 1949 German Basic Law (Article 1.1 of which reads: 'Human dignity is inviolable. To protect and to respect it shall be the duty of all state authority'). Bearing in mind the European context in which the concept developed and the methodological framework underpinning this study, Chapter 3 opens up this mainstream narrative in order to include other states in addition to Germany, as human dignity is now codified in the vast majority of EU Member States' constitutions. This makes it possible to include and to consider other moments of constitutional foundation, such as the post-communist transition, which is particularly significant due to the scope of the transformation and its impact on the construction of dignity, confirming it as the key foundation of democracy in Europe. As a result, the codification of dignity in the Lisbon Treaty takes its full significance both as a supranational endorsement of constitutional evolutions at national levels and as a new beginning for European constitutionalism. While providing a clear normative definition of human dignity, the Lisbon Treaty and the EU Charter shed new light on the connections between dignity and constitutional foundations, throwing dignity's transformative role into sharp relief.

Studying human dignity's construction as a constitutional concept would not be complete without including constitutional judges' active role in bringing it to life and opening up an unexpectedly rich range of meanings, considering the terse phrasing of constitutional provisions in this respect. Chapter 4, entitled 'Human Dignity: A Judge-Made Concept', therefore approaches this dimension of the construction of dignity by raising the questions 'when?' and 'how?' instead of seeking an ever elusive (and frustrating) answer to the question 'what?'. Often prompted by applicants, judges have tended to be particularly imaginative and prolific when interpreting human dignity provisions. As a result, a complex and rich picture has emerged of dignity as a compelling judicial principle underpinning all human rights interpretation that judges have sought to embed at the heart of their respective constitutional orders, while interlocking their own construction with that of fellow judges in other European legal systems. Consequently, human dignity has gradually acquired its full European dimension in positive law, albeit in the absence of a matching theoretical framework.

B. Human Dignity, Constitutionalism and Democracy

Having shed light on a fuller construction of human dignity at the heart of European constitutionalism up to its latest codification in the Lisbon Treaty, the second part of this study reflects on this concept's potential roles in the twenty-first century. As mentioned above, with the codification of human dignity in the EU Charter (adopted in 2000) and subsequently in the Lisbon Treaty, this concept has reached a paradoxical situation, with its strongest normative strength so far not being matched by an equally strong theoretical understanding and clear sense of how it can be used in constitutional adjudication. If anything, this concept has never been subjected to such a degree of scholarly scepticism and doubt. This part of the book is based on the methodological assumption that the apparent inflation of human dignity, as well as its alleged misuses by judges, reveals a deeper transformation of European constitutionalism, and that seeking to make sense of these changes will help to understand human dignity and to construct it further in a meaningful way. Building on the previous part of the book, it is argued that two key transformations are affecting both the construction of human dignity and European constitutionalism.

The first transformation involves the construction of human beings by constitutionalism, which has been a driving factor in the development of human dignity since 1789 or so. Most scholarly studies on this issue have focused on the genetic dimension of humanity; shifting the discussion into the field of bioethics and away from constitutionalism and human rights. Chapter 5, entitled 'Hidden in Plain View: Workers' Human Dignity', brings to the fore the constitutional identity of man as worker. Taking strength from the recognition of workers' dignity at the highest normative level (under Article 31 EU Charter), this chapter proposes theoretically to anchor their dignity in their humanity, as constructed by European constitutionalism. On this basis the chapter reflects on the potential meaning of workers' dignity, using the EU Charter as a platform for its exploration.

Chapter 6 of this book, entitled 'Defining Dignity, Protecting Human Time', focuses on the temporal dimension of European constitutionalism and on human dignity's role in shaping it in particular ways. Inspired by the work of legal philosopher François Ost, this chapter argues that human dignity can play a role in moving European constitutionalism out of a sort of existential crisis, diagnosed by Ost as 'detemporalisation', when constructed as the kairos of human rights, refocusing constitutional time on new beginnings and on making space at the heart of the present for the future to unfold towards a time of enhanced protection of humanity and greater democracy.

Finally, Chapter 7, entitled 'Re-thinking Constitutionalism: Dignity, Humanism, Democracy', draws out the distinctive features of dignity-based constitutionalism as they have been discussed throughout this book. The first part of the chapter argues that European constitutionalism is a form of humanism, characterised by a very sophisticated definition of humanity, constructed as a deliberate project which has driven the development of European constitutionalism, giving it its unique identity and purpose. As a result, the chapter's second part discusses the rise of dignity-democracy, a richer version of liberal democracy characterised by its particular construction of time, the central role played by constitutional courts and, ultimately, by the inviolability of human dignity, which binds constitution-makers, thus guaranteeing a smooth flow of constitutional time from a rejected past of inhumanity towards the possibility of a future, or futures, in which the protection of humanity may be enhanced.

2

We are Not Born in Dignity

I. INTRODUCTION

THE LEGAL SYSTEM of human rights protection in Europe (and more generally in the West) rests on the assumption that, as human beings, we are born with the unique quality of dignity that distinguishes us from other beings (primarily animals), justifying and explaining the special protection of our rights The emblematic text here is Article 1 of the UN Universal Declaration of Human Rights which reads: 'All human beings are born free and equal in dignity and rights. They are endowed with reason and conscience and should act towards one another in a spirit of brotherhood'.

It is suggested that the connection between dignity and humanity, the immediate origin of which can be explained as a response to the inhumanity of the Second World War, would not however have been possible without the more ancient and complex process of construction of the concept of human dignity, which was also on the drafters' minds.[1] Students of human dignity have not ignored the importance of its history and have tended to emphasise the length and complexity of its evolution, agreeing on the determinant role of the Second World War in propelling the concept onto the constitutional stage. Most historical reconstructions, however, have taken the shape of a (variously exhaustive) catalogue of key dignity thinkers,[2] leading to some frustration due to the apparent failure of history to clarify the concept's meaning.[3]

[1] J Morsink, *The Universal Declaration of Human Rights: Origins, Drafting, and Intent* (Philadelphia, PA, University of Pennsylvania Press, 1999) 281–327.

[2] B Giese, *Das Würde-Konzept: Eine normfunktionale Explikation des Begriffes Würde in Art.1 Abs 1 GG* (Berlin, Duncker und Humblot, 1975); P Kondylis, 'Würde' in O Brunner, W Conze and R Koselleck (eds), *Geschichtliche Grundbegriffe: Historisches Lexikon zur politisch-sozialen Sprache in Deutschland* (Stuttgart, Klett-Cotta, 1992) vol 7, 645–77; FJ Wetz (ed), *Texte zur Menschenwürde* (Stuttgart, Reclam, 2011); and M Mahlmann, *Elemente einer ethischen Grundrechtstheorie* (Baden-Baden, Nomos, 2005) ch 3 'Die Menschenwürde im Wechsel der historischen Reflexion', 97–178. See also U Vincenti, *Diritti e Dignità Umana* (Rome, Editori Laterza, 2009) 41–89.

[3] 'Infolge dieses vielfachen und widersprüchlichen philosophischen und politischen Sprachgebrauchs ist "Menschenwürde" zu einer Leerformel neben anderen geworden': Kondylis, above n 2, 677.

This chapter proposes a different approach to reconstructing human dignity's history based on three methodological assumptions. First, the principal underlying assumption is that in order to construct a meaning of human dignity, we must make fuller sense of its history, by bringing together thinkers, contexts and legal texts. Considering the overall context is particularly important in the early stages, before human dignity became a phrase used by lawyers and codified in constitutions and human rights declarations. In fact, as will be discussed, human dignity (or rather dignity) was used by philosophers and political thinkers before lawyers. Seen in this light human dignity's codification in normative texts is not the starting point of this concept's history. This raises the second methodological issue, inherent in all historical reconstructions, and particularly crucial here, namely, the identification of a suitable commencement.[4] Literature on human dignity tends to approach this in two different ways, either by emphasising the significance of the 1948 UN Universal Declaration as a sort of dignity 'big bang', heralding the start of a new era after the war; or by highlighting the ancientness of its roots, generally traced back to the writings of Cicero. It is suggested here that identifying the commencement of human dignity's history as a constitutional concept must be guided by today's uses of the concept, namely, in its connections with human rights and democracy,[5] and in particular with its foundational role in European constitutionalism.[6] This points towards two crucial periods in European history: the Renaissance, for its emphasis on the human and humanism, and the Enlightenment, with its attempt to codify human rights and to control the sovereign's power. An exhaustive and linear account of the history of human dignity across centuries falls outside this study's scope. Instead, and this is the third methodological assumption, this chapter seeks to identify some of the concept's 'tipping points', namely, its most salient moments and the key ideas that ultimately led to its codification in legal texts.[7] This chapter therefore focuses on the transformations

[4] HG Gadamer, *Au commencement de la philosophie, pour une lecture des Présocratiques* (Paris, Seuil, 2001).

[5] C Dupré, 'Dignity, Democracy, Civilisation' (2013) 33 *Liverpool Law Review* 264.

[6] C Dupré, 'Human Dignity in Europe: A Foundational Constitutional Principle' (2013) 19 *European Public Law* 319.

[7] P Rosanvallon, *Le sacre du citoyen: histoire du suffrage universel en France* (Paris, Gallimard, 1992): 'La méthode que nous voulons suivre, à l'inverse, n'a d'autre visée que de comprendre *de l'intérieur* les certitudes, les tâtonnements ou les aveuglements qui gouvernent l'action et l'imagination des hommes' (at 19) and 'Faire l'histoire du suffrage universel, c'est d'abord se glisser dans un problème, pour en suivre de l'intérieur le travail, et non pas repérer une sorte de mystérieux germe démocratique initial dont on raconterait la croissance et l'arrivée à maturité ... Il s'agit plus d'entrer dans une question que de fixer a priori un point de départ. La question première? Elle est d'essayer de repérer *les points de basculement* et de différenciation [pour fragmenter le champ] au sens ou l'on casse un noyau pour mieux en analyser la matière' (at 21–22) (emphasis added).

introduced by human dignity, in the ways in which men[8] thought about themselves, their form of government and their ability to shape their destiny.

As a result, this chapter suggests that the history of human dignity can be understood as that of a powerful ideal that captured the imagination and dreams of philosophers across centuries. Among the many philosophers who have influenced the concept, two are singled out here for the lasting contribution they arguably made to shaping it. The first is Giovanni Pico della Mirandola, whose famous *Oratio* was a breakthrough, particularly for his re-thinking of the Imago Dei paradigm in the light of man's new freedom constantly to shape and determine his identity. The second philosopher considered here is Immanuel Kant, without whom the concept of human dignity might never have emerged in its modern form. While his heritage and his philosophy are still much discussed today, his so-called object formula has been adopted by German constitutional judges as one of the first constitutional definitions of human dignity after the Second World War.

Grounded in the Renaissance and in the Enlightenment, the ideal of dignity was arguably so central to the image of man and of a just society that it took the momentous change of the French Revolution and its 1789 Declaration of the Rights of Man and the Citizen to start realising this ideal. This chapter's central section discusses and reflects on the 1789 Declaration, which played a crucial role in founding European constitutionalism at the time and in shaping it since then.[9] In relation to human dignity, as is argued here, the Declaration marks a 'tipping point', namely, a pivotal moment in the concept's construction, from the Ancien Regime understanding of 'dignities', to laying the foundation for its modern understanding as equal dignity shared by all human beings. The last section therefore reconstructs the first constitutional definition of dignity on the basis of the Declaration's definition of human beings and shows that despite not using the word dignity in the concept's current understanding, that first definition already captures and attempts to protect a complex multi-layered definition of humanity.

II. HUMAN DIGNITY AS IDEAL

Idealism is a core component of human dignity, one without which it is not possible to understand its current meanings and historical transformations.

[8] I am using the term 'men' or 'Man' to refer to human beings in general and certainly not to exclude women from this discussion and from the benefit of human dignity.

[9] P Häberle, '1789 als Teil der Geschichte, Gegenwart und Zukunft des Verfassungsstaates' in P Häberle (ed), *Rechtsvergleichung im Kraftfeld des Verfassungsstaates: Methoden und Inhalte, Kleinstaaten und Entwicklungsländer* (Berlin, Duncker und Humblot, 1992) 685–720. See also L Hunt, *Inventing Human Rights: A History* (NewYork/London, WW Norton & Company, 2008).

Built into the concept of dignity is a belief that life can be (even) better, that it is possible to construct a more just world. This belief is deeply connected to hope,[10] a crucial and (perhaps) unique human capacity not to reduce life to its current experience of unfairness and suffering, and to be able to imagine (for instance) that the future can be better: that justice can be restored after injustice, that peace comes after war, that equality can replace discrimination and segregation, or that food will be available to end hunger. By definition, idealism does not have much to do with the actual possibility of these futures, but the first step in the process of their always uncertain realisation is the freedom and capacity to imagine a different world, particularly in contexts and circumstances where everything seems to be stacked against the odds of these dreams becoming reality. It is suggested that, over the centuries, human dignity has captured three broad ideals that have sustained its construction: freedom, autonomy and equality. Although it is hard to disentangle them from one another, for the sake of presentational clarity each of them is discussed below by association with a particularly prominent thinker or historical moment.

A. Freedom

We owe the connection between freedom and dignity to Giovanni Pico della Mirandola,[11] a young Italian count born in 1463,[12] whose thinking and work shaped Renaissance philosophy to the point of becoming one of its emblems.[13] Embarking on the project of radically scrutinising the accepted philosophical and theological knowledge of his time, Pico della Mirandola wrestled with the definition of man in relation to both God and animals. Breaking away from the definition of man as microcosmos prevailing at the time, Pico argued that man was ontologically undetermined, that it was not

[10] E Bloch, *The Principle of Hope* (N Plaice and P Knight (trans), Cambridge, MA, Massachusetts Institute of Technology Press, 1986).

[11] Christoph Goos observed that Pico's thinking on human dignity is influential on some of today's legal scholars, such as Hasso Hofmann, Martin Morlock and Rolf Gröschner, *Innere Freiheit: Eine Rekonstruktion des grundgesetzlichen Würdebegriffs* (Bonn, Bonn University Press, 2011) 34–35.

[12] *L'Opera e il Pensiero di Giovanni Pico dell a Mirandola nella Storia dell'Umanesimo* (conference proceedings) (Florence, Istituto Nazionale di Studi sul Rinascimento, 1965); and A Klein, *La Dignità dell'Uomo nel Pensiero del Rinascimento* (Turin, Giappichelli, 1976). Generally see P Steenbakkers, 'Human Dignity in Renaissance Humanism' in M Düwell, J Braarvig, R Brownsword and D Mieth (eds), *The Cambridge Handbook of Human Dignity* (Cambridge, Cambridge University Press, 2014) 85–94.

[13] MA Gukosvkj, 'Giovanni Pico della Mirandola: "Uomo del Medioevo o del Rinascimento"?' in *L'Opera e il Pensiero di Giovanni Pico dell a Mirandola nella Storia dell'Umanesimo* (conference proceedings) (Florence, Istituto Nazionale di Studi sul Rinascimento, 1965) 457–67.

possible to determine man *a priori*, and that man can only be by doing.[14] This ontological indetermination gives man the freedom to self-determine, and this special freedom was called dignity. Both the term and the idea were so novel and striking at the time that in 1557 this was chosen as the posthumous title for his famous oration, *De Hominis Dignitate*.[15] While this *Oratio* has fascinated many scholars, Ernst Cassirer is perhaps the philosopher who captured most eloquently this ideal of freedom, pre-figuring the post-Second World War development of human dignity:[16]

> The freedom of man consists in the uninterrupted creativity he exercises upon himself, which can at no point come to a complete cessation. Such a cessation is in a certain sense the lot of every other nature except man ... But this uncertainty [caused by the constant self-creativity], this perpetual peril of human existence—not in the physical but in the moral and religious sense—at the same time constitutes for Pico man's real greatness ... What he [Pico] here sets up as the distinctive privilege of man is the almost unlimited *power of self-transformation* at his disposal. Man is that being to whom no particular form has been prescribed and assigned. He possesses the power of entering into any form whatever. What is novel in this idea lies not in its content, but rather in the *value* Pico places on this content. For it is an extraordinarily bold step of Pico's to reverse at this point the conventional metaphysical and theological estimate.[17]

Man's special freedom called dignity was not, however, absolute as it ultimately reflected God's freedom under the Imago Dei paradigm.[18] The full realisation of this human freedom is therefore ultimately determined, as the more similar to God man becomes, the more free he is too.[19] Despite these limitations, Pico's definition of dignity as human freedom constantly to

[14] FS Pignagnoli (ed), *Giovanni Pico della Mirandola: La Dignità dell'Uomo* (Bologna, Edizioni Scolastiche Pàtron, 1969) 33–43.

[15] For an annotated translation in Italian see FS Pignagnoli (ed), *Giovanni Pico della Mirandola: La Dignità dell'Uomo* (Bologna, Edizioni Scolastiche Pàtron, 1969) 71.

[16] Ernst Cassirer died in 1945. On dignity after 1945, see Chapter 3.

[17] E Cassirer, 'Giovanni Pico della Mirandola: A Study in the History of Renaissance Ideas' (1942) 2 *Journal of History of Ideas* 123, 331 (original emphasis). This definition of man entertains particular, and novel, connections with time, history and fate: '[Pico] does not simply wish to elevate the mind above time, he wishes rather to locate it in the midst of time: he sees the mind in its actual "history" ... For to him history is no mere fate, and time is not merely the external frame within which this fate is worked out ... In his own history therefore man is not simply subject to the temporality and transitoriness of things; in it he rather reveals his own nature—a nature indeed mutable, but in this very mutability free, because it is the self-changing, the eternal "Proteus"' (at 334). The connections between time and dignity are discussed in Chapter 6.

[18] Pico had enough trouble with Pope Innocent III, who banned the debate he had wanted to initiate with his 900 Theses in 1486.

[19] FS Pignagnoli (ed), *Giovanni Pico della Mirandola: La Dignità dell'Uomo* (Bologna, Edizioni Scolastiche Pàtron, 1969) 37.

self-transform and self-create, which gave man a chameleon-like quality,[20] still resonates in current human dignity case law, characterised by its great versatility. As will be seen in Chapter 4, this is arguably one hermeneutic technique deployed by judges today in order to acknowledge and protect a diversity of human identities and personalities.

B. Autonomy

The next building block of the dignity ideal is autonomy, understood as the capacity to set one's own rules, which can be contrasted with heteronomy, namely, the dependence on norms set by somebody else, usually a higher authority. Historically and philosophically, severing the ties between God's authority as the ultimate source of nomos was a key step in the conquest of autonomy.[21] In this respect the Enlightenment was a crucial moment in re-thinking the core assumptions on which philosophy and political power had so far rested,[22] with Immanuel Kant as one of its emblematic philosophers.[23] At the risk of simplifying the rich and complex work of the Königsberg scholar, Kant can be remembered here for having made and explored the connections between autonomy and humanity, and in this process he gave the concept of dignity its modern significance as a uniquely human quality. In particular, he is remembered for his categorical imperative that men should 'so act as [they] use humanity, whether in [their] own person or in the person of any other, always at the same time as an end, and never merely as a means'.[24]

This formulation follows Kant's reflection on the core distinction between means/things on the one hand, and ends/rational beings on the other hand, namely, while persons are rational beings and exist as ends in themselves,

[20] 'Who will not look with awe upon this our chameleon, or who, at least, will look with greater admiration on any other thing? This creature, man, whom Asclepius the Athenian, by reason of this very mutability, this nature capable of transforming itself, quite rightly said was symbolized in the mysteries by the figure of Proteus': available at www.cscs.umich.edu/~crshalizi/Mirandola/. For a comment on this image, see FS Pignagnoli (ed), *Giovanni Pico della Mirandola: La Dignità dell'Uomo* (Bologna, Edizioni Scolastiche Pàtron, 1969) 79.

[21] More recently, see the concept of autonomous societies developed by Cornelius Castoriadis, *Domaines de l'Homme: les carrefours du labyrinthe (2)* (Paris, Points Seuil, 1999).

[22] See also E Cassirer, *The Philosophy of the Enlightenment* (Princeton, NJ, Princeton University Press, 1951).

[23] For classic studies of Kant's work, see O O'Neill, *Constructions of Reason, Explorations of Kant's Practical Philosophy* (Cambridge, Cambridge University Press, 1989) and TE Hill, *Dignity and Practical Reason in Kant's Moral Theory* (Ithaca, NY, Cornell University Press, 1992). Recent re-interpretations of Kant include O Sensen, *Kant on Human Dignity* (Berlin, De Gruyter, 2011) and M Rosen, *Dignity: Its History and Meaning* (Cambridge, MA, Harvard University Press, 2012).

[24] I Kant, *Groundwork of the Metaphysics of Morals* (M Gregor (trans and ed), Cambridge, Cambridge University Press, 1991) 4:429, 38.

other beings which are merely a means, Kant calls 'things' (and sometimes 'animals') as they only have a 'relative worth'. A bit later in the text, Kant elaborates on the idea of 'relative worth', contrasting it with 'inner worth', which he calls 'dignity' (*Würde*):[25]

> In the kingdom of ends everything has either a *price* or a *dignity* (*Würde*). What has a price can be replaced by something else as its *equivalent;* what on the other hand is raised above all price and therefore admits of no equivalent has a dignity. What is related to general human inclinations and needs has a *market price*; that which, even without presupposing a need, conforms with a certain taste, that is with a delight (*Wohlgefallen*) in the mere purposeless (*zwecklosen*) play of our mental powers, has a *fancy price* (*Affectionspreis*); but that which constitutes the condition under which alone something can be an end in itself has not merely a relative worth that is, a price, but an inner worth, that is *dignity*.[26]

We are here at the philosophical roots of the constitutional concept of human dignity as it is largely understood today, namely, a concept that is exclusive to human beings, so that it can be used to distinguish them from other beings, which do not have dignity but a relative worth. Important to note here is that the implicit definition of humanity is not a biological one, but one which assumes the capacity to reason, that is to set one's own ends. This focus, while it has been criticised from a modern perspective of (gender) equality,[27] has remained crucial in shaping the concept of dignity as a source of sovereignty and as a philosophical basis for citizenship.

In *The Metaphysics of Morals*, 12 years later, Kant went back to these points and developed them further in what has perhaps remained its most synthetic and modern formulation of humanity as dignity:

> Humanity itself is a dignity; for a human being cannot be used merely as a means by any human being (either by others or even by himself) but must always be used at the same time as an end. It is just in this that his dignity (personality) consists, by which he raises himself above all other beings in the world that are not human beings and yet can be used, and so over all *things*. But just as he cannot give himself away for any price (this would conflict with his duty of self-esteem), so neither can he act contrary to the necessary self-esteem of others, as human beings, that is,

[25] 'Now I say that the human being and in general every rational being *exists* as an end in itself, *not merely as a means* to be used by this or that will at its discretion; instead he must in all his actions, whether directed to himself or to other rational beings, always be regarded at the same time as an end.... Beings the existence of which rests not on our will but on nature, if they are beings without reason, still only have a relative worth, as means, and are therefore called *things* (*Sachen*), whereas rational beings are called *persons* because their nature already marks them out as an end in itself, that is, as something that may not be used merely as a means, and hence so far limits all choice (and is an object of respect)': Kant, above n 24, 4:428, 37.

[26] ibid 4:435, 42.

[27] TE Hill, 'Kantian Perspectives on the Rational Basis of Human Dignity' in M Düwell, J Braarvig, R Brownsword and D Mieth (eds), *The Cambridge Handbook of Human Dignity* (Cambridge, Cambridge University Press, 2014) 215, 218.

> he is under obligation to acknowledge, in a practical way, the dignity of humanity in every other human being. Hence there rests on him a duty regarding the respect that must be shown to every other human being.[28]

Three points can be retained from this paragraph. First of all, dignity does not proceed from God, it is not a quality given by God to man as a divine creation and creature; dignity proceeds from man's inner worth and his unique ability to set his own ends, namely, to make his own laws. By locating dignity in humanity and no longer in God, Kant makes the philosophical transition from dignity as being heteronomous and teleological, as formulated by Pico, to dignity as autonomy and ontology. It has therefore often been described as 'unconditional', 'incomparable' and 'without equivalent'.[29] The second point to note is that dignity is used to define humanity not with reference to God, but by distinction from other beings which only have a 'relative worth', namely, animals or things. Unlike human beings, their worth can be compared and assessed in terms of price, they can be treated as mere objects. Consequently and thirdly, although Kant has also used the term dignity in its Ancien regime sense of (social) rank,[30] it is very clear from the above extract that dignity is not used to distinguish among human beings, but to distinguish human beings from other beings, such as animals. By defining human beings through their inner worth, Kant put all human beings on a basis of equality, from which follows their duty to respect the dignity of fellow human beings (formulated in the above quotation) and never to treat them as mere means, as this, would go against his own dignity and therefore humanity. In so doing, what Kant also did was to position human beings in relationships of reciprocity or reflexivity with each other.[31] Moreover, this new dignity-led logic is no longer based on the fundamen tal inequality and hierarchy which distinguished God and, importantly his lieutenant on earth, the King (or Emperor) and by extension the aristocracy, from human beings.[32] Instead, as discussed further below, it is based on the assumption of a fundamental equality between all human beings, who are equal participants in the moral law. Men can set their own ends, and only men can do so. Dignity therefore defines men both as human beings, with their own raison d'être, and as citizens, ie capable of making their own

[28] Doctrine of Virtue: para 38, M Gregor (ed), *The Metaphysics of Morals* (Cambridge, Cambridge University Press, 2009) 209. See also the luminous discussion by P Manent, *Cours familier de philosophie politique* (Paris, Gallimard, 2001) 317–20.

[29] Hill, above n 27, 215, 217.

[30] As will be discussed below, when Kant was writing, the use of the term 'dignity' was in flux between an Ancien Regime 'dignity-as-social-rank' and modern democratic 'dignity-as-equality' meanings.

[31] On Kant's concept of common sense (*Gemeinsinn*) see R Beiner (ed), *Hannah Arendt: Lectures on Kant's Political Philosophy* (Brighton, Harvester Press, 1982), 68–77.

[32] See J Waldron, *Dignity, Rank and Rights* (Oxford, Oxford University Press, 2012) 30–36 and S Hennette-Vauchez, 'A Human Dignitas? Remnants of the Ancient Legal Concept in Contemporary Dignity Jurisprudence' (2011) 9 *International Journal of Constitutional Law* 32.

law.[33] This presupposed the invention of an institutional framework, about which Kant said little, but, as will be discussed below, that the French Revolutionaries had started establishing.

Of this sophisticated thinking, twentieth century (constitutional) lawyers[34] and judges have primarily retained what is called in German the 'object formula',[35] according to which treating a human being as an object or an instrument to pursue goals not set by him (but by the state) breaches his human dignity.[36] The concept of autonomy has remained a key component in the current discussions and definitions of humanity, with some authors seeing autonomy and dignity as antagonistic concepts,[37] and others arguing for the possibility of deploying the argument of dignity in order to protect those human beings who have lost their autonomy.[38]

Moral philosophical readings of Kantian autonomy have sometimes tended to forget that this concept was also a powerful call for liberating moral decision-making from extraneous factors and actors. As one of the conditions of what Kant calls the universal law, this autonomy can arguably also be seen from a political angle, and understood as a possible way to limit the sovereign's power. This topic was certainly very high in Kant's mind, as well as on the Enlightenment's philosophical and political reform agenda, out of which modern constitutionalism was born. The quest for autonomy in democratic law-making has arguably since then evolved to respond to a transformation in the nature of heteronomy, which nowadays in Europe is no longer primarily about rejecting God and religion as ultimate sources of constitutional authority and legitimacy. Instead capitalist ideology represents perhaps the dominant threat to autonomous and democratic law-making in the twenty-first century.[39]

[33] See J Waldron, 'Citizenship and Dignity' in C McCrudden (ed), *Understanding Dignity* (Oxford, Oxford University Press, 2013) 327–43.

[34] G Dürig, 'Der Grundrechtssatz von der Menschenwürde: Entwurf eines praktikabeln Wertsystems der Grundrechte aus Art.1. Abs.I in Verbindung mit Art. 19 Abs. II des Grundgesetzes' (1956) 81 *Archiv für öffentliches Recht* 127. See also GP Fletcher, 'Human Dignity as a Constitutional Value' (1984) 22 *University of Western Ontario Law Review* 171.

[35] See, eg the first two rulings of the German Constitutional Court BVerfGE 27, 1 [6]; and BVerfGE 45, 187 [228] *Nachschlagewerk des Bundesverfassungsgerichts*, edited by the German Federal Constitutional Court (Karlsruhe, R v Decker's Verlag, CF Müller, 2004). More generally, see E Daly, *Dignity Rights: Courts, Constitutions and the Worth of the Human Person* (Philadelphia, PA, University of Pennsylvania Press, 2013) 44–49.

[36] For a recent example see the controversial German Aviation Security Act case decided by the German Federal Constitutional Court in 2006 and discussed by K Moller, 'On Treating Persons as Ends: The German Aviation Security Act, Human Dignity, and the German Federal Constitutional Court' (2006) *Public Law* 457 and R Youngs, 'Germany: Shooting Down Aircraft and Analyzing Computer Data' (2008) 6 *International Journal of Constitutional Law* 331.

[37] C Foster, *Human Dignity in Bioethics and Law* (Oxford, Hart Publishing, 2011).

[38] C Dupré, 'Human Dignity and the Withdrawal of Medical Treatment: A Missed Opportunity?' (2006) 6 *European Human Rights Law Review* 687.

[39] Generally see A Supiot, *The Spirit of Philadelphia, Social Justice v the Total Market* (S Brown (trans), London, Verso, 2012). On a Marxist approach to this discussion, see

C. Equality

The third dignity ideal discussed here is that of equality among all human beings, which has arguably played a crucial role in shaping a modern concept of human dignity, namely, one that was gradually separated away from its earlier dominant meaning of dignity as rank.[40] As it underpins the entire representation of human relationships, society and ultimately a certain vision of democracy, this ideal has been perhaps the most easily and vocally translated into political claims and terms. This section does not purport to reconstruct a complete lineage of this ideal, but instead it brings together some of the more frequently cited authors and ideas in dignity scholarship. Chronologically, Leveller John Lilburne (c.1614–57) is perhaps the first to have used dignity in 1646 in support of a powerful argument that 'all men by nature are the children of Adam, and regardless of religious differences, they are all equal and alike in power, dignity, authority and majesty'.[41] The context was the English Civil War and radical claims to political equality in a republic headed by Cromwell that Lilburne found did not grant enough equality and liberty. Writing in a different context and a little later, Samuel Pufendorf (1632–94) connected dignity to man's ability to reason, that is to distinguish good from bad. Accordingly, all men equally share this dignity as it is ultimately God's gift.[42] Interestingly, Pufendorf developed the idea of equality into a rule of sociability based on reciprocity according to which, since they are equal in dignity, men have to respect each other's dignity, using it as one basis of his theory of duties.[43] Writing in 1740, the prominent natural law thinker, Christian von Wolff (1679–1754) also read equality into the God-given dignity, distinguishing this natural dignity from social dignities (*dignitates civiles*) that could only be recognised and awarded on the basis of '*merita*'.[44]

W Bonefeld and K Psychopedis (eds), *Human Dignity: Social Autonomy and the Critique of Capitalism* (Aldershot, Ashgate, 2005). More generally see C Joerges's discussion of the management of the Euro crisis: 'Europe's Economic Constitution in Crisis and the Emergence of a New Constitutional Constellation' (2014) 15 in *German Law Journal* 985.

[40] On a socialist reading and re-interpretation of dignity as equality, see G Lohmann, 'Human Dignity and Socialism' in M Düwell, J Braarvig, R Brownsword and D Mieth (eds), *The Cambridge Handbook of Human Dignity* (Cambridge, Cambridge University Press, 2014) 126–34.

[41] J Lilburne, *The Free-Mans Freedome Vindicated* (1646), CW Firth (ed), *The Clarke Papers*, vol 3, 351, quoted by MR Ishay, *The History of Human Rights: From Ancien Times to the Globalization Era* (Berkeley, CA, University of California Press, 2004) 77. See also Kondylis, above n 2, 664.

[42] Kondylis, above n 2, 662–63.

[43] S Pufendorf, *Über die Pflicht des Menschen und des Bürgers nach dem Gesetz der Natur* (K Luig (trans and ed), Frankfurt am Main, Insel Verlag, 1994) quoted in FJ Wetz (ed), *Texte zur Menschenwürde* (Stuttgart, Reclam, 2011) 106.

[44] Kondylis, above n 2, 663.

Seen in this context, Kant's approach to dignity as equality mentioned above builds on these ideas (his concept of dignity as resting in human reason only) while cutting the last tie with God as the ultimate source of (equal) dignity.[45] As will be recalled, for Kant, the crucial distinction was between animals or beasts (who cannot set their own ends, and have only an externally set price or value) and men (who can set their own ends, and should not treat each other as mere means, but always as ends). Men's intrinsic dignity put them on an equal footing with each other, raising them above animals that they could instrumentalise in order to pursue certain ends. The categorical imperative arguably therefore becomes both a rule of sociability (perhaps in an echo of Pufendorf) and the ultimate source of normativity. These dignity-as-equality ideals challenged, each in their own way, the established political order and representations of human beings and their relationships, calling for a different way of thinking, and a new society based on equality to replace the existing one based on distinctions and hierarchies. Dignity as an ideal and political claim became instrumental in the powerful shift from rank to equality that characterised the spirit of the French Revolution and its Declaration.

III. 1789: FROM DIGNITIES TO DIGNITY

It is suggested here that the French Revolution and the 1789 Declaration of the Rights of Man and the Citizen marked a 'tipping point' in the construction of human dignity[46] as the modern constitutional concept that we understand today to be the foundation of Western liberal human rights. The 1789 Declaration is neither the only, nor the first bill of rights, and the 1215 Magna Carta[47] and the 1776 Virginia Bill of Rights have of course also contributed to shaping today's human rights. However, despite the Terror that followed, as Peter Häberle has persuasively argued, the 1789 Declaration has had a lasting and profound impact not only on the construction of human rights, but also on the emergence of constitutionalism in Europe.[48]

As will be recalled, the term dignity was in flux between a 'dignity as rank' meaning, and a 'dignity as equality' meaning, which was in the process of becoming the new (modern) and constitutional understanding of this

[45] This debate seems to have picked up again, see, eg GP Fletcher, 'In God's Image: The Religious Imperative of Equality under the Law' (1999) 99 *Columbia Law Review* 1608; and H Bielefeldt, *Philosophie der Menschenrechte: Grundlagen eines weltweiten Freiheitsethos* (Darmstadt, Primus Verlag, 1992) 175–201.

[46] A 'point de basculement' in the sense of Rosanvallon, see above n 7.

[47] A Arlidge and I Judge, *Magna Carta Uncovered* (Oxford, Hart Publishing, 2015).

[48] Häberle, above n 9, 685–720. Generally see Ishay, above n 41 and Hunt, above n 9.

term.[49] In 1754, the famous *Encyclopédie* of Diderot and d'Alembert recognised two types of dignity, one connected with forms of public office and the exercise of public power, and the other with the holding of fiefs and related prerogatives of justice.[50] This definition is arguably a typical Ancien Regime one, corresponding to the public offices which were the monopoly of the aristocracy and the feudal organisation of society at the time.[51] As is discussed below, the 1789 Declaration, while retaining the meaning of dignity as social distinction, set up the constitutional framework for the foundations of the modern dignity-as-equality concept. This powerful conceptual transformation would not have been possible without what can be called the spirit of dignity underpinning the French Revolution and the Enlightenment, and that can be read, as a watermark, in the 1789 Declaration

A. The Spirit of Dignity

The Declaration of the Rights of Man and the Citizen contains the term dignity (in the plural form) under Article 6:

> Statute law is the expression of the general will. All citizens have the right to take part in person or through their representatives in its enactment. Whether it protects or punishes, it must be the same for all. Since *all citizens are equal in its eyes*, they are likewise eligible for all *dignities* (dignités), *positions and posts* according to ability and without distinctions other than their merits and abilities.[52] (emphasis added)

This provision reflects the transition between ancient and modern meanings of dignity: on the one hand, it is a resounding and revolutionary statement of equality ('all citizens ... without distinction'), on the other hand, the term 'dignities', clearly referring to specific professional and social positions, is used in its Ancien Regime meaning, reflecting the mainstream sense of the term as recorded by the *Encyclopédie* some years before. This drafting can be partly explained by the fact that Article 6 was adopted a few days after the abolition of the aristocracy's privileges, also referred to as 'dignities',

[49] MJ Meyer, 'Kant's Concept of Dignity and Modern Political Thought' (1987) 8 *History of Political Ideas* 319. See also A Simonin, 'La dignité de la personne humaine n'est pas une idée révolutionnaire' in C Girard and S Hennette-Vauchez (eds), *La dignité de la personne humaine: recherche sur un processus de juridicisation* (Paris, Presses Universitaires de France, 2004) 309.

[50] *Encyclopédie*, T4 (1754), 1004, Article 'Dignité', quoted by Kondylis, above n 2, 656.

[51] In 1651, Thomas Hobbes famously wrote: 'the public worth of a man, which is the value set on him by the Commonwealth is that which men commonly call dignity. And this value of him by the Commonwealth is understood by offices of command, judicature, public employment; or by the names and titles introduced for distinction of such values': *Leviathan, or the Matter, Form and Power of A Commonwealth* (AP Martinich and B Battiste (eds), Peterborough, Broadview, 2010) 98. See also Kondylis, above n 2, 662.

[52] The English translation used here is that of SE Finer *et al* (eds), *Comparing Constitutions* (Oxford, Clarendon Press, 1995).

during the night of 4 August. The wording of Article 6 may therefore be read as a deliberate echo of the 'decree related to the abolition of privileges' which provided: 'All citizens, without distinction by birth, may be eligible for all offices and ecclesiastical, civil and military dignities'.[53] Read in this light, the term 'dignities' under Article 6 refers to specific professional positions, namely, those of the clergy and of the aristocracy, and has to be distinguished very clearly from the overall claim to equality of the 1789 Declaration. While the Declaration did not refer to dignity in the modern sense of this term, the spirit of dignity as equality arguably underpins the whole text, and the term 'dignities' can be understood as an echo of the common language of the time used to refer to specific professional and social positions (*dignitas* as *officium*), and not as a statement of dignity as rank. This is confirmed by the revised version of this provision under the 1793 Constitution, which dropped the reference to 'dignities' and replaced it by the more general and neutral phrase 'public offices' ('*emplois publics*').[54]

While dignity was not used in its modern sense in the 1789 and 1793 Declarations, it was used in this sense at the time by some of the leading political commentators on the French Revolution. MJ Meyer identified two such (English) authors.[55] Thomas Paine in *The Rights of Man* was perhaps one of the first political commentators on the French Revolution to refer to 'the natural dignity of man' as the reason to protect individual rights that transcend authoritative rule.[56] Writing almost at the same time, Mary Wollstonecraft in her *Vindication of the Rights of Women* (1792) referred to dignity as being 'native' and emphasised what she called 'dignity of character', to contrast it with its mainstream meaning, social dignity and (in a very Kantian manner according to Meyer) she related this 'native dignity' to the definition of human beings as 'rational beings'. Going further than Paine and than most of the Revolutionaries, she defined women as equally rational as men.[57] Meyer, presenting these commentaries in the context of the debate triggered by Burke's anti-revolutionary positions, illustrates very

[53] 'Tous les citoyens, sans distinction de naissance, pourront être admis à tous les emplois et dignités ecclésiastiques, civiles et militaires, et nulle profession utile n'emportera dérogeance'. Quoted by J Morange, *La Déclaration des Droits de l'Homme et du Citoyen (26 août 1789)* (Paris, Presses Universitaires de France, 1989) 19–20.

[54] Article 5: 'Tous les citoyens sont également admissibles aux emplois publics. Les peuples libres ne connaissent d'autres motifs de préférence, dans leurs élections, que les vertus et les talents' in J Godechot (ed), *Les Constitutions de la France depuis 1789* (Paris, Garnier Flammarion, 1979) 80.

[55] Meyer, above n 49, 319–32.

[56] 'The Patriots of France have discovered in good time that rank and dignity in society must take a new ground. The old one has fallen through. It must now make the substantial ground of character instead of the chimerical ground of titles': T Paine, *The Rights of Man* (New York, Anchor, 1973) 320, quoted by Meyer, above n 49, 324. See also RD Glensy, 'The Right to Dignity' (2011) 66 *Columbia Human Rights Law Review* 65, 77–78.

[57] Meyer, above n 49, 325.

well how the concept of dignity was at the heart of two opposite visions of society, ie the Ancien Regime based on dignity-as-rank, and the new order being created based on 'native' dignity-as-equality.[58] These contrasting uses of dignity arguably underline the significance of the rights of man and citizens declared in 1789 as providing the necessary constitutional cradle out of which dignity could emerge as the foundation of human rights, nearly two centuries later in 1948.

B. Constitutionalism as the Cradle of Human Dignity

It is suggested that the 1789 Declaration further contributed to the construction of human dignity in its modern meaning by providing the basis for an institutional framework, within which rights and (later) human dignity could acquire their full constitutional status. Although the Declaration distinguishes between the rights of man and the rights of citizen in its title, in its text, rights are not identified one way or the other.[59] Rather, the more significant distinction made by the Declaration is arguably between, on the one hand, the 'natural, inalienable and sacred human rights' (Preamble) with which human beings are born and, on the other hand, the man-made constitutional framework, which is designed to protect these rights.[60]

[58] This significance is arguably confirmed *a contrario* in a constitutional text using dignity to indicate and create an extreme form of dignity-as-rank. The Senatus Consulte of 7 November 1852, which constituted Napoleon as Emperor, proclaimed in its Art 1 that: '[l]a dignité impériale est rétablie. Louis Napoléon Bonaparte est Empereur des Français sous le nom de Napoleon III'. Its Art 2 confirms and strengthens this connection: 'La dignité impériale est héréditaire dans la descendence directe et légitime de Louis Napoleon Bonaparte, de mâle en mâle, par ordre de primogéniture, et à l'exclusion perpétuelle des femmes et de leur descendance'. Quoted in J Godechot (ed), *Les Constitutions de la France depuis 1789* (Paris, Garnier Flammarion, 1979) 298. Erin Daly observes a similar connection between dignity and hereditary monarchy under the 1879 Constitution of the Kingdom of Bulgaria: Daly, above n 35, 11.

[59] As Marcel Gauchet explained, what we now call 'social rights' were very closely connected to what we now call 'civil and political rights': 'la véritable racine des droits sociaux se trouve là, dans le devoir secret de la société des individus de faire en sorte que ses membres deviennent ou demeurent de ces êtres indépendants et autosuffisants dont elle est censée procéder, qu'il s'agisse de l'affirmation de leur autonomie (éducation), de leur protection contre la dépendance (secours) ou de la préservation de leur capacité à subsister par eux-mêmes (travail)': *La Révolution des droits de l'Homme* (Paris, Gallimard, 1989) xxiii. See also P Unruh, 'Kant—Menschenwürde—Sozialstaat: Notizen zu einem Begründungsprogramm' in R Grote *et al* (eds), *Die Ordnung der Freiheit: Festschrift f. Christian Starck zum 70. Geburtstag* (Tübingen, Mohr Siebeck, 2007) 133–50.

[60] N Bobbio noted that '[The Revolutionaries] also needed to consider the individual on his own, free from all social ties and, more to the point, all political ties, in a state like the state of nature, although this was a rational hypothesis which intentionally ignored the historic origins of human societies ... This meant that civil society was no longer a natural state like the family or other social groupings, but something artificial and intentionally built on the voluntary union of natural individuals': N Bobbio, *The Age of Rights* (A Cameron (trans), Cambridge, Polity Press, 2005) 103.

The Declaration rights are well-known and flow from the foundational cluster of freedom and equality (Article 1), together with liberty, property, security and resistance to oppression (Article 2). These rights cannot be guaranteed outside a specific institutional framework which includes a parliament (the word is not mentioned) to adopt statute law 'as the expression of the general will',[61] a court system to carry out justice and decide on punishment (Articles 7, 8, 9, 10), a 'police force' (*force publique*) 'to safeguard the rights of man and citizen' (Articles 12 and 13) funded by a 'common contribution' determined and controlled by citizens (Article 14) and the requirement that 'every public servant' be accountable for his administrative conduct (Article 15).

Closing this arrangement is Article 16, the penultimate Article, which provides the overarching structure and significance of this new order: 'A society where rights are not secured or the separation of powers established has no constitution at all'.[62] In this context, the word 'constitution' can be understood as confirming the distinction between the rights of man and the rights of citizen, and emphasising the importance of this distinction, as without an institutional arrangement, there can be no 'society' and man is reduced to the fictional state of nature (a much discussed topic among Enlightenment philosophers). This provision can also be read as meaning that in the absence of 'society' there can be no free and equal 'citizens', but only subjects deprived of all political rights and control over their destiny. Thirdly, this provision has further been constructed as identifying the two key substantive ingredients of a democratic constitution, understood as the supreme norm setting up a political order, namely as a set of rights, and the principle of separation of powers.[63]

As a result, while these rights can be understood as the historical basis out of which human dignity could subsequently arise as a constitutional concept, the significance of the institutional framework sketched out in the Declaration—a parliament, a court system, a free press, a police force, a fair and transparent tax system, and an accountable administration—must be borne in mind. At the centre of this new constitutional framework is its new principal actor, man as a citizen.

[61] Article 6 continues: 'All citizens have the right to take part in person or through their representatives in its enactment'.

[62] Article 17 defines and protects the right to individual property as 'inviolable and sacred'.

[63] Mounier defined a good constitution in the following terms: 'il faut qu'elle soit fondée sur les droits des hommes, et qu'elle les protège évidemment, il faut donc, pour préparer une constitution, connaître les droits que la justice naturelle accorde à tous les individus, il faut rappeler les principes qui doivent former la base de toute espèce de société, et que chaque article de la constitution puisse être la conséquence d'un principe. Un grand nombre de publicistes modernes appellent l'exposé de ces principes une déclaration des droits' quoted in Morange, above n 53, 14.

IV. DIGNITY AS HUMANITY

By creating humanity as a new constitutional entity and positioning man at the centre of its institutional and human rights framework,[64] the 1789 Declaration arguably created the substantive core of the concept of human dignity, which only became part of the (mainstream) human rights language after 1945. Chronologically, therefore, the word came after the substance it was created to identify. However, from the start in 1789, the constitutional construction of human beings was characterised by its complexity and its ability to evolve so as to capture a range of intertwined identities, which acknowledge (and protect) the uniqueness of human beings in a democratic constitutional order. As is well known, the 1789 Declaration constructed two of these identities in an explicit manner, ie man and citizen; a third identity, the human being as worker, was discussed by the drafters in 1789 (but ultimately not adopted) and developed more fully over the following centuries, albeit in a less central position within constitutionalism than the two other constitutional identities of human beings.

A. Man: Equality, Relationality and Abstraction

Until 1789, and from a philosophical point of view, man had been broadly defined in two complementary ways, by distinction from beasts or animals, and by reference to his Creator, as Imago Dei. Politically and socially, man was defined by his belonging to one of three orders, the aristocracy, the clergy or the third estate. The 1789 Declaration broke away from these definitions by constructing man as a self-referential individual: to be a 'man' and worthy of constitutional protection, it was enough to be born out of a woman.

This ontological definition echoes some of the debates on the fictitious state of nature: man pre-exists society and society's aim is to protect man's natural and inalienable rights according to Article 1. Therefore, the freedom of the 1789 Declaration can also be understood as an ontological freedom, man being no longer made in the image of God is not expected to conform to any pre-determined model set by a higher authority. In particular, man is free to think what he wants, especially in religious matters. Man is also free to communicate and express his thoughts. The sole limit to man's new freedom is the freedom of other men (Article 4), in that man can only be limited by fellow human beings and no longer by God. All men are equal and this

[64] Pierre Manent reminds us that the 'crime of lèse-humanité' started to emerge during the French Revolution, acknowledging the new importance of (ordinary) human beings, complementing and perhaps meant to replace the 'crime de lèse-majesté': Manent, above n 28, 206.

equality forms a crucial part of the revolutionary definition of humanity, as discussed above. This axiomatic equality constitutes the basis of a new social order, breaking away from the previous order resting on inequality and discrimination. The ontological equality of men therefore becomes both the foundation and the ultimate aim of the nascent democratic constitutional order. Built into human rights, this equality is the condition of democracy. Distinctions are still possible, but they can only be justified by 'public utility' ('*utilité commune*', Article 1), and no longer by birth. Furthermore, the 1789 Declaration created man as individual, recognising his constitutional and social existence on his own;[65] in other words, man is no longer defined by reference to groups, social orders, or his belonging to an exclusive community. As a result, man is free to shape his own social identity according to his own beliefs and thoughts.

Importantly, however, man's recognition as individual must not be confused with a selfish and extreme version of individualism. The man born out of the French Revolution and Declarations is arguably defined in his singularity, arguably so that he can better engage in a complex set of relationships with others, with man's equality feeding into the fundamental reciprocity of these interactions. The invention of 'man' therefore went together with the invention of another central component of liberal democracy, ie society, freely and self-consciously constituted by equal men considered in their singularity. The complex connections between man, understood on his own, and society were at the heart of the Enlightenment philosophical and political discussions.

The spirit of dignity arguably makes it possible to capture the particular type of interaction among men that human rights and constitutionalism have promoted since 1789. The resulting constitutional definition of human beings emphasises their dynamic interactions on a reciprocity and equality basis, rather than their static and isolated position in society. This has been captured by the idea of 'fraternity', one of the slogans of the Revolutionaries, and, more recently, by the 'spirit of brotherhood' of the 1948 UN Universal Declaration of Rights, and is at the root of the wider idea of solidarity. From a more theoretical perspective, this dignity-based solidarity of human relationships has been eloquently expressed by scholars like Peter Häberle, who observed that the concept of dignity immediately brings to the fore the connection with the other (*der Du-Bezug*).[66] In a similar vein, former president of the Italian Constitutional Court, Giovanni Maria Flick, noted that human dignity takes its full constitutional significance in its capacity to integrate human beings in society by promoting their mutual relationships; regardless of their uniqueness and their diversity, they are brought

[65] Bobbio, above n 60, 104–5 and Manent, above n 28, 183–201.

[66] P Häberle, *Europäische Verfassungslehre*, 6th edn (Baden-Baden, Nomos, 2009) 288.

together by their ties of solidarity, the only way by which diversity and equality can be reconciled.[67] In terms of human rights, this has important implications, namely, that the 1789 rights, while they are 'natural, inalienable and sacred', are not absolute. Rights are therefore always relative in the sense that they are enjoyed and exercised in a social and relational context. Rights, by definition, can and have to be limited, the crucial question being about the authority and justification for these limitations. As will be seen in the following chapter, this has evolved into a distinction between the core rights of human dignity, which are protected in absolute ways by European constitutionalism, and the non-core rights, which are meant to promote this complex set of human interactions and relationships.

Finally, it has to be noted that the Declaration 'man' is strangely abstract compared to the rich political and philosophical discussions about reason and passions (or inclinations as they were called at the time):[68] the 1789 man has no passion or inclinations, no religion, no social identity, and his wealth is not an issue. This abstraction was subsequently criticised, first by Marx and more recently by feminists. The criticism is no doubt well deserved, but it tends to overlook the conceptual strength of abstraction.[69] While most (if not all) drafters had in mind a white male 'man', the abstract 'man', as a constitutional concept, has a number of advantages from the theoretical point of view of the conceptual foundation of human dignity.[70] The first advantage is its openness and inclusiveness, which has arguably made it possible, many years, if not centuries, later, for this 1789 white 'man' to become female and black, poor and sick, old and young, with each time reliance on the concept of human dignity in human rights texts being used to acknowledge these newly recognised human identities. In other words, the concept of man, like the concept of dignity, could evolve gradually to include and protect a whole range of human identities as they have become socially and politically accepted, opening up the framework of constitutionalism to include them. Therefore, the abstraction of humanity built into the concept of man is arguably what made it a valuable constitutional tool to discuss and protect new dimensions or forms of humanity, such as human embryos (or even 'just' cells) or future generations. Finally

[67] GM Flick, 'Dignità Umana e Tutela dei Soggetti Deboli: Una Riflessione Problematica' in E Ceccherini (ed), *La Tutela della Dignità dell'Uomo* (Naples, Editoriale Scientifica, 2008) 55–56.

[68] S Rials (ed), *La Déclaration des Droits de l'Homme et du Citoyen* (Paris, Hachette, 1988) 326–27.

[69] HG Gadamer, *Au commencement de la philosophie: pour une lecture des Présocratiques* (Paris, Seuil, 2001) 18–19.

[70] Revolutionaries abolished slavery in 1794, and some of the drafters, such as Condorcet were quite 'feminist' for their time. However, the gender bias of the Declaration did not escape Olympe de Gouges who drafted the Declaration of the Rights of Women in September 1791 and died—like a man—by decapitation in 1793.

and importantly, conceptual abstraction is key to promoting a language that can be spoken by all across time and space and that has therefore provided the broad basis of communication necessary for the foundation and protection of human rights, making it possible for this language to evolve over time, and to address new concerns.

B. Citizen: Dignity as Sovereignty

The 1789 Declaration invented the citizen as a constitutional twin of 'man'. As a result, this text is often remembered for the modern invention of civil and political rights, such as freedom (Article 4), participation in law-making (Article 6), presumption of innocence (Article 9), freedom of religion (Article 10), freedom of thought and speech (Article 11) and a right to property (Article 17). Above all, and mentioned first as a natural and inalienable right, is the right to resist oppression (Article 2). All these rights, particularly perhaps the latter, have provided a basis for human dignity as a constitutional concept.

As will be recalled, these rights could not have developed their full constitutional and political significance without the autonomy that the 1789 Declaration both assumed and created as a basis for the rights of man and citizen. This fundamental autonomy contrasts with the heteronomy of the Ancien Regime, where the ultimate source of power and legitimacy rested in God.[71] The text of the Declaration made it very clear that it was drafted by 'the representatives of the French people convened in National Assembly' and did not refer to God as its source.[72] The choice of the phrase 'Supreme Being' (in the Declaration's Preamble) has been understood as a sort of compromise, meant to include other religions than the majority Catholicism.[73] It can further be understood as a gradual step towards eventually severing all ties with the divine as supreme authority, paralleling the choice of a constitutional monarchy as paving the way towards a republic, designed as a secular regime. With the Declaration, sovereignty therefore ceased to be divine and unquestionable, becoming instead human and embodied in the individual citizen, whose new civil rights were primarily about discussing and challenging political power. The right to vote was included as a mechanism to take part in the enactment of statute law (Article 6), but it only subsequently became the paradigmatic civil and political right that we know today, masking perhaps its historical foundation in the freedom to

[71] Gauchet, above n 59, 17: 'L'homme des droits de l'homme surgit de la sécession divine, qui le laisse en sa solitude d'origine devant un univers vacant où librement déployer ses pouvoirs'.
[72] Rials, above n 68, 341.
[73] Morange, above n 53, 32–33.

question.[74] Similarly, the subsequent identification of sovereignty with the nation (and nowadays almost exclusively located in the state), has arguably masked the importance of its individual source in singular human beings. This civic sovereignty was explicitly directed towards the 'preservation of the natural and imprescriptible rights of man' but has no other constitutional finality and, in this sense, is open-ended and totally free constantly to re-invent its own finality.[75]

Finally, it is suggested that this civic sovereignty has had far-reaching consequences on the perception and construction of constitutional time. While the connections between time, constitutionalism and dignity will be discussed more closely in Chapter 6 below, they can be noted here by way of overall reflection on the wider significance of these transformations. Citizens, by taking charge of their law-making, also took charge of their political destiny.[76] This arguably deeply transformed constitutional time, which acquired two new dimensions, past and present, with the past explicitly set out and defined in the Preamble to the 1789 Declaration, as the time of 'public misfortune and government depravity'. By rejecting the unwanted past, the Revolution created the possibility of the present, which was imagined as a better time than the past, namely, a time where the 'ignorance, forgetfulness, or contempt of human rights' (Preamble) could be addressed and remedied. In short, with the invention of the citizen, constitutional time ceased to be divine and eternal in order to become human and changeable, ie triggering a move out of the past into the present.[77]

C. Worker: Dignity as Self-Determination and Social Justice

The third constitutional identity of human beings to emerge out of the French Revolution was arguably as workers. Although there is now a distinction between labour rights and social rights, it is suggested that historically the constitutional definition of man as worker was located at the crossroads of two strands of human dignity: one echoing Kant's self-determination and the other reflecting aspirations and struggles for a life worthy of dignity, which came to be associated with the socialist movements of the following centuries.

[74] Rosanvallon, above n 7.

[75] N Bobbio reminds us that the 1789 Declaration did not enshrine happiness as a specific constitutional goal, and in this differed from the American text: Bobbio, above n 60, 78–80.

[76] With reference to today's context, Erin Daly observes that some constitutions connect dignity and citizenship: Daly, above n 35, 130, 139.

[77] C Dupré and J-r Yeh, 'Constitutions and Legitimacy over Time' in M Tushnet, T Fleiner and C Saunders (eds), *Routledge Handbook of Constitutional Law* (Oxford/New York, Routledge, 2013) 45–56.

The first component of workers' dignity arguably follows the Kantian maxim or, rather perhaps, its spirit (for it is doubtful that the drafters had read Kant) as discussed above. While it does not appear in the 1789 Declaration, it is very explicitly articulated four years later in the 1793 Declaration of Rights, under Article 18:

> Every man can contract his services and his time, but he cannot sell himself nor be sold: his person is not an alienable property (une propriété aliénable). The law knows of no such thing as the status of a servant (domesticité); there can exist only a contract for services and compensation between the man who works and the one who employs him.[78]

In addition to reflecting (at least on paper if not in its implementation) what could be called today a much more social spirit of the 1793 Declaration,[79] this provision illuminates the tight connections between the three constitutional identities of man. The core connection between these three identities is arguably the ideal of dignity. While the term itself is not mentioned, this definition of workers clearly echoes the Kantian distinction between things and men, whereby things have a price and can be sold, while men have no price and can never be reduced to a commercial value. According to Article 18 of the 1793 Declaration, the 'human person may not be an alienable property (*propriété aliénable*)'. Quite clearly, this also reflects a key concern at the time, which is made explicit in the text, namely, the condition of domestic servants (*domesticité*) and serfs. The provision, however, goes further than addressing these issues: it sets out a new constitutional definition of workers, which is directed at all types of workers and not just at servants. While workers can sell 'their services and their time', they may never sell themselves. The prohibition is reflexive and affects both the work-giver who can neither own a worker nor sell him, and the worker himself, who may not renounce his status of man and of citizen by selling himself. Article 18 further acknowledges that, while the work relationship between the 'man who works' and the employer is not one of equality, it is one of mutual recognition (*reconnaissance*) and of respect (*engagement de soin*). Work is therefore about exercising one's fundamental freedom and right to engage in meaningful relationships with fellow human beings, which include but may not be reduced to their economic dimension.

[78] Translation in FM Anderson (ed), *The Constitutions and Other Selected Documents Illustrative of the History of France, 1789—1901* (Minneapolis, MN, HW Wilson, 1904); reprinted in JR Censer and L Hunt (eds), *Liberty, Equality, Fraternity: Exploring the French Revolution* (American Social History Productions, 2001) available at www.columbia.edu/~iw6/docs/dec1793.html.

[79] See, eg Art 21: 'Public relief is a sacred debt. Society owes maintenance to unfortunate citizens, either procuring work for them or in providing the means of existence for those who are unable to labor'. Same source as above n 78.

The fundamental connections explicitly made by Article 18 of the 1793 Declaration between constitutionalism and the definition of work, that is as being respectful of the workers' identity as man and as citizen, continued to be developed after the revolutionary period. Discussion and promotion of working conditions, social justice and, ultimately, of workers' identity and role within a political system were key issues in the socialist movement,[80] which eventually led to what is often identified as the first constitutional codification of human dignity. Drafted under the direct influence of Lassale, Article 151 of the 1919 Weimar Constitution provides that 'The organisation of the economic life must conform to the principles of social justice with a view to guaranteeing a dignified existence (*menschenwürdiges Dasein*) to all'. While this provision was not constructed as a right (either objective or subjective), its codification confirmed the importance of promoting a 'dignified existence' as a social aim for the state. Its impact on the Weimar Constitution was, however, limited due to a lack of binding force and confusion about the exact meaning of the phrase 'dignified existence'.[81] What this provision did, however, was to make the quality of 'economic life' an issue of constitutionalism and to highlight the constitutional importance of a 'dignified existence'.[82]

The same year saw the codification of another work-related facet of the idea of dignity, at a very different normative level, namely, in the part of the Versailles Peace Treaty which established the International Labour Organization (ILO). The foundational principle of this newly created international body was 'labour should not be regarded merely as a commodity or an article of commerce'.[83] Capturing the ILO's overarching concern for 'the well-being, physical, moral and intellectual, of industrial wage-earners' (Preamble to the ILO Constitution), this provision is therefore arguably tightly connected to the promotion of dignity. While the phrase 'human dignity' is not mentioned, the Kantian principle seems to be clearly echoed in these lines and comes to light when the word 'labour' is replaced by labourer

[80] M Mahlmann, *Elemente einer ethischen Grundrechtstheorie* (Baden-Baden, Nomos, 2005) 166–67; see also G Lohmann, 'Human Dignity and Socialism' in M Düwell, J Braarvig, R Brownsword and D Mieth (eds), *The Cambridge Handbook of Human Dignity* (Cambridge, Cambridge University Press, 2014) 126–34.

[81] D Jaber, *Über den mehrfachen Sinn von Menschenwürde-Garantien: Mit besonderer Berücksichtigung von Art.1 Abs. 1 Grundgesetz* (Frankfurt, Ontos Verlag, 2003) 157–73. See also P Unruh, *Weimar Staatslehre und Grundgesetz: ein verfassungstheoretischer Vergleich* (Berlin, Duncker und Humblot, 2004); and HC Nipperdey (ed), *Die Grundrechte und Grundpflichten der Reichsverfassung: Kommentar zum zweiten Teil der Reichsverfassung* (1930) (Kronberg, Scriptor Verlag, 1975) vol 3, 125–49.

[82] As discussed in the following chapter, this connection reappeared in the first constitutional codification of dignity after the Second Word War, under Art 36 of the 1947 Italian Constitution.

[83] International Labour Organization Constitution 1919, first general principle, Part XIII of the Treaty of Versailles, Art 427.

or worker. In fact, the principal objective of the ILO since its creation has arguably been to promote workers' dignity and social justice in the world.[84]

The last provision discussed here by way of closing these initial reflections concerns a slightly different strand of human dignity development and was adopted in 1848 in the French Decree prohibiting slavery:

> Considering that *slavery is an assault upon human dignity; that in destroying man's free will*, it destroys the natural source of law and duty; that it is a flagrant violation of the republican creed: Liberty, Equality, Fraternity.[85] (emphasis added)

This provision is not highlighted here due to its French provenance,[86] but because it is perhaps the very first provision of constitutional significance to enshrine explicitly the phrase 'human dignity'. Moreover, it constructs a very strong and elaborate definition of human dignity, bringing together key threads of that concept, as discussed in this chapter, and making them explicit. The first point to note is perhaps that while slaves' working conditions were (and still are) very harsh and physically inhumane, human dignity's definition focuses on 'man's free will': the Decree prohibits an extreme form of objectification of workers, which reduces them to the condition of a thing or an animal, under the total control of their owners. The second point is the conceptual and normative continuity between human dignity, on the one hand, and liberty, equality, fraternity, on the other, which weaves the spirit of dignity (discussed at the start of this chapter) tightly into the fabric of the political regime promoting the prohibition of slavery. The last point to observe is the connection between respect for human dignity (in the form of prohibition of slavery) and the republican type of the regime, thus confirming that the principle of human dignity goes together with a particular concept of sovereignty, in which individual citizens, as opposed to the monarch, play the key role in adopting the law and shaping the collective destiny.

V. CONCLUSION

This chapter has sought to reconstruct the emergence and complex trajectories of the concept of human dignity since its early incarnation as a

[84] G Rodgers, E Lee, L Swepston and J Van Daele, *The ILO and the Quest for Social Justice, 1919—2009* (Geneva, ILO, 2009). See also A Supiot, *The Spirit of Philadelphia: Social Justice v the Total Market* (S Brown (trans), London, Verso, 2012) and CW Jenks, *Human Rights and International Labour Standards* (London, Stevens & Sons Ltd, 1960).

[85] Rebecca J Scott, 'Dignité/Dignidade: Organizing Against Threats to Dignity in Societies after Slavery' in C McCrudden (ed), *Understanding Human Dignity* (Oxford, Oxford University Press, 2013) 61–77. The original provision reads: 'le gouvernement provisoire, considérant que l'esclavage est un attentat contre la dignité humaine, qu'en détruisant le libre arbitre de l'homme, il supprime le principe naturel du droit et du devoir, qu'il est une violation flagrante du dogme république, liberté, égalité, fraternité [...]'. The above translation is by RJ Scott (at 61).

[86] It was brought to my attention by Rebecca Scott, above.

powerfully evocative and subversive ideal, capturing men's simple and yet unreachable dreams to live their lives as whole human beings, and ultimately to take control over their singular and collective destinies. Human dignity as a concept has evolved out of two fundamental and interconnected transformations: one is from the historical and ordinary meaning of dignity as denoting special social distinction into a constitutional meaning of dignity-as-equality; and the second is the break away from the Ancien Regime, with its absolute monarchy ultimately deriving its authority from God. The French Revolution was a key moment in this process and the 1789 Declaration, while not codifying human dignity, put in place, on paper and in people's minds, the necessary framework out of which the modern concept of human dignity could arise at a later stage.

The first codification of human dignity in the 1919 Weimar Constitution, focusing on social justice and an 'existence worthy of dignity', can be seen as completing human beings' constitutional definition as man and citizen that was started by the 1789 Declaration, by adding to it man as worker. The resulting definition of human dignity is still a hybrid one, with on the one hand aspirations and claims for social justice and equality, and on the other hand a number of emerging normative elements. It is clear that dignity is constructed as a uniquely human quality, with humanity being defined both by the capacity to reason and by birth (biology). This makes human dignity the foundation of citizenship and associated rights; the same logic of self-determination and prohibition of degradation underpins the constitutional definition of man as worker, making human dignity the foundation of (what we now call) labour rights. There is a clear sense that dignity gives human beings a special political status, but human dignity's constitutional status for the period considered in this chapter is still limited, with very few mentions in constitutional texts, uncertain normative value and a substantive meaning that is more about aspirations for greater justice than specific justiciable rights. In this respect, the prohibition of slavery on the explicit ground that it breaches human dignity can be noted as the first instance of giving this concept a constitutional substance, and a clear normative strength, namely, the absolute prohibition of slavery.

While this chapter could not include all struggles that have contributed to the rise of human dignity, focusing on the most momentous and persistent ones,[87] such as the French Revolution and socialist movement, it has confirmed the connections between the rise of human dignity as a constitutional concept, and social and political struggles, or indeed war. In this respect, it has to be highlighted that the first codification of human dignity took place after the First World War in 1919 in the Weimar Constitution and as part of

[87] M Mahlmann, 'Six Antidotes to Dignity Fatigue in Ethics and Law' in C McCrudden (ed), *Understanding Dignity* (Oxford, Oxford University Press, 2013) 593, 596–97.

the Treaty of Versailles for the ILO. As is well known, it took the systematic and savage destruction of humanity caused by the Second World War and totalitarian regimes to propel human dignity to the fore of constitutionalism and human rights, and to complete its construction as a constitutional tool to protect humanity and democracy, paving the way for a systematic process of codification.

3

The Foundations of European Constitutionalism: 1949, 1989, 2009

I. INTRODUCTION

THE LONG LINEAGE of human dignity as a philosophical and political ideal and concept discussed in the previous chapter contrasts with its comparatively short history as a constitutional concept, which is generally understood to have started after the Second World War, when the constitutional concept of human dignity took shape as a kind of manifesto for a new era of peace and democracy.[1] In human rights and human dignity scholarship, two dates are often identified with this beginning. 1948 marked the adoption of the United Nations Universal Declaration of Human Rights, article 1 of which reads: 'All human beings are born free and equal in dignity and rights. They are endowed with reason and conscience and should act towards one another in a spirit of brotherhood'. 1949 marked the adoption of the West German Basic Law, article 1.1 of which reads: 'Human dignity is inviolable. To protect and to respect it shall be the duty of all state authority'.[2]

There is no doubt that the codification of human dignity in these contexts is an extremely important element in understanding both that particular

[1] MA Glendon, *A World Made New: Eleanor Roosevelt and the Universal Declaration of Human Rights* (New York, Random House, 2002). See also H Bielefeldt, 'Die Menschenwürde als Fundament der Menschenrechte' in V Deile, FJ Hutter, S Kurtenbach and C Tessmer (eds), *Jahrbuch Menschenrechte 2005* (Frankfurt am Main, Suhrkamp, 2004) 143–54. At a more philosophical level see JC Isaac, 'A New Guarantee on Earth: Hannah Arendt on Human Dignity and the Politics of Human Rights' (1996) 90 *American Political Science Review* 61 and the recent study of C Menke, 'Dignity as the Right to Have Rights: Human Dignity in Hannah Arendt' in M Düwell, J Braarvig, R Brownsword and D Mieth (eds), *The Cambridge Handbook of Human Dignity* (Cambridge, Cambridge University Press, 2014) 332–42.

[2] The full text of Art 1 continues: '2. The German people therefore acknowledge inviolable and inalienable human rights as the basis of every community, of peace and of justice in the world. 3. The following basic rights shall bind the legislature, the executive and the judiciary as directly applicable law'. For a recent review of the key interpretations of human dignity in German scholarship and the history of this concept see C Goos, *Innere Freiheit: Eine Rekonstruktion des grundgesetzlichen Würdebegriffs* (Bonn, Bonn University Press, 2011).

concept and European constitutionalism more generally.[3] However, the pride of place these dates and texts occupy in the general narrative on post-war democracy in Europe tends to overlook other dates and starting points, thereby simplifying the complexities and richness of human dignity's history and meaning. In order to form a fuller picture of this concept and hopefully to understand it better in the context of European constitutionalism, the scholarly gaze must therefore embrace a wider range of dates and constitutions, before and—significantly—after 1948–49.

The first mention of dignity before 1948[4] is to be found in the Preamble to the Irish Constitution adopted in 1937:

> In the name of the most Holy Trinity, from Whom is all authority and to Whom, as our final end, all actions both of men and States must be referred. [W]e the people of Eire … [G]ratefully remembering their heroic and unremitting struggle to regain the rightful independence of our Nation, [A]nd seeking to promote the common good, with due observance of Prudence, Justice and Charity, so that the dignity and freedom of the individual may be assured, true social order attained, the unity of our country restored, and concord established with other nations.[5]

As will be recalled from the Introduction, this approach to human dignity has not been repeated in the post-war period and subsequent codifications.[6] The 1947 Italian Constitution was the first post-war constitution to enshrine human dignity,[7] as it did so before the adoption of the 1948 UN Universal Declaration, it offers an original approach to codifying dignity, which, while not being so influential as the German model, needs to be noted here as illustrating the possible formulations and uses of (human) dignity in a codified constitution. The Italian Constitution contains three references to dignity: first, Article 3 connects the principle of equality before the law with the

[3] LE Weinrib, 'Human Dignity as Rights-protecting Principle' (2004) 17 *National Journal of Constitutional Law* 325.

[4] The development of human dignity up to 1919 is discussed in the previous chapter. This chapter focuses only on the democratic uses of dignity in European constitution.

[5] T Iglesias, 'The Dignity of the Individual in the Irish Constitution: The Importance of the Preamble' (2000) 89 *Studies* 19; and S Moyn, 'The Secret History of Constitutional Dignity' in C McCrudden (ed), *Understanding Human Dignity* (Oxford, Oxford University Press, 2013) 95–113.

[6] What may be seen in some Irish scholarly writing, however, is a current trend to construct human dignity with a focus on equality and humanity, and perhaps closer to the continental pattern of interpretation developed in the post-war years. In particular see W Binchy, 'Dignity as a Constitutional Principle' in O Doyle and E Carolan (eds), *The Irish Constitution: Governance and Values* (Dublin, Thomson Round Hall, 2008) 307–26; more generally see TJ O'Dowd, 'Dignity and Personhood in Irish Constitutional Law' in G Quinn, A Tingram and S Livingstone (eds), *Justice and Legal Theory in Ireland* (Dublin, Oak Tree Press, 1995) 163–83.

[7] The very first post-war constitutional codification of human dignity can be found in the first draft of the French Constitution, adopted and rejected in 1946. Two key provisions can be noted here: Art 22 reads: 'Tout être humain possède, à l'égard de la société, les droits qui garantissent, dans l'intégrité et la dignité de sa personne, son plein développement physique, intellectuel et moral'. Article 27 provided: 'La durée et les conditions du travail ne doivent porter atteinte ni à la santé, ni à la dignité, ni à la vie familiale du travailleur'.

concept of 'social dignity';[8] secondly, Article 36 refers to dignity in the very specific context of workers' fair remuneration;[9] and thirdly, Article 41 codifies human dignity as a possible boundary to the freedom of 'private economic enterprise'.[10] These provisions approach (human) dignity in a rather social manner, reflecting the immediate post-war spirit as well as the influence of the Communist Party at the time in Italy. While they technically differ from the codification of human dignity since 1949, recent doctrinal writing has tended to read the Italian constitutional approach to human dignity in the light of the mainstream approach to the concept, which has been developed since 1949.[11]

The period after 1949 is particularly interesting for it shows how the codification of human dignity has gradually spread to almost all constitutions in Europe,[12] in three broad waves.[13] The first wave corresponds to democratic

[8] Article 3 reads: '1. 'All citizens have equal social dignity and are equal before the law, without distinction of sex, race, language, religion, political opinions, personal and social conditions. 2. It is the duty of the Republic to remove those obstacles of an economic and social nature which in fact limit the freedom and equality of citizens, impede the full development of the human person and the effective participation of all workers in the political, economic and social organization of the country'. See GP Dolso, 'Articolo 3' in S Bartole and R Bin (eds), *Commentario Breve alla Costituzione* (Padua, CEDAM, 2008) 14–37 and A Celotto, 'Articolo 3' in R Bifulco, A Celotto and M Olivetti (eds), *Commentario alla Costituzione* (Turin, UTET, 2006) 65–87.

[9] Article 36.1 reads: 'Workers are entitled to remuneration commensurate with the quantity and quality of their work, and in any case sufficient to ensure to them and their families a free and dignified existence (*un'esistenza libera e dignitosa*)'. See F Gambini, 'Il Principio di Dignità' in P Cendron *et al* (eds), *I Diritti della Persona* (Turin, Utet, 2005) 231–42; and A Ruggeri and A Spadaro, 'Dignità dell'Uomo e Giurisprudenza Costituzionale (Prime Notazione)' (1991) 3 *Politica del Diritto* 343, 359–62.

[10] Article 41.2 reads: '[Private economic enterprise] may not be carried out against the common good or in a way that may harm public security, liberty, or human dignity'. See R Nira, 'Articolo 41' in R Bifulco, A Celotto and M Olivetti (eds), *Commentario alla Costituzione* (Turin, UTET, 2006) 846–63; M Giampierretti, 'Articolo 41' in S Bartole and R Bin (eds), *Commentario Breve alla Costituzione* (Padua, CEDAM, 2008) 403–19; A Ruggeri, 'Appunti per uno Studio sulla Dignità dell'Uomo, Secondo Diritto Costituzionale' (2011) 1 *Rivista Telematica dell'Associazione Italiana dei Costituzionalisti* 1; and A Mattioni, 'Profili Costituzionali della Dignità Umana' (2008) 2–3 *Rivista di Scienze Giuridiche* 251.

[11] See, eg E Ceccherini (ed), *La Tutela della Dignità dell'Uomo* (Naples, Editoriale Scientifica, 2008); and M Di Ciommo, *Dignità Umana e Stato Costituzionale* (Florence, Passigli Editori, 2010).

[12] As a result, the constitutions which do not explicitly include a reference to human dignity have become the exception to this rule. They include Denmark, the Netherlands, the constitution of which does not include fundamental rights; the constitutions of Malta and Cyprus, possibly because of the British influence on their drafting; and the United Kingdom, which has no codified constitution. This is not to say, however, that human dignity is completely absent from these constitutional orders, as it may have been developed in case law (as in the French, UK and Austrian constitutional orders). On Austria, see K Burger, *Das Verfassungsprinzip der Menschenwürde in Österreich* (Frankfurt am Main, Peter Lang, 2002).

[13] For brief and selective comparative overviews of human dignity in Europe, see N Rao, 'On the Use and Abuse of Dignity in Constitutional Law' (2008) 14 *Columbia Journal of European Law* 201; S Riley, 'Human Dignity: Comparative and Conceptual Debates' (2010) 6 *International Journal of Law in Context* 117.

transitions in the South of Europe, with Greece (Article 2), Portugal (Articles 1, 26 and 59) and Spain (Article 10) between 1975 and 1978. The second wave also marks a democratic transition, this time from Communism in Central and Eastern Europe, with Hungary (Article 54), Croatia (Articles 25 and 35), Bulgaria (Articles 4, 6 and 32), Romania (Article 1), Slovenia (Articles 21 and 34), Estonia (Article 10), Slovakia (Articles 12 and 19), Lithuania (Articles 21 and 25), the Czech Republic (Articles 1 and 10), Latvia (Article 95) and Poland (Article 30) enshrining human dignity in their new or revised constitutions between 1989 and 1997. The 1990s wave of human dignity codification further included Belgium (Article 23) in 1994, as well as Finland, which codified human dignity under Article 1 largely following the German Basic Law in 1995 as part of a major constitutional revision.[14] Finally, and very importantly, the last dignity codification took place at the supranational level, first with the adoption of the European Union Charter of Fundamental Rights in 2000 and then with the Lisbon Treaty, which gave the Charter a constitutional status equal to that of the Treaties and enshrined human dignity as its first foundational value under Article 2 in 2009.

The 'never again' pledge that propelled human dignity into the field of constitutionalism in the immediate post-war years was notoriously strong in West Germany.[15] As can be seen from the subsequent waves and contexts of human dignity codification, this response was not limited to Germany and this chapter therefore argues that human dignity has been used as a constitutional tool to make sense of the past in a range of ways.[16] In constitutional texts human dignity expresses the drafters' promise to leave this unwanted past behind and provides a formal source of rights. While the exact legal substance of human dignity has, as a result, remained open and, according

[14] Article 1 of the Finnish Constitution reads: 'Finland is a sovereign Republic. The Constitution of Finland is established in this constitutional act. The constitution shall guarantee the inviolability of human dignity and the freedom and rights of the individual and promote justice in society…'. Generally, see J Husa, *The Constitution of Finland: A Contextual Analysis* (Oxford, Hart Publishing, 2011) 177.

[15] Horst Dreier points out that dignity was a key ideal of the German resistance since 1943 and figured on the political agenda of the German social democrats (Kreisauer memorandum) in 1944: H Dreier (ed), *Grundgesetz-Kommentar* (Tübingen, Mohr Siebeck, 2004) 153. See also, eg the life and work of Stéphane Hessel: born to a Jewish family in Berlin, he became actively involved in the resistance after miraculously escaping death on several occasions. After the war, he worked with Eleanor Roosevelt to edit the UN Universal Declaration of Human Rights. S Hessel, *Indignez-vous!* (Montpellier, Editions Indigènes, 2010). Hessel died in 2013.

[16] GM Flick, 'Dignità Umana e Tutela dei Soggetti Deboli: Una Riflessione Problematica' in E Ceccherini (ed), *La Tutela della Dignità dell' Uomo* (Naples, Editoriale Scientifica, 2008) 41: 'Insomma, la valorizzazione esplicita e preliminare della dignità—quale momento di apertura e di fondazione di un sistema costituzionale—esprime con molta efficacia la considerazione di essa come valore essenziale e ponte rispetto ad un passato che si vuole non già cancellare e dimenticare, ma rifiutare e rinnegare esplicitamente attraverso l'impegno a che non possa mai più verificarsi'.

to some critics, vague and empty,[17] since 2009 the concept has acquired a very clear and rich substantive core definition at the highest normative level in Europe, ie under Title I of the EU Charter. The last section thus discusses this core meaning and its significance in relation to the idea of humanity in the wider framework of European constitutionalism.

II. MAKING SENSE OF THE PAST

The Second World War and the Nazi regime have had an unprecedented and lasting impact on the law, especially on the ways in which we think about, use and develop it.[18] After the war and the Holocaust, (most) lawyers have become much more critical about the possible abuse and instrumentalisation of the law to serve evil causes. In the immediate post-war years, human rights soon crystallised the new hopes and aspirations for a better world, as well as providing potentially powerful legal tools to make it happen, and in particular to guarantee that the destruction of humanity should never again start in the midst of a formally democratically elected regime.[19] For obvious historical reasons these connections were spelt out with particular strength in the West German context, both in the drafters' discussions and by the Federal Constitutional Court, particularly in the 1950s. Subsequent codifications in other EU Member States also show a tight correlation between codifying human dignity and moving away from dictatorship and civil war, so it is therefore suggested that human dignity has been used as a constitutional tool to leave behind an unwanted past and to lay the foundations of democracy, present and future. This is discussed with reference to three different types of approaches. The first one is the 'never again' pledge as formulated in West Germany, gradually endorsed in subsequent democratic transitions across Europe. The second approach is that of the Hungarian Constitutional Court, which used human dignity as an hermeneutic tool to filter out the unwanted law inherited from Communism. Thirdly, this section discusses the approach adopted by the European Court of Human Rights (ECtHR), which has used the core prohibitions under Articles 2, 3 and 4 of

[17] See, eg C McCrudden, 'Human Dignity and Judicial Interpretation of Human Rights' (2008) 19 *European Journal of International Law* 655, 698: 'All that is left of human dignity, it might be said, is a relatively empty shell provided by the minimum core, but when the concept comes to be applied the appearance of commonality disappears, and human dignity (and with it human rights) is exposed as culturally relative, deeply contingent on local politics and values, resulting in significantly diverging, even conflicting conceptions'.

[18] D Fraser, *Law after Auschwitz: Towards a Jurisprudence of the Holocaust* (Durham, NC, North Carolina Academic Press, 2005).

[19] J Morsink, *The Universal Declaration of Human Rights: Origins, Drafting and Intent* (Philadelphia, PA, University of Pennsylvania Press, 1999), ch 2 'World War II as a Catalyst', 36–91; see also G Hughes, 'The Concept of Dignity in the Universal Declaration of Human Rights' 2011 (39) *Journal of Religious Ethics* 1.

the European Convention on Human Rights (ECHR) to build a firm barrier against the unwanted past and developed a technique of interpretation making space for a better future to unfold at the heart of its human rights construction.

A. 'Never Again'

Capturing the particular post-war determination to rebuild the world on a new basis, 'dignity' arguably became the rallying call in support of a human rights-based democracy.[20] It therefore featured prominently in the preparation of the UN Universal Declaration and in its promotion. The Declaration positioned human dignity at the heart of the nascent international system of human rights protection and, while it provides no definition of this new phrase, its semantic constellation clearly revolves around the uniqueness of humanity, a connection that bears a Kantian resonance as made explicit by one of its drafters.[21] Furthermore, this post-war human rights system was born out of an acute sense of humanity's vulnerability and of the need to ensure that democratic law would never again lead to the systematic destruction of human beings. This 'never again' spirit was particularly strong in the West German Federal Republic where the Basic Law was adopted to move away from the 'horrors of Nazism' and was described in the following way by Edward J Eberle:

> The adoption of the Basic Law in 1949, following the debacle of World War II, signalled a new constitutional order in Germany. Seeking distance from the horrors of Nazism, the Basic Law makes a sharp break from this immediate past, instead drawing deeply upon German tradition to found the legal order on moral

[20] See, eg the seminal 'Four Freedoms' speech delivered before the US Congress by FD Roosevelt: 'Just as our national policy in internal affairs has been based upon a decent respect for the rights and the dignity of all our fellow-men within our gates, so our national policy in foreign affairs has been based on a decent respect for the rights and dignity of all nations, large and small'. Message to Congress, 6 January 1941, reproduced in MR Ishay (ed), *The Human Rights Reader: Major Political Essays, Speeches, and Documents from Ancient Times to the Present* (New York, Routledge, 2007) 480.

[21] Jacques Maritain who played an active role in the preparation of the UDHR appeared to endorse completely the Kantian definition of dignity: 'The human person possesses rights because of the very fact that it is *a person, a whole, master of itself and of its acts, and which consequently is not merely a means to an end, but an end, an end which must be treated as such.* The dignity of the human person? The expression means nothing if it does not signify that by virtue of natural law, the human person has the right to be respected, is the subject of rights, possesses rights. There are things which are owed to man because of the very fact that he is man' (emphasis added): *The Rights of Man and Natural Law* (London, G Bles/ Centenary Press, 1944) 37, quoted by A Sajó, *Limiting Government: An Introduction to Constitutionalism* (Budapest, Central University Press, 1999) 248. See also P Valadier, 'Jacques Maritain's Personalist Conception of Human Dignity' in M Düwell, J Braarvig, R Brownsword and D Mieth (eds), *The Cambridge Handbook of Human Dignity* (Cambridge, Cambridge University Press, 2014) 260–68.

> and rational idealism, particularly that of Kant ... Thus, the Basic Law is a value-oriented constitution that obligates the state to realise a set of objectively ordered principles, rooted in justice and equality that are designed to restore the centrality of humanity to the social order and thereby secure a stable democratic society on this basis.[22]

In addition to being endorsed and developed in German scholarship,[23] this foundation in dignity as rejection of the unwanted past and of all forms of (possible) totalitarianism was developed by the Federal Constitutional Court in several rulings, principally, but not exclusively in the 1950s. In this respect, the 1952 ruling on the unconstitutionality of the Socialist Reich Party (Sozialistische Reichspartei), which established itself in 1949 as a successor of the infamous NSDAP, is especially clear.[24] In that judgment, constitutional judges in particular identified a number of features of the total state, including the Führer principle; the complete insignificance of the individual human being regarding the Volk; the absence of law and the rule of discretion; the desecration of human dignity;[25] and the breach of international treaties and rights of free states, which ultimately created the domination of fear and terror under the NSDAP.[26] While this enumeration is not exhaustive, it gives a clear indication of the legal substance of the 'never again' commitment. This ruling makes it clear that human dignity is used by the German Constitutional Court to move away from the Nazi state described as a 'total state', which subordinated the individual to the 'Volk' and its 'Führer' and created a regime of fear and terror (*Furcht und Schreken*). In this specific judicial construction, the concept of human dignity is therefore meant to avoid a return of the negation of humanity and individuals by making sure that the state cannot become 'total' again, but that it will leave people free to set their own ends, which in this case meant the banning of the disputed party.

[22] EJ Eberle, 'Observations on the Development of Human Dignity and Personality in German Constitutional Law: An Overview' (2013) 33 *Liverpool Law Review* 203. See also N Knoepffler and M O'Malley, 'Human Dignity: Regulative Principle and Absolute Value' (2010) 21 *Journal International de Bioéthique* 63, and more recently C Goos, 'Würde des Menschen: Restoring Human Dignity in Post-Nazi Germany' in C McCrudden (ed), *Understanding Human Dignity* (Oxford, Oxford University Press, 2013) 79–94.

[23] The 'never again' spirit has remained a very significant part of human dignity's definition, including in its use in relation to bioethics, as illustrated by E-W Böckenförde, 'Menschenwürde als normatives Prinzip' (2003) 17 *JuristenZeitung* 809: 'Das Grundgesetz proklamiert und gewährleistet das Grundrecht auf Leben und die Unantastbarkeit der Menschenwürde. Daß diese Garantien in der Verfassung vorhanden sind, kommt nicht von ungefähr. Es waren die bitteren Erfahrungen aus der NS-Zeit, die dazu führten, daß gerade die Unverletzlichkeit und das Achtungsgebot der Menschenwürde in das Grundgesetz aufgenommen wurden, und ebenso das Grundrecht auf Leben, das frühere Verfassungen so nicht kannten'.

[24] BVerfGE 2, 1 of 23 October 1952.

[25] The word '*Schändung*' is translated as desecration by reference to the work of Giorgio Agamben, *Homo Sacer, Sovereign Power and Bare Life* (D Heller-Roazen (trans), Stanford, Stanford University Press,1998). An alternative translation is 'violation'.

[26] BVerfGE 2, 1, 19–20.

A few years later, faced with the issue of the constitutionality of the Communist Party of Germany, the Federal Constitutional Court famously held that human dignity was the highest value of democracy, emphasising that individuals have to develop their personality in the ways they choose, that is free from any social class imposed identity.[27] Significantly, it is in this ruling that the Federal Constitutional Court is understood to have constructed human dignity for the first time as the prohibition on depriving human beings of the freedom to set their own ends and on reducing them to an object, even if allegedly for their own good.[28] This formula echoing the Kantian imperative was to become the hallmark of the German understanding of human dignity,[29] which (as discussed below) has now been endorsed by the EU Commission in its Annual Report on the EU Charter.

The development of post-war constitutionalism, in Germany and in other post-war and post-dictatorship states, can be understood as an attempt to ban each of these elements and to use their exact opposites as foundations for the new democratic order, with the promotion of human dignity as a tool to prevent the desecration of humanity. While not always articulated so expressly or so eloquently, it is noted here that constitutional codification of human dignity in other EU Member States took place in similar contexts. In fact, many constitutions adopted constitutions adopted since 1945 in Europe marked the end of a war (Second World War in France, Italy, Germany), or civil wars (Spain and Greece), as well as long regimes of (in most cases) harsh dictatorships (Portugal, Spain, Greece, Hungary, Bulgaria, Romania, Slovakia, Lithuania, Czech Republic, Latvia and Poland). Several constitutional Preambles explicitly reflect these other manifestations of a 'never again' spirit. They identify the 'regimes that had sought to enslave and degrade humanity' (France 1946), 'the fascist regime … dictatorship, oppression and colonialism' (Portugal 1976) and 'the bitter experiences of the times when fundamental freedoms and human rights were violated in our Fatherland' (Poland 1997) as what the constitution is designed to

[27] BVerfGE 5, 85, 204 of 17 August 1956: 'In der freiheitlichen Demokratie ist die Würde des Menschen der oberste Wert. Sie ist unantastbar, vom Staate zu achten und zu schützen. Der Mensch is danach eine mit der Fähigkeit zur eingenverantwortlicher Lebensgestaltung begabte "Persönlichkeit". Sein Verhalten und sein Denken können daher durch seine Klassenlage nicht eindeutig determiniert sein. Er wird viel mehr als fähig angesehen, und es wird ihm demgemäß abgefordert, seine Interessen und Ideen mit denen der anderen auszugleichen. Um seiner Würde willen muß ihm eine möglichst weitgehende Entfaltung seiner Persönlichkeit gesichert werden'.

[28] BVerfGE 5, 85, 205, see M Mahlmann, *Elemente einer ethischen Grundrechtstheorie* (Baden-Baden, Nomos Verlag, 2008) 234.

[29] The so-called object formula has been repeated and developed in a number of constitutional rulings, including BVerfGE 27, 1 [6]; 45, 187 [228]; 50, 125 [133]; 50, 166 [175]; 72, 105 [116]; 109, 133 [150]; 115, 118 [153]. See E-W Böckenförde, *Recht, Staat, Freiheit: Studien zur Rechtsphilosophie, Rechtstheorie und Verfassungsgeschichte* (Frankfurt am Main, Suhrkamp, 2006) 382–83. For a more recent illustration see R Youngs, 'Germany: Shooting Down Aircraft and Analyzing Computer Data' (2008) 6 *International Journal of Constitutional Law* 331.

protect against. In short, the 'never again' pledge can be understood as a commitment to guard against the advent of (civil) war, oppression, deprivation of liberty, institutionalised inequality, lack of freedom and inhumanity. Significantly, human dignity was enshrined in a prominent position in these constitutions, either as the first of their respective human rights chapters,[30] or as a key feature of the new constitutional order listed at the start of constitutions,[31] thus establishing a strong connection between the rise of a new type of democracy developed through post-Second World War constitutionalism and human dignity.

Against the background of the EU Charter's adoption and after providing an outline of key stages in the development of human rights protection in Europe, Klaus Günther's observation aptly summarises the Europe-wide significance of the foundation of human rights in the 'never again' pledge:

> This brief and cursory European history of human rights has already led several authors to the conclusion that human rights have to do with the negative historical experiences of collective traumata. They are embedded in a *memory of injustice and fear*. Of course, this memory is not explicitly incorporated in the text of human rights. But it forms an important, perhaps even the most important, part of the political culture in which these rights are accepted and criticized, given, claimed, interpreted, applied and enforced. If you want to know what is meant by 'human dignity' or 'equal concern and respect' for every human being, you can either look at the various kinds of definitions, at a huge record of legal cases, or you can think of the German Gestapo torturing a political opponent or the Holocaust of European Jews. Human beings differ in wealth, gender, ethnicity, and other properties, but what they all have in common is the experience of pain and humiliation.[32]

Post-war constitutionalism in Europe, deeply rooted in this memory of inhumanity and dictatorship, can therefore be understood as a process of 'learning by disaster',[33] which to a large extent explains the meteoric rise of human dignity in the field of constitutionalism and human rights. While it has undoubtedly been foundational, this 'never again' rejection of the past has, however, not been the only way of making sense of the past through the prism of human dignity.

[30] Key examples of human dignity as first constitutional provision of human rights sections include Germany (1949), Spain (1978), Hungary (1989) and Poland (1997). Alternative first provisions under these sections include citizenship/nationality, equality and life.

[31] Human dignity as a key feature of a new democratic regime: Germany (Art 1); Sweden (Art 2); Greece (Art 2); Portugal (Art 1); Bulgaria (Art 4); Romania (Art 1); Czech Republic (Art 1).

[32] K Günther, 'The Legacies of Injustice and Fear: A European Approach to Human Rights and their Effects on the Political Culture' in P Alston (ed), *The EU and Human Rights* (Oxford, Oxford University Press, 1999) 126 (emphasis in original). See also Susan Marks, 'The European Convention on Human Rights and its "Democratic Society"' (1996) 66 *British Yearbook of International Law* 209.

[33] J Habermas, 'Learning by Disaster? A Diagnostic Look Back on the Short 20th Century' (1998) 5 *Constellations* 307.

B. Filtering the Past

As a constitutional tool to make sense of the past, the concept of human dignity has also been used to filter the law inherited from previous and undemocratic regimes. This situation was typical of post-communism where, for a mixture of pragmatic and political reasons, communist law could not be rejected en bloc when the new democratic parliaments were elected and the communist constitutions were gradually revised or replaced by democratic ones. While parliaments adopted new law in compliance with the new democratic standards, it fell to the newly created constitutional courts[34] to undertake this filtering process.

The Hungarian Court created by the 1989 constitutional revision soon established itself as the front-runner of constitutional justice during the post-communist transition.[35] In this context, its deliberate use of human dignity as a tool to make sense of the past is exemplary of an attempt gradually to reconstruct democratically sound foundations for human rights. The Hungarian context involved a peaceful political and constitutional transition, or rather a 'change of system' as it was called (*rendszerváltás*), closely monitored by the newly created constitutional court. During these years, the challenge faced by Hungarian constitutionalism was to 'rebuild the ship at sea'.[36] Constructing the present out of the past, the Hungarian Constitutional Court devised a novel 'revolution under the rule of law' doctrine of interpretation. The Court opted for a very gradual process of sorting the communist heritage, considering each (challenged) rule on its merits and assessing its constitutionality by reference to the new democratic requirements. Central to this filtering process was the concept of human dignity, modelled on the 1949 German Constitution and enshrined in the 1989 constitutional revision at the head of the fundamental rights section.[37] As a result, rules on issues as diverse as trade union representation, capital punishment, participation in sport competitions, determination of one's biological father, public prosecutors' powers, the right to a healthy environment, civil servants' private life, and access to higher education were subjected to the human dignity constitutional filter. In each case, the constitutional court refrained from a blanket rejection of the contested rule on the sole basis of

[34] H Schwartz, *The Struggle for Constitutional Justice in Post-Communist Europe* (Chicago, IL, Chicago University Press, 2000).

[35] Generally, see C Boulanger, *Hüten, Richten, Gründe: Rollen der Verfassungsgerichte in der Demokratisierung Deutschlands und Ungarns* (Berlin, Epubli, 2013).

[36] J Elster, C Offe and UK Preuß, *Institutional Design in Post-communist Societies: Rebuilding the Ship at Sea* (Cambridge, Cambridge University Press, 1998).

[37] Article 54.1 read: 'In the Republic of Hungary every human being has the innate right to life and human dignity, and no one may be arbitrarily deprived of these rights'. Generally, see C Dupré, *Importing the Law in Post-communist Transitions: The Hungarian Constitutional Court and the Right to Human Dignity* (Oxford, Hart Publishing, 2003) 129–54.

its (temporal) communist origin, and endeavoured instead to scrutinise it carefully in order to decide whether it met the new democratic standard of human dignity. While the outcome of this process was very generally the nullification of what had been key pillars of communist law and control over society (typically, for instance, the public prosecutors' power and state control over associations), this process of filtering was at least as important as its (perhaps predictable) outcome. In this context of democratic transition, human dignity was therefore used as a constitutional tool to re-interpret some of the fundamental rights inherited from the previous communist constitution. This technique of interpretation arguably constitutes a more nuanced way of filtering out the unwanted past, by re-orienting in a liberal democratic way some of its more typically communist rights, such as children's right to receive care and protection from the state, access to higher education or the provision of maternity benefits and childcare. This new and human dignity-compatible interpretation of fundamental rights could then be used as a new constitutional basis for rights, thus creating a sort of starting point for the present to unfold. This interpretation further contributed to come to terms with a difficult past by acknowledging the wrongfulness of some of the past laws. The constitutional present gradually emerging out of this process is as a result tightly linked to the past, being an (albeit incompletely) corrected and improved version of it and developing through a constant constitutional conversation with it. Constructed in this way, the constitutional present is never closed, as it is not exempt from human dignity-based scrutiny and re-interpretation.

C. Constructing Temporal Boundaries

The ECHR adopted in 1950 in order to guarantee a set of civil and political rights at the core of liberal democracy across Europe also reflects the scars left by the war and the Holocaust. As is well known, the ECHR did not enshrine human dignity,[38] but it is hard to imagine that its drafters did not

[38] Jean-Paul Costa (former president of the ECtHR) notes that the absence of 'human dignity' in the ECHR text is surprising and it might be explained by a 'more practical, pragmatic and mechanism-oriented' nature of the ECHR compared to that of the UN Universal Declaration adopted two years before. J-P Costa, 'Human Dignity in the Jurisprudence of the European Court of Human Rights' in C McCrudden (ed), *Understanding Human Dignity* (Oxford, Oxford University Press, 2013) 393–94. It has to be noted that, since 1950, human dignity has been enshrined in some Additional Protocols to the ECHR, notably in the Preamble to Additional Protocol 13 abolishing the death penalty, the first paragraph of which reads 'Convinced that everyone's right to life is a basic value in a democratic society and that the abolition of the death penalty is essential for the protection of this right and for the full recognition of the inherent dignity of all human beings'. Moreover, dignity figures prominently in the title of the Oviedo Convention of 1997: Convention for the Protection of Human Rights and Dignity of the Human Being with regard to the Application of Biology and Medicine.

think this concept to be crucial.[39] What the ECHR did enshrine, however, is a set of three very strong prohibitions on killing, on torturing and on subjecting people to inhuman and degrading treatment or punishment, and on holding people in slavery and forced labour (under Articles 2, 3 and 4). These three core prohibitions arguably also reflect the 'never again' spirit of the post-war period discussed above and, as was confirmed half a century later by the EU Charter, constitute the human rights core of human dignity.[40] The ECtHR, it is suggested, has used these prohibitions in order to set very clear temporal boundaries, and to construct what could be called a 'time wall' between the past and the present. As it targets a specific set of practices, the ECtHR's approach to the past is more specific than the general 'never again' logic, which is about the whole structure and operation of the state. Moreover, it is argued that the ECtHR construction of the past has led to the present being understood not just as a negative past,[41] but as the preparation towards a future. Three temporalities have therefore arguably emerged out of the ECtHR construction of these provisions: a past, a present and the possibility of a future. These three temporalities are both connected and distinguished from each other by reliance on the living instrument doctrine of interpretation, a novel technique of interpretation first used in relation to Article 3, and which constructs the future as a better present, namely as a time where human rights will be better protected.[42] This is perhaps no more visible than in relation to the ECtHR's hermeneutic approach to torture under Article 3.[43] This is well illustrated in the *Selmouni v France* case, in which the Court held:

> However, having regard to the fact that the Convention is a 'living instrument which must be interpreted in the light of the present-day conditions' ..., the

[39] 'It is likely that the drafters nevertheless had the concept of dignity in their minds, especially because the very establishment of the Council of Europe in 1949 and the elaboration of the Convention, the first treaty prepared within its framework, were the work of persons firmly opposed to the atrocities and barbarity of the Second World War': Costa, above n 38, 394.

[40] Discussed below.

[41] 'Again, to restrict art 3 to treatment which might have been regarded as torture or inhuman or degrading in the immediate aftermath of the atrocities of World War II would have robbed the article of the vital protection which it has provide to those in custody in every part of the Continent': N Bratza, 'Living Instrument or Dead Letter: The Future of the ECHR' (2014) 2 *European Human Rights Law Review* 116, 120.

[42] G Letsas, *A Theory of Interpretation of the European Convention on Human Rights* (Oxford, Oxford University Press, 2007) 58–79 and A Mowbray, 'The Creativity of the European Court of Human Rights' (2005) 5 *Human Rights Law Review* 57. See also Chapter 7.

[43] On Art 3 ECHR, generally see C Grabenwarter, *European Convention on Human Rights: A Commentary* (Munich/Oxford, Verlag CH Beck/Hart Publishing, 2014) 31–52. With regard to Art 4 ECHR, the small number of rulings make it difficult to draw wider conclusion; the landmark ruling in *Siliadin v France* of 26 October 2005, Application no 73316/01, is discussed further in Chapter 5 but can be noted here as illustrating a similar approach. Article 2 case law does not tend to refer to human dignity; however, since *McCann v United Kingdom* in 1995 its construction is closely related to that of democracy; see S Skinner, 'The Core of McCann: Lethal Force and Democracy under the ECHR' in C Ovey *et al* (eds), *The Right to*

> Court considers that certain acts which were classified in the past as 'inhuman and degrading treatment' as opposed to 'torture' *could be classified differently in future. It takes the view that the increasingly high standard being required in the area of the protection of fundamental rights and liberties correspondingly and inevitably requires greater firmness* in assessing breaches of the fundamental values of democratic societies.[44] (emphasis added)

On this basis the ECtHR held that the French Government had breached Article 3. While this extract can be understood as a stern warning to Member States, it also reflects a particular construction of time, which aims to increase the distance between the past and the present, by lowering the threshold of severity, and to pave the way towards a better future. This sense of dynamic built into the ECtHR interpretation arguably implies that the past is never closed and that it can and must constantly be revisited. This constant critical (re-)interpretation is arguably crucial as it is only by making sense of the past that constitutionalism can make space for the present and the future to unfold, without being limited to the prohibition on repetition of the unwanted past.[45] Finally, the ECtHR construction of the 'present-day conditions' is built on Member States' practice and standards (as well as on international law). In so doing therefore, the ECtHR has brought into its own construction of time that of the Member States, gradually setting out the wider and dynamic time structure for European constitutionalism.[46]

The three approaches to the past considered above (the 'never again' logic, the filtering process, and the time wall) are complementary, and are by no means the only strategies put forward by constitutionalism and democracy to address the injustice of the past, both in relation to issues of compensation for material loss and in terms of accepting the wrong and the hurt caused.[47] What they have in common is the aim of promoting a constitutional discussion on, and ultimately an assessment of, the past by reference

Life: Twenty Years of Legal Developments since McCann v The United Kingdom, Publication in Honour of the Deputy Registrar of the European Court of Human Rights Michael O'Boyle (2015, forthcoming).

[44] *Selmouni v France*, Application no 25803/94, ECtHR, 28 July 1999, para 101.

[45] With this in mind, the torture practices that have formed part of the war against terrorism and the academic discussions on the possibility of the lawfulness of torture are particularly concerning, because they arguably abolish the boundaries between past and present. Generally, see G Frankenberg, 'Torture and Taboo: An Essay Comparing Paradigms of Organised Cruelty' (2008) 56 *American Journal of Comparative Law* 403.

[46] It has to be noted that in the EU, the European Court of Justice/Court of Justice of the European Union (ECJ/CJEU) does not operate on an assumption that the past is necessarily bad and has to be rejected or filtered out. Rather, its construction of constitutional traditions common to the Member States considers the past as a reservoir of good practice and models to turn to for inspiration. The term 'traditions' is ambiguous as it denotes both the past and current practices or even aspiration.

[47] See, eg I Pogany, *Righting Wrongs in Eastern Europe* (Manchester, Manchester University Press, 1997) and more generally R Teitel, *Transitional Justice* (Oxford, Oxford University Press, 2010).

to a particular understanding and ideal of humanity at the foundation of post-war constitutionalism. Their other shared feature is to be activated by individual applicants. This construction of time therefore depends (to some degree) on individual vigilance and on a certain democratic activism, as well as on the existence of appropriate remedies (such as individual petition before the ECtHR or constitutional complaint at the national level), and effective access to justice, facilitated for instance by legal aid provision.

III. HUMAN DIGNITY AS CONSTITUTIONAL FOUNDATION

The role of human dignity as a tool of constitutional foundation is, however, not limited to the critical memory characteristic of European constitutionalism, for foundation necessarily also calls for the possibility of imagining a future. By definition, at the moment of foundation, namely, the drafting and adopting of the new constitutional text, the substance of this future is not determined, so while the future remains (deliberately perhaps) undefined, it bears two characteristics. The first is the future's mere existence, that is having established that the present must be different from the past, constitutionalism is founded on the assumption that the present is meant to change, making way for the future to happen. The second characteristic of the future is about its substance, which is envisaged as an enhanced quality of democracy and of human rights protection. We find here again the concept of human dignity used as a powerful rhetorical device to formulate this commitment in constitutional texts adopted since 1945 in Europe. As is discussed in the second part of this section, this solemn commitment is supported by, and finds its practical dimension in, the use of dignity as a source of constitutional rights, which have given European constitutionalism its particular structure and identity since the Second World War.

A. The Promise of Dignity

The end of the Second World War and of dictatorships broke cycles of violence and cruelty, opening up a new prospect of peace and democracy. The foundation of European constitutionalism rests in the promise that a new beginning is possible, that a time of humanity can actually follow the time of inhumanity, and that the time of democracy can replace the time of dictatorship and totalitarianism. This promise is arguably what has given European constitutionalism both its principal foundation and sense of direction. In practice, this promise was made by the drafters, first of the UN Universal Declaration of Human Rights in 1948 and, subsequently, of the Member States' constitutions, particularly of those adopted after (civil) war and dictatorship across Europe.

While the promise of dignity is very striking in this post-1945 context, it is a technique of constitutional foundation which arguably goes back to perhaps what can be called the beginning of human rights in Europe with the 1789 French Declaration of the Rights of Man and the Citizen. Its drafters deliberately and explicitly positioned the text at a key temporal junction, between a past that had to be rejected, but which must always be remembered, and the promise of a new beginning and a better future:

> The representatives of the French convened in National Assembly,
>
> Considering that ignorance, *forgetfulness* (*l'oubli*), or contempt of human rights are the sole causes of public misfortune and government depravity,
>
> Have resolved to set out in a *solemn declaration* the natural, inalienable and sacred human rights,
>
> In order that this declaration, *ever present* to all members of the body social, may *call constantly to mind* their rights and duties,
>
> So that the acts of the legislature and of the executive, measured at any moment *against the final end of all political institutions*, be rendered more respectful thereof. (emphasis added)

In 1948, when human dignity was explicitly codified for the first time, the drafters of the post-war foundational bill of rights adopted a very similar approach to those of the 1789 Declaration, positioning human dignity at the interface of past and present:

> Whereas *recognition of the inherent dignity* and of equal and inalienable rights of all members of the human family is *the foundation of freedom, justice and peace in the world*; whereas *disregard and contempt for human rights have resulted in barbarous acts which have outraged the conscience of mankind* ...; whereas the people of the United Nations reaffirmed their faith in fundamental human rights, in the dignity and worth of the human person ..., whereas Member States *have pledged to achieve the promotion of universal respect for and observance of human rights and fundamental freedoms*. (emphasis added)

The parallels are clear between these two foundational texts: memory of inhumanity and 'barbarous acts', the beginning of a new era, an explicit promise to protect human rights henceforth which constitutes a promise of a better future. The key distinction between these two texts is the phrase 'human dignity' that appears in the 1948 text, prompting its subsequent uses in national constitutions and international human rights conventions.[48] While the reasons for choosing this particular phrase will possibly always

[48] On dignity in international law, see A Marhaun, *Menschenwürde und Völkerrecht* (Tübingen, Köhler-Druck, 2001); P Capps, *Human Dignity and the Foundation of International Law* (Oxford, Hart Publishing, 2009); and R Andorno, 'International Policy and a Universal Conception of Human Dignity' in NJ Palpant and S Dilley (eds), *Human Dignity in Bioethics: From World Views to the Public Square* (New York, Routledge, 2013) 127–41.

remain a little mysterious, comparing both texts highlights a crucial semantic and political shift between the definition of human beings as 'man and citizen' in 1789 and as 'the members of the human family' in 1948. This shift is of wider significance as it is suggested that human beings are from then on explicitly defined as belonging to humanity.[49] As might be recalled from the previous chapter, the constitutional definition of human beings as part of humanity had already been formulated during the Enlightenment with the 1789 Declaration's emphasis on the 'natural rights' or the 'rights of Man', as well as by Kant's definition of humanity on the basis of reason and dignity. The 1948 Declaration confirms these connections and elaborates on them, defining humanity at the crossroads of biology, equality and the 'spirit of brotherhood'.[50] In the context of the post-war period, this is a significant addition as the war and in particular the labour and concentration camps had demonstrated that reducing people to their mere biological existence and survival could destroy their humanity. What makes people human is also their belonging to the human family on a basis of equality among all and 'a spirit of brotherhood'. The definitions of humanity and dignity remain abstract and open, which may be understood as humanity becoming a constitutional project, namely, a self-aware open process of (re) construction, instead of its past destruction,[51] in which human rights have a key role to play within the framework of constitutionalism.

Promises are typical and powerful acts of foundation, and in the immediate post-war context, the foundational priority was arguably to ban in the most absolute way possible those 'barbarous acts' which destroyed human beings in their physicality and in the spirit of equality and brotherhood in which they relate to each other. As a result, the ECHR prohibitions on killing, on torture and the infliction of inhuman and degrading treatment or punishment, and slavery, servitude and forced labour represent without doubt the political core of human dignity. Yet, however crucial these prohibitions were at the time and have since been, complying with them does not arguably exhaust the promise of dignity on which European constitutionalism rests. It is therefore suggested here that these prohibitions are part of the wider project of post-war constitutionalism, which aims to give (back) to humanity its own fate and the power to shape its own destiny. This has been particularly powerfully expressed by Imre Kertész, winner of

[49] On the dignity of the human species see D Feldman, 'Human Dignity as a Legal Value, Part I' (1999) *Public Law* 682, 684.

[50] See, eg H Hoffmann, 'Die versprochene Menschenwürde' (1993) 118 *Archiv für öffentliches Recht* 370, 376; and E Daly, *Dignity Rights: Courts, Constitutions and the Worth of the Human Person* (Philadelphia, PA, University of Pennsylvania Press, 2013) 11–25.

[51] G Agamben, *Sovereign Power and Bare Life* (D Heller-Roazen (trans), Stanford, CA, Stanford University Press, 1998); see also D Fraser, *Law After Auschwitz: Towards a Jurisprudence of the Holocaust* (Durham, NC, Carolina Academic Press, 2005), in particular ch 3 'Dead Man Walking: Law and Ethics after Auschwitz', 51–76.

the Nobel Prize for Literature, in relation to the Jewish people in his book *Fateless*.[52] This state of 'fatelessness' (*sorstalanság*) is one that has deprived other human beings of their dignity too; in this respect one can mention the situation of stateless persons,[53] asylum-seekers and minorities. While it was originally made in the particular post-war and post-dictatorship contexts, the appeal of human dignity as a foundational promise for a new and fairer era has arguably also extended to other contexts of constitutional foundation, not characterised by the end of war or dictatorship, such as in Belgium in 1994 or Finland in 1995 and 2000.[54] As will be discussed in the following section, the EU Charter adopted in 2000 closes this phase of human dignity codification by endorsing Member States' constitutional approach to human dignity.[55]

The human dignity promise is anchored in a powerful sense of idealism shared by the human rights movement, in the belief that life can be better and that human beings can make a better life for themselves by using the toolkit of democracy and human rights.[56] In this sense the post-war dignity promise has its roots in the Enlightenment belief in emancipation and in humanity's capacity and willingness to better itself.[57] The whole post-war re-foundation in human dignity can therefore be understood as being driven by what can be called, by reference to Ernst Bloch's work, the principle of hope,[58] and by a constitutional commitment not to deprive human beings of this (as far as we know) exclusively human capacity to dream of better worlds.[59] We must, of course, not fool ourselves that the beautiful words of

[52] I Kertész, *Être sans destin* (Paris, Actes Sud, 1998); in English: *Fateless* (N and C Zaremba (trans), London, Vintage, 2006).

[53] Which originally prompted Hannah Arendt to reclaim dignity as the right to have rights, see A Kesby, *The Right to Have Rights: Citizenship, Humanity and International Law* (Oxford, Oxford Scholarship Online, 2012).

[54] As explained in the Introduction.

[55] C Dupré, 'Article 1: Human Dignity' in S Peers, T Hervey, J Kenner and A Ward (eds), *The EU Charter of Fundamental Rights: A Commentary* (Oxford, CH Beck/Hart Publishing, Nomos, 2014) 3.

[56] G Frankenberg, 'Human Rights and the Belief in a Just World' (2014) 12 *International Journal of Constitutional Law* 35.

[57] P Allott, *Eunomia: New Order for a New World* (Oxford, Oxford University Press, 1990).

[58] E Bloch, *The Principle of Hope* (N Plaice, S Plaice and P Knight (trans), Cambridge, MA, Massachusetts Institute of Technology Press, 1986).

[59] The connections between hope and dignity were made explicit by German, ECHR and then UK judges in relation to prisoners' right to have a review of their life-long sentence, see *Vinter v United Kingdom*, ECtHR, 9 July 2013: 'The [German Federal Constitutional] court found that the State could not turn the offender into an object of crime prevention to the detriment of his constitutionally protected right to social worth … The State struck at *the very heart of human dignity if it stripped the prisoner of all hope of ever earning his freedom*' (para 69, emphasis added); see also para 113. In *Hutchinson v United Kingdom*, Application no 57592/08, ECtHR, 3 February 2015, the Fourth Section of the ECtHR repeated the reference to human dignity, but made no connection to hope and found no violation of Art 3 ECHR due to recent UK case law on life sentences adopted following *Vinter*. This is discussed further in Chapter 6.

human rights declarations (or constitutional provisions) will suffice to keep evil at bay and to construct a better democracy that we hope can materialise. Against naive romanticism, the promise of human dignity brings to light the awareness that there is no guarantee that the future will be better, and this may be seen as an encouragement or an empowerment (some may say a duty) to take action to bring this future into existence. Therefore in today's Europe, the *Sapere Aude* Kantian appeal might well be translated as an empowering call for dignity.[60] In any event, European constitutionalism has arguably endeavoured to substantiate this promise by creating a distinct institutional framework for liberal democracy revolving around sophisticated human rights guaranteed in constitutions, thus making human dignity the 'highest moral notion of democratic humanity'[61] and the source of all constitutional rights.

B. Dignity as a Source of Constitutional Rights

While, as discussed in the previous chapter, the concept of human dignity could not possibly have emerged as a constitutional concept without the Enlightenment and French Revolutionaries declaring human rights in the first place, in the post-war context and human rights texts, human dignity is the basis of human rights. In that sense, post-war European constitutionalism marked the beginning of a new era. By putting state power after the commitment to human rights and 'reconfiguring the relationship between the individual and the state',[62] post-war constitutionalism has created new normative hierarchies and priorities. To paraphrase Article 1 of the draft German Basic Law, individuals do not exist for the state, but the state exists for the individual.[63] This has led to human dignity being positioned at the very heart of Member States' constitutions, largely following the German model in this respect, and among the defining principles of a state and/or

[60] This *Sapere Aude* (Dare to know) call could be understood now as 'dare to speak up against indignity'. See P Allott, 'Kant or Won't: Theory and Moral Responsibility: The BISA Lecture, December 1995)' (1997) 23 *Review of International Studies* 339, 356.

[61] '"La dignité humaine" est la notion morale la plus haute de l'humanité démocratique': P Manent, *Cours familier de philosophie politique* (Paris, Gallimard, 2011) 317.

[62] LE Weinrib, 'Human Dignity as Rights-protecting Principle' (2004) 17 *National Journal of Constitutional Law* 325, 330.

[63] '(1) Der Staat ist um des Menschen willen da, nicht der Mensch um des Staates willen. (2) Die Würde der menschlichen Persönlichkeit ist unantastbar. Die öffentliche Gewalt is in allen ihren Erscheinungsformen verpflichtet, die Menschenwürde zu achten und zu schützen', quoted by Mahlmann who lists the other versions of what became Art 1 of the German Basic Law: M Mahlmann, *Elemente einer ethischen Grundrechtstheorie* (Baden-Baden, Nomos Verlag, 2008) 244–47. See also R Will, 'Die Menschenwürde: Zwischen Versprechen und Überforderung' in F Roggan (ed), *Mit Recht für Menschenwürde und Verfassungsstaat: Festgabe für Dr Burkhart Hirsch* (Berlin, Berlin Wissenschaftsverlag, 2006) 29–31.

under the first provision of the constitution's section or chapter on rights.[64] This approach was endorsed by the European Union when it drafted its own Charter of Fundamental Rights in 2000, which enshrined human dignity under its very first Article, thus formally endorsing the human rights milestones of the ECHR and the West German Basic Law.

The immediate and practical consequence of enshrining human dignity in prime position in constitutions has been to make it the source of all other constitutional rights. In political philosophy, dignity was famously described by Hannah Arendt as the right to have rights, calling for a re-foundation of democracy on a new political principle after the failure of the Weimar Republic.[65] More recently and in the field of constitutional jurisprudence, this has led scholars to define human dignity as a kind of 'mother right': '*Muttergrundrecht*' or '*anyajog*',[66] or a matrix principle ('*principe matriciel*')[67] needed for the continuous protection of constitutional rights.[68] These images express the fact (and the claim) that human dignity can 'give birth' to new rights, for instance rights that were not codified in a constitution at the time of drafting because they had not been formalised as such.[69] What is important to note here is that human dignity is thus the normative and theoretical source of all types of rights, regardless of their belonging to so-called 'generations', thus promoting a holistic protection of humanity.

As a result and in recent years, case law development and academic discussions have tended to focus on the connection between human dignity and social, economic and cultural rights, particularly with regard to the issue of entitlement to welfare protection from the state.[70] In this sense, the Belgian Constitution makes the most explicit connections between human dignity and social, economic and cultural rights,[71] but it is not the only example. In fact, human dignity provisions in post-1945 constitutions have arguably picked up, in their own ways, on some of the nineteenth century social issues

[64] This is very clear in the case of Spain, Portugal, 1989 Hungary and Finland.

[65] Generally see Kesby, above n 53.

[66] Dupré, above n 37, 67–71.

[67] B Mathieu, 'Pour une reconnaissance de "principes matriciels" en matière de protection constitutionnelle des droits de l'homme (1)' (1995) *Recueil Dalloz Sirey (Chronique)* 211.

[68] A Barak, *Human Dignity: The Constitutional Value and the Constitutional Right* (Cambridge, Cambridge University Press, 2015) ch 9 'Human Dignity as a Framework Right (Mother Right)', 156–69.

[69] Judicial constructions of human dignity are discussed in the next chapter.

[70] B Klein Goldewijk, A Contreras Baspineiro and PC Carbonari (eds), *Dignity and Human Rights: The Implementation of Economic, Social and Cultural Rights* (Antwerp, Intersentia, 2002). In relation to recent German constitutional case law, see I Leijten, 'The German Right to an *Existenzminimum*, Human Dignity and the Possibility of a Minimum Core Socioeconomic Rights Protection' (2015) 16 *German Law Journal* 23.

[71] Belgian Constitution, Art 23 reads: 'Everyone has the right to lead a life in conformity with human dignity. To this end, the laws, decrees and rulings alluded to in Article 134 guarantee, taking into account corresponding obligations, economic, social and cultural rights, and determine the conditions for exercising them. These rights include notably: (1) the right

relating to dignity, such as social equality, decent pay and decent work.[72] In addition, post-communist constitutions have retained some of the social and welfare protection from the communist era, although these provisions were not necessarily phrased in terms of human dignity.[73] The welfare dimension of dignity in European constitutionalism, however, is certainly not communist in spirit or in practice and encompasses a much wider range of 'welfare traditions', including that of the United Kingdom and those developed by the Nordic States.[74] Acknowledging this European heritage, the drafters of the EU Charter enshrined in it a section entitled 'Solidarity' including rights ranging from specific labour rights to provisions for social security and social assurance, health care and on access to 'services of general economic interests'.[75]

By contrast, the role of human dignity as the foundation of civil and political rights tends to be less discussed, perhaps because they have become a taken-for-granted component of constitutionalism and liberal democracy. It is important, however, not to forget that the constitutional commitment to human dignity is also the foundation of these rights. At a philosophical level and as will be recalled from the previous chapter, Kant made the connection between humanity, dignity and participation in the making of the universal law. The capacity to set one's own ends therefore became both the definition of human dignity and a philosophical foundation for the right to vote and other crucial civil and political rights, such as freedom of conscience, expression, religion and protest (which were just emerging in the wake of the French Revolution). Building on this in the post-war period, Hannah Arendt derived the 'right to have a place in the world' and to belong to a political community from human dignity.[76] Seen in this light, it is arguably important to distinguish between the source of sovereignty, resting in the

to employment and to the free choice of a professional activity in the framework of a general employment policy, aimed among others at ensuring a level of employment that is as stable and high as possible, the right to fair terms of employment and to fair remuneration, as well as the right to information, consultation and collective negotiation; (2) the right to social security, to health care and to social, medical and legal aid; (3) the right to have decent accommodation; (4) the right to enjoy the protection of a healthy environment; (5) the right to enjoy cultural and social fulfillment': Legal Department of the Belgian House of Representatives, January 2009, translated by A MacLean.

[72] See, eg the Italian Constitution mentioned above.

[73] The approach to welfare rights in post-communist constitutionalism led to intense discussion, see, eg A Sajó, 'How the Rule of Law Killed Hungarian Welfare Reform' (1996) 5 *East European Constitutional Review* 31.

[74] See, eg 2000 Finnish Constitution, Art 19.1, which reads 'Those who cannot obtain the means necessary for a life in dignity have the right to receive the indispensable care'. See J Husa, *The Constitution of Finland: A Contextual Analysis* (Oxford, Hart Publishing, 2011) 169–210 and, more generally, M Scheinin (ed), *The Welfare State and Constitutionalism in the Nordic Countries* (Århus, Phønix -Trykkeriet A/S, 2001).

[75] T Hervey and J Kenner (eds), *Economic and Social Rights under the EU Charter of Fundamental Rights* (Oxford, Hart Publishing, 2003).

[76] H Arendt, *The Origins of Totalitarianism* (New York, Harcourt, Brace, 1973) ch 9 'The Decline of the Nation-State and the End of the Rights of Man', 267–304.

individual, and the constitutional framework for its exercise, set up at the national and supranational levels in Europe. In practical terms, therefore, emphasising the foundation of civil and political rights in human dignity may well be a way forward in constructing a concept of EU citizenship and in conceptualising the connections between the others (for instance, the non-EU citizens) and the 'nationals', as well as in refining the existing rights flowing out of EU citizenship.[77]

Last but not least, human dignity is the foundation of rights that do not yet exist or have not yet been fully formulated as such. This is clear in its judicial uses, where human dignity is deployed as a hermeneutic tool to draw new rights out of the existing ones. Significantly, it has also been the intellectual tool used to try to conceive, and give normative substance to, the so-called third generation rights. This is well illustrated in relation to aspects of bioethics,[78] future generations rights, and environmental protection.[79] Overall therefore, the commitment of European constitutionalism to human dignity is a constant reminder of the principle of indivisibility of human rights, and that emerging human rights must arguably be crafted with reference to the protection of human beings understood, not just as singular biological units, but rather as part of the human family, and in order to promote constructive and fulfilling interrelationships, including with the generations yet to come.

This section has shown that while the post-war promise of dignity was necessarily full of indeterminacy,[80] it is by no means empty. On the contrary, it has re-configured the power relationships between states and individuals, giving human beings the possibility to regain and (so it is hoped) maintain control of their destiny. In this process, human dignity has technically been a crucial font (or matrix) of specific constitutional rights, making it possible to ensure a continuous and evolving protection of human beings' complex and unpredictable lives. While the constitutional definition of human dignity can arguably never be exhausted in the sum of these rights, European constitutionalism nevertheless provides a synthetic definition for human dignity, which as discussed below, is now located at the highest normative level of Europe.

[77] D Kochenov, 'The Right to Have What Right? EU Citizenship in Need of Clarification' (2013) 19 *European Law Journal* 502; and AJ Menéndez, 'Which Citizenship? Whose Europe: The Many Paradoxes of European Citizenship' (2014) 15 *German Law Journal* 907.

[78] D Beyleveld and R Brownsword, 'Human Dignity, Human Rights and Human Genetics' (1998) 61 *Modern Law Review* 661 and R Andorno, 'Human Dignity as a Common Ground for a Global Ethics' (2009) *Journal of Medicine and Philosophy* 1.

[79] In this respect, the work of Hans Jonas has lost none of its relevance: *Prinzip Verantwortung* (Frankfurt am Main, Suhrkamp, 1989). More recently, see Felix Ekardt, 'Toward a New Approach in Discourse Theory in Justice and Law' (2012) *Archiv für Rechts- und Sozialphilosophie* 377 and M Düwell, 'Human Dignity and Future Generations' in M Düwell, J Braarvig, R Brownsword and D Mieth (eds), *The Cambridge Handbook of Human Dignity* (Cambridge, Cambridge University Press, 2014) 551–58.

[80] F Ost, *Le temps du droit* (Paris, Odile Jacob, 1999) 17.

IV. NORMATIVE DEFINITION OF HUMAN DIGNITY

While (nearly) all constitutions since the post-war era have enshrined human dignity, none of them have provided any definition for this complex constitutional concept, thus leaving the phrase 'human dignity' without apparent normative substance, a situation perceived as a weakness by some of its critics.[81] This gap has, however, been filled by what may be considered here as Europe's latest constitutional text adopted at the supranational level, namely, the Lisbon Treaty, and crucially the EU Charter, which came into force in December 2009.[82] The Lisbon Treaty makes human dignity the first foundational value of the EU under Article 2, which reads:

> The Union is founded on the *values of respect for human dignity*, freedom, democracy, equality, the rule of law and respect for human rights, including the rights of persons belonging to minorities. These values are common to the Member States in a society in which pluralism, non-discrimination, tolerance, justice, solidarity, and equality between women and men prevail.[83] (emphasis added)

This provision echoes and endorses Member States' constitutional construction of human dignity as a foundational value[84] and enshrines it as the first of its foundational values, giving it the highest possible ranking. This prominence is confirmed and strengthened in the EU Charter, which enshrines dignity as its first provision, under its first title dedicated to 'dignity'.[85] The EU definition of human dignity, as deriving both from Article 2 TEU and the first Title of the EU Charter, therefore arguably provides a long awaited missing link[86] in the concept's construction in European constitutionalism.

[81] See notably R Macklin, 'Dignity is a Useless Concept: It Means No More than Respect for Persons or their Autonomy' (2003) 327 *British Medical Journal* 1419.

[82] K Schwarzburg, *Die Menschenwürde im Recht der Europäischen Union* (Baden-Baden, Nomos, 2012).

[83] As part of the drafting process of the Treaty Establishing a Constitution for Europe, there were many individual proposals for the phrasing of Art 2, all of which enshrined human dignity as the first foundation. There were three different views. One from Lord Tomlinson who favoured an emphasis on democracy rather than on dignity as '[it] arise[s] from the other values'. Second, the Rt Hon David Heathcoat-Amory MP proposed to delete the mention of human dignity from the text as 'although a worthy concept, dignity is a subjective term once placed in a lawyer's brief'. The third jointly came from two Portuguese MPs (Maria Eduarda Azevedo and Alberto Costa): it focused on respect for human rights, equality between men and women, rule of law, tolerance, justice and solidarity.

[84] C Dupré, 'Dignité dans l'Europe constitutionnelle: entre inflation et contradiction' in J Ziller (ed), *L'Européanisation des droits constitutionnels à la lumière de la Constitution pour l'Europe* (Paris, l'Harmattan, 2002) 121–35.

[85] K Wolfram, 'Die Rolle der Menschenwürde in der EU-Verfassungsdebatte' in M Fisher (ed), *Der Begriff der Menschenwürde: Definition, Belastbarkeit und Grenzen* (Frankfurt am Main, Peter Lang, 2005) 27–46; and J Meyer (ed), *Kommentar zur Charta der Europäischen Union* (Baden-Baden, Nomos, 2003); and M Borowsky, 'Würde des Menschen' in MJ Meyer (ed), *Kommentar zur Charta der Grundrechte der Europäischen Union*, 4th edn (Baden-Baden, Nomos Verlag, 2014) 1–124.

[86] Two key dignity ECJ rulings can be mentioned here: C-377/98 *Kingdom of the Netherlands v European Parliament*, 9 October 2001 and C-36/02 *Omega Spielhallen-und*

Moreover and as a result, the EU Charter provides the first detailed substantive definition of human dignity as a constellation of core prohibitions.

A. A Constellation of Core Prohibitions

The first striking feature of the EU Charter's definition of human dignity is its textual similarity with the ECHR core prohibitions on killing, torturing and on holding in slavery as the Charter explicitly endorses these. Indeed, the first Title of the Charter can be described as a cluster or constellation of core prohibitions. Explicitly presented as a mere codification of existing law,[87] this approach to human dignity differs from the domestic constitutional drafting and builds on it by bringing together under the dignity label a set of core rights, thus giving human dignity an explicit normative substance:

- Article 1: 'Human dignity is inviolable. It must be respected and protected.'
- Article 2: 1. 'Everyone has the right to life.' 2. 'No one shall be condemned to the death penalty, nor executed.'
- Article 3: 1. 'Everyone has the right to respect for his or her physical and mental integrity.' 2. 'In the field of medicine and biology, the following must be respected in particular: (a) the free and informed consent of the person concerned, according to the procedures laid down by law; (b) the prohibition of eugenic practices, in particular those aiming at the selection of persons; (c) the prohibition of making the human body and its parts as such a source of financial gain; (d) the prohibition of reproductive cloning of human beings.'
- Article 4: 'No one shall be subjected to torture or to inhuman or degrading treatment and punishment.'
- Article 5: 1. 'No one shall be held in slavery or servitude.' 2. 'No one shall be required to perform forced or compulsory labour.' 3. 'Trafficking of human beings is prohibited.'

Automatenaufstellung GmbH v Oberbürgermeisterin der Bundestadt Bonn, 14 October 2004. Both rulings contain explicit dignity-based arguments, apparently brought before the ECJ by the applicants and the Advocates General. It has to be noted that the ECJ made no reference to the EU Charter in either of these rulings. This is discussed further in Chapter 4.

[87] The last sentence of the Preamble is very explicit: 'To this end, it is necessary to strengthen the protection of fundamental rights in the light of changes in society, social progress and scientific and technological developments *by making those rights more visible* in a Charter' (emphasis added). The explanatory notes to the Charter specify the sources of Title 1 provisions as being a combination of the ECHR (Arts 2, 4 and 5) as complemented by Art 1 of Additional Protocol 6 to the ECHR in relation to Art 2 EU Charter. The other main source is the 1998 Convention on Human Rights and Biomedicine and its Additional Protocol ETS 168 which prompted the inclusion of Art 3 EU Charter (originally not included under the ECHR).

This set of core prohibitions follows the Union's commitment to 'place the individuals at the heart of its activities', announced in the Preamble to the Charter and confirmed since then in the *Annual Reports on the Application of the Charter*, starting in 2010:

> Human dignity is *the basis of all fundamental rights*. It guarantees the *protection of a person from being treated as a mere object by the State or by its fellow citizens*. The rights and freedoms under the title Dignity, such as the right to life, and the prohibition of torture and slavery, must be respected so we can exercise other rights and freedoms in the Charter, for example freedom of expression and freedom of association. None of the rights laid down in the Charter may be used to harm the rights of another person.[88] (emphasis added)

This definition follows that of the ECHR[89] and embraces the Member States' approach to human dignity as the overarching prohibition on instrumentalising human beings. While endorsing the constitutional heritage, the Charter goes further in a number of ways. For a start, by comparison to Article 2 ECHR, the protection of the right to life is considerably strengthened in the wording of Article 2 EU Charter which explicitly mentions the abolition of the death penalty under Article 2.2, thus acknowledging the two Additional Protocols 6 and 13, ratified by all the EU Member States. Similarly, Article 3 EU Charter codifies the existence of 'a right to respect for his or her physical and mental integrity', developed both by the ECtHR at the crossroads of Article 3 (prohibition of inhuman and degrading treatment) and Article 8 (protection of privacy and personality), and by the 1997 Oviedo Convention on Human Rights and Biomedicine.[90] Article 5 EU Charter updates Article 4 ECHR by adding the now well-recognised and major human rights issue that human trafficking represents for the EU and its Member States. The only ECHR provision that has remained untouched by the EU Charter's drafters is the prohibition of torture, inhuman and degrading treatment or punishment under Article 4 EU Charter, perhaps a sign that the ECtHR's living instrument approach has provided a sufficiently robust technique of protection and a benchmark for the EU.[91]

Moreover, it has to be noted that the right to life loses the prime position it has under the ECHR, which in the EU Charter is now occupied by human

[88] *2010 Annual Report from the Commission on the Application of the EU Charter of Fundamental Rights* (2010) 21. The same definitional paragraph is repeated in the Reports of 2011, 2012 and 2013.

[89] Under Art 52.3 EU Charter, the meaning and scope of these provisions have to be constructed as the same as those laid down by the Convention.

[90] See S Michalowski, 'Article 3: The Right to Integrity of the Person' in S Peers, T Hervey, J Kenner and A Ward (eds), *The EU Charter of Fundamental Rights: A Commentary* (Oxford, CH Beck/Hart Publishing/Nomos, 2014) 39.

[91] M Nowak and A Charbord, 'Article 4: Prohibition of Torture and Inhuman or Degrading Treatment or Punishment' in S Peers, T Hervey, J Kenner and A Ward (eds), *The EU Charter of Fundamental Rights: A Commentary* (Oxford, CH Beck/Hart Publishing/Nomos, 2014) 61.

dignity. This is largely in line with national constitutions where human dignity tends to appear before the right to life, but is a novelty in relation to the ECHR. This reversal of normative hierarchies, by putting life after dignity, is therefore bound to affect both the construction of the principle of sanctity of life (which underpins the ECHR system of human rights protection) and the construction of human dignity, presented in the Charter as a right both separate from and superior to the right to life.[92] Overall, the EU definition of human dignity endorses the 'never again' commitment discussed above, by making human dignity both its first foundational value, and substantiating it under the Charter with a set of core prohibitions, most of which were originally enshrined in the ECHR. The EU Charter therefore adopts the ECHR approach to constructing the constitutional present as separated from the unwanted past by a 'time wall', made of these absolute prohibitions.

B. Embracing Humanity

In addition to the rights discussed above, the EU Charter's codification of human dignity brings to light dimensions of humanity that had until then not been acknowledged and explicitly protected in national constitutions. The first new development explicitly acknowledges the elderly as a category of humanity in need of specific human rights protection under Article 25, which provides that 'the Union recognises the rights of the elderly to lead a life of dignity and independence and to participate in social and cultural life'. This codification reflects a growing awareness that the population appears to be ageing and that elderly people are increasingly vulnerable to a number of human rights abuses, such as discrimination, neglect or degrading and harmful treatment at the hands of their carers.[93] The phrase 'a life in dignity and independence' is not defined, but arguably includes a core quality of life as protected by the Title I human dignity rights. In addition, this provision acts as a crucial reminder that ageing should not deprive people of their humanity, their ability to engage with and enjoy a range of positive interactions with fellow human beings, and the possibility of remaining active members in society and in the political community to which they belong. While children have been acknowledged as subjects and beneficiaries of human rights since the 1990s, in particular under the 1990 UN Convention

[92] In the absence of case law, the significance of this change of hierarchies has yet to unfold; see Dupré, above n 55, 3.

[93] C O'Cinneide, 'Article 25: The Rights of the Elderly' in S Peers, T Hervey, J Kenner and A Ward (eds), *The EU Charter of Fundamental Rights: A Commentary* (Oxford, CH Beck/Hart Publishing/Nomos, 2014) 693. See also B Mikołajczyk, 'Is the ECHR Ready for Global Ageing?' (2013) 17 *International Journal of Human Rights* 511.

on the Rights of the Child, explicit acknowledgement of 'the elderly' is a recent normative development in human rights law is and not yet protected by a matching convention at the UN or EU levels.[94] The concept of human dignity is arguably instrumental in extending and refining the constitutional definition of humanity so as to include older people.

The second development in humanity's constitutional definition through the concept of human dignity is the recognition of a worker's 'right to working conditions which respect his or her health, safety and dignity' under Article 31.1 of the EU Charter. This is also a significant development in relation to most Member States' constitutions,[95] which do not acknowledge workers' dignity in such an explicit manner, as well as in relation to EU labour law, which had until then mainly focused on (sexual and racial) harassment as a narrow definition of human dignity.[96] Highlighting the normative connections between Articles 1, 3 and 31 of the EU Charter, labour lawyer Alan Bogg understands this provision as being 'the most fundamental of labour rights of the EU Charter'[97] and constructs it as providing overall protection for 'norms of civility' in the workplace.[98] Moreover, with this provision, the Charter's drafters (perhaps unwittingly) arguably continued the process of constitutional recognition of workers' humanity led by the socialist critique of human rights and capitalist economy in the nineteenth century and discussed in the previous chapter. As a result, it is suggested that the so-called object formula, endorsed by the European Commission in its annual reports on the EU Charter as a broad definition of human dignity, equally applies to human beings in the context of work situations and relationships, and that workers' humanity is now fully recognised (at least on paper) at the highest normative level of European constitutionalism.[99]

Overall, the codification of human dignity in the EU Charter has arguably led to a fuller recognition (and protection) of humanity by European constitutionalism, confirming that it is not limited to specific nationality or citizenship, but is inclusive of everyone. Furthermore, reliance on human dignity serves to extend the hitherto almost exclusively biological and

[94] Colm O'Cinneide refers to the United Nations Principles for Older Persons of 1991 and the more recent 'Chung Report' prepared by the Advisory Committee to the Human Rights Council in January 2010. In Europe, the point of reference is Art 23 European Social Charter on the right of elderly persons to social protection: see O'Cinneide, above n 93, 697–98.

[95] The exception is the 1947 Italian Constitution, with its Art 36.1, mentioned above.

[96] A Bogg, 'Article 31: Fair and Just Working Conditions' in S Peers, T Hervey, J Kenner and A Ward (eds), *The EU Charter of Fundamental Rights: A Commentary* (Oxford, CH Beck/Hart Publishing/Nomos, 2014) 833–68. See also R O'Connell, 'The Right to Work in the ECHR' (2012) 2 *European Human Rights Law Review* 176. These issues are discussed in more detail in Chapter 5.

[97] Bogg, above n 96, 837.

[98] ibid 855.

[99] This is discussed in more detail in Chapter 5.

'natural' definition of humanity[100] to encompass (under Article 3) its genetic dimension and the reality that it can now be engineered, sometimes with specific aims, such as ridding human beings of genetic 'imperfections'.[101] This provision may therefore be understood as an attempt to prevent abusive manipulations of the human genome. Arguably and importantly, this provision can further be understood as an attempt to preserve the mystery of human attractions and affinities, as well as the role of chance that is so crucial to human reproduction, and to humanity itself. Finally, for all its effort and innovation in embracing an expanding definition of humanity, the EU Charter remains silent on the latter's beginning and end, namely, the issue of the constitutional status of human embryos and the constitutionality of euthanasia and assisted suicide, three well-known dignity issues, which are equally controversial and divisive.

What is clearly coming to light in the EU Charter definition of humanity through the concept of human dignity is its temporal dimension. The impact of time on human life, specifically, in relation to ageing, is acknowledged for the first time, and the emphasis on workers' dignity has its roots in the Working Time Directive.[102] Moreover, the ECtHR's construction of temporal boundaries between the past and the present is retained and consolidated by the EU Charter, which explicitly builds in the prohibition on the death penalty and on human trafficking. Standing out in this context, the prohibition of human reproductive cloning adds a new element to this construction of human and constitutional time, which had so far focused on keeping the past of inhumanity away from the constitutional present. Unlike most of the practices prohibited under the first title on Dignity, which are associated with an unwanted past, reproductive cloning of human beings is not a practice of the past. Rather, it is a possibility of the (perhaps very near) future. Therefore, what is appearing under the EU Charter is a new dimension of

[100] The Portuguese Constitution (as revised in 1997) was exceptional in its recognition of the genetic identity of human beings under Art 26.2: 'The law shall guarantee the personal dignity and genetic identity of the human being, particularly in the creation, development and use of technology and in scientific experimentation'.

[101] 'L'AMP, qui s'est ouverte à la détection des caratéristiques avec le tri des embryons, n'a pas su inventer une régulation internationale (en témoigne l'extension du tourisme médical) et a fini par devenir un enjeu financier, idéologique. Loin de se contenter de compenser un handicap affectant cette fonction essentielle qu'est la procréation, elle se transforme aujourd'hui en moyen de "dépasser" certaines propriétés de notre espèce, de la différence sexuelle au vieillissement, et représentera finalement une solution de rechange généralisable à la procréation—depuis toujours aléatoire—. ... L'homme augmenté sera la créature d'une société nécessairement policée, dont l'ordre est déjà annoncé par les dispositifs d'identification et de surveillance': J Testard, 'Repenser la procréation médicalement assistée', *Le Monde Diplomatique* (April 2014) 28. See also J Testard, *Faire des enfants demain* (Paris, Seuil, 2014).

[102] Originally Directive 93/104/EC, amended by Directive 2000/34/EC and Directive 2003/88/EC, see Bogg, above n 96, 835. See also D McCann, 'Decent Working Hours as a Human Right: Intersections in the Regulation of Working Time' in C Fenwick and T Novitz (eds), *Human Rights at Work: Perspectives on Law and Regulation* (Oxford, Hart Publishing, 2010) 509–28.

constitutional time, that of a negative future as a result of this prohibition on human reproductive cloning. Whether this is an effective approach to regulating human cloning and reproduction is a separate question.[103] What is interesting to note, however, is the negative construction of the future as a 'never ever' temporality, paralleling that of the present constructed in terms of a 'never again' past. This provision can further be understood as an attempt to freeze the artificial development of humanity in its current genetic state. Overall, the EU Charter has endorsed the construction of time developed by the ECtHR and added to it the idea of a future, which is also constructed by reference to human dignity.

V. CONCLUSION

The codification of human dignity in the 1948 UN Universal Declaration made this concept visible to all, connecting it explicitly with human rights and humanity. The chapter has discussed how the apparently tautological and vague construction of human dignity, the definition of humanity through dignity, has in fact made it possible to speak the unspeakable, anchoring the traumatic experience and memory of the Second World War, particularly that of the Holocaust, into the foundation of constitutionalism. As a result, post-war constitutionalism has introduced a new dimension of human dignity, namely, its inviolability, first asserted by the West German Basic Law in 1949 and subsequently endorsed by the EU Charter in 2000, in force since 2009. While the idea of inviolability deserves closer attention, two points can be noted here: one is its tight normative correspondence with a set of absolute prohibitions, first established by the ECHR and then endorsed by the EU Charter under its first Title on human dignity; the other is its more ancient roots in the inalienability of the natural rights of man as they were declared in 1789.

In addition, the post-war uses of human dignity have confirmed the constitutional definition of man inherited from 1789 and from the nineteenth century's social struggles, by emphasising the right to life under Article 2 ECHR and related Additional Protocols, together with workers' dignity explicitly enshrined in the EU Charter. This chapter has further shown how the concept of human dignity is gradually replacing that of 'man' to define humanity, as a result of two related movements. One has involved the increasing concretisation of 'man' (presented in very abstract terms in the 1789 Declaration) into a range of specific incarnations, such as workers, the elderly, children, the disabled and women, who are now explicitly protected

[103] See for instance: S Vöneky and R Wolfrum (eds), *Human Dignity and Human Cloning* (Leiden, Martinus Nijhoff Publishing, 2004).

by constitutional texts, as well as the explicit acknowledgment of the genetic dimension of humanity, which since the 1990s has complemented humanity's biological definition, as illustrated under Article 4 EU Charter. The other movement is the increasing awareness of dimensions of humanity that are not yet existent or identifiable (because they cannot yet be defined in precise terms), nevertheless combined with the increasing sense that this 'not yet' humanity needs to be acknowledged and protected by constitutions and human rights instruments. The phrase human dignity is therefore becoming a primary constitutional tool to protect a concept of humanity going much beyond the existing individual human beings, to include the whole of mankind, future generations, as well as a form of humanity that for now we cannot even imagine.

Finally, post-war constitutionalism has confirmed the constitutional framework inherited from the 1789 Declaration, namely a codified constitution guaranteeing the separation of powers and protection of rights, and strengthened these by adding two features to European constitutionalism, the creation of a level of normativity above that of the state and the development of human rights protection at a European level, first with the ECHR and now with the EU Charter (albeit with a different scope). As is discussed in the following chapter, constitutional codification of human dignity has therefore given human beings a concept, a voice and an institutional framework to challenge the sovereign law and alleged breaches of their humanity and perceived injustice. In this process, (constitutional) courts have provided a new forum of discussion for human dignity, wherein judges are key actors in developing the concept's meanings.

4

Human Dignity: A Judge-Made Concept

I. INTRODUCTION

THIS CHAPTER CONTINUES to explore the making of human dignity as a constitutional concept after its emergence in post-war codified constitutions as a solemn promise to protect humanity and always to remember times and causes of inhumanity. As discussed in the previous chapter, this commitment was eventually codified at the highest normative level in the European Union, namely, under Article 2 TEU, making human dignity the EU's first 'foundational value', and under the first Article of the EU Charter, which enshrined human dignity as 'inviolable'. While these provisions can be seen as the culmination of a process of national and supranational codification, they do not mark the end of the wider process of transformation of human dignity from a philosophical and political ideal into a constitutional concept.

Crucial in the making of human dignity have been its uses by constitutional judges. In fact, it is the judicial construction of human dignity that first attracted scholarly attention. Indeed, courts' prolific and imaginative interpretation of human dignity has significantly contributed to making this concept a part of every day human rights adjudication. When considered in its world-wide extension, however, this judicial dimension of human dignity may not always indicate a clear substantive meaning.[1] Yet, when considered in the framework of European constitutionalism, a much clearer picture of human dignity's meanings and uses begins to appear.[2] While at the time of writing it is too soon for the CJEU to have developed a substantial body

[1] See, eg C McCrudden, 'Human Dignity and Judicial Interpretation of Human Rights' (2008) 19 *European Journal of International Law* 655; LR Barroso, 'Here, There and Everywhere: Human Dignity in Contemporary Law and in the Transnational Discourse' (2012) 35 *Boston College International and Comparative Law Review* 332.

[2] Generally see L Burgogne Larsen (ed), *La dignité saisie par les juges* (Brussels, Bruylant, 2010); and M Di Ciommo, *Dignità Umana e Stato Costituzionale* (Florence, Passigli Editori, 2010).

of human dignity case law on the basis of Article 1 EU Charter,[3] national constitutional courts and the European Court of Human Rights (ECtHR) have already produced sufficient case law to make this study possible. The selection of courts considered here is based on two criteria. In line with the focus on constitutionalism, and as explained in the Introduction, this chapter focuses on constitutional courts and the two supranational European courts, the ECtHR and the European Court of Justice/Court of Justice of the European Union (ECJ/CJEU). Importantly, these have also been chosen because they represent different types of courts and a range of constitutional contexts, so as to include developments beyond the immediate post-war foundation discussed in the previous chapter.[4] The selection of courts is therefore representative of most (if not all) judicial approaches to human dignity within the EU. The chapter considers common law (mainly the UK Supreme Court, but also the High Court) and civil law (German, French and Hungarian) courts; national courts and the two supranational courts; courts operating in the immediate post-Second World War context (the German Federal Constitutional Court) and a court emblematic of post-communist transitions (the Hungarian Constitutional Court between 1990 and 1998);[5] typical constitutional courts (the German and Hungarian courts) and an atypical one (the French Constitutional Council); finally, a generalist supranational court (the ECJ/CJEU) and a specialist supranational human rights court (the ECtHR). Not all constitutional courts operating in the EU could be included in this study, but the above selection arguably provides a solid basis for understanding human dignity's significance as a judge-made concept.

In order to counter the difficulty triggered by the question 'what is human dignity in case law?' found in many studies of this concept, this chapter focuses instead on the question 'why?' have judges developed the concept of human dignity, which is notoriously abstract and therefore presumably very difficult to use in a context of adjudication.[6] As a result, the chapter does not propose to reconstruct human dignity's substantive meaning out of a

[3] The first case decided on Art 1 by the CJEU was C-411/10 *NS v Secretary of State for the Home Department* jointly with C- 493/10 *ME, ASM, MT, KP, EH v Refugee Applications Commissioner, Minister for Justice, Equality and Law Reform* of 21 December 2011. See the case note by J Buckley in (2012) 2 *European Human Rights Law Review* 205.

[4] Selecting these courts has also depended on my linguistic abilities to read the case reports in the original languages, as well as my familiarity with the various legal systems from which they are extracted, so that I could understand the significance of case law more fully and accurately.

[5] For a discussion of Hungarian dignity developments since 2010, see C Dupré, 'Human Dignity: Rhetoric, Protection and Instrumentalisation' in GA Tóth (ed), *Constitution for a Disunited Nation: On Hungary's 2011 Fundamental Law* (Budapest, Central European University Press, 2012) 143–70.

[6] C Dupré, 'Constructing the Meaning of Human Dignity: Four Questions' in C McCrudden (ed), *Understanding Human Dignity* (Oxford, Oxford University Press, 2013) 113–22.

comprehensive survey of case law in Europe. Rather, it is deliberately selective and focuses on the first rulings in which human dignity was deployed in a significant way by judges. The methodological assumption underlying this approach is that the 'first-time rulings' are driven by compelling reasons and can therefore illuminate the concept's significance and its impact on human rights adjudication, and beyond this, on European constitutionalism as a whole. In numerous rulings the word 'dignity' is mentioned in passing, without having any apparent impact on the reasoning, while in other cases, where judges seem to focus more on dignity, they do not develop it. In constitutional orders where dignity is not codified, such as the European Convention on Human Rights (ECHR), the UK common law and EU law up until 2009, it is even more difficult to identify a 'first-time ruling', as dignity has been used in a very diffuse manner. It has nevertheless been possible to select a range of such rulings, and reasons for specific choices are made clear in each case discussed below. With this in mind, the period considered here stretches from 1951 to 2013, that is from the early years of German constitutional case law to (at the time of writing) a recent ECtHR ruling.

Judges' role in constructing human dignity has been particularly crucial in the constitutional orders where it is not enshrined in the constitution or the founding Treaty, such as France, the ECtHR, the EU and the United Kingdom.[7] Looking at this set of cases, the first section argues that judges have constructed dignity by reference to the post-war dignity commitment, endorsing it and re-activating it. The second striking feature of the judicial construction of human dignity is that it has been explicitly constructed by drawing on what can be called a European heritage; in practice, as discussed in the central section of this chapter, this has been done through the reliance on comparative law drawing on European norms and case law. This use of European and comparative materials is not just motivated by the search for inspiration, but as argued in the last part of this chapter, judges have understood and constructed the protection of human dignity as the essence of European constitutionalism.

II. ENDORSING AND RE-ACTIVATING THE FOUNDATIONAL PROMISE

Studies of dignity case law are often quick to highlight its apparent directionlessness and messiness and they are also quick to criticise judges for their apparent or possible misuse of judicial discretion.[8] The significance of

[7] On dignity in Austrian constitutional law, see K Burger, *Das Verfassunsprinzip der Menschenwürde in Österreich* (Frankfurt am Main, Peter Lang, 2002).

[8] 'La dignité humaine est en passe de devenir la notion la plus agaçante de la litérature judiciaire, tant elle se prête à des utilisations variées. Elle est l'alibi des caprices des juges, et, par voie de conséquence, la bête noire de la doctrine': Ph Martens, 'Encore la dignité humaine: réflexion

the very existence of such case law itself is often missed and deserves closer attention. Indeed, it was not obvious that such an abstract concept, which crystallised so many and often inconsistent dreams, aspirations and values, could be used by judges at all, especially considering that its legal nature (neither clearly a subjective right, nor a clear-cut value or principle) did not facilitate their task.[9] Despite these difficulties, judges have risen to the challenge and used dignity to endorse the post-war foundational promise of European constitutionalism, re-activating its use in relation to contexts and facts very different from those that influenced its initial formulation.

A. Significance of Human Dignity Case Law

Human dignity case law in Europe is notable both in terms of quantity and quality. A simple key word search in the ECtHR database will bring up hundreds of references; even in the United Kingdom, where the concept is still largely underused compared to other European constitutional orders, such a search nevertheless brings up a similar amount of recent case law.[10] In Germany, where human dignity has tended to be used very selectively as a kind of *ultima ratio* of judicial reasoning, case law is nevertheless quite substantial in quantity and, more to the point, in quality, having shaped German constitutional law and culture perhaps more than any other provision of the constitution.[11] In terms of human dignity issues arising in case law, Erin Daly's book provides a fair sense of their wide span across the whole human rights spectrum ranging from equality, to welfare,

d'un juge sur la promotion par les juges d'une norme suspecte' in *Mélanges en Hommage à P Lambert* (Brussels, Bruylant, 1999) 561, quoted by X Bioy, 'Le concept de dignité, rapport introductif' in L Burgogne-Larsen (ed), *La dignité saisie par les juges en Europe* (Brussels, Bruylant, 2010) 13–54, at 49. See also N Rao, 'On the Use and Abuse of Dignity in Constitutional Law' (2008) 14 *Columbia Journal of European Law* 201.

[9] The Spanish Constitutional Court deliberately excluded the possibility that human dignity on its own could serve as a ground for the constitutional remedy against fundamental rights breaches (*recurso de amparo*): STC 64/1986. It has nevertheless found other ways to use this concept in its case law: M Revenga Sánchez, 'La dignité dans la jurisprudence constitutionnelle Espagnole' in L Burgogne-Larsen (ed), *La dignité saisie par les juges en Europe* (Brussels, Bruylant, 2010) 199–216. By contrast, on (German) judges' ability and willingness to use dignity, see D Grimm, 'Dignity in a Legal Context: Dignity as an Absolute Right' in C McCrudden (ed), *Understanding Human Dignity* (Oxford, Oxford University Press, 2013) 381–93.

[10] On dignity in the common law, see the PhD thesis of Daniel Bedford, *Constructing Human Dignity: an Investment Concept* (PhD thesis, University of Exeter, 2015, manuscript on file with the author).

[11] D Kommers, *The Constitutional Jurisprudence of the Federal Republic of Germany* (Durham, NC, Duke University Press, 1997) remains a good source in English, even though it is nearly 20 years old. See also EJ Eberle, 'Observations on the Development of Human Dignity and Personality in German Constitutional Law: An Overview' (2013) 33 *Liverpool Law Review* 203 and M Mahlmann, 'The Basic Law at 60: Human Dignity and the Culture of Republicanism' (2010) 11 *German Law Journal* 9.

including self-determination and freedom,[12] and reflects the fact that almost every aspect of human interaction and identity could be, in one way or another, translated and adjudicated in terms of human dignity. To add to this difficulty, even when specific issues have recurred in case law as dignity issues, such as in relation to abortion, euthanasia or medical treatment, this argument has not provided one answer, but a range of (often) conflicting perspectives.[13] Attempting to extract a clear and self-contained substantive meaning out of this case law, especially embraced in its full European scope, is therefore perhaps not the most effective methodology.

Nevertheless, it is argued that case law can be very helpful for understanding human dignity better, but in terms of how and why it has been deployed in judgments. The first thing that we learn from such cases is that the concept has been granted a full normative existence, which goes way beyond its codification in constitutions. The phrase 'human dignity' is therefore not only an important rhetorical device enshrined in constitutions in a context of democratic foundation, as discussed in the previous chapter, but it has also acquired through judicial interpretation its own semantic and normative reality. In other words, it has left the realm of constitutional drafting to be appropriated by judges and (a point that is often forgotten) by applicants and alleged victims of human dignity breaches, and has therefore become everybody's concept, rather than a 'founding fathers' concept. The development of human dignity through case law therefore confirms the concept's continued relevance today, that is well beyond the special foundation period that originally led to its codification in the aftermath of war and dictatorship in Europe. This takes human dignity into the real world of everyday constitutionalism arising out of sometimes apparently very mundane issues of human life and death, giving human dignity a fuller and sometimes unexpected range of meanings. For it must not be forgotten that, although judges are ultimately those who decide on cases and write up their reasoning, they do not do this in isolation, but in the context of a dispute and after having heard the arguments put before them and taking into account the relevant constitutional provisions. In this sense, judicial reasoning distills the views of a multitude of other human dignity-makers and numerous other meanings into a single narrative construction. In this context, human dignity can be understood as an always temporary solution to a difficult conflict and one that has been crafted by judges with a view to resolving this situation.

[12] E Daly, *Dignity Rights: Courts, Constitutions and the Worth of the Human Person* (Philadelphia, PA, University of Pennsylvania Press, 2013).

[13] Typically on abortion see R Siegel, 'Dignity and Sexuality: Claims on Dignity in Transnational Debates over Abortion and Same-sex Marriage' (2012) 10 *International Journal of Constitutional Law* 355; DP Kommers, 'Autonomy, Dignity, Abortion' in T Ginsburg and R Dixon (eds), *Comparative Constitutional Law* (Cheltenham, Edward Elgar, 2011) 441–58.

These micro-constructions of human dignity by judges have complemented and developed the macro-construction of dignity at the constitutional level, through the struggles discussed in the previous two chapters, reminding us that human dignity is a deliberate and complex human construction taking place in a specific historical and social context and the particular framework of constitutionalism, with a view always to protecting the uniqueness of humanity against destruction and instrumentalisation.

B. Endorsing Human Dignity

Cutting across the diversity of human dignity case law is the endorsement by judges of the foundational promise enshrined in constitutions adopted after war and dictatorship. For historical and contextual reasons, this judicial approach to human dignity can be expected in constitutional orders such as those of (West) Germany or post-communist Hungary and indeed it is to be found in their case law. Less expected perhaps and therefore all the more interesting, this approach was also adopted by French constitutional judges and UK judges in very different contexts. As discussed below, in both instances judges constructed a concept of dignity as an endorsement of this foundational promise, albeit in quite different ways.

Chronologically, the first case considered is that of the French Constitutional Council which, in 1994, discovered the principle of protection of human dignity ('principe de sauvegarde de la dignité humaine contre toute forme d'asservissement et de dégradation') in a complex ruling on the constitutionality of two bioethics Bills,[14] one on 'the respect for the human body' and the other on the use of products (mainly gametes and embryos) of the human body, medically assisted procreation and pre-implantation diagnosis.[15] Highlighted as a 'major event' by a leading constitutional law scholar at the time,[16] the reference to the principle of human dignity was surprising, considering that this phrase is not enshrined in the 1958 Constitution. Being very aware of this, the Constitutional Council derived its newly discovered principle of human dignity protection from the

[14] Constitutional Council, 27 July 1994, No 94/343/344 DC. Commented by B Mathieu in [1995] *Dalloz* 237 and L Favoreu in [1995] *Dalloz*, Sommaire, 299. See also B Mathieu, 'Bioéthique: un juge constitutionnel réservé face aux défis de la science' [1994] *Revue Française de Droit Administratif* 1019.

[15] In the 1994 ruling, the Council was petitioned by 60 MPs together with the President of the National Assembly; while complying with the constitution, in practice this joint petition has been rare and demonstrated here the political significance of the issue.

[16] L Favoreu in [1995] *Dalloz*, Sommaire, 299.

post-war dignity commitment originally enshrined in the 1946 Constitution. This widening of the benchmarks of constitutionality is itself a creation of the Constitutional Council, dating from a ruling on freedom of association delivered in 1971, and is known as the 'bloc of constitutionality' (*bloc de constitutionnalité*).[17]

Among other sources, the constitutionality bloc includes the Preamble to the 1946 Constitution, from which the Council derived the human dignity principle in its 1994 decision, quoting *in extenso* the relevant sentence of the Preamble ('in the morrow of the victory achieved by the free peoples over the regimes that had sought to enslave and degrade humanity'). While there was at the time of the ruling certainly much discussion about the implications of some bioethics issues for human dignity, the connections between the immediate post-war and liberation context referred to in the 1946 Preamble and the bioethics issues at stake in the ruling, namely, the use and selection of embryos as well as access to the gametes' donor's identity for children born as a result of IVF, are not self-evident. In fact, the Council did not really elaborate on the meaning of the newly discovered human dignity principle in its reasoning. What seemed to matter was to establish a connection between human dignity and a politically very symbolic source of constitutionality, thus arguably giving it strong political resonance and legitimacy.[18] In so doing, the Constitutional Council endorsed the post-war dignity commitment made by the drafters of the 1946 Constitution and re-activated it, as it was nowhere enshrined in the subsequent constitution. This process of re-activation is crucial to legitimising the creation of the new human dignity principle. It further shows how human dignity is constructed as a shield against a new threat to humanity (even though there was ultimately no finding of unconstitutionality in that case). In this process, human dignity has therefore acquired a new normative and semantic depth and the post-war human dignity commitment has been extended to protect dimensions of humanity that the 1946 drafters almost certainly did not have in mind.

Following this ruling, the human dignity principle was spelt out in the statute of 29 July 1994 and enshrined in article 16 of the Civil Code.[19] Since this decision, the principle of human dignity has been used by the

[17] DC 71-44 of 16 July 1971 on freedom of association and DC 74-54. Generally see A Stone, *The Birth of Judicial Politics in France* (Oxford, Oxford University Press, 1992).

[18] M Borgetto, 'Préambule de la Constitution de 1946' in D Chagnollaud and G Drago (eds), *Dictionnaire des droits fondamentaux* (Paris, Dalloz, 2006) 593–601.

[19] Article 16 of the Code Civil reads: 'Legislation ensures the primacy of the person, prohibits any infringement of the latter's dignity and safeguards the respect of the human being from the outset of life.' Trans by G Rouhette and A Rouhette-Berton, www.legifrance.gouv.fr.

Constitutional Council,[20] as well as by other courts in France.[21] However, it has still not been codified in the 1958 Constitution, despite various opportunities to do so.[22] Therefore, in French constitutionalism human dignity has remained a purely judge-made principle, the substantive content of which has never been fully explicated and can only be understood and legitimated by reference to the re-activated post-war human dignity commitment.

Operating in a very different constitutional context and in response to very different questions, namely, the appropriate ways of lifting severely disabled adults, the UK High Court nevertheless adopted a very similar approach in its ruling of 18 February 2003 in *R (on the application of (1) A and (2) B (by their litigation friend the Official Solicitor) (3) X (4) Y) v East Sussex County Council*.[23] While not the very first common law ruling with a reference to dignity,[24] this arguably is the first explicit construction of human dignity in a UK ruling. We find here the same logic of constructing human dignity by reference to the post-war human dignity commitment.

[20] Xavier Bioy's thesis on these developments has remained one of the most comprehensive and enlightening studies in the French context, *Le concept de personne humaine en droit public* (Paris, Dalloz, 2003). See also ML Pavia and T Revet (eds), *La dignité de la personne humaine* (Paris, Economica, 1999); C Girard and S Hennette-Vauchez (eds), *La dignité de la personne humaine: recherche sur un processus de juridicisation* (Paris, Presses Universitaires de France, 2004).

[21] The best-known example is the ruling on dwarf throwing delivered by the Supreme Administrative Court a year later: Conseil d'Etat, *Commune de Morsang sur Orge*, 27 October 1995, discussed by P Frydman, 'L'atteinte à la dignité de la personne humaine et les pouvoirs de police municipale' (1995) 6 *Revue Française de Droit Administratif* 1204; see also J Morange, 'La dignité humaine en tant que composante de l'ordre public: l'inattendu retour en droit administratif Français d'un concept controversé' (2008) 5 *Revue Française de Droit Administratif* 979. For a recent critical reflection on the uses of human dignity by the French Supreme Administrative Court, see V Champeil-Desplats and S Slama, 'Qu'elle protège ou qu'elle punisse, la dignité n'est pas la même pour tous' (2014) *Revue des Droits de l'Homme, Actualités Droits-Libertés*, available at http://revdh.revues.org/828, 30 May 2014.

[22] S Veil, *Redécouvrir le Préambule de la Constitution: Rapport au Président de la République* (Paris, La Documentation Française, 2008) 85–96. The proposed revised Art 1 read: 'La France est une République indivisible, laïque, démocratique et sociale. Elle assure l'égalité devant la loi de tous les citoyens sans distinction d'origine, de race ou de religion. Elle reconnaît l'égale dignité de chacun. Elle respecte toutes les croyances. Son organisation est décentralisée'.

[23] [2003] EWHC 167 (Admin). Munby LJ has also written a number of essays on human dignity, see 'Dignity, Happiness and Human Rights' (2011) *Elder Law Journal* 32; and 'What Price Dignity?' (2012) 15 *Community Care Law Report* 5. Generally see S Graumann, 'Human Dignity and People with Disabilities' in M Düwell, J Braarvig, R Brownsword and D Mieth (eds), *The Cambridge Handbook of Human Dignity* (Cambridge, Cambridge University Press, 2014) 484–91.

[24] The House of Lords ruling in the case of Bland about the withdrawal of life support is often mentioned as containing the first dignity reference: *Airedale NHS Trust v Bland* [1993] AC 789. Generally see D Feldman, 'Human Dignity as a Legal Value, Part I' (1999) *Public Law* 682 and 'Human Dignity as a Legal Value, Part II' (2000) *Public Law* 61; C Dupré, 'Dignity, Democracy, Civilisation' (2013) 33 *Liverpool Law Review* 263; and C Gearty, *Principles of Human Rights Adjudication* (Oxford, Oxford University Press, 2004) 84–115 and 'Socio-economic Rights, Basic Needs, and Human Dignity: A Perspective from Law's Front Line' in C McCrudden (ed), *Understanding Human Dignity* (Oxford, Oxford University Press, 2013) 155–72.

In the absence of a codified constitution in the United Kingdom, Munby LJ referred to the (European) foundational human rights texts, namely, the UN Universal Declaration, the EU Charter and the ECHR:

> The first [particularly important concept] is human dignity. True it is that the phrase is not used in the [European] Convention [on Human Rights] but *surely it is immanent in article 8, indeed in almost every one of the Convention's provisions* ... The invocation of the dignity of the patient in the form of declaration habitually used when the court is exercising its inherent declaratory jurisdiction in relation to the gravely ill or dying is not some meaningless incantation designed to comfort the living or to assuage the consciences of those involved in making life and death decisions: it is a *solemn affirmation of the law's and society's recognition of our humanity and of human dignity as something fundamental.* Not surprisingly, human dignity is extolled *in article 1 of the [EU] Charter*, just *as it is in article 1 of the Universal Declaration.* And the latter's call to us to 'act towards one another' is nothing new ... Dignity interests are also, of course, at the core of the rights protected by *article 3* [ECHR].[25] (emphasis added)

The task of re-constructing human dignity by reference to the foundational commitment of the post-war era faced by Munby LJ is particularly arduous: the ECHR does not contain the phrase 'human dignity'; the UN Declaration does, but is not legally binding; finally the EU Charter, which is the latest human rights texts and does contain a specific dignity provision, had no legal force in the United Kingdom as this was before the Lisbon Treaty became binding. Nonetheless, the judge successfully manages to draw out a human dignity commitment and to substantiate it much more precisely than the French Court did in its 1994 ruling. The three texts of reference, each of which is quite tenuous in terms of human dignity normativity, are held together by the human dignity commitment expressed in the judge's own words as 'a solemn affirmation of the law's and society's recognition of our humanity and of human dignity as something fundamental'. The absence of human dignity in the text of the ECHR is counterbalanced by the 'immanence' of this commitment permeating the whole ECHR and located in particular under Article 3 and Article 8, which are discussed at length in the ruling. From the UN Declaration, the judge retains and highlights the relationality of dignity and the pledge to act towards each other in a spirit of brotherhood,[26] which is at the core of the dispute, ie how the carers and the applicants should relate to each other in relation to physical and mechanical lifting and how the latter could be lifted by the former. The solemn affirmation of humanity and human dignity was brought closer to home by Munby LJ's reference to the EU Charter. In so doing, the High Court judge not only anticipated the coming into force of the Charter (a development which was

[25] [2003] EWHC 167 (Admin) para 86.
[26] Discussed in the previous chapters.

not quite definite at the time), but he also brought to the fore the ECHR's immanent commitment to human dignity. Finally, in this way, the possible critique that this judicial construction of human dignity is conjured up out of thin air is effectively preempted by the judge's emphasis on human dignity's fundamental nature.

By going back to these foundational texts, ie the 1946 French Constitution, the ECHR, and the UN Universal Declaration, both sets of judges have sought to ascertain the meaning of a notoriously difficult concept that they deployed for the first time in their respective case law. By referring to European texts they further constructed human dignity as a fully European concept, from which they derived a specific concept meant to address the issue at stake.

III. MAKING HUMAN DIGNITY EUROPEAN

While most human dignity studies have identified case law as a key location for the concept's development,[27] few have paused to reflect on the fact that it is mainly constitutional judges who have constructed human dignity. This is arguably significant as constitutional courts have also been an innovation of post-Second World War constitutionalism, one of its achievements and one of its distinguishing features. What is also important to note here is that these courts have not operated in isolation, ignoring each other's case law, rather they have initiated a sort of spontaneous communication among themselves and referred to their respective case law. This has given rise to a particular method of interpretation which draws on comparative and European law, which, it is argued, has been instrumental for the construction of human dignity, making it a fully European concept, tightly woven into the fabric of European constitutionalism.

A. A Network of Constitutional Courts

Much has been written on constitutional justice,[28] but some of its key characteristics are worth noting here as they have arguably influenced the construction of human dignity. Within the framework of European constitutionalism, constitutional judges occupy a particular institutional position

[27] For a focus on the law-maker, see J Waldron, 'How Law Protects Dignity' (2012) 71 *Cambridge Law Journal* 200.

[28] On the rise of constitutional courts, see R Hirschl, *Towards Juristocracy: The Origins and Consequences of the New Constitutionalism* (Cambridge, MA, Harvard University Press, 2004). More recently see M Tushnet, *Advanced Introduction to Comparative Constitutional Law* (Cheltenham, Edward Elgar, 2014) 40–69; and M De Visser, *Constitutional Review in Europe: A Comparative Analysis* (Oxford, Hart Publishing, 2014).

above the law-maker and below the authority of the codified constitution (or foundational treaty), of which they are the authoritative interpreters. Establishing constitutional courts, designed to rebalance the political preponderance of democratically elected parliaments and to strengthen the authority of the codified constitution as the supreme law of a given state, was a further and complementary innovation meant to keep dictatorship at bay.[29] This transformed European democracy from a (largely if not exclusively) majoritarian type with Parliament at its heart, to one where law-making could be judicially reviewed and the minority could be heard and protected, mainly through judicial remedies for human rights breaches.[30] As, by and large, this new institutional design, first adopted in the two main former dictatorships, Italy and West Germany, successfully contributed to developing a new democratic framework, safeguarding rights and protecting minorities, it was then also followed in other post-dictatorial regimes, such as Spain and Portugal. When the last dictatorial regimes eventually collapsed in Central and Eastern Europe, most post-communist constitutions established a constitutional court, positioning it squarely at the heart of their institutional design, and entrusting it with a clear mission to protect human rights and to break away from the communist dogma and practice of unity of power.[31]

While they may not be *stricto sensu* constitutional courts, the two supranational courts arguably also form part of this effort to protect human rights and to provide authoritative interpretation of primary law. This role is very clear in relation to the ECtHR, which was established to protect a range of core civil and political rights enshrined in the ECHR so that High Contracting Parties can petition the Court against violations allegedly committed by other state signatories. Moreover, innovating on international law mechanisms, the ECHR made it possible for individual applicants to apply to the ECtHR against a state. Originally optional, this remedy eventually became compulsory and proved crucial in the development of ECHR justice.[32] The

[29] L Weinrib, 'Human Dignity as Rights-protecting Principle' (2004) 17 *National Journal of Constitutional Law* 325.

[30] See, eg *Gorzelik and others v Poland* (2005) 40 EHRR 75, ECtHR, Grand Chamber: '[N]ot only is political democracy a fundamental feature of the European public order but the Convention was designed to promote and maintain the ideals and values of a democratic society ... democracy does not simply mean that the views of the majority must always prevail: a balance must be achieved which ensures the fair and proper treatment of minorities and avoids any abuse of a dominant position'. Generally see A Barak, *The Judge in a Democracy* (Princeton, NJ, Princeton University, 2006); and J Komárek, 'National Constitutional Courts in the European Constitutional Democracy' (2014) 12 *International Journal of Constitutional Law* 525.

[31] See, eg M Verdrussen (ed), *La justice constitutionnelle en Europe centrale* (Brussels, Bruylant, 1997); H Schwartz, *The Struggle for Constitutional Justice in Post Communist Europe* (Chicago, IL, University of Chicago Press, 2000); G de Vergottini (ed), *Giustizia Costituzionale e Sviluppo Democratico nei Paesi dell'Europa Centro-Orientale* (Turin, G Giappichelli, 2000).

[32] As is well-known, the ECHR is the victim of its own success and various reforms have been introduced in an attempt to deal with the huge number of individual petitions received

ECJ/CJEU, although not originally designed to have a human rights adjudication role, has ended up developing such a role, prompted by applicants[33] and Member States.[34] Under the Lisbon Treaty, human rights have become (at least on paper) a central component of the European Union, with the EU Charter acquiring the same constitutional rank as the Treaties.[35]

A further characteristic of these courts is that they are connected to each other by what can be called a loose and largely, but not exclusively, spontaneous network of communication. In other words, these European courts 'talk' to each other.[36] While this process of judicial communication is not fully understood yet, it appears to be increasing,[37] and if it does not affect all areas of law to the same extent, human dignity has certainly proved to be a particular favourite 'conversation topic' for courts.[38] This 'spontaneous' judicial communication is taking place in a constitutional framework where judges are encouraged to seek each other's opinion in an increasing number of ways,[39] gradually establishing formal communication channels at all levels: the well-established preliminary references before the ECJ/CJEU for domestic courts and the right for individuals to petition the ECtHR against a contracting party are now complemented by a form of preliminary reference before the ECtHR under Additional Protocol 16 to the ECHR.[40] This

every year. Generally see R Blackburn and J Polakiewicz (eds), *Fundamental Rights in Europe: The European Convention on Human Rights and its Member States, 1950–2000* (Oxford, Oxford University Press, 2001) and K Lörcher, 'The Future of the European Court of Human Rights in the Light of the Brighton Declaration' in F Dorssemont, K Lörcher and I Schömann (eds), *The European Convention on Human Rights and the Employment Relation* (Oxford, Hart Publishing, 2013) 93–104.

[33] Notably and for the first time: Case 29/69 *Stauder v City of Ulm* [1969] ECR 419.

[34] M Kumm, 'Who is the Final Arbiter of Constitutionality in Europe?: Three Conceptions of the Relationship between the German Federal Constitutional Court and the European Court of Justice' (1999) 36 *Common Market Law Review* 351; and A Pliakos and G Agnanostaras, 'Who is the Ultimate Arbiter? The Battle over Judicial Supremacy in EU Law' (2011) 36 *European Law Review* 109.

[35] M Varjú, *European Union Human Rights Law: The Dynamics of Interpretation and Context* (Cheltenham, Edward Elgar, 2014).

[36] MA Glendon, *Rights Talk: The Impoverishment of Political Discourse* (New York, Free Press, 1991).

[37] See B Markesinis and J Fedtke (eds), 'The Judge as a Comparatist' (2005) 80 *Tulane Law Review* 11, Special Issue; A Barak, *The Judge in a Democracy* (Princeton, NJ, Princeton University Press, 2006) ch 10 'Comparative Law', 197–204; and T Groppi and MC Ponthoreau (eds), *The Use of Foreign Precedents by Constitutional Judges* (Oxford, Hart Publishing, 2013).

[38] This is also taking place outside Europe: VC Jackson, 'Constitutional Dialogue and Human Dignity: States and Transnational Constitutional Discourse' (2004) 65 *Montana Law Review* 15.

[39] W Weiß, 'Human Rights in the EU: Rethinking the Role of the European Convention on Human Rights after Lisbon' (2011) 7 *European Constitutional Law Review* 64.

[40] Article 1 of Additional Protocol 16 reads: 'Highest courts of a High Contracting Party, as specified in accordance with Article 10, may request the Court to give advisory opinions on questions of principle relating to the interpretation or application of the rights and freedoms defined in the Convention or the protocols thereto'. Additional Protocol 16 was adopted on 2 October 2013, and has not yet been ratified.

method of interpretation by reference to comparative law has so far largely been left to judges's discretion; however, due to the formalisation of judicial communication across Europe it is safe to assume that the use of comparative law by courts will gradually become more systematic.

First studied in detail in relation to Hungarian constitutional case law between 1990 and 1998, this method of constructing human dignity by reference to comparative law amounted to a process of importation of German constitutional case law, used by the Hungarian Court to lay new foundations for human rights and constitutionalism after the fall of communism. As this was closely discussed elsewhere,[41] the next section focuses on other contexts and courts, in which judges have constructed human dignity by comparative reference to the case law of other European courts, both national and supranational.

B. Interlocking Human Dignity

As a result of this process of judicial communication amongst constitutional courts in Europe and their reliance on comparative law, the judge-made concept of human dignity, particularly in those systems where dignity was not originally codified, is fully European, broadly combining or interlocking three types of sources, namely, ECHR case law, EU law and Member States' law.[42] This section focuses on the supranational courts, the ECJ/CJEU and the ECtHR, partly due to their particular trans-European importance, as well as because of the pivotal or mediation role that both courts have played in translating the concept of human dignity from a domestic constitutional order into their respective supranational order, with the resulting construction of the concept being ultimately binding on Member States. The first instance discussed below involves the ECJ and Germany (the *Omega* ruling of 2004) and the second and more recent example discussed involves Germany, the ECtHR and the United Kingdom (*Vinter v United Kingdom* of 2013).

Until the coming into force of the EU Charter, the EU concept of human dignity was entirely judge-made and constructed by reference to comparative law.[43] While it was not the first ECJ case considering the argument of

[41] C Dupré, *Importing the Law in Post-Communist Transitions: The Hungarian Constitutional Court and the Right to Human Dignity* (Oxford, Hart Publishing, 2003).

[42] K Lenaerts, 'Interlocking Legal Orders in the European Union and Comparative Law' (2003) 52 *International and Comparative Law Quarterly* 873.

[43] J Jones, 'Human Dignity in the EU Charter of Fundamental Rights and Before the European Court of Justice' (2012) 33 *Liverpool Law Review* 281; generally see K Schwarzburg, *Die Menschenwürde im Recht der europäischen Union* (Baden-Baden, Nomos, 2012).

human dignity,[44] the *Omega* ruling[45] was the first in which this approach was both explicitly spelt out in the Opinion of the Advocate General (AG) and endorsed by the ECJ, and determinant for the construction of the EU concept of human dignity. The dispute was triggered by a peculiar form of entertainment, known as a 'laserdrome' involving the use of 'sub-machine-gun type laser targeting devices against players'. Omega, the German company operating these games, turned to the UK-based Pulsar company for the supply of the equipment. In response to people's concerns about this killing game, the Bonn police got involved and banned these activities on the ground that they 'constituted a danger to public order, since the acts of simulated homicide and trivialisation of violence thereby engendered were contrary to fundamental values prevailing in public opinion'.[46] Omega's legal challenge eventually reached the Bundesverwaltungsgericht (Federal Administrative Court) arguing that it breached freedom to provide services under Article 49 of the EC Treaty (TEC). The German court referred the issue to the ECJ for a preliminary ruling as the gist of the question was a clash between freedom of services and human dignity.

Encouraged by its Advocate General, the ECJ constructed its own concept of human dignity, combining a range of sources:

> *As the Advocate General argues in paragraphs 82 to 91 of her Opinion*, the Community legal order undeniably strives to ensure respect for human dignity as a general principle of law. There can be therefore no doubt that the objective of protecting human dignity is compatible with Community law, it *being immaterial* in that respect that, in Germany, the principle of respect for human dignity has a particular status as an independent fundamental right.[47] (emphasis added)

In these few lines, the ECJ conjured up human dignity without any kind of reference to EU primary law, not even to the EU Charter adopted four years

[44] Chronologically, the first dignity ruling by the ECJ is C-377/98 *Kingdom of the Netherlands v European Parliament*, 9 October 2001, involving the protection of biotechnological inventions; see K Frahm and J Gebauer, 'Patent auf Leben? Der Luxemburger Gerichtshof und die Biopatent-Richtlinie' (2002) 1 *Europa Recht* 78; and M Rau and F Schorkopf, 'Der EuGH und die Menschenwürde' (2002) 34 *Neue Juristische Wochenschrift* 2448; and TM Spranger, 'Case Note' (2002) 39 *Common Market Law Review* 1147. The very first ECJ ruling on dignity may well be the famous *Stauder v City of Ulm* case, which was originally raised by the applicant as a human dignity issue before the German courts; the ECJ, however, did not mention it. Generally see E Dubout, 'La dignité dans la jurisprudence de la Cour de Justice des Communautés' in L Burgogne-Larsen (ed), *La dignité saisie par les juges en Europe* (Brussels, Bruylant, 2010) 56–79.

[45] C-36/02 *Omega Spielhallen-und Automatenaufstellungs-GmbH v Oberbürgermeisterin der Bundesstadt Bonn*, 14 October 2004. The ruling was discussed by CT Smith and T Fetzer, 'The Uncertain Limits of the European Court of Justice's Authority: Economic Freedom versus Human Dignity' (2004) 10 *Columbia Journal of European Law* 445; and by T Ackermann, 'Case C-36/02 Omega Spielhallen-und Automatenaufstellungs-GmbH v Oberbürgermeisterin der Bundestadt Bonn' (2005) 42 *Common Market Law Review* 1107.

[46] *Omega*, above n 45, para 7.

[47] ibid para 34.

before and which was duly mentioned in the Opinion under paragraph 91. It appears, therefore, that the ECJ human dignity concept is entirely constructed out of comparative materials identified by the Advocate General. These include the 1948 Universal Declaration of Human Rights, the two 1966 Covenants, a reference to the ECHR case of *Pretty v United Kingdom*, and Article 1 of the German Basic Law. In addition to this, the Advocate General noted two Regulations and the ruling in *Kingdom of the Netherlands v European Parliament*.[48] While the ECJ was obviously aware both of the weight of this principle in German constitutional law and of the importance of German law for the development of human dignity (as outlined by AG Stix Hackl), it emphasised the distinction between the German and EU concepts of human dignity.

Technically justified by the fact that 'as far as human dignity in Community law is concerned, therefore, it is clear that it has not found express (written) mention in valid primary legislation',[49] this use of comparative law reflects the ECJ's general comparative curiosity and attitude.[50] In a fairly typical way, the ECJ did not explicitly engage with a comparative overview, leaving this task to its Advocate General. While German constitutional law on human dignity was obviously influential both on the Opinion and the judgment, the ECJ appears to have been keen to minimise or hide this influence (which can only be identified in the Opinion) or to dilute it by making reference to ECtHR case law,[51] which, while being relevant, does not articulate the concept of human dignity either. The ECJ might have had its own (good) reasons for downplaying German constitutional law as a model, for instance, that it is arguably crucial that the EU concept of human dignity arising out of this use of comparative law is of a unique EU nature and clearly distinct from the German concept, ie from any of the individual components of the comparative law survey. Even so, the resulting EU concept of human dignity could not have been crafted without a comparative law analysis.

Operating in a very different context, the ECtHR has relied on a similarly comparative approach in its construction of human dignity, as illustrated by the *Vinter v United Kingdom* case.[52] This case, decided in 2013, is not the first human dignity ruling by the ECtHR (which is identified below as the

[48] See AG Opinion para 89.

[49] ibid 87.

[50] K Schiemann, 'A Response to *The Judge as a Comparatist*' (2005) 80 *Tulane Law Review* 281. See also F Jacobs, 'Judicial Dialogue and the Cross-Fertilization of Legal Systems: The European Court of Justice' (2003) 38 *Texas International Law Journal* 547.

[51] This approach is particularly clear in relation to the ECJ's protection of transsexuals' right not to be discriminated against on the ground of sex: see C-13/94 *P v S and Cornwall County Council*, 30 April 1996 and C-117/01 *KB v National Health Service Pensions Agency and Secretary of State for Health*, 7 January 2004.

[52] *Vinter and others v United Kingdom*, Applications no 66069/09, 130/10 and 3896/10, ECtHR Grand Chamber, 9 July 2013.

so-called marital rape case), as the Strasbourg court has used human dignity in a number of ways from early on in its case law.[53] This is, however, one of the first rulings where human dignity is constructed as part of an explicit comparative survey and reflection. The ECtHR's use of comparative law is not limited to human dignity and is much more overt and systematic than in ECJ case law (perhaps due to the absence of an equivalent to an AG Opinion).[54] In the case of *Vinter*, it considered a whole range of examples, including Council of Europe texts, provisions of international criminal law, EU law, contracting states law, with Germany and Italy being covered in far more detail including relevant case law, in addition to references to non-European jurisdictions. The comparative overview was presented at the start of the judgment, before the Court outlined its own assessment.[55] The gist of its reasoning was based on whether life orders, which do not include the prospect of release or the possibility of reviewing the sentence, breach Article 3 ECHR prohibiting inhuman and degrading treatment and punishment. As part of this discussion, the ECtHR went back to German law, referring explicitly to the leading case on the subject:

> Furthermore, as the German Federal Constitutional Court recognised in the *Life Imprisonment* case ..., it would be incompatible with the provision of human dignity in the Basic Law for the State forcefully to deprive a person of his freedom without at least providing him with the chance to someday regain that freedom. It was that conclusion which led the Constitutional Court to find that the prison authorities had the duty to strive towards a life sentence prisoner's rehabilitation and that rehabilitation was constitutionally required in any community that established human dignity as its centrepiece ... *Similar considerations must apply under the Convention system* the very essence of which, as the *Court has often stated*, is respect for human dignity ... *Indeed, there is also now clear support in European* and international law for the principle that all prisoners, including those serving life sentences be offered the possibility of rehabilitation and the prospect of release if that rehabilitation is achieved.[56] (emphasis added)

While technically the ECtHR reasoning was based on Article 3, the core of the ECtHR's reasoning arguably rested on human dignity, in that the connection between a breach of Article 3 and life orders without review was made thanks to reliance on that concept. This connection was explicitly

[53] B Maurer, *Le principe du respect de la dignité humaine dans la Convention Européenne des Droits de l'Homme* (Paris, La Documentation Française, 1999); L Jeannin, 'Le principe de dignité dans l'espace de la Convention Européenne des Droits de l'Homme' in C Girard and S Hennette-Vauchez (eds), *La dignité de la personne humaine, recherche sur un processus de juridicisation* (Paris, Presses Universitaires de France, 2005) 176–88; and J-P Costa, 'Human Dignity in the Jurisprudence of the European Court of Human Rights' in C McCrudden (ed), *Understanding Human Dignity* (Oxford, Oxford University Press, 2013) 393–402.

[54] CL Rozakis, 'The European Judge as a Comparatist' (2005) 80 *Tulane Law Review* 257.

[55] *Vinter*, above n 52, paras 59–76.

[56] ibid para 113.

inspired by German case law, to which the ECtHR gave clear references. Nevertheless, the ECtHR was keen to construct its concept of dignity not as German, but as a well-established concept in its own case law and, importantly, as being in line with 'European law'. In this context, dignity was closely related to hope, a connection that the ECtHR noted in the German *Life Imprisonment* case,[57] and endorsed as the underlying assumption of its reasoning.[58]

By way of conclusion, a number of issues can be briefly discussed. The first one arising out of these two supranational rulings on human dignity is the apparent influence of German law: in the ECJ case, the comparative survey largely focused on Germany and in the ECtHR ruling the only domestic case law cited in the Grand Chamber's assessment was German. The influence of German case law on an EU concept of human dignity can and has been discussed.[59] What seems to matter, however, and this is the second issue to note, is that both supranational courts endeavoured to distinguish their concept of dignity from that of Germany in a fairly similar fashion, ie by emphasising that their respective legal order strives to protect human dignity, but as part of a well-recognised European trend, rather than because Germany does it.

This can, of course, be explained by a range of reasons, including the importance of developing autonomous legal concepts at the supranational levels, as well as perhaps the wish to pre-empt the critique of merely copying German law. Beyond that, however, what both courts have endeavoured to do through their respective comparative construction of their own human dignity concept is arguably to lock it into a wider cross-European concept of dignity and related standards of protection, which involves three broad components: Member States law, ECHR case law and provisions and EU law, in particular the EU Charter. The importance of fitting into this cross-European—or full European (to distinguish it from the too restrictive EU or ECHR labels)—dimension of dignity is such that it arguably outweighs the difficulty of the comparative endeavour of its construction. Interestingly,

[57] ibid para 69.

[58] Soon afterwards the UK Court of Appeal had to re-examine this issue, and while it underlined the importance of hope, it dissented from the ECtHR in no uncertain language: 'In our judgment, the law of England and Wales therefore does provide to an offender "hope" or the "possibility" of release in exceptional circumstances which render the just punishment [whole life sentence] originally imposed no longer justifiable': *R v Ian McLoughlin* and *R v Lee William Newell*, [2014] EWCA Crim 188, 18 February 2014, para 35. In *Hutchinson v United Kingdom*, Application no 57592/08, 3 February 2015, the ECtHR reiterated the importance of human dignity under para 19, but, taking note of recent UK case law, found no violation of Art 3. This case is further discussed in Chapter 6.

[59] J Jones, '"Common Constitutional Traditions": Can the Meaning of Human Dignity under German Law Guide the European Court of Justice?' (2004) *Public Law* 167; and C Dupré, 'Article 1: Human Dignity' in S Peers, T Hervey, J Kenner and A Ward (eds), *The EU Charter of Fundamental Rights: A Commentary* (Oxford, Hart Publishing, 2014) 3, 19 and 21–22.

both the ECJ/CJEU and ECtHR acknowledged the lack of specific codification of human dignity in the ECHR, which, however, did not seem to be problematic for their respective construction of this concept.

Finally, and importantly, this comparative construction of human dignity, with its reliance on a range of different legal systems (as opposed to a unique and specific source of inspiration) and its emphasis on a particular spirit of dignity (as opposed to specific codification which cannot be found in the ECHR) might also have the advantage of providing this European concept of human dignity with some permanence and of protecting it against possible drastic changes in (for instance domestic) case law. As both courts have made clear, protecting human dignity is of prime importance because it is the essence of European constitutionalism.

IV. THE ESSENCE OF EUROPEAN CONSTITUTIONALISM

In European case law, the concept of human dignity arising out of the comparative construction discussed above is distinct from each of its individual components, with each court developing and using it making it clear that it is not to be found in the sum of its various parts. The reason why courts have deployed human dignity despite the lack of codified constitutional basis at the supranational level until 2009 and the difficulties of constructing it through the comparative method is, in the words of the ECtHR in the 1995 marital rape ruling discussed below, because 'respecting human dignity is the essence' of European constitutionalism.

This section therefore starts with a close discussion of the ECtHR's resounding statement, which is arguably emblematic of human dignity's defining role in European constitutionalism. In addition, adopting the 'first time' approach set out above brings to light some of the core issues of human dignity as constructed in case law decided between 1951 and 2011. These rulings, discussed in a chronological order, have each been a significant milestone in the construction of a European concept of human dignity, structuring and informing its substantive meaning and, beyond that, European constitutionalism.

A. Civilisation, Rule of Law and Consent to Sex

The so-called marital rape ruling of 1995[60] is perhaps the first ruling in which the ECtHR elaborated its concept of human dignity in an explicit and

[60] *SW v United Kingdom*, Application no 20166/92, ECtHR, 22 November 1995.

significant way.[61] This ruling emphasised the importance of always renewed consent to sexual intercourse within a marital relationship.

The applicant, who had raped his wife, argued that the common law had never explicitly defined forced sexual intercourse between husband and wife as rape and that this was one of the immunities against prosecution.[62] As his argument was rejected by the House of Lords, he appealed before the ECtHR claiming a breach of Article 7 (non-retroactivity of criminal punishment). The ECtHR started by highlighting the significance of Article 7, 'which is an essential element of the rule of law, occupies a prominent place in the Convention system of protection'.[63] It further noted that whilst 'an offence must clearly be defined in the law' (para 35), an 'element of judicial interpretation is inevitable' (para 36). Consequently, Article 7 'cannot be read as outlawing the gradual clarification of the rules of criminal liability through judicial interpretation from case to case' (para 36). The Court considered closely the evolution of the common law on rape and concluded that 'this evolution had reached a stage where judicial recognition of the absence of immunity had become a reasonably foreseeable development of the law' (para 43). In so doing, the ECtHR largely followed and endorsed the UK courts' approach and closed its examination and interpretation of Article 7. However, it went back to the core of the dispute, the offence of rape in the following terms:

> What is more, the abandonment of the unacceptable idea of a husband being immune against prosecution for rape of his wife was in conformity, not only with a *civilised concept of marriage* but also, and *above all, with the fundamental objectives of the Convention, the very essence of which is respect for human dignity* and human freedom.[64] (emphasis added)

Technically, the ECtHR did not need to make this statement, because on its own, the reasoning on Article 7 ECHR was sufficient to support the lawfulness of prosecution in that case. Therefore, the statement was clearly meant to strengthen and tighten the ECtHR interpretation of Article 7, cutting short any kind of criticism about the exact dating or foreseeability of the offence in question. Prompted by the 'unacceptable idea' of marital rape and the compelling necessity to re-draw the normative boundaries of a 'civilised marriage', the ECtHR statement has also arguably a much wider significance.

[61] This is not necessarily the very first mention of human dignity, which is often identified as the Commission opinion in *East African Asians (Citizens of the UK and Colonies) v United Kingdom*, Application no 4626/70, 6 March 1978, Eur Comm HR Report, 14 December 1973, (1974) 78-A DR.5.

[62] The applicant relied on a common law principle as stated by Sir Matthew Hale CJ in his *History of the Crown* published in 1736.

[63] *SW v United Kingdom*, above n 60, para 34.

[64] ibid para 44.

Importantly, the Court positioned human dignity very firmly at the heart of the ECHR system of human rights protection, making it 'its very essence', a phrase that has subsequently been regularly repeated by the ECtHR[65] and has now crystallised human dignity's status within the ECHR system,[66] no doubt increasing the visibility and uses of this concept by the ECtHR. The word 'essence' is significant too. In practical terms, it was made necessary by the absence of human dignity from the ECHR. In normative and political terms, it acknowledges that this concept is so fundamental that not only can courts protect it without a specific codified basis, as the ECtHR has done, but also that they have a duty to protect human dignity, whenever it is threatened. In this regard, it is significant that the ECtHR phrased its human dignity commitment in such broad and abstract terms, without narrowing them down to the facts of the case and to the raped wife's dignity. As seen in the first chapter of this book, this broad and abstract approach to the concept is in line with the post-war foundational human dignity commitment. In practice and in ECtHR case law, it has made it possible for the ECtHR to deploy human dignity in a whole range of situations, which are very different from rape, and have included a request for assisted suicide (as in the *Pretty v United Kingdom* case), and the importance of rehabilitation and review of sentence for prisoners serving a life order (as in the *Vinter v United Kingdom* case discussed above).

This statement about human dignity in the *SW v United Kingdom* ruling is further significant in that it connects what is perhaps one of the most intimate human activities, sexual intercourse, with a wider concept of civilisation based on consent. This definition of human dignity is characterised not only by consent, but by consent that is always sought and given anew: the marital vows on the wedding day must not be understood as applying to the whole duration of married life and the many occasions of sexual intercourse and intimacy that this involves. This is of course a crucial and very positive step in the construction, and punishment, of rape.[67] Importantly too, as political philosopher Pierre Manent reminds us, this is crucial for democracy:

> The horizon of democracy [its long-term goal] is a society which would consist only of free individuals, that is individuals linked solely by freely undertaken ties. The ambition of democracy is to move us from an imposed, received or inherited

[65] Notably in *Pretty v United Kingdom*, Application no 2346/02, 29 April 2002, para 65.

[66] This is how it has been understood from outside: see the Opinion of AG Stix Hackl in *Omega*, discussed above n 45, and how Munby LJ presented it in his judgment on appropriate lifting techniques for disabled adults in *R (on the application of (1) A and (2) B (by their litigation friend the Official Solicitor) (3) X (4) Y) v East Sussex County Council*, discussed above n 23.

[67] This is also a good illustration of courts' crucial role in correcting the law-maker's omissions, and of the much needed judicial dimension of human dignity protection, which may not be left to a single branch of power.

> life, to a chosen life. Democracy is the volontarisation of all relations and all ties. Historically, the principle of consent was first affirmed and institutionalised in the central order of human life, that is the political order ... Despite temporary setbacks, this empire of consent has never ceased to expand, while symmetrically, the empire of command has never ceased to decrease.[68]

The ECtHR mention of human dignity in the marital rape ruling therefore not only promotes a particular type of civilisation that the Court intends to protect,[69] but also stretches the boundaries of democracy a little further to include a most intimate sphere of life, which has to be based on the same principle of continuously re-asserted consent. The connections between human dignity and democracy were elaborated 10 years later by the UK House of Lords in one of its first human dignity rulings, *Ghaidan v Godin-Mendoza*, with an emphasis on equality, which was triggered by a dispute involving tenancy rights of a deceased man's surviving homosexual partner. Baroness Hale held:

> Such a guarantee of equal treatment is also essential to democracy. Democracy is founded on the principle that each individual has equal value. Treating some as automatically having less value than others not only causes pain and distress to that person but also violates his or her dignity as a human being. *The essence of the [European] Convention, as has often been said, is respect for human dignity and human freedom*: see Pretty v UK (2002) 35 EHRR 1, 37, para 65. Second, *such treatment is damaging to society as a whole* ... It also damages social cohesion, creating not only an under-class, but an under-class with a rational grievance. Third, it is *the reverse of the rational behaviour we now expect of government and the state*. Power must not be exercised arbitrarily. If distinctions are to be drawn, particularly upon a group basis, it is an important discipline to look for a rational basis for those distinctions. Finally, it is a purpose of all human rights instruments to secure the protection of the essential rights of members of minority groups, *even when they are unpopular with the majority. Democracy values everyone equally even if the majority does not.*[70] (emphasis added)

This extremely rich statement extends the ECtHR connection between human dignity and civilisation to democracy.[71] We find in it some of the key components of human dignity discussed so far, namely, equality as a concept built into human dignity, the power relationship between individuals and state, and the emphasis on minorities rights, particularly 'unpopular minorities'. As will be seen below, human dignity has been recurringly used to protect those on the margins of society and whose voices are otherwise little heard, such as (raped) women, homosexuals (as in the above case),

[68] P Manent, *Cours familier de philosophie politique* (Paris, Gallimard, 2001) 192. Author's translation with thanks to S Skinner.

[69] C Dupré, 'Dignity, Democracy, Civilisation' (2013) 33 *Liverpool Law Review* 263.

[70] *Ghaidan v Godin-Mendoza (FC)* [2004] UKHL 30, 21 June 2004, para 132.

[71] The last chapter of the book discusses these issues in greater detail.

disabled people, the poor, or foreigners, to name a few categories of claimants in human dignity case law across Europe. The relational dimension of human dignity is particularly eloquently brought to the fore in the above statement: rooted in equality, it implicitly builds on the 'spirit of brotherhood' of the 1948 UN Declaration, and highlights the state's requirement to justify the unequal treatment it imposes on some people. Above all, breaching human dignity by discriminating against a singular human being due to their differences 'damages society as a whole and social cohesion'. It is the sense and knowledge that what is at stake in a given dispute brought before a judge is not just about addressing an individual grievance, but involves the wider make-up of society, a certain quality of civilisation and of democracy, that has arguably made uses of human dignity particularly compelling for judges.

B. Core Issues of Dignity and of Constitutionalism

The rulings discussed below have each contributed to defining and shaping a substantive dimension of human dignity within their respective constitutional order, as well as a dimension that has since then been well established in case law across Europe. In order to avoid a pointless ranking of these core issues that have gradually shaped a European concept of human dignity, and to provide instead a sense of its gradual construction by judges, they are presented chronologically, bearing in mind that the ECtHR marital rape case discussed above (but not again below) would be situated roughly at the mid-point of this development.

i. Welfare

The first dignity case in (West) Germany was delivered on 19 December 1951 and was brought to the German Federal Constitutional Court as a claim of breach of constitutional rights (*Verfassungsbeschwerde*, under Article 93 of the Basic Law). The applicant was the widow of a solicitor who had died during the war, she was unfit for work and had three children aged six to 16.[72] The gist of her complaint was that under the welfare statute (*Versorgungsgesetz*) she only received 3 Deutsche Marks more for herself and her children than other war widows who, unlike her, could earn a living. While the applicant ultimately lost her case, this ruling is significant as the Constitutional Court derived from the second sentence of Article 1 ('the duty to respect and protect human dignity') a positive obligation to protect human beings. However, this did not include protection against

[72] BVerfGE 1, 97.

material deprivation (*Schutz vor materieller Not*),[73] which the Court went on to derive from the social state principle.[74] On this basis, the applicant could have been vindicated in principle. In the case, however, the Constitutional Court found no evidence that the law-maker had set the various amounts of welfare in an arbitrary manner, rendering the applicant's claim groundless.

Despite the rejection of the application, this case has shaped the concept of human dignity in two very significant ways: the first was to derive from human dignity a positive duty to protect human beings, and the second was to relate this concept to the provision of welfare and to the guarantee of a subsistence minimum. This ruling has since been confirmed by the German Constitutional Court, thus demonstrating its ongoing validity.[75] Connecting human dignity to claims of welfare benefits has sometimes been objected to both on political and on technical legal grounds (with a range of critiques including issues of the separation of powers, cost and the allegedly exclusive verticality of human rights application).[76] Inspite of this, there seems to have been a shift in approach and an increasing call to provide protection against destitution on the basis of human dignity, both in academic literature[77] and in case law across Europe.[78] In particular, the prohibition of inhuman and degrading treatment under Article 3 ECHR has been constructed in

[73] The Court held: 'The second sentence [of Article 1] "to respect and to protect [human dignity] is the obligation of all state power" does create for the state a positive duty of "protection", which however does not include protection against material deprivation, but rather protection against human dignity attacks committed by others, such as degradation (*Erniedrigung*), denunciation (*Brandmarkung*), persecution (*Verfolgung*) and ostracism (*Ächtung*) and so on' (at 104).

[74] C Bommarius, 'Germany's *Sozialstaat* Principle and the Founding Period' (2011) 12 *German Law Journal* 1879.

[75] See BVerfGE 1, 332 (348) and BVerfGE 1, 418 (423). Recent case law includes the so-called Hartz IV ruling of 9 February 2010 (BVerfG, 1, BvL 1/09); and the decision of 18 July 2012 on asylum-seekers (1BvL 10/10 -1 BvL 2/11). See IT Winkler and C Mahler, 'Interpreting the Right to a Dignified Minimum Existence: A New Era in German Socio-Economic Rights Jurisprudence?' (2013) 13 *Human Rights Law Review* 388; and I Leijten, 'The German Right to an *Existenzminimum*, Human Dignity and the Possibility of a Minimum Core Socio-economic Rights Protection' (2015) 16 *German Law Journal* 23.

[76] The European Commission of Human Rights at first refused to rely on Art 3 ECHR in situations of destitution: *Van Volsem v Belgium*, Commision EHR, 9 May 1990, discussed by A Cassese, 'Can the Notion of Inhuman and Degrading Treatment be Applied to Socio-Economic Conditions?' (1994) 2 *European Journal of International Law* 141.

[77] C O'Cinneide, 'A Modest Proposal: Destitution, State Responsibility and the ECHR' (2008) 5 *European Human Rights Law Review* 583; and S Fredman, 'Positive Duties and Socio-economic Disadvantage: Bringing Disadvantage onto the Equality Agenda' (2010) 3 *European Human Rights Law Review* 290. See also K Steigleder, 'Human Dignity and Social Welfare' in M Düwell, J Braarvig, R Brownsword and D Mieth (eds), *The Cambridge Handbook of Human Dignity* (Cambridge, Cambridge University Press, 2014) 472–76.

[78] See, eg the Portuguese Constitutional Court's ruling of 19 December 2002, No 509/02. Extracts reproduced in P Bon and D Maus (eds), *Les grandes décisions des cours constitutionnelles Européennes* (Paris, Dalloz, 2008) 173. See also *R (on the application of Adam) v Secretary of State for the Home Department*; *R (on the application of Limbuela) v Secretary of State*

domestic case law to protect people against state-caused destitution, as in a recent UK House of Lords ruling on asylum-seekers:

> The only question, therefore, is whether the degree of suffering endured or imminently to be endured by these people [the asylum-seekers and applicants] reaches the degree of severity prohibited by Article 3 ... But to have to endure the indefinite prospect of both [rooflessness and cashlessness], unless one is in a place where it is both possible and legal to live off the land, is in today's society both inhuman and degrading. *We have to judge matters by the standards of our own society in the modern world, not by the standards of a third world society or a bygone age.*[79] (emphasis added)

Key to this reasoning is the standard of assessment used in deciding whether Article 3 is breached. This reflects the ECtHR living instrument approach, as well as an increasing concern and consensus that wide-spread poverty can be detrimental not only to those personally suffering from destitution, but also to the functioning of democracy as a whole.[80] The guarantee of minimum welfare is arguably therefore a core component of the concept of human dignity because it protects the most vulnerable, allowing them to live and to be included in society. This particular construction of human dignity is obviously therefore related to promoting a certain sense of social justice, which was very high on the post-war constitutional agenda. As explained by Erin Daly, promotion of human dignity-based welfare is also crucial to sustaining a healthy level of democratic participation and dialogue:

> Where the equal dignity of each individual is recognised and appreciated, the public can take part directly in the constitutional democratic dialogue, with the court as facilitator to ensure that all parties respect the rules of the game. The more empowered each member of the public, each participant, is—that is, the more work each person does to assure the development and implementation of policies that are consistent with constitutional democracy—the less work the court needs to do.[81]

for the Home Department; *R (on the application of Tesema) v Secretary of State for the Home Department*, [2005] UKHL 66, House of Lords, 3 November 2005. See also the ruling of the Spanish Supreme Court: JUR/2015/17371, Tribunal Supremo (Sala de lo Social), 22 December 2014. With thanks to Miguel Ángel M Badenes for bringing this to my attention. In relation to the ECHR, see J Kenny, 'European Convention and Social Welfare' (2010) 5 *European Human Rights Law Review* 495; and A Frohwerk, *Soziale Not in der Rechtssprechung der EGMR* (Tübingen, Mohr Siebeck, 2012).

[79] Per Baroness Hale of Richmond, *R (on the application of Adam)*, above n 78, para 78.

[80] D Roman, *Le droit public face à la pauvreté* (Paris, Librairie Générale de Droit et de Jurisprudence, 2002); and D Schnapper, *La démocratie providentielle: essai sur l'égalité contemporaine* (Paris, Gallimard, 2002). See also Stephen P Marks, 'Poverty' in D Moeckli, S Shah and S Sivakumara (eds), *International Human Rights Law*, 2nd edn (Oxford, Oxford University Press, 2014) 567–89.

[81] E Daly, *Dignity Rights: Courts, Constitutions, and the Worth of the Human Person* (Philadelphia, PA, University of Pennsylvania Press, 2013) 154.

Living in fear of being evicted from one's home or in humiliation of having to rely on charity for food, enduring cold and hunger, or being unable to obtain medical treatment and care is affecting too many Europeans, and 'is leading to a quiet desperation ... resulting in depression, resignation and the loss of hope for their future' according to a 2013 Red Cross Report.[82] Over six decades after the German war widows ruling, the relevance and usefulness of human dignity as a tool of social and democratic inclusion has therefore lost none of its significance and its urgency.

ii. Workers' Self-Determination

The next human dignity core issue was elaborated by the Hungarian Constitutional Court.[83] Its first human dignity ruling, Case 8/1990 of 23 April 1990, was delivered a few months after the Court started operating. The case involved trade unions' right of representation, and the Court called on human dignity in the following terms:

> The Constitutional Court considers the right to human dignity as one of the formulations of the general personality right. Modern constitutions and constitutional case law identify the general personality right in terms of several of its aspects, such as the right to free fulfillment of personality, the right to self-determination, the general freedom of action or the right to a private sphere.[84]

In addition to providing the first syncretic definition of human dignity at the time,[85] this ruling brought to the fore the right to self-determination, a right with a particularly strong political resonance in Hungary at the time, considering the context of this case, in that it was decided within months of the collapse of the communist system and involved a key pillar of the political control exercised by the ruling party, ie trade unions. On this basis, the Constitutional Court concluded that trade unions could no longer automatically represent employees, and certainly not against their will, as the

[82] International Federation of Red Cross and Red Crescent Societies, *Think Differently: Humanitarian Impact of the Economic Crisis in Europe* (Geneva, 2013) 2.

[83] The apparently huge time gap between the two rulings and dates (1951 and 1989), is due to the focus on 'first dignity rulings'. As will be recalled, dignity constitutional case law has played a considerable role in shaping the practice of German democracy since 1949, see DP Kommers, *The Constitutional Jurisprudence of the Federal Republic of Germany* (Durham, NC, Duke University Press, 1997).

[84] C Dupré, *Importing the Law in Post-Communist Transitions: The Hungarian Constitutional Court and the Right to Human Dignity* (Oxford, Hart Publishing, 2003) 66–67.

[85] This is further nuanced and discussed in Dupré, above n 84, 66–68 and 82. On Hungarian constitutional case law, see L Sólyom and G Brunner (eds), *Verfassungsgerichtsbarkeit in Ungarn: Analysen und Enscheidungssammlung, 1990–1993* (Baden-Baden, Nomos, 1995); L Sólyom and G Brunner (eds), *Constitutional Judiciary in a New Democracy: The Hungarian Constitutional Court* (Ann Arbor, MI, University of Michigan Press, 2000); and A Holló and Á Erdei (eds), *Selected Decisions of the Constitutional Court of Hungary (1998–2001)* (Budapest, Akadémiai Kiadó, 2005).

disputed communist regime had required until then. With its focus on autonomy and self-determination, this construction of human dignity arguably reflects the essence of the new constitutional order that the Hungarian Court was involved in rebuilding, namely, an order where people are free from ideologically driven policies imposed from above by the ruling party. It may not be surprising that one of the first rulings connecting human dignity and workers' rights should come from a post-communist constitutional court. Above all what this Hungarian ruling did, was to apply the right to self-determination and the freedom to 'master one's fate', which lies at the core of human dignity,[86] to the specific context of work, thereby extending the reach of European constitutionalism to the work sphere. This process can also be observed across Europe in the way that working conditions are increasingly being assessed by reference to human dignity[87] and human rights.[88]

iii. Defining Humanity

Chronologically, the next 'first time ruling' is that of the French Constitutional Council delivered in 1994 and discussed above. It is noted again here for the connections it established between dignity and the definition and protection of humanity, in forms that were emerging at the time due to medical and scientific developments. The French Court held:

> The legislation referred sets out a number of principles including the primacy of the human being, respect for the human being from the inception of life, the inviolability, integrity and non-marketability of the human body and the integrity of the human race; these principles help to secure the constitutional principle of the protection of human dignity.[89]

This typically terse statement by the French Court has arguably been a major contribution to the definition of human dignity in that it proposed a more sophisticated definition of humanity, which includes the genetic dimension of humanity.[90] This definition built on the post-war definition of humanity, which, as will be recalled, focused on biology and belonging to the human

[86] E Daly, *Dignity Rights: Courts, Constitutions and the Worth of the Human Person* (Philadelphia, PA, University of Pennsylvania Press, 2013) ch 4 'Master of One's Fate', 71–100.

[87] A Bogg, 'Article 31: Fair and Just Working Conditions' in S Peers, T Hervey, J Kenner and A Ward (eds), *The EU Charter of Fundamental Rights: A Commentary* (Oxford, Hart Publishing/Nomos, 2014) 833–68.

[88] R O'Connell, 'The Right to Work in the ECHR' (2012) 2 *European Human Rights Law Review* 176; and C Fenwick and T Novitz (eds), *Human Rights at Work: Perspectives on Law and Regulation* (Oxford, Hart Publishing, 2010). The next chapter discusses further the connections among work, dignity and constitutionalism.

[89] Constitutional Council, No 94/343/344 DC, 27 July 1994. English translation provided by the official website of the Constitutional Council: www.conseil-constitutionnel.fr.

[90] Compare with Art 26.3 of the Portuguese Constitution which provides: 'The law shall guarantee the personal dignity and genetic identity of the human being, particularly in the creation, development and use of technology and in scientific experimentation'.

family (Article 1 UN Universal Declaration of Human Rights). Importantly, the 1994 expanded definition of humanity was not just genetic, it was also normative, ie shaped by constitutional principles explicitly listed as 'the primacy of the human being, respect for the human being from the inception of life, the inviolability, integrity and non-marketability of the human body and the integrity of the human race'. While the court formulating them was French, these principles are broadly shared by European constitutionalism, in particular by the 1997 Oviedo Convention and the EU Charter which have since come into force and prohibit reproductive human cloning, as discussed in the previous chapter. It is important, however, to note that this substantive aspect of human dignity is still very much under construction and is being continuously shaped and refined by courts.[91] Despite, or perhaps because of, its unfinished status, this particular aspect of human dignity arguably lies at the heart of European constitutionalism, as protecting humanity means constantly refining the definition of human rights and inventing new mechanisms, a process arguably best undertaken through transparent and democratic reflection and discussion.[92]

iv. Setting the Boundaries of Capitalism

The ruling considered here involves a different but equally essential dimension of European constitutionalism, namely, its relationship with capitalism, which has been the dominant ideology underpinning the construction of Europe since 1945, and even more so since the fall of Communism in 1989. Historically presented as a way out of war and towards democracy, Europe was primarily devised as an economic community. When Communism collapsed in Central and Eastern Europe, the transformation of these planned economies into liberal ones became a key aspect of the democratic transition, as well as, crucially, a political requirement for joining the European Union. While the connections between constitutionalism and capitalism are numerous,[93] they have often been articulated in terms of human dignity and it is hardly surprising that the *Omega* ruling,[94] one of the first dignity

[91] See for instance: C-34/10 *Brüstle v Greenpeace eV*, CJEU, 18 October 2011. See S H E Harmon, G Laurie and A Courtney, 'Dignity, Plurality and Patentability: The Unfinished Story of Brüstle v Greenpeace' (2013) 38 *European Law Review* 92; and B v Roermund, 'The Embryo and its Rights: Technology and Teleology' (2013) 14 *German Law Journal* 1939.

[92] Ultimately, this is a universal task, the problem in practice being size and the related difficulty of reaching world-wide consensus (eg on the constitutional status of human embryos), as well as issues of implementation and compliance with whatever rules may have been adopted at the international level.

[93] D Nicol, *The Constitutional Protection of Capitalism* (Oxford, Hart Publishing, 2010).

[94] C-36/02 *Omega Spielhallen-und Automatenaufstellungs-GmbH v Oberbürgermeisterin der Bundestadt Bonn*, First Chamber, 14 October 2004. See J Morijn, 'Balancing Fundamental Rights and Common Market Freedoms in Union Law: *Schmidberger* and *Omega* in the Light of the European Constitution' (2006) 12 *European Law Journal* 15.

rulings delivered by the ECJ, should involve precisely this tension, which is at the heart of the EU.

As will be recalled from the discussion above, at the core of this ruling was the tension between respect for human dignity (constructed as part of public policy) and the freedom of services and free movement of goods, two of the four fundamental freedoms structuring the common market. In this respect, it is significant that human dignity was interpreted as a general principle of EU law and found to be a valid ground of public policy for restricting the freedom of services and banning the laserdrome entertainment on German territory. Without referring to human dignity as the essence of the EU legal order, the ECJ expressed a similar point as the ECtHR when it held that 'the Community legal order *undeniably strives to ensure respect for human dignity* as a general principle of law' (emphasis added).[95] In this sentence, the ECJ arguably identified human dignity as a new imperative of the EU legal order, in addition to the four economic freedoms. The difficulty, temporarily resolved in this case, is about solving the conflicts that will inevitably arise out of these two dimensions of the EU constitutional order.

What the *Omega* ruling powerfully demonstrates is the impact that the protection of human dignity can have on a given constitutional order. This approach to dignity has, however, not been confirmed by the ECJ/CJEU, and the *Laval* and *Viking* rulings delivered afterwards seem to indicate that the EU's priority has remained the protection of the economic freedoms.[96] With the coming into force of the Lisbon Treaty and its explicit commitment to human dignity as the first of its foundational values under Article 2, reinforced by Title 1 of the EU Charter, the EU has arguably reached a crossroads in respect of re-balancing its (sometimes) conflicting core values.[97] At the time of writing, the impact of the economic and financial crisis which is shaking the EU cannot be ignored in this discussion. However, it is suggested that the tension is also a deeper and more theoretical one, which raises issues about the respective purposes of the EU and of European constitutionalism. On the basis of the *Omega* ruling, together with the human dignity commitment in the Lisbon Treaty, it is suggested that this tension ought to be solved in favour of human dignity in order to reflect the EU's intention 'to place the individual at the heart of its activities' (to refer to the

[95] *Omega*, above n 94, para 34.

[96] C-341/05 *Laval un Partneri v Svenska Byggnadsarbetareförbundet*, 18 December 2007 and C-438/05 *International Transport Workers' Federation and Finnish Seamen's Union v Viking Line ABP and OÜ Viking Line Esti*, Grand Chamber, 18 December 2007. See C Joerges and F Rödl, 'Informal Politics, Formalised Law and the "Social Deficit" of European Integration' (2009) 15 *European Law Journal* 1.

[97] LFM Besselink, 'The Parameters of Constitutional Conflict after Melloni' (2014) 39 *European Law Review* 531.

words of the Charter's Preamble), confirming and strengthening the essence of EU constitutionalism as the protection of humanity.[98]

v. Protecting Asylum-Seekers

This overview of 'first time rulings' would not be complete without considering the CJEU case law since the coming into force of the Lisbon Treaty, as until then the ECJ was reluctant to refer to the EU Charter. The first dignity ruling of the CJEU involves the way in which asylum-seekers are treated by the EU and its Member States, and in particular the possibility of refoulement to the country of entry.[99] While discussion of Article 1 EU Charter by the CJEU in these cases was very brief,[100] the argument of human dignity nevertheless played a key role in support of the asylum-seekers. The CJEU held that Member States could not send them back to the country of entry on the basis that they were not aware of the specific conditions of their treatment. The CJEU contrasted the issue of 'slightest infringement' of the Directives at stake by a Member State, which is 'not sufficient to prevent the transfer of an asylum seeker to the Member State primarily responsible',[101] with that of 'systemic flaws in the asylum procedure and reception conditions for asylum applicants in the Member State responsible, resulting in inhuman and degrading treatment, within the meaning of Article 4 of the Charter'.[102] With regard to the latter, the CJEU held that Member States may not transfer an asylum-seeker back to the Member State responsible 'where they cannot be unaware of [these] systemic deficiencies'.[103] This logic, the CJEU continued, applies in the same way in relation to the other relevant EU Charter Articles, namely and significantly, Article 1 on human dignity, as well as Article 18 on the right to asylum and Article 47 on the right to an effective remedy.[104]

Treatment of asylum-seekers (under Directive 2003/9/EC on the minimum standards for the reception of asylum-seekers) has since been a recurring theme brought before the CJEU on the ground of a human dignity breach

[98] In this respect, it may be regretted that the CJEU found that the EU Charter did not apply to Member States qua parties to the ESM Treaty: C-370/12 *Thomas Pringle v Government of Ireland and Attorney General*, 27 November 2012.

[99] C-493/10 *NS v Secretary of State for the Home Department* and C-411/10 *ME, ASM, MT, KP, EH v Refugee Applications Commissioner and Minister for Justice, Equality and Law Reform*, 21 December 2011. See J Buckley, 'NS v Secretary of State for the Home Department (C-411/10)' (2012) 2 *European Human Rights Law Review* 205.

[100] Compare with the degree of engagement of the ECtHR in a ruling on the same issue, brought by the same applicants and delivered previously: *MSS v Belgium and Greece*, Application no 30696/09, Grand Chamber, 21 January 2011.

[101] *NS v Secretary of State for the Home Department*, above n 99, para 84.

[102] ibid para 86.

[103] ibid paras 94 and 106.

[104] ibid para 115.

under Article 1 EU Charter, including minimum standards of living in the Member State where the application is originally lodged, understood with reference to the requirement that 'the amount of financial aid granted [must be] sufficient to ensure a standard of living adequate for the health of applicants and capable of ensuring their subsistence'.[105] More recently, the CJEU held that applicants seeking asylum on the grounds of persecution for being homosexuals should not be expected to provide documentary (eg film) evidence of their intimate sexual acts as part of their application.[106] Considering how asylum-seekers tend to be treated and considering the Directive's explicit requirement that their human dignity should be respected at their reception and throughout the duration of their application process, it is not surprising that asylum-seekers' treatment was the first human dignity issue brought before the CJEU.

What is interesting from the perspective of this study is that this case law confirms the irrelevance of nationality (or citizenship) with regards to human dignity protection and that the CJEU issued a resounding reminder that Articles 1 and 4 EU Charter protect all human beings. With this, we are on the now familiar terrain of the connections between humanity and dignity, on the one hand, and the connections between dignity and equality, on the other. Moreover, this CJEU case law highlights a crucial issue of constitutionalism and democracy, namely, the way in which aliens are treated: while the reality is far from perfect, case law is consistently clear that being a non-national with a yet uncertain legal status (namely, pending the asylum application or its outcome) may never justify treatment that infringes human dignity, and does require Member States to provide minimum welfare assistance.[107] Dignified living conditions guaranteed in this way allow asylum-seekers to subsist while their application is being considered. More importantly perhaps, the provision of such conditions substantiates the recognition of asylum-seekers' existence by the state, which is the first step for them to regain a sense of their identity and some control over their lives.[108]

Overall, the rulings selected and discussed above arguably illuminate what constitutes the core or essence of European constitutionalism. What can be seen, arising out of this case law, is not only a clear substantive

[105] Case C-79/13 *Federal agentschap voor de opvang asielzoekers v Selver Saciri et al*, 27 February 2014, paras 38–40; see also: Case C-179/11 *Cimade and GISTI v Ministre de l'intérieur, de l'outre-mer, des collectivités territoriales et de l'immigration*, 27 September 2012.

[106] Cases C-148/13 and C-150/13 *A, B, C v Staatssecretaris van Veiligheid en Justitie*, 2 December 2014, para 65. Generally see G Collste, 'Human Dignity, Immigration and Refugees' in M Düwell, J Braarvig, R Brownsword and D Mieth (eds), *The Cambridge Handbook of Human Dignity* (Cambridge, Cambridge University Press, 2014) 461–68.

[107] See, eg the ruling of the German Constitutional Court, 18 July 2012 (1BvL 10/10-1 BvL 2/11); and the UK Supreme Court ruling in *R (on the application of Adam)*, above n 78.

[108] A Kesby, *The Right to Have Rights: Citizenship, Humanity and International Law* (Oxford, Oxford Scholarship Online, 2012).

definition of what human dignity means on a day to day basis (as opposed to the exceptional foundational moments of constitutionalism), but also—and crucially—that the construction of human dignity by judges is rarely innocuous or neutral as it implies finding a way to decide among conflicting priorities in a manner that is often novel and alters the status quo ante of European constitutionalism.

V. CONCLUSION

The selection of cases and courts discussed here was not based on the similarity of their approach to human dignity, but because they represent a wide range of contexts and types of judicial reasoning. Yet the similarity of human dignity definitions and of ways in which this concept has been constructed by judges is striking: while each first time human dignity ruling epitomised a particular issue faced by the court in the case before it, it also illustrates broader European concerns.

What is further striking in judicial uses of human dignity is that it has often been driven by an explicit attempt to bring a given constitutional order up to date with 'modern constitutions' (as in Hungary) or with 'the present day conditions' (in ECtHR case law). In this sense, constitutional courts have arguably played a key role in re-activating the foundational commitment to human dignity, and testing it against current developments and new threats to humanity. Related to this and similarly striking is the way in which courts have tended to anchor their individual construction of human dignity in what can be called a pan or trans-European understanding of this concept, drawing on and combining three main sources (Member States' constitutions, the ECHR and the EU Charter). This cross-European concept of dignity brings together individual European constitutional orders, and it arguably acts as a locking mechanism, securing human dignity deep at the heart of European constitutionalism and ensuring that the foundational commitment to its protection on which constitutionalism is grounded can be sustained despite changes and emerging threats and concerns. This locking mechanism is also an effective tool of constitutional integration, with each constitutional order making up European constitutionalism being rooted in human dignity both as its own foundation and its connection to the whole.

5

Hidden in Plain View: Workers' Human Dignity

I. INTRODUCTION

WORK AND DEMOCRACY have had an uneasy relationship. This has perhaps been the case since the 'invention' of democracy in 5 BC Athens, where what we would now consider as work was done essentially by women, slaves and aliens, namely, all the non citizens. As Cornelius Castoriadis observed, Athenian democracy was explicitly built on the practice (and rationale) that citizens were not supposed to work, so as to be free to debate and take part in public decision-making. In this sense, being a citizen and a 'worker' were two mutually exclusive constitutional identities.[1] As a result, work was also by and large left out of the democracy theories, which have used Athens (implicitly or explicitly) as a model or inspiration. The absence of work in this initial democratic thinking and related practices was magnified by the fact that, as André Gorz reminded us, until the late eighteenth century and the rise of early capitalism, work did not exist in its modern, ie industrial form.[2] This partly explains why human rights and constitutionalism, which had by then started to be developed, could not fully integrate the dimension of work and workers' rights as constitutional rights, to the same degree as civil and political rights. In the twentieth century, the discussion on the constitutional status of work and workers' rights within the framework of liberal democracy was arguably greatly limited by the rival model of communist dictatorships, in which workers and their rights occupied pride of place. This ideological conflict at the heart of Europe ended with the collapse of Communism in Central and Eastern Europe, a process consolidated by accession to the European Union of most of those countries in two main waves, in 2003 and 2007, with Croatia being the latest new Member State since 2013. Hopefully, this therefore makes it possible to consider the relationship between work and democracy without ideological fear or prejudice.

[1] C Castoriadis, *Domaines de l'homme: les carrefours du labyrinthe (2)* (Paris, Seuil, 1999).
[2] A Gorz, *Métamorphoses du travail: critique de la raison économique* (Paris, Gallimard, 1988) 29–46.

Work as it has evolved under capitalism is now central to human identity, whether people are in employment or out of work, whether they are pre-work and being trained with a view to finding work, or post-work and retired, enjoying (or not as may be the case) the benefits of having worked. Moreover, people derive certain rights from their status as workers and, conversely, their ability to enjoy some human rights is affected by their work situation. Despite work's undeniable role in shaping human lives and identities, the constitutional status of workers has often been overshadowed by constitutionalism's emphasis on citizenship together with civil and political rights. In fact, as will be recalled from the previous three chapters, the constitutional identity of human beings as citizens has developed in connection with that of workers. Chapter 2 sketched out the key features of workers' constitutional identity, the development of which can be traced back to the French Revolution.[3] Chapter 3 brought to the fore the EU Charter's focus on the importance of workers' rights explicitly codified under Article 5 (prohibition of slavery, forced labour and human trafficking), and Article 31 (respect for workers' health, safety and dignity). Chapter 4 confirmed the position of worker's rights, rooted in their right to self-determination and the pursuit of social justice, at the core of European constitutionalism.

In this respect the EU Charter' explicit codification of workers' dignity under Article 31 and implicit codification under Articles 4 and 5 has to be welcomed as the first supranational normative step towards bringing workers' rights within the mainstream of human rights and European constitutionalism. Therefore, using the EU Charter as a platform to reflect on and discuss the constitutional identity of workers, this chapter argues that human dignity can serve both as a theoretical and practical link between labour law and constitutionalism in order to shape workers' constitutional identity as human beings. In so doing, the chapter draws on a stream of case law and academic reflection that seeks to bridge the gap between labour rights and human rights,[4] and between constitutionalism and workers' rights.[5] In particular, this chapter was inspired by more recent developments

[3] The term 'worker' is used in a generic sense for the purposes of this chapter, which does not develop the technical nuances of this term according to (European and domestic) labour law. It is primarily understood in contrast and comparison with the two other constitutional identities of human beings, qua 'man' and qua citizen as discussed in Chapter 2. Moreover, this term is used by reference to the EU Charter, which uses 'worker' in its Art 31. I also use the term 'employee' in the general sense of 'worker' and not in the technical meaning this term can have under labour law.

[4] P Alston (ed), *Labour Rights as Human Rights* (Oxford, Oxford University Press, 2005); see also R Allen QC, R Crasnow and A Beale, *Employment Law and Human Rights*, 2nd edn (Oxford, Oxford University Press, 2006); and S Fredman, *Human Rights Transformed: Positive Rights and Positive Duties* (Oxford, Oxford University Press, 2008).

[5] P Häberle, 'Aspekte einer Verfassungslehre der Arbeit' in P Häberle (ed), *Rechtsvergleichung im Kraftfeld des Verfassungsstaates: Methoden und Inhalte, Kleinstaaten und Entwicklungsländer* (Berlin, Duncker und Humblot, 1992) 524–51.

in ECHR case law and related academic commentary.[6] The approach to European constitutionalism adopted here, bringing together the ECHR, the EU and their Member States' constitutional orders considered from a longer-term historical perspective, sheds light on the important continuum existing across human beings' three constitutional identities, as man, as citizen and as worker, as well as on the fundamental connections among European constitutionalism, democracy and workers' human dignity. Moreover, the coming into force of the EU Charter at the same time as the worst economic and financial crisis in the EU's entire history, with far-reaching negative consequences for workers' rights, provides a timely opportunity to reflect on these issues,[7] bringing into sharp relief the potential and actual impacts of—deteriorating—workers' constitutional status and rights on the overall quality of democracy.

While this chapter will touch on issues of welfare and social rights, it is not primarily about them.[8] It starts by observing that workers' rights and constitutionalism are rooted in shared struggles for human dignity and are now developing on converging lines. In its central part, the chapter sketches out the key features of workers' constitutional identity anchored in human dignity, and discusses them through the prism of the EU Charter such as Articles 4 and 5 and Article 31.1. The chapter closes with a critical reflection on the connection between workers' human dignity and democracy.

II. WORKERS ARE HUMAN BEINGS

It is argued here that the main reason for bringing workers' rights under the protective scope of constitutionalism and human rights is workers' humanity, understood here not just in the biological sense of this term, but in the sense that it has acquired in European constitutionalism over centuries,

[6] Chronologically: C Fenwick and T Novitz (eds), *Human Rights at Work: Perspectives on Law and Regulation* (Oxford, Hart Publishing, 2010); R O'Connell, 'The Right to Work in the ECHR' (2012) 2 *European Human Rights Law Review* 176; F Dorssemont, K Lörcher and I Schömann (eds), *The European Convention on Human Rights and the Employment Relation* (Oxford, Hart Publishing, 2013); V Mantouvalou, 'Labour Rights in the European Convention on Human Rights: An Intellectual Justification for an Integrated Approach to Interpretation' (2013) 13 *Human Rights Law Review* 529.

[7] E Achtsioglou and M Doherty, 'There Must be Some Way Out of Here: The Crisis, Labour Rights and Member States in the Eye of the Storm' (2014) 20 *European Law Journal* 219.

[8] Despite obvious connections between welfare and human dignity: see D Schnapper, *La démocratie providentielle: essai sur l'égalité contemporaine* (Paris, Gallimard, 2002); G Katrougalos and P O'Connell, 'Fundamental Social Rights' in M Tushnet, T Fleiner, T and C Saunders (eds), *Routledge Handbook of Constitutional Law* (London, Routledge, 2013) 375; and B Klein Goldewijk, A Contreras Baspineiro and PC Carbonari (eds), *Dignity and Human Rights: The Implementation of Economic, Social and Cultural Rights* (Antwerp, Intersentia, 2002).

rooted in Kantian philosophy as the ability to self-determine and the prohibition on instrumentalisation, as discussed in Chapter 2.[9] After briefly setting out the converging lines between work and constitutionalism, this section therefore highlights the key features of workers' humanity constructed through the prism of their dignity.

A. Work and Constitutionalism: Converging Parallels

As will be recalled from Chapter 2, the milestones in the development of constitutionalism also marked key stages in the development of workers' rights and of their constitutional identity. These include 1793, with the adoption of workers' first constitutional definition anchored in self-determination, the balance of power between the employer and the worker, and the inalienability of the worker (who may not be bought or sell himself);[10] 1848, with the abolition of slavery on the ground of human dignity;[11] and 1919, with the creation of the International Labour Organization (ILO) founded on the overarching principle that 'labour should not be regarded merely as an article of commerce'.[12] 1919 also marked the adoption of the first constitutional provision, namely, Article 151 of the Weimar Republic Constitution, which mentioned workers' rights and the idea of a 'dignified existence' with reference to 'economic life', stating that 'The organisation of economic life must conform to the principles of social justice with a view to

[9] An alternative approach consists in considering workers' rights as a type of social citizenship, originally proposed by TH Marshall, *Citizenship and Social Class and other Essays* (Cambridge, Cambridge University Press, 1950). This has been developed in relation to the EU more recently by French labour lawyer Sandrine Maillard, *L'émergence de la citoyenneté sociale Européenne* (Aix en Provence, Presses Universitaires de Aix-Marseille, 2008).

[10] Article 18 of the 1793 Constitution reads: 'Every man can contract his services and his time, but he cannot sell himself nor be sold: his person is not an alienable property (*une propriété aliénable*). The law knows of no such thing as the status of a servant (*domesticité*); there can exist only a contract for services and compensation between the man who works and the one who employs him'. See Chapter 2.

[11] Décret relatif à l'abolition de l'esclavage dans les colonies et les possessions françaises du 27 Avril 1848, discussed in Chapter 2. See also RJ Scott, 'Dignité/Dignidade: Organizing Against Threats to Dignity in Societies after Slavery' in C McCrudden (ed), *Understanding Human Dignity* (Oxford, Oxford University Press, 2013) 61–77.

[12] G Rodgers, E Lee, L Swepston and J Van Daele, J, *The ILO and the Quest for Social Justice, 1919–2009* (Geneva, International Labour Organization, 2009); see also T Ramm, 'Epilogue: The New Ordering of Labour Law 1918–45' in B Hepple (ed), *The Making of Labour Law in Europe: A Comparative Study of Nine Countries Up to 1945* (London, Mansell Publishing, 1986) 277. Its Preamble reads: 'And whereas conditions of labour exist involving such injustice, hardship and privation to large numbers of people as to produce unrest so great that the peace and harmony in the world are imperilled'; opening sentence of the Constitution of the ILO, available at www.ilo.org/ilolex/english/constq.htm.

guaranteeing a dignified existence to all [*menschenwürdigen Dasein*]'.[13] It is suggested that the historical fate of this particular provision is emblematic of the wider status of work in European constitutionalism. In 1949, while it was incorporated almost verbatim into the East German Constitution under Article 19,[14] this provision disappeared from the new West German Basic Law at the same time as the codification of human dignity under its first article, which was to become so influential.[15] Exeunt work and dignified existence, enter abstract inviolability of human dignity, with the result that workers' human dignity and rights have developed along separate tracks.

This divide was also at the foundation of Europe arising out of the EEC and the Council of Europe, characterised by a deliberate division of responsibility. Thus, the EEC was in charge of creating a common market, and primarily concerned with the economy, and the Council of Europe was in charge of promoting democracy and human rights. As will also be recalled, the latter's main Convention, the European Convention on Human Rights (ECHR), deliberately and almost exclusively focuses on civil and political rights, leaving economic, social and cultural rights in a sort of vacuum[16] which the adoption of the European Social Charter in 1961 (revised in 1996) has not managed to address.[17] Moreover, within the EEC, workers'

[13] HC Nipperdey (ed), *Die Grundrechte und Grundpflichten der Reichsverfassung: Kommentar zum zweiten Teil der Reichsverfassung, Dritter Band* (Kronberg, Scriptor Verlag, 1930) 125; and P Häberle, 'Aspekte einer Verfassungslehre der Arbeit' in P Häberle (ed), *Rechtsvergleichung im Kraftfeld des Verfassungsstaate: Methoden und Inhalte, Kleinstaaten und Entwicklungsländer* (Berlin, Duncker und Humblot, 1992) 533. On the Weimar Republic, see also P Unruh, *Weimar Staatslehre und Grundgesetz: ein verfassungstheoretischer Vergleich* (Berlin, Duncker und Humblot, 2004); and 'Kant—Menschenwürde—Sozialstaat' in R Grote *et al* (eds), *Die Ordnung der Freiheit: Festschrift f. Christian Starck zum 70. Geburtstag* (Tübingen, Mohr Siebeck, 2007) 133. See also O Kahn-Freud (ed) (with an introduction and appendices by R Lewis and J Clark), *Labour Law and Politics in the Weimar Republic* (Oxford, Basil Blackwell, 1981).

[14] Article 19 reads: 'Organisation of economic life must conform to the principles of social justice; it must guarantee to all an existence compatible with the dignity of man ... It is incumbent upon the economy to contribute to the benefit of the whole people and to the satisfaction of its wants and to ensure that everybody will obtain, in accordance with his performance, a just share in the yield of production'. This provision remained in the 1968 version of the East German Constitution under Art 19: 'Achtung und Schutz der Würde und Freiheit der Persönlichkeit sind Gebot für alle staatlichen Organe, alle gesellschaftliche Kräfte und jeden einzelnen Bürger', as quoted by FJ Wetz, 'Die Würde des Menschen—Ein Phantom?' (2001) 87 *Archiv für Rechts-und Sozialphilosophie* 315.

[15] See Chapter 3.

[16] Rory O'Connell points out that social rights were also on the mind of some ECHR drafters and quotes the French representative, M Teitgen, as observing that 'What is the value of sacred family rights and family liberties for the father who is permanently haunted by the spectre of unemployment?': 'The Right to Work in the ECHR' (2012) 2 *European Human Rights Law Review* 176.

[17] The 1961 European Social Charter (revised in 1996) was adopted under the Council of Europe. See APCM Jaspers and L Betten (eds), *25 Years European Social Charter* (Deventer, Kluwer Law and Taxation Publishers, 1988), and L Samuel, *Fundamental Social Rights: Case Law of the European Social Charter* (Strasbourg, Council of Europe Publishing, 1997).

rights were largely left out of the treaties, in the belief that their working conditions would be addressed by an 'upward harmonisation'.[18]

Despite these fragmentations and divisions along ideological and institutional lines, human rights have remained, in principle, indivisible, with human dignity acting as a bridge among the various types of rights. Case law started evolving in an attempt to protect workers' (human) rights more effectively as a response to concerns about the deterioration of working conditions, and a rough chronology of this process can be put together. While it may not be the exclusive factor, the end of the Cold War mentioned above seems to have had an impact on the greater convergence between workers' rights and constitutionalism, with the 1990s appearing as a significant decade in this respect. The first ECHR case to mention in this respect was *Niemietz v Germany* delivered in 1992, which extended the protection of the right to privacy under Article 8 to the workplace and work relationships.[19] In EC/EU primary law the first mention of human dignity can be found a few years later, in the revised Social Charter adopted in 1996 under Article 26, which provided that: 'With a view to ensuring the effective exercise of the right of all workers to protection of their dignity at work, the Parties undertake…'. At the EU level, human dignity starts appearing in secondary legislation in 2000 in Directives on harassment at work.[20] Moreover, as will be recalled from Chapter 4, in *Omega* the European Court of Justice (ECJ) used the argument of human dignity for the first time, finding it a lawful ground to restrict freedom of establishment.[21] As will also be recalled, this construction of human dignity echoes domestic case law holding peepshow performing[22] and prostitution[23] to be a breach of human

[18] F Rödl, 'Constitutional Integration of Labour Constitutions' in EO Eriksen, C Joerges and F Rödl (eds), *Law, Democracy and Solidarity in a Post-national Union: The Unsettled Political Order of Europe* (Oxford, Routledge, 2008) 152, 155: 'The original idea for European labour law was written into the Treaty of Rome. It consisted of only two elements: the free movement of workers, and the right of women to equal pay for equal work. Apart from this, the founding Member States restricted themselves to expressing a belief in an upward harmonisation of working conditions, ie 'harmonisation while the improvement is being maintained'. According to this belief there was no need for further European labour regulation'.

[19] *Niemietz v Germany*, Application no 72/1991/324/396, ECtHR, 16 December 1992. Generally see R O'Connell, 'The Right to Work in the ECHR' (2012) 2 *European Human Rights Law Review* 176. More generally, see F Dorssemont, K Lörcher and I Schömann (eds), *The European Convention on Human Rights and the Employment Relation* (Oxford, Hart Publishing, 2013).

[20] Article 2.3 of Council Directive 2000/78/CE: harassment is 'a form of discrimination … when unwanted conduct related to any of the grounds referred to in Article 1 takes place with the *purpose or effect of violating the dignity of a person and of creating an intimidating, hostile, degrading, humiliating or offensive environment*' (emphasis added).

[21] C-36/02 *Omega Spielhallen-und Automatenaufstellungs-GmbH v Oberbürgemeisterin der Bundestadt Bonn* [2005] 1 CMLR 5, ECJ. See Chapter 4.

[22] German so-called peep show cases include one decided in 1981 (BVerwG 64, 274) and the other in 1990 (BVerwG 84, 314).

[23] *Diário da República*, Case no 144/2004, 2nd series, no 42, 19 April 2004, 6082–2873, quoted and commented by Jorge Miranda and José M Alexandrino in P Bon and D Maus (eds),

dignity, on the ground that they turn women into mere objects. A similar kind of logic was applied in the much-discussed French administrative ruling on dwarf throwing.[24] These instances are arguably a very significant development in the field of constitutionalism and human rights, with each individual case apparently arising randomly across the EU bringing to the fore the connections among human dignity, work and working conditions, and European constitutionalism. Under EC/EU law, workers' rights started being shaped before the *Omega* ruling, as early as 1964[25] with the case of *Hoekstra*,[26] followed by a number of cases such as *Levin* in 1982,[27] *Lawrie-Blum* in 1986,[28] *Allonby* and *Trojani*, both in 2004,[29] the same year as *Omega*.

In parallel, a number of proposals have been made by legal academics to fit workers' rights within the framework of human rights.[30] For instance, the work of Sandra Fredman can be mentioned here as she has argued for a greater and more effective use of human rights against private parties, by emphasising the role of positive duties imposed on states.[31] The work of German constitutional law scholar, Peter Häberle, stands out for his endeavour to fit work and workers' rights within the wider framework of constitutionalism. In particular, he has argued that human beings' constitutional identity should not be reduced to being a mere *homo economicus*,[32] and he has emphasised the necessity of constitutionalism to keep the market within certain boundaries, in order to avoid breaches of human dignity and human rights. More recently and without reference to Häberle's work, the 'integrated' approach proposed by Virginia Mantouvalou is particularly

Les grandes décisions des cours constitutionnelles européennes (Paris, Dalloz, 2008) 181. See also *Tremblay v France*, Application no 37194/02, ECtHR, 11 December 2007.

[24] *Cne de Morsang sur Orge*, Conseil d'Etat, Ass, 27 October 1995 (1995) *Dalloz Jur* 257. See Chapter 4.

[25] With thanks to Jeff Kenner for shedding light on this line of case law: J Kenner, 'New Frontiers in EU Labour Law: From Flexicurity to Flex-Security' in M Dougan and S Currie (eds), *50 Years of European Treaties: Looking Forward and Thinking Back* (Oxford, Hart Publishing, 2009) 279, 290–95.

[26] ECJ, C-75/63 *Hoekstra v Bedrijfsvereiniging Detailhandel*, 19 March 1964.

[27] ECJ, C-53/81 *Levin v Staatssecretaris van Justitie*, 23 March 1982.

[28] ECJ, C-66/85 *Deborah Lawrie-Blum v Land Baden-Württenberg*, 3 July 1986.

[29] Respectively: C-256/01 *Debra Allonby v Accrington and Rossendale College*, 13 January 2004; and C-456/02 *Michel Trojani v Centre Public d'Aide Sociale de Bruxelles*, Grand Chamber, 7 September 2004.

[30] P Alston (ed), *Labour Rights as Human Rights* (Oxford, Oxford University Press, 2005).

[31] S Fredman, *Human Rights Transformed: Positive Rights and Positive Duties* (Oxford, Oxford University Press, 2008) and 'Positive Duties and Socio-economic Disadvantage: Bringing Disadvantage onto the Equality Agenda' (2010) 3 *European Human Rights Law Review* 290.

[32] P Häberle, 'Aspekte einer Verfassungslehre der Arbeit' in P Häberle (ed), *Rechtsvergleichung im Kraftfeld des Verfassungsstaates: Methoden und Inhalte, Kleinstaaten und Entwicklungsländer* (Berlin, Duncker und Humblot, 1992) 524; see also P Häberle, 'Un jurista universal nacido en Europa: Interview with F Balaguer Callejón' (2010) 13 *Revista de Derecho Costitucional Español*, available at www.ugr.es/~redce/REDCE13/ReDCEportada13.htm.

worth noting here for her endeavour to read workers' rights into the ECHR civil and political rights.[33] In constructing an 'intellectual justification' for this, she brings together a range of arguments, such as the principle of indivisibility of rights, the idea of 'positive freedom', and the theory of capabilities promoted by Sen and Nussbaum.[34] While Mantouvalou does not rely on the concept of human dignity in this process, it is suggested that her arguments seen together come very close to the concept of human dignity as constructed in this book.

Overall, while scholars have considered these issues from their respective areas of specialism, be it labour law, constitutional law or human rights, their meeting point is arguably workers' identity as human beings and their shared concern that workers' human dignity should not be breached by unbridled free market economics. The following section builds on these approaches and considers this issue from the perspective of European constitutionalism. Bringing together the ECHR, the EU and their Member States, it is argued that the key features structuring the constitutional definition of humanity and the concept of human dignity can justify granting workers a fuller constitutional identity, thus contributing to connecting workers' rights to human rights and European constitutionalism.

B. Structuring Features of Workers' Humanity

The concept of human dignity has been used in academic literature in order to promote workers' rights and enhanced working conditions.[35] In law, human dignity has also been a key argument to prohibit slavery, forced labour and human trafficking. This section suggests that the principal argument for bringing workers' rights and protection within the framework of European constitutionalism is their humanity, namely, the fact that one does not cease to be a human being in the workplace. As discussed in previous chapters, human dignity is the constitutional concept used to capture and protect the complexity of humanity and human identities. It can therefore be used as an attempt to build a theoretical bridge between workers' rights and constitutionalism on the basis of three key elements, namely, the 'never

[33] Mantouvalou, above n 6: 'It is an *integrated* approach, because it integrates certain socio-economic rights into a civil and political rights document. This integrated approach characterises the work of the ILO more generally and has been described as a "holistic approach". Applied to the ECHR, it means that certain social and labour components are essential elements of the Convention, and should therefore be protected as such' (original emphasis) (at 536).

[34] Mantouvalou, above n 6, 545–55.

[35] O Tissot, 'Pour une analyse juridique du concept de "dignité" du salarié' (1995) *Droit Social* 972. More recently see F Héas, 'Observations sur le concept de dignité appliqué aux relations de travail' (2010) 746 *Le Droit Ouvrier* 1.

again' promise, the imbalance of power between the worker and her or his work-giver, and the importance of human relationships.

First of all, it is suggested that the protection of workers' humanity proceeds from the same 'never again' spirit and construction of time that were discussed in Chapter 3. While domestic constitutions have not always (explicitly) connected human dignity and work, this spirit was arguably the driving force behind the revival of labour law after the Second World War, with the 1944 Declaration of Philadelphia as its emblem. Convened by Roosevelt with the aim of bringing the ILO back into action, it is a solemn affirmation that 'labour is not a commodity' (Article Ia) and that 'all human beings, irrespective of race, creed or sex, have the right to pursue both their material well-being and their spiritual development in conditions of freedom and dignity, of economic security and equal opportunities' (Article IIa). The Kantian prohibition on instrumentalising human beings potently resonates in the ILO's foundational principle.[36] Moreover, as argued by French labour lawyer, Alain Supiot, the ILO commitment is clearly connected to the principle of dignity through its emphasis on social justice and economic security:

> The principle of dignity additionally implies linking the imperative of freedom and of security. Human beings are able to exercise their 'freedom of speech and belief' and to be free from 'tyranny and oppression' (Universal Declaration of Human Rights) only if they have sufficient material security and 'economic security' (Declaration of Philadelphia).[37]

The ILO's commitment to dignity was explicitly reiterated in that body's 1958 Resolution marking the tenth anniversary of the UN Universal Declaration of Human Rights. This Resolution, clearly building on the 1944 Philadelphia Declaration, expressed its pledge for 'the continued co-operation of the ILO with the UN in the promotion of universal respect for and observance of human rights and fundamental freedoms on the basis of the dignity and the worth of the human person'.[38]

As a result, since the post-war era workers' identity and dignity have been shaped by the memory of inhuman working conditions, certainly those of Nazi labour and concentration camps, as well as going further back to the time when the ILO prohibited forced labour with its 1930 Convention.[39] Often unnoticed, it is through workers' rights and working conditions that

[36] In *Rantsev v Cyprus and Russia* (Application no 25965/04, ECtHR, 10 May 2010) the ECtHR notes that human trafficking 'treats human beings as commodities to be bought and sold and put to forced labour' (at para 281).

[37] A Supiot, *The Spirit of Philadelphia: Social Justice v the Total Market* (S Brown (trans), London, Verso, 2012) 12.

[38] CW Jenks, *Human Rights and International Labour Standards* (London, Stevens & Sons Ltd, 1960) 5–6.

[39] Forced Labour Convention, adopted on 28 June 1930 by the General Conference of the ILO.

human dignity made its first entry into the field of human rights and constitutional rights in some of the founding Member States of the then EC after the war, such as France with the draft Constitution of 1946,[40] and Italy with the 1947 Constitution, which came into force in 1948.[41] Workers' dignity was intended to protect them in their normal working conditions, and not only against the extreme dehumanising forms of work such as slavery or forced labour.[42] Adopted six years after the Declaration of Philadelphia, and two years after the UN Declaration, the ECHR enshrined the absolute prohibition on servitude, slavery and forced labour. It is perhaps not surprising, therefore, that the European Court of Human Rights' (ECtHR) turning point in its construction of labour rights was linked to its reliance on ILO regulations,[43] confirmed in the famous case of *Siliadin v France*.[44] Articles 5 and 31 EU Charter protecting workers' rights can therefore be read as forming part of this lineage, and carrying the memory of work that destroyed humanity and as echoing the 'never again' pledge at the foundation of European constitutionalism.

The second structuring feature of humanity in which workers' human dignity can theoretically be grounded flows from the imbalance of power inherent in workers' position in their contractual relationship with the employer, as well as in their day to day dealings.[45] As will be recalled from Chapter 3, in European constitutionalism since 1945 human dignity has been the key tool used both to acknowledge the extreme imbalance of power between the state and individual, and to invert it for the benefit of

[40] Two key provisions can be noted here: Art 22 read: 'Tout être humain possède, à l'égard de la société, les droits qui garantissent, dans l'intégrité et la dignité de sa personne, son plein développement physique, intellectuel et moral' and Art 27 provided: 'La durée et les conditions du travail ne doivent porter atteinte ni à la santé, ni à la dignité, ni à la vie familiale du travailleur'.

[41] Article 36.1 of the 1947 Italian Constitution reads: 'Workers are entitled to remuneration commensurate with the quantity and quality of their work, and in any case sufficient to ensure to them and their families a *free and honourable existence* (*un'esistenza libera e dignitosa*)' (emphasis added). Generally see P Grossi, 'La Dignità nella Costituzione Italiana' in E Ceccherini (ed), *La Tutela della Dignità dell'Uomo* (Naples, Editoriale Scientifica, 2008) 79, 82–97; and G Ferrara, 'La Pari Dignità Sociale' in *Studi in Onore di Giuseppe Chiarelli, Tomo Secondo* (Milan, Giuffrè, 1974) 1087–105.

[42] Jenks, above n 38, 8.

[43] K Lörcher, 'The New Social Dimension in the Jurisprudence of the European Court of Human Rights (ECtHR): The *Demir and Baykara* Judgment: its Methodology and Follow-up' in F Dorssemont, K Lörcher and I Schömann (eds), *The European Convention on Human Rights and the Employment Relation* (Oxford, Hart Publishing, 2013) 4–46.

[44] *Siliadin v France*, Application no 73316/01, ECtHR, 26 October 2005, paras 51 and 85: 'In those circumstances, the Court considers that limiting compliance with Article 4 of the Convention only to direct action by the State authorities would be inconsistent with the international instruments specifically concerned with [forced labour] and would amount to rendering it ineffective' (at para 89).

[45] O de Schutter, 'Human Rights in Employment Relationships: Contracts as Power' in F Dorssemont, K Lörcher and I Schömann (eds), *The European Convention on Human Rights and the Employment Relation* (Oxford, Hart Publishing, 2013) 105–39.

human beings, whom the state may no longer degrade into instruments for the sole purpose of achieving its own ends.[46] The same logic can arguably be applied in relation to workers, whereby human dignity is used to redress, if not to eliminate completely, the imbalance of power which characterises work relationships. While this is no novelty,[47] it is important to note that the imbalance of power is not 'just' between the employer and the employee, but it is ultimately and increasingly, between workers and capitalism, which since the collapse of Communism in the 1990s has become the unrivalled economic ideology in Europe, to the point of becoming total.[48] Ultimately, as argued by Sheldon Leader, the quality of work and working conditions, together with workers' constitutional status and protection, reflect states' ability and willingness to control and minimise the most detrimental effects of capitalism on human rights and human beings.[49] Particularly perhaps in the economic crisis unfolding at the time of writing, it is difficult to ignore the increase in private parties' power to inflict harm and affect some very basic rights, such as physical integrity, privacy, home or freedom of expression. The diminution of state power as the overall source of normativity and protection of human rights has so far not been matched by an increasing protection of workers' rights against possible abuse by private parties, such as their employers. These apparently contextual considerations are in fact the very foundation of labour law, as set out in an early academic reflection on its scope, confirming the shared concerns of labour law and constitutionalism with regard to the protection of workers' human dignity and 'human personality':

> [The unity of the goal of labour law] is based on the prevailing principle of the unity of human labour as the embodiment of the human personality and on the special function of the law which governs it as the guardian of human beings in an age of almost unrestrained materialism.[50]

In the twenty-first century, this comment has lost none of its significance and it has arguably become integrated in the field of constitutionalism and human rights through the prism of human dignity. Adapting the Kantian

[46] See also L Weinrib, 'Human Dignity as Rights-protecting Principle' (2004) 17 *National Journal of Constitutional Law* 325.

[47] Oliver de Schutter, above n 45, quotes Adam Smith writing in 1776: 'A landlord, a farmer, a master manufacturer, or merchant, though they did not employ a single workman, could generally live a year or two upon the stocks which they have already acquired. Many workmen could not subsist a week, few could subsist a month, and scarce any a year without employment. In the long run the workman may be as necessary to his master as his master is to him; but the necessity is not so immediate' (at 109–10).

[48] Supiot, above n 37.

[49] S Leader, 'Inflating Consent, Inflating Function, and Inserting Human Rights' in J Dine and A Fagan (eds), *Human Rights and Capitalism: A Multidisciplinary Perspective on Globalisation* (Cheltenham, Edward Elgar, 2006) 28–47.

[50] H Sinzheimer 'Die Fortentwicklung des Arbeitsrechts und die Aufgabe der Rechtslehre' (1910–1911) 20 *Soziale Praxis* 1237, quoted by Hepple, above n 12, 9.

imperative of non-instrumentalisation, Peter Häberle argued that human beings may not be reduced to a mere 'economic factor'.[51] In the context of work relationships, where employees tend to be considered by employers as disposable and interchangeable production units, increasingly exclusively identified as mere figures, such as their economic cost for the employer or the financial income they generate, the Kantian distinction (discussed in Chapter 2) between value or market price (*pretium*) that can be attributed to things and animals, and dignity or intrinsic worth which is an exclusively human quality, has never been more relevant.[52]

The third and last feature of workers' humanity that can be captured and protected in terms of human dignity is the importance of fostering relationships at work, namely, workers' ability to interact with fellow workers and employers, as well as with the outside world. This has been highlighted by Virginia Mantouvalou who draws on the concept of capabilities.[53] Considering ECtHR case law, she observes that the Strasbourg Court acknowledged and protected this relational dimension in two cases.[54] In *Niemietz v Germany*, the ECtHR protected Niemietz's professional relationships with his clients by holding that searching the filing cabinet in his office was an unlawful breach of Article 8 ECHR on private life.[55] In *Sidabras and Džiautas v Lithuania*, the ECtHR went further and held that dismissal can have a negative impact on Article 8 by generating social isolation for the unemployed.[56] This rather creative interpretation of Article 8 ECHR with

[51] Peter Häberle emphasised this aspect, connecting it very strongly with human dignity: 'Der Mensch darf nicht zum blossen Wirtschaftsfaktor degradiert werden. "Menschlische Faktoren", viel zitiert, sind in das Wirtschaftsleben spezifisch einzubeziehen. Die Arbeits-und Wirtschaftswelt muß menschenwürdig sein bzw. werden' in *Das Menschenbild im Verfassungsstaat*, 4th edn (Berlin, Duncker und Humblot, 2008) 68.

[52] 'Today's process of globalisation is guided by quite the opposite goals. The goal of social justice has been replaced by that of the free circulation of goods and capital and the hierarchy of ends and means has been inverted ... Instead of indexing the economy to human needs and finance, and finance to the needs of the economy, the economy obeys the demand of finance and human beings are treated as "human capital" at the disposal of the economy': Supiot, above n 37, 14.

[53] 'A positive idea of freedom as capability is not individualistic. It views the ability to relate to others as central': Mantouvalou, above n 6, 552.

[54] ibid 552.

[55] *Niemietz v Germany*, above n 19: 'Respect for private life must also comprise to a certain degree the right to establish and develop relationships with other human beings. There appears, furthermore, to be no reason of principle why this understanding of the notion of "private life" should be taken to exclude activities of a professional or business nature since it is, after all, in the course of their working lives that the majority of people have a significant, if not the greatest, opportunity of developing relationships with the outside world'. (at para 29)

[56] *Sidabras and Džiautas v Lithuania*, Applications nos 55480/00 and 59330/00, ECtHR, 27 October 2004: 'The ban [from engaging in professional activities in various branches of the private sector on account of their status as a "former KGB officer"] has, however, affected [the applicants'] ability to develop relationships with the outside world to a very significant degree and has created serious difficulties for them in terms of earning their living, with obvious repercussions on the enjoyment of their private lives'. (at para 14)

reference to work and unemployment takes us to the heart of the constitutional concept of human dignity. As will be recalled, while the concept is used to acknowledge and protect the uniqueness of each human person, European constitutionalism does not consider human beings in social isolation, but rather and fundamentally in their ability to engage in a range of free and meaningful relationships with others. Moreover, human dignity promotes a particular quality of relationships, referred to as the 'spirit of brotherhood' in the UN Universal Declaration of Human Rights. The same logic arguably animates labour law's first attempts to protect workers' dignity through the prohibition on discrimination and harassment, which can be understood as promoting supportive, inclusive and tolerance-based relationships at work. In other words, these are relationships that consider fellow workers, regardless of their place, status or seniority in the workplace, on a basis of equality and reciprocity. Labour lawyer Alan Bogg aptly summarises this by noting that human dignity (as enshrined under the EU Charter) provides overall protection for 'norms of civility' in the workplace.[57] While dignity has also been associated with 'decency',[58] the term civility is arguably more appropriate as it echoes that of civilisation, which the ECtHR used in relation to the concept of 'civilised marriage' in the marital rape ruling discussed in Chapter 4. Its Latin root, *civis*, brings to the fore the significance of civil relationships at work, not just as a matter of being nice to each other, but also and crucially, as the process through which workers' self-determination and ability to influence their work are both encouraged and made possible. Ultimately, it is also the quality of relationships at work that arguably makes work humane and meaningful, and distinguishes human workers from animals and from robots.

Consequently, as this section has shown, the three key pillars, or structuring features, of workers' humanity are fundamentally related to the core components of the constitutional concept of human dignity and point to what is a key conceptual connection and a necessity: namely, the linkage between work and citizenship, that is, between the rights of workers and constitutionalism through human dignity.

III. CONSTRUCTING WORKERS' DIGNITY: THE EU CHARTER AS A BASIS

Using the EU Charter as a platform for exploring how workers' human dignity may be constructed, this section suggests that the gap between the theoretical

[57] A Bogg, 'Article 31: Fair and Just Working Conditions' in S Peers, T Hervey, J Kenner and A Ward (eds), *The EU Charter of Fundamental Rights: A Commentary* (Oxford, CH Beck/Hart Publishing/Nomos, 2014) 833, 855.

[58] A Margalit, *The Decent Society* (N Goldblum (trans), Cambridge, MA, Harvard University Press, 1996).

underpinning of their human dignity discussed above and its potential protection under the Charter is perhaps not so wide as one might think. This section is based on the underlying assumption that the rights enshrined under the Dignity Title apply equally to all human beings, including workers. As the latest constitutional codification of many labour law rights,[59] the EU Charter is a significant development in closing the gap between workers' rights and constitutionalism, in that codification of workers' human dignity, under the combined reading of Article 31.1 and Title 1 (on human dignity), anchors their rights at the heart of European constitutionalism.[60] Article 31.1 ('Every worker has the right to working conditions which respect his or her health, safety and dignity')[61] while not being the first labour right provision under the Solidarity Title,[62] is the first explicit codification of workers' dignity in EU primary law. It may therefore be read as an umbrella provision in relation to working conditions, and arguably constitutes as such a sufficiently broad basis for exploring the connections now apparent in EU law between work, dignity and constitutionalism.

A. Inviolability of Workers' Dignity

First of all, the principle of inviolability of dignity under Article 1 EU Charter[63] applies to workers as well as to the construction of their rights. In particular, it requires that close attention be paid to the power relationship between the employer and the employee (as well as among employees), so as to soften the negative consequences of its structural imbalance in the employer's favour.[64] As suggested above, the overall purpose of constitutional

59 B Bercusson, 'Episodes on the Path towards the European Social Model: The EU Charter of Fundamental Rights and the Convention on the Future of Europe' in C Barnard, S Deakin and G Morris (eds), *The Future of Labour Law: Liber Amicorum Bob Hepple QC* (Oxford, Hart Publishing, 2004) 179. See also B Bercusson (ed), *European Labour Law and the EU Charter of Fundamental Rights* (Baden-Baden, Nomos, 2006).

60 Discussed in Chapter 3.

61 T Blanke, 'Fair and Just Working Conditions (Article 31)' in B Bercusson (ed), *European Labour Law and the EU Charter of Fundamental Rights* (Baden-Baden, Nomos, 2006) 357–78.

62 The first provision under Title IV 'Solidarity' is Art 27 guaranteeing a right to information and consultation within the undertaking.

63 C Dupré, 'Article 1: Human Dignity' in S Peers, T Hervey, J Kenner and A Ward (eds), *The EU Charter of Fundamental Rights: A Commentary* (Oxford, CH Beck/Hart Publishing/Nomos, 2014) 3–24. See also M Borowsky, 'Artikel 1' in J Meyer (ed) *Charta der Grundrechte der EU* (Baden-Baden, Nomos, 2011) 94–121; P Grossi, 'Dignità Umana e Libertà nella Carta dei Diritti Fondamentali dell' Unione Europea' in M Siclari (ed), *Contributi allo Studio della Carta dei Diritti Fondamentali dell' Unione Europea* (Turin, Giappichelli, 2003) 41–60 and M Olivetti, 'Article 1: Human Dignity' in WBT Mock and G Demuro (eds), *Human Rights in Europe: Commentary on the Charter of Fundamental Rights of the European Union* (Durham, NC, North Carolina University Press, 2010) 3–11.

64 'The crucial element in the making of labour law is *power*. Many of the demands made by labour movements and social reformers were unsuccessful because they were unacceptable to

protection of workers' dignity is to attenuate this imbalance and to ensure that workers may not be turned into mere tools used to pursue work objectives (exclusively) set by the employer, particularly with regard to what can be called here vulnerable workers. Moreover, the principle of inviolability applied to the work context can arguably be construed as making unlawful any systematic departure from, or exception to, the rules on workers' dignity on the ground of an emergency situation, such as a wide-ranging economic crisis or smaller-scale financial issue affecting a given employer. This well-established principle under the ECHR, specifically under Article 15,[65] according to which, for instance, Member States may never derogate from their obligations not to breach Article 3 ECHR, arguably applies in a similar manner to workers' rights and work context on the basis of Article 1 EU Charter. In other words, it is suggested that the obligation to respect and protect human dignity under Article 1 implies that states have to guarantee that workers may not be treated in a degrading or inhuman manner, or may not lose their self-determination at work due to an economic crisis and related austerity measures.

The second feature of workers' human dignity is equality. While it is not enshrined under Title 1 on human dignity,[66] the rights contained in the Solidarity Title arguably apply to 'every worker' equally.[67] Historically, labour law has strived to protect all workers regardless of their singular identity. This is particularly important for all those who do not appear to fit the norm, such as women, children, indigenous people[68] and foreigners in general, whether they are in a legal or illegal situation. Consequently, it is suggested that regardless of where workers are based and who their employer is, they are equally entitled to Article 31 EU Charter protection, and this clearly points to the horizontal reach of this provision.[69] In the context of the

those with greater economic and political power. From this perspective labour law as it developed in Europe can be seen as an alternative both to laissez-faire capitalism and to the abolition of wage labour and the creation of some form of socialism. The powerfulness of the opponents of reforms was the decisive factor in the making of labour law. It is in power relationships, which are rooted in social structure, that we may find a key to understanding both the common tendencies and the divergencies in the labour laws of societies which have shared the experience of capitalist industrialisation': Hepple, above n 12, 5.

65 Article 15.2 ECHR reads: 'No derogation from Article 2, except in respect of deaths resulting from lawful acts of war, or from Articles 3, 4 (paragraph 1) and 7 shall be made under this provision'.

66 It appears under Art 20, the first provision of Title III 'Equality'.

67 A Giorgis, 'Article 31: Fair and Just Working Conditions' in WBT Mock and G Demuro (eds), *Human Rights in Europe: Commentary on the Charter of Fundamental Rights of the European Union* (Durham, NC, Carolina Academic Press, 2010) 187–97.

68 L Swepston, 'Human Rights and Rights at Work' in G Rodgers, E Lee, L Swepston and J Van Daele, *The ILO and the Quest for Social Justice, 1919–2009* (Geneva, ILO, 2009) 37.

69 De Schutter, above n 45, 105; see also B Bercusson, 'Episodes on the Path towards the European Social Model: The EU Charter of Fundamental Rights and the Convention on the Future of Europe' in C Barnard, S Deakin and G Morris (eds), *The Future of Labour Law: Liber Amicorum Bob Hepple QC* (Oxford, Hart Publishing, 2004) 179–200.

ECtHR, this same principle has already been established by the Strasbourg Court in relation to the prohibition of slavery and forced labour (under Article 4 ECHR) in the *Siliadin v France*, and in the *Rantsev v Cyprus and Russia* rulings, where the 'employer' was a private party.[70] Finally, equal dignity implies that the distinction between nationals and non-national workers, in other words (political) citizenship, becomes irrelevant for the purpose of protecting their human dignity at work.

Thirdly, the inviolability of workers' human dignity implies that they are also entitled to the absolute protection derived from Title 1 EU Charter. While the discussion of Articles 2, 3 and 4 is developed below, the importance of Article 5 on the prohibition of servitude, slavery, forced labour and human trafficking has to be noted here as this provision was specifically designed to protect workers, and therefore may be seen as underpinning the very core of their human dignity, that is, the protection against being completely deprived of their self-determination and instrumentalised for the exclusive benefit of their employers.[71] Despite the known difficulty for modern slaves to access justice and the rarity of case law on this issue, the significance of Article 5 must not be underestimated. In the same way as human dignity constitutional provisions carry the memory of times of inhumanity, Article 5 carries the memory of times of inhuman work and, moreover, the addition of the prohibition of human trafficking in the EU Charter (a mention not included in the ECHR) is a stern reminder that the time of inhuman work is not over and that protecting against the annihilation of workers' human dignity is a paramount concern and aim of constitutionalism in the twenty-first century.

B. Human(e) Working Conditions

Workers' human dignity is also protected in relation to the normal working conditions, that is, those falling outside the scope of Articles 4 and 5 mentioned above. While this provision is presented as a codification of the existing legislation on harassment and discrimination, reading it from the perspective of workers' dignity, namely, in combination with Title 1 rights, brings to light a much wider scope of protection that is explored below.

First, reading Article 31 in the light of Article 2 EU Charter highlights the importance of the right to life at work. It is suggested that workers' right to

[70] *Siliadin v France*, above n 44, and *Rantsev v Cyprus and Russia*, above n 36.

[71] *Siliadin v France*, above n 44 paras 117–20 and *Rantsev v Cyprus and Russia*, above n 36: 'The Court considers that trafficking in human beings, by its very nature and aim of exploitation, is based on the exercise of powers attaching to the right of ownership. *It treats human beings as commodities to be bought and sold* and put to forced labour, often for little or no payment, usually in the sex industry but also elsewhere' (at para 281) (emphasis added).

life arguably goes much further than the right not to be killed at work (by one's employer, fellow workers or dangerous working conditions). Working conditions that are human dignity-compliant should therefore ensure that the protection of workers' lives is not limited to the physical location of the workplace, but extends outside the workplace against the lasting, delayed and sometimes invisible negative effects of some working conditions, such as prolonged exposure to toxic or radioactive substances, and that employers may still be held responsible for their employees' health if it deteriorates, or if employees die as result of a disease triggered by working conditions.

Secondly, Article 31 can be interpreted in conjunction with Article 3 EU Charter, protecting the right to physical and mental integrity. While Article 3 refers to medical treatment and informed consent,[72] the general wording of Article 3.1 leaves open the possibility of using it in the work context and in a more general sense, namely, as the general personality right and right to privacy, both understood as protecting autonomy, or the right to make up one's own mind and to be involved in the key decisions concerning one's life. There is no reason why this logic may not be extended to protect consent in relation to decisions affecting one's work and working conditions, especially perhaps considering the connections between the required protection of physical and mental integrity (protected under Article 3) and workers' health and dignity (protected under Article 31).[73] Connecting workers' human dignity with Article 3 EU Charter arguably gives labour law rules concerning consent, information and participation in decisions affecting work and working conditions particular constitutional importance, with their ultimate aim being to protect workers' physical and mental integrity, a core component of their human dignity under Title 1 EU Charter. Failing to do so may amount, in serious situations, to a breach of Article 4 EU Charter which prohibits inhuman and degrading treatment or punishment at work.

In addition, the protection of workers' mental integrity under Article 3 EU Charter may be connected to the idea of fulfilment of one's personality at and through work. This issue has been explored by a team of Belgian labour lawyers, according to whom work and working conditions should allow workers the 'pleasure to be themselves' (*le plaisir d'être soi-même*).[74] This understanding of work as a form of self-fulfilment provides a refreshing

[72] The Explanations to the EU Charter point to the Convention for the Protection of Human Rights and Dignity of the Human Being with regard to the Application of Biology and Medicine (Oviedo Convention) as the key source of inspiration for Art 3.

[73] Philippe Davezies defines workers' dignity breaches as including vexations, denying workers' suffering, denying their individual personality, overall psychological hurt which negatively affects their health. P Davezies, 'Évolution des organisations du travail et atteintes à la santé. Contribution au séminaire interdisciplinaire "Les Nouvelles Organisations du Travail"' (1999) 3 *Travailler* 87. With thanks to Véronique Daubas-Letourneux for bringing this to my attention.

[74] A Cieslar, A Nayer and B Smeesters, *Le droit à l'épanouissement de l'être humain au travail: métamorphoses du droit social* (Brussels, Bruylant, 2007).

alternative to the classic capitalist definition of work based on financial profit. As will be recalled from above, the ECtHR has already acknowledged this dimension of work, phrasing it in terms of personality development derived from the right to privacy under Article 8, and including the protection of relationships developed at and through work. In particular the ECtHR emphasised that '[it] is after all in the course of their working lives that the majority of people have a significant opportunity of developing relationships with the outside world'.[75] The EU Charter does not enshrine a general personality right, but its privacy provision (Article 7) can be interpreted in line with ECtHR case law on Article 8, with Article 3 EU Charter arguably strengthening the importance of this right due to its connections with the concept of human dignity.

Finally, in addition to the above discussion on Article 4 EU Charter, it is suggested that this provision can be read in the light of Article 3 ECHR and may be used as a basis for a requirement of decent remuneration, that is, a remuneration which makes it possible for workers to afford accommodation, food, health care and sanitation, therefore protecting them against destitution. This reading would reactivate some domestic constitutional provisions,[76] giving them a strong normative and persuasive force at a time when the growing number of the so-called working poor makes them urgently relevant.

Overall, this brief survey of EU Charter provisions has shown that it is possible to identify a clear normative substance for workers' human dignity by connecting the Charter's human dignity core (as defined under Title 1) to a range of other rights specifically directed at workers. Interpreted in this way, the obligation to respect workers' dignity under Article 31 extends far beyond its mainstream scope[77] and certainly beyond the protection against harassment, with which it is most often associated.[78] Moreover, seen in the light of human dignity, the protection of workers' rights as constitutional rights is arguably not just the protection of workers' bare life (namely, the right not to be killed and the obligation to minimise threats to life in the workplace). Rather, it is far more than that as it captures a powerful and necessary reminder that workers are human beings, and that their humanity

[75] *Campagnano v Italy*, Application no 77955/01, ECtHR, 3 July 2006 (at para 54), confirming its 1992 landmark ruling in *Niemietz v Germany*, above n 19.

[76] Notably Art 36 of the 1947 Italian Constitution, see above n 41. See also the recent ruling of the Spanish Supreme Court: Tribunal Supremo (Sala de lo Social), 22 December 2014, JUR/2015/17371.

[77] T Blanke, 'Fair and Just Working Conditions (Article 31)' in B Bercusson (ed), *European Labour Law and the EU Charter of Fundamental Rights* (Baden-Baden, Nomos, 2006) 357; Giorgis, above n 67, 187; HD Jarass (ed), *Charta der Grundrechte der Europäischen Union unter Einbeziehung der vom EUGH entwickelten Grundrechte und der Grundrechtsregelungen der Verträge: Kommentar* (Munich, CH Beck, 2010) 276–80.

[78] JQ Whitman, 'The European Transformation of Harassment Law: Discrimination versus Dignity' (2003) 9 *Columbia Journal of European Law* 241.

should be fully protected in the workplace so as to empower them to be active participants in making the decisions affecting them and their working conditions.

C. Solidarity and the Pursuit of Social Justice

The codification of workers' human dignity in the EU Charter brings together a whole range of rights from which labour rights had previously tended to be dissociated. The Charter also contextualises workers' rights, by positioning them within the general aims of human rights and constitutionalism, thus opening their interpretation and possible application beyond their very technical dimensions. As a result, it is suggested that the codification of workers' human dignity under the Solidarity Title of the EU Charter underscores the key role of workers' rights and human dignity in the pursuit of social justice, which historically and politically has shaped human rights as well as labour law, as will be recalled from Chapter 2. While this raises complex issues, which regrettably must fall beyond the scope of this study, the following points can nevertheless be made to highlight the fuller ramifications of workers' human dignity. In this context, solidarity may be understood in two broad ways.

First, the connection between human dignity and solidarity may be understood in an abstract or principled manner, as illustrated by the 1948 UN Universal Declaration's famous 'spirit of brotherhood'. As discussed above, the same spirit applies to relationships in the workplace and the codification of human dignity in the EU Charter can be understood as creating an expectation of civility in the workplace. Workers' human dignity further integrates them in the wider society, which is (according the foundational principle of constitutionalism and human rights) composed of equal individuals. In the beautiful words of Giovanni Maria Flick, former president of the Italian Constitutional Court:

> Dignity is inherent in man not as a singular being, in the emptiness of his solitude, but as a person integrated in society and who is fulfilled through relations with others who, at the same time, are equal to and different from him. And, precisely because of the specificity and diversity of each person, there cannot be equality without solidarity, since only the latter can overcome diversity with a view to achieving equality.[79]

Secondly, the idea of social justice has a specific meaning in relation to work, which was shaped by the 1944 Philadelphia Declaration. Building on its 1919 foundational text, which mentioned that 'lasting peace can be

[79] GM Flick, 'Dignità Umana e Tutela dei Soggetti Deboli: Una Riflessione Problematica' in E Ceccherini (ed), *La Tutela della Dignità dell'Uomo* (Naples, Editoriale Scientifica, 2008) 55–56. Translation with thanks to Stephen Skinner.

established only if it is based on social justice', the 1944 Declaration brought together the key issues of equality, dignity and material well-being.[80] It is therefore suggested that the codification of workers' dignity under the Solidarity Title of the EU Charter has to be read as being part of this lineage. The Solidarity Title is a rather mixed bag, revealing perhaps the fragmented approach to this issue adopted by the EU since its creation, as well as the reluctance of drafters and Member States to commit to a social or welfare European Union. Yet with all its faults and imperfections, this Title brings to the fore what can be called a concrete type of solidarity, which is work-based or work-related, and which complements the abstract type of solidarity mentioned above. This raises the issue of workers' pay, which has been explicitly addressed from the perspective of dignity in some domestic constitutions, such as under Article 36.3 of the 1947 Italian Constitution.[81] The EU Charter makes no reference to 'decent income' or minimum income, although this could arguably be read into Article 31, in the combination of the dignity requirement (Article 31.1) and the 'annual period of paid leave' (Article 31.2). What the EU Charter does, however, is to codify rights to social security and social assistance 'in the case of loss of employment' (Article 34.1) and the right to have a 'decent existence for all those who lack sufficient resources' (Article 34.3).[82] These provisions put the human dignity requirement in the wider perspective of a 'life worthy of human dignity', a concept discussed in its explicit connections to work by Georg Lohmann, with reference to Martha Nussbaum's writing.[83]

Ultimately, defining workers' human dignity and protecting it involves reflecting on the boundaries between capitalism and European constitutionalism, as well as on the overall purpose of the latter in relation to the former.[84] The construction of the European Union has largely been driven

[80] Supiot, above n 37, 13.

[81] See also Chapter 3.

[82] R White, 'Article 34: Social Security and Social Assistance' in S Peers, T Hervey, J Kenner and A Ward (eds), *The EU Charter of Fundamental Rights: A Commentary* (Oxford, CH Beck/ Hart Publishing/Nomos, 2014) 927–49. Generally see D Roman, 'Le principe de la dignité dans la doctrine de droit social' in C Girard and S Hennette-Vauchez (eds), *La dignité de la personne humaine, recherche sur un processus de juridicisation* (Paris, Presses Universitaires de France, 2004) 70–87.

[83] G Lohmann, 'Human Dignity and Socialism' in M Düwell, J Braarvig, R Brownsword and D Mieth (eds), *The Cambridge Handbook of Human Dignity* (Cambridge, Cambridge University Press, 2014) 126, 130–32.

[84] Generally see D Nicol, *The Constitutional Protection of Capitalism* (Oxford, Hart Publishing, 2010); J Dine and A Fagan (eds), *Human Rights and Capitalism: A Multidisciplinary Perspective on Globalisation* (Cheltenham, Edward Elgar, 2006); as well as W Bonefeld and K Psychopedis (eds), *Human Dignity: Social Autonomy and the Critique of Capitalism* (Aldershot, Ashgate, 2005).

by economic objectives of a capitalist nature (free and fair competition, freedom of movement, etc), and now the specific financial targets derived from the so-called golden rule. Constitutionalism, to a large extent, has therefore provided the toolkit for undertaking this economic project, as well as a narrative of rights, freedom and peace to support the democratic legitimacy of this enterprise. This however is not the sole purpose of constitutionalism, and workers' human dignity acts as a crucial reminder that constitutionalism's overarching purpose is to ensure that human beings' life and work may not totally be dictated by the capitalist logic, creating therefore a precious space within which human beings must be considered and treated in terms of their humanity and must not reduced to their capitalist value (or lack of). Consequently, including workers and their rights within the framework of European constitutionalism promotes an understanding of work as a key human activity, meant to generate a decent income for workers, as well as to give them a meaningful life and ultimately control over their destiny. In short, workers' constitutional identity as human beings constructed by reference to their human dignity in the EU Charter provides a foundation for workers' constitutional status, and thus a much needed benchmark to assess the quality of their rights and of their working conditions, as well as, ultimately and as discussed below, of democracy.

IV. WORKERS' DIGNITY AND DEMOCRACY

Examining the connections between work and human dignity, which is considered here as a core attribute of constitutionalism, leads to the need to consider the wider implications of this relationship. Although that linkage raises a number of important issues that cannot be addressed here,[85] it is argued that the central question is the significance for democracy of protecting workers' human dignity through constitutionalism. In that regard, three points are discussed here: the significance of protection at constitutional level, workers' rights and liberal democracy, and the dynamic of emancipation common to workers' rights and human rights.

[85] This section does not consider these issues from the angle of what Florian Rödl calls a 'constitution of work' as the '*Arbeitsverfassung*' under the German system: F Rödl, 'Constitutional Integration of Labour Constitutions' in EO Eriksen, C Joerges and F Rödl (eds), *Law, Democracy and Solidarity in a Post-national Union: The Unsettled Political Order of Europe* (Oxford, Routledge, 2008) 152–71. The issues of the institutional implications of protecting workers' rights at the constitutional level need to be borne in mind, as do the issues of the appropriate normative location of this protection, namely, whether at the domestic level or at the EU supranational level.

A. Significance of Protection at Constitutional Level

Bringing workers' dignity within the scope of European constitutionalism raises the protection of workers' right to a constitutional level by positioning them on the same plane as civil and political rights, thus creating a duty imposed on the law-maker to guarantee workers' rights regardless of political and—crucially—economic circumstances. Whereas some of the workers' rights obviously remain subject to being refined and implemented through statutory (or secondary) legislation, as well as regulations adopted in the workplace, it is suggested that the core of workers' human dignity may not be subject to the discretion of law-makers or of employers. In particular and in practice, guaranteeing workers' rights to life, physical and mental integrity, not to be treated in an inhuman and degrading manner, not to be tortured, and above all, not to be held in slavery, forced labour or subject to human trafficking, should not be made dependent, and variable, on resource allocation and political preferences.

The second implication of raising the protection of workers' human dignity to the constitutional level of protection is to make workers normatively visible within constitutionalism, thus complementing their protection qua human beings and qua citizens. This brings constitutionalism closer to reality, acknowledging that work occupies a very substantial part, both in quantity and in quality, in shaping human identities and lives, both positively and negatively. Acknowledging workers' human dignity at the heart of European constitutionalism therefore gives workers not only constitutional visibility, it also and crucially gives them a constitutional voice. It is true that labour law is largely about giving workers a voice, with, for instance, the rights to join a trade union or to engage in collective bargaining. This labour law voice tends, however, to be heard mainly within the workplace and relationships. Seen from the perspective of constitutionalism and human dignity, it is therefore suggested that managing the economy is not exclusively about setting and achieving financial and budgetary targets, it is also about making sure that the importance of workers' humanity and lives is not lost in this process.

Moreover, in an increasingly globalised economy characterised by (among other things) greater movement of workers across national boundaries within the EU (and elsewhere), giving workers a constitutional voice might usefully complement political citizenship, which for many workers in the EU does not overlap with their work status, either because they are non-EU citizens, or because they are nationals of a Member State other than the one in which they are working. In this respect human dignity-based workers' rights could make it possible for them to be more actively involved in the discussion of the law affecting them, but that they cannot currently influence through the ballot box. As a result, in the specific context of the EU, acknowledging workers' human dignity at the constitutional level might go some way towards complementing EU citizenship created by the Maastricht Treaty, which has fallen short of successfully addressing the 'social' and the democratic deficits, that have limited the EU construction and increasingly call its legitimacy into question.[86]

B. Workers' Rights and Liberal Democracy

The connections between the quality of workers' rights and the quality of democracy are so important that the ECtHR has very firmly constructed the prohibition of slavery, servitude and forced labour (under Article 4 ECHR) as 'one of the most fundamental values of democratic societies'.[87] Elaborating on this fundamental connection, this section briefly discusses three issues for democracy that arise out of acknowledging the constitutional importance of workers' human dignity and their rights.

The first issue might already have taken the shape of a concern in the critical reader's mind, that the emphasis on workers' constitutional identity is a form of crypto-communist argument. While the risk of a revival of communist ideology is minimal, this issue requires attention primarily so as to avoid misunderstanding. It is not suggested here that human beings' constitutional identity as constructed through the prism of human dignity should usurp their constitutional identity as citizens, nor is it suggested that workers' rights should take precedence over civil and political rights.[88] What is suggested is that the constitutional identity of human beings should also include that of workers and that constitutionalism should more explicitly make space for protecting workers' human dignity, especially with respect for the core rights as enshrined under Title 1 EU Charter. In the same way that rights should be considered and protected in their indivisibility, the

[86] Generally AJ Menéndez, 'Which Citizenship? Whose Europe: The Many Paradoxes of European Citizenship' (2014) 15 *German Law Journal* 907.

[87] *Siliadin v France*, above n 44. This prohibition is so important that the Court emphasised that: 'Unlike most of the substantive clauses of the Convention and of Protocols Nos 1 and 4, Article 4 makes no provision for exception and no derogation from it is permissible under Article 15.2' (at para 112). See V Mantouvalou, 'The Prohibition of Slavery, Servitude and Forced Labour and Compulsory Labour under Article 4 ECHR' in F Dorssemont, K Lörcher and I Schömann (eds), *The European Convention on Human Rights and the Employment Relation* (Oxford, Hart Publishing, 2013) 143–58.

[88] For a typically communist approach to workers' rights see for instance Art 3 of the 1949 Hungarian Constitution (very heavily influenced by the 1936 Soviet Constitution): 'The Hungarian People's Republic defends the power and liberty of the Hungarian working people and the independence of the country; it opposes every form of the exploitation of man by man and organises the forces of society for socialist construction. In the Hungarian People's Republic the close alliance of the workers and working peasantry is made a reality under the leadership of the working class', quoted in JF Triska (ed), *Constitutions of the Communist Party-States* (Stanford, CA, Hoover Institution Publications, 1968) 182. See also the first clause of the USSR Civil Code: 'The law guarantees the rights of citizens, except in cases where exercising them would contradict state-socialist goals', quoted in Supiot, above n 37, 7.

constitutional identities of human beings in the sense of man, citizen and worker, form a continuum, with human dignity providing a shared core of absolute rights and a conceptual connection among them. The implication of this continuum is that breaching or undermining one of its components negatively affects the others.[89]

The second issue which has to be noted is that anchoring workers' constitutional identity in human dignity brings to the fore their freedom to shape their own identity, in the sense that workers' constitutional protection does not depend on a constitutionally pre-determined, closed or reductive definition of work (in the same way that humanity is not given a closed definition under constitutionalism). As will be recalled, the emphasis here has been on workers' self-determination and the related prohibition on instrumentalising or reducing them to mere tools of production. This, of course, is meant to protect them against abusive employers and, importantly, it also protects them against instrumentalisation by the government in power. In addition, the concept of work itself has been left deliberately undefined, partly due to the technical complexities of doing so, but above all because the emphasis is on the person doing the work (and this may include a whole range of activities) and her human dignity, and not on the work activity itself. Focusing on the latter, especially if on the basis of a definition which excludes some activities, might lead to excluding those undertaking such activities from benefitting from such human dignity protection.

In fact, it is suggested that European constitutionalism does not promote a single type of work, rather the emphasis is on a particular quality of work, namely, work that makes it possible to lead a dignified existence as discussed above in relation to the EU Charter. This was made explicit under Article 23 of the UN Universal Declaration of Human Rights, which provides that remuneration should ensure the worker and his family 'an existence worthy of dignity'.[90] Although this provision has no normative force, as recalled by Johannes Morsink in his commentary on the Declaration,[91] it has been influenced by the long-standing work of the ILO, which applies to EU Member States.[92] As discussed above, the issue of income is crucial for workers' human dignity. This is not, however, the sole rationale, and deriving a dignified existence from work is also a crucial condition for healthy

[89] V Mantouvalou, 'Workers Without Rights as Citizens at the Margins' (2013) 16 *Critical Review of International Social and Political Philosophy* 366.

[90] Article 23.3 reads: 'Everyone who works has the right to just and favourable remuneration ensuring for himself and his family and existence worthy of human dignity, and supplemented, if necessary, by other means of social protection'.

[91] J Morsink, *The Universal Declaration of Human Rights: Origins, Drafting and Intent* (Philadelphia, PA, University of Pennsylvania Press, 1999) 157–81.

[92] P Herzfeld Olsson, 'The ILO Acquis and EU Labour Law' in M Rönnman (ed), *Labour Law, Fundamental Rights and Social Europe* (Oxford, Hart Publishing, 2011) 27–55.

democracy, as highlighted by Nelson Mandela, speaking at the ILO Conference on Decent Work in 2007, in the following terms:

> Decent work is based on the efforts of personal dignity, on *democracies that deliver* for people, and economic growth that expands opportunities for productive jobs and enterprise development ... *Decent work is about the right not only to survive but to prosper and to have a dignified and fulfilling quality of life.* This right must be available to all human beings.(emphasis added)[93]

This quotation brings to light the third issue arising out of the connections between workers' rights and democracy, namely, that the quality of work not only affects the quality of workers' life, but also the quality of democracy. In other words, what the connections between work and human dignity emphasise is the connection between the nature and quality of a political order and the working conditions and status of those subject to it. Consequently, political orders which do not protect workers' core human dignity rights and which support slavery, forced labour or human trafficking, do not qualify as liberal democracies. In fact, the quality of workers' rights and the quality of democracy in a given political system are intertwined. For instance, in this respect, the Soviet labour camps were arguably as much a feature of the communist dictatorship as the rules on the unity of powers and the impossibility of political opposition. While inhuman working conditions on a systematic scale often go together with no or limited political rights, improving working conditions may have an overall positive impact on the democratic quality of a regime. In this respect, the ILO work on improving labour conditions in non-democratic regimes has shown that the two can be mutually supportive.[94]

In relation to European constitutionalism, two points can be derived from this observation. First is the argument that the quality of European democracy does not solely depend on the quality of its civil and political rights, but also on the social and economic rights flowing from the core human dignity rights discussed here. Secondly, and conversely, acknowledging this and seeking to improve workers' rights is arguably one way to promote democracy in Europe, and bearing in mind the context at the time of writing, it may well be one way of keeping authoritarian temptations at

[93] As quoted in G Rodgers, E Lee, L Swepston and J Van Daele, *The ILO and the Quest for Social Justice, 1919–2009* (Geneva, ILO, 2009) 205. The 'decent work agenda' includes creating jobs, guaranteeing rights at work, extending social protection and promoting social dialogue.

[94] For examples of the interconnections of democracy and work, think of the ILO's role in campaigning against the Apartheid regime, or the role of the Polish trade union Solidarnosc in bringing down the communist dictatorship. Generally see G Rodgers, E Lee, L Swepston and J Van Daele, *The ILO and the Quest for Social Justice, 1919–2009* (Geneva, ILO, 2009) 50–51 and 54–57; see also T Ramm, 'Epilogue: The New Ordering of Labour Law 1918–45' in B Hepple (ed), *The Making of Labour Law in Europe: A Comparative Study of Nine Countries Up to 1945* (London, Mansell Publishing, 1986) 277, 285–95.

bay. In the meantime, considering working conditions and the quality of workers' human dignity under a particular constitutional order may be an effective way of assessing the quality of its democracy.

C. Human Rights and Workers' Rights: A Shared Dynamic of Emancipation

The last implication of anchoring workers' humanity and rights in dignity is that this arguably triggers a particular dynamic of interpretation as discussed in Chapter 3, namely, the living instrument doctrine developed by the ECtHR. Following this logic, workers' rights are not to be interpreted by reference to the time of their adoption, nor is the quality of their working conditions to be assessed in relation to what was acceptable at that time. Rather, it is suggested that workers' rights have to be understood and protected with reference to present-day conditions and to standards that are acceptable nowadays in a liberal democracy. This is particularly well illustrated by the landmark ruling of *Rantsev v Cyprus and Russia* in which the ECtHR constructed Article 4 as including the prohibition on human trafficking:

> The Court notes that trafficking in human beings as a global phenomenon has *increased significantly in recent years* ... In Europe, its growth has been facilitated in part by the collapse of former Communist blocs ... In light of *the proliferation of both trafficking itself and of measures taken to combat it*, the Court considers it appropriate in the present case to examine the extent to which trafficking itself may be considered to run counter to *the spirit and purpose of Article 4* of the Convention such as to fall within the scope of the guarantees offered by that Article without the need to assess which of the three types of proscribed conduct are engaged by the particular treatment in the case in question ... There can be *no doubt that trafficking threatens the human dignity* and fundamental freedoms of its victims and *cannot be considered compatible with a democratic society* and the values expounded in the Convention. *In view of its obligation to interpret the Convention in light of present-day conditions, the Court ... considers that trafficking itself ... falls within the scope of Article 4* of the Convention. (emphasis added)[95]

Compared to the ECtHR, the ECJ/CJEU engagement with this approach has so far been limited, as indicated in its interpretation of Article 4 EU Charter prohibiting inhuman and degrading treatment or punishment and

[95] *Rantsev v Cyprus and Russia*, above n 36 paras 278–82.

torture.[96] However, under Article 52.3 EU Charter, the scope and meaning of the Charter rights, which correspond to rights guaranteed by the ECHR, 'shall be the same as those laid down by the said Convention'. The endeavour to achieve consistency across the case law of the two supranational courts is, of course, crucial, even more so since EU accession to the ECHR is unlikely to take place any time soon. Seeking consistency in the judicial construction of similar rights by the ECtHR and the CJEU further emphasises the emancipation dynamic that underscores the development of EU Charter rights and of labour rights, which have also been driven by a constant endeavour to improve working conditions and workers' lives. While in the foundational years of European constitutionalism in the immediate aftermath of the Second World War, the memory of inhuman work was on the mind of drafters and politicians alike, it seems to have faded away with the more recent treaty revisions. Consequently, it is important that this emancipation dynamic both seeks to keep EU Charter rights evolving to reflect current conditions and continues to conserve this essential memory of what must not be allowed to repeat itself, ie past 'bitter experiences'. Forgetting these would not just be damaging for the collective memory of Europeans, it could also arguably undermine the foundations of European constitutionalism.[97]

V. CONCLUSION

It has become increasingly difficult to think about constitutionalism's significance without thinking about how it protects workers and about the wider position of work in the doctrine of constitutionalism. At a theoretical level, it is increasingly hard to justify the protection gap between, on the one hand, civil and political rights guaranteed almost in eternity and at the very top of the constitutional normative pyramid and, on the other hand, social and economic rights, which depend very much on the political agenda of the government in power (and on the employer's willingness).[98]

[96] In relation to refugees' human dignity, compare the ECtHR ruling in *MSS v Belgium and Greece*, Application no 30696/09, Grand Chamber, 21 January 2011 with the CJEU ruling in C-411/10 *NS v Secretary of State for the Home Department* and C-493/10 *ME, ASM, MT, KP, EH v Refugee Applications Commissioner and Minister for Justice, Equality and Law Reform*, 21 December 2011.

[97] C Joerges, 'Working Through "Bitter Experiences" Towards a Purified European Identity? A Critique of the Disregard for History in European Constitutional Theory and Practice' in EO Eriksen, C Joerges and F Rödl (eds), *Law, Democracy and Solidarity in a Post-national Union: The Unsettled Political Order of Europe* (Oxford, Routledge, 2008) 173–91.

[98] C Dupré, 'Unlocking Human Dignity: Towards a Theory for the 21st Century' (2009) 2 *European Human Rights Law Review* 190.

In broad exploratory strokes, and from the perspective of European constitutionalism, this chapter has attempted to construct workers' human dignity as a bridge between labour law and constitutionalism, and between labour rights and human rights. In practice, connecting these fields are workers themselves, whose humanity deserves full constitutional protection regardless of whether they are located in the polling booth or in the workplace. As discussed in this chapter, workers' humanity is not merely biological, but also and importantly it is what protects workers from being degraded into the bare life of the *homo sacer*.[99]

There are many issues that this chapter could not discuss, such as the technicalities of EU labour law and the full range of work-related ECHR case law. Similarly, Member States' approaches to workers' human dignity could only be superficially raised. It is nevertheless hoped that the proposed construction of workers' human dignity is sufficiently persuasive. Above all, the chapter has shown that, while human dignity has often been associated with the guarantee of a minimum existence to protect people against destitution or with the prohibition of harassment and discrimination, it can also be used as a powerful tool for reflecting on the boundaries between constitutionalism and capitalism, and for re-imagining work as personal fulfilment and workers' political empowerment to protect and develop democracy. This involves both a politically-shaped critique of existing parameters, using human dignity as a compass for normative development, and a substantive reading of the implications of human dignity as the foundation for the burgeoning web of constitutional connections at the European level.

Finally, centred in their humanity, workers' human dignity carries the memory of past inhumane types of work and its development is arguably driven by a similar emancipatory spirit that can be observed in the ECtHR case law with the living instrument doctrine. Bringing this to light, this chapter has confirmed the connection between protecting human dignity and constructing constitutional time in a particular way, thus inviting further exploration of the temporal dimensions of human dignity and European constitutionalism.

[99] With reference to G Agamben, *Homo Sacer: Sovereign Power and Bare Life* (D Heller-Roazen (trans), Stanford, CA, Stanford University Press, 1998).

6

Defining Dignity, Protecting Human Time

Es ist Zeit, daß es Zeit wird.[1]

I. INTRODUCTION

TIME ENTERTAINS NUMEROUS and complex connections with law that have been variously discussed and studied in legal scholarship. In particular, the memorial function of (constitutional) law is well-known[2] and has played a crucial role in the process of facing up to Europe's darker past.[3] Indeed, acknowledging past hurt and violence has been one way of mending time and constructing a more just democracy. Another temporal dimension of law, and in particular of constitutionalism, lies at the heart of the rule of law principle, which seeks to ensure that law does not repeat past injustice, that it promotes a safe and continuous present, on the basis of clear rules accessible to all and, finally, that the future can be predicted to the extent that the law can only be changed within a certain procedural framework (with due notice and discussion) and (for some theories) in compliance with certain substantive requirements.[4]

Human dignity, as indicated over the previous chapters, enjoys a privileged relation with time.[5] As the foundation of post-war constitutionalism, it carries the memory of the inhuman times and the promise of a better

[1] P Celan, 'Corona' in B Wiedemann (ed), *Die Gedichte: Kommentierte Gesamtausgabe* (Frankfurt am Main, Suhrkamp, 2005) 39. See also HG Gadamer, *Wer bin Ich und wer bist Du: Kommentar zu Celans 'Atemkristall'* (Frankfurt am Main, Suhrkamp, 1986).

[2] E Christodoulidis and S Veitch (eds), *Lethe's Law: Justice, Law and Ethics in Reconciliation* (Oxford, Hart Publishing, 2001).

[3] C Joerges and NS Ghaleigh (eds), *The Darker Legacies of Law in Europe* (Oxford, Hart Publishing, 2003); see also the Special Issue on 'Memory, Politics and Law' (2005) 6 *German Law Journal*. More generally, see K Palonen, T Pulkkinen and JM Rosales (eds), *The Ashgate Research Companion to the Politics of Democratization in Europe* (Farnham, Ashgate, 2008).

[4] More generally, see L Cuocolo, *Tempo e Potere nel Diritto Costituzionale* (Milan, Giuffrè, 2009) and J Rubenfeld, *Freedom and Time: A Theory of Constitutional Self-Government* (New Haven, CT, Yale University Press, 2001).

[5] First explored in C Dupré, 'Unlocking Human Dignity: Towards a Theory for the 21st Century' (2009) 2 *European Human Rights Law Review* 190.

future. Indeed, human dignity has been used in case law in order to make sense of the unwanted past and to make space at the heart of European constitutionalism for a time that has yet to unfold.[6] The marked increase in constitutional codification of human dignity since the 1990s has corresponded to a new stage in constitutional time in Europe, with the end of communist dictatorships in Central and Eastern Europe and a new beginning for liberal democracy in these countries, as well as enhanced democratic expectations within the European Union, with, for instance, the creation of an EU citizenship in the Maastricht Treaty in 1992 and express commitment to democracy under Article 6 of the 1996 Amsterdam Treaty.[7] At about the same time, in constitutional orders without a codified human dignity provision, judges started 'discovering' it, constructing it by reference to the post-war dignity commitment, endorsing the 'never again' pledge and confirming human dignity's foundational importance for European constitutionalism. Over the same period, human dignity uses in case law and legal scholarship have also increased with regard to changes in defining humanity, prompting interrogations about the beginning and the end of human life, together with the definition of humanity itself.[8] This has led to a multiplication of human dignity case law and a diversification of its judicial constructions to such an extent as to make the concept visible to scholars and to trigger critique and scepticism about its meaning and usefulness.[9]

It is suggested here that this apparently inflationary increase in dignity uses in relation to constitutionalism and human rights echoes deep changes in time, both in its perception and its construction by constitutionalism. In other words, there is a sense that time is beginning to overflow its familiar constitutional boundaries, namely and primarily, the clear demarcations between the past, the present as a 'never again' rejection of the past, and the future as the possibility of enhanced human rights protection as constructed by the European Court of Human Rights (ECtHR) as discussed above, which had so far managed to contain and orient it.[10] This profound change has many causes. For instance, globalisation scholars have informed

[6] In the eloquent words of Giovanni Maria Flick, human dignity is a bridge between the past and the anxieties triggered by an unknown future: 'Dignità Umana e Tutela dei Soggetti Deboli: Una Riflessione Problematica' in E Ceccherini (ed), *La Tutela della Dignità dell'Uomo* (Naples, Editoriale Scientifica, 2008) 39, 40–45.

[7] A von Bogdandy and J Bast (eds), *Principles of European Constitutional Law*, 2nd edn (Oxford, Hart Publishing, 2010) 48.

[8] See, eg R Andorno, 'Human Dignity and Human Rights as Common Ground for a Global Ethics' (2009) *Journal of Medicine and Philosophy* 1; and D Beyleveld and R Brownsword, *Human Dignity in Bioethics and Biolaw* (Oxford, Oxford University Press, 2001)

[9] For instance and chronologically: R Macklin, 'Human Dignity is a Useless Concept: It Means No More than Respect for Persons or their Autonomy' (2003) 327 *British Medical Journal* 1419; N Rao, 'On the Use and Abuse of Dignity in Constitutional Law' (2008) 14 *Columbia Journal of European Law* 201; and C McCrudden, 'Human Dignity and Judicial Interpretation of Human Rights' (2008) 19 *European Journal of International Law* 655.

[10] See Chapter 3.

us that with legal space becoming global, time too has changed, also becoming global and escaping the familiar boundaries of (national) democracy.[11] Sociologists have confirmed the deep transformations of our perception of time largely due to technological changes[12] and, for instance, Hartmut Rosa identified and studied what many of us have experienced and suspected for a while: time is speeding up.[13] A more radical diagnosis is perhaps about time becoming instantaneous and thus non-existent.[14]

The epistemological premise of this chapter is that it is neither possible, nor desirable, to try to fit the new time of humanity and constitutionalism into the old boundaries, as changes are too deep and far-reaching. Rather, this chapter suggests that human dignity raises the question of how we might understand the connections between human time and the time of constitutionalism and democracy. It is furthermore suggested that dignity, as the conceptual bridge between human beings and constitutionalism, can play a key role both in acknowledging human time and re-directing the time of constitutionalism so as to protect the time of humanity.

In developing my reflection on time and constitutionalism, the work of two scholars has been particularly inspirational. The book by the Belgian legal philosopher, François Ost, *Le Temps du Droit* (1999),[15] which analysed the time changes in law as a 'detemporalisation of law' (time overflowing its established and familiar boundaries) is fascinating and originally triggered my interest in time and law, which I started exploring in relation to human dignity and human rights. In relation to the specific connections between time and constitutions, I have found German constitutional law scholar Peter Häberle's work particularly illuminating and thought-provoking: developed in the 1970s, it has lost none of its significance and relevance for the current context.[16] Drawing on these two main sources of inspiration, this chapter approaches the connections between time, dignity and democracy in three stages.

[11] S Wolin, 'What Time is It?' (1997) 1 *Theory & Event* 1; WE Conolly, *Theory Out of Bounds* (Minneapolis, MN, University of Minnesota Press, 2002); K Hutchings, *Time and World Politics: Thinking the Present* (Manchester/New York, Manchester University Press, 2008).

[12] H Nowotny, *Eigenzeit, Enstehung und Strukturierung eines Zeitgefühles* (Frankfurt am Main, Surhkamp, 1989) translated in English by N Plaice as *Time: The Modern and Postmodern Experience* (Cambridge, Polity Press, 1994).

[13] H Rosa, *Accélération: une critique sociale du temps* (Paris, La Découverte, 2010).

[14] P Virilio, *Le futurisme de l'instant* (Paris, Galilée, 2009).

[15] F Ost, *Le temps du droit* (Paris, Odile Jacob, 1999); see also F Ost and M Van Hoecke (eds), *Time and Law: Is it the Nature of Law to Last?* (Brussels, Bruylant, 1998).

[16] P Häberle, 'Zeit und Verfassung' (1974) 21 *Zeitschrift für Politik* 111; P Häberle, 'Zeit und Verfassungskultur' in P Häberle (ed), *Rechtsvergleichung im Kraftfeld des Verfassungsstaates: Methoden und Inhalte, Kleinstaaten und Entwicklungsländer* (Berlin, Duncker und Humblot, 1992) 627. More generally see P Häberle, *Europäische Verfassungslehre*, 6th edn (Baden-Baden, Nomos, 2009) and *L'État constitutionnel* (Aix en Provence, Presses Universitaires d'Aix-Marseille, 2004).

The chapter starts by discussing how the transformations affecting European constitutionalism and our understanding of humanity are also affecting the constitutional boundaries of time. With this in mind, the chapter proposes a two-way definition of human dignity as time of one's own,[17] '*Eigenzeit*' (literally 'proper time'),[18] and as *kairos* of human rights, ie the possibility of change and new beginnings. It is therefore suggested that human dignity can be interpreted as a key tool in protecting the plurality of human time by re-imagining the constitutional present as a plurality of futures, the construction of which can be assessed by reference to human dignity's inviolability, understood here as its unique position outside time.

II. CONSTITUTIONAL TIME OVERFLOWS

Time and constitutions interact through a complex dialectic relationship: time has triggered specific constitutional concerns and responses, in particular the need to control and shape it; and, in so doing, constitutions have shaped time in a particular way through their attempt to appropriate and control it. Indeed, the emergence of modern constitutionalism can arguably be dated from the claim that time belongs to men and democracy, and no longer to God and absolute monarchs.[19] In his seminal work, Peter Häberle identified many connections between time and constitutions. Above all perhaps he argued that constitutions are a bridge between the past (with its cultural heritage) and the future, and he likened constitutions to a contract between generations. According to him, constitutions have therefore made it possible to insert democracy in a particular time frame, through the creation of a number of tools and procedures in an attempt to ensure a smooth unfolding and control of time.[20]

It is suggested here that time that had been so carefully constructed and tamed by European constitutionalism (as discussed in Chapters 2, 3 and 4) is now being fragmented into a plurality of temporalities that can no longer fully be given meaning and direction by the original 'never again' spirit that informed European constitutionalism in the aftermath of war and

[17] The echo of Virginia Woolf's *A Room of One's Own* (London, Penguin Books, 1928, reprinted 2000) is deliberate here and will be discussed below.

[18] H Nowotny, *Time: The Modern and Postmodern Experience* (N Plaice (trans), Cambridge, Polity Press, 1994).

[19] C Dupré and J-r Yeh, 'Constitutions and Legitimacy over Time' in M Tushnet, T Fleiner and C Saunders (eds), *Routledge Handbook of Constitutional Law* (Oxford/New York, Routledge, 2013) 45.

[20] Häberle, 'Zeit und Verfassungskultur', above n 16, 627. These ideas were furthered and more systematically explored by S Kirste, 'Die Zeit der Verfassung' (2008) 56 *Jahrbuch des öffentlichen Rechts der Gegenwart* 35.

dictatorship.[21] Constitutional time is therefore undergoing a process of deep transformation, first diagnosed and identified by François Ost as 'detemporalisation':[22] a four-way process involving a certain denial of time understood as change and ultimately mortality; surrendering to physical time and its irreversible process of destruction; a deterministic mis-representation of time as being homogenous and smoothly continuous; and, finally, a mismanagement of social time ignoring its plurality and different rhythms. While Ost was writing in more general terms as a philosopher, his diagnosis is helpful in bringing to light and understanding a deeper transformation of constitutional and human time.

A. Human Time as Fragmented Plurality

Human time is becoming fragmented and its plurality can no longer be fully known or understood through the lenses of human rights and constitutionalism.[23] This has many causes that affect human beings in their identity as workers and as citizens. Above all, the root cause is arguably to be found in the new medical and technological possibilities that are questioning our understanding of what humanity is, thus altering human time which is understood by human rights law as starting with birth. Due to medical developments, human time now starts with conception, which can occur as the result of sexual intercourse or in a petri dish under a microscope, with the latter making the pre-birth dimension of human time particularly visible and problematic. While human rights have generally not been extended in full to these early stages of embryo formation, nor to the foetus in the womb,[24] these new possibilities have arguably profoundly affected the constitutional perception and measure of human time. Not only is it now possible to make human time start before birth, but it is also possible to suspend it (by freezing gametes and embryos for instance), or to set human time artificially, for instance, by deciding when to implant the *in vitro* embryo(s). This has given rise to the field of bioethics and related discussions in which human dignity has been deployed as a key argument

[21] It is not the first time that men have tried to regain control over time and to make it theirs; at a philosophical level see, eg G Deleuze, 'Kant—Synthèse et Temps' (1978) *Les Cours de Gilles Deleuze*, available at www.webdeleuze.com.

[22] Ost, above n 15, 14–15: 'Il s'agit tout d'abord du refus même du temps entendu comme changement, évolution, finitude et donc aussi mortalité. [Deuxièmement] l'abandon au cours du temps physique dont le mouvement, irréversible, conduit toute chose à la destruction. [Troisièmement] la pensée déterministe que genère la représentation d'un temps homogène et uniforme, plein et continu … une quatrième menace de détemporalisation tient à la gestion de la polychronie, car le temps social se décline de toute évidence au pluriel'.

[23] See, eg B Edelman, *La personne en danger* (Paris, Presses Universitaires de France, 1999).

[24] See in particular *Vo v France*, Application no 53924/00, ECtHR, 8 July 2004. In the absence of consensus, the ECtHR recognises a margin of appreciation to Member States.

in an attempt to find appropriate ways for (re)setting human time.[25] Importantly, this has also challenged the concept of human rights at the core of European constitutionalism, which until now has dated the beginning of human time from birth, due to the Enlightenment and natural law heritages as well as the impossibility of knowing or doing otherwise. At the other end of human existence, the time and timing of death have also been profoundly transformed, mainly due to medical developments, which have made it possible to keep people artificially alive and to develop new life-prolonging therapies. As a result, fewer people than ever before die of a 'natural' death at their spontaneous time; and dying has become for many a very closely monitored medical process. These changes to the timing of death have led an increasing number of people to seek to reclaim control over their death, prompting discussion on euthanasia and assisted suicide. Human dignity has been a core argument in these debates, promoted both by those who want to maintain a 'natural timing' of death and dying, and by those who want to make use of their last opportunity to be free and control their life by controlling their death too.[26]

Furthermore, with human time becoming the time of humankind in addition to the time of individual human beings, a new dimension of time is beginning to appear in constitutionalism, challenging its representation and boundaries. Again, human rights, primarily designed to operate and protect human beings between their individual birth and death, have proved to be ill-equipped to recognise and protect these new temporalities. Seen in this light, the concept of future generations can be understood as an attempt to acknowledge and protect the time of mankind: however, while it is a concept supported by a growing body of academic literature, it has so far not found its place within the framework of European constitutionalism.[27]

[25] For instance in Germany, Matthias Herdegen triggered a nationwide controversy with his new interpretation of human dignity, by moving away from the 'never again' approach that had so far structured this concept's understanding in German scholarship: M Herdegen, 'Artikel 1' in T Maunz and G Dürig (eds), *Grundgesetz Kommentar*, looseleaf edn (Munich, CH Beck Verlag, 2003) 1, with a vigorous critique by EW Böckenförde, 'Abschied von den Verfassungsvätern: Die Neukommentierung von Art.1 des Grundgesetzes markiert einen Epochenbruch' *Frankfurter Allgemeine Zeitung*, 3 September 2003, 33; and *Recht, Staat, Freiheit: Studien zur Rechtsphilosophie, Staatstheorie und Rechtssgeschichte* (Frankfurt am Main, Suhrkamp, 2006) 379. In English (and with no relation to these discussions), see R Brownsword, 'Human Dignity, Human Rights and Simply Trying to Do the Right Thing' in C McCrudden (ed), *Understanding Human Dignity* (Oxford, Oxford University Press) 345–58.

[26] M Düwell, 'On the Border of Life and Death: Human Dignity and Bioethics' in M Düwell, J Braarvig, R Brownsword and D Mieth (eds), *The Cambridge Handbook of Human Dignity* (Cambridge, Cambridge University Press, 2014) 526–34. See also H Biggs, *Euthanasia, Death with Dignity and the Law* (Oxford, Hart Publishing, 2001). More generally and critically see E Picker, *Menschenwürde und Menschenleben: Das Auseinderdriften zweier fundamentaler Werte als Ausdruck der wachsenden Relativierung des Menschen* (Stuttgart, Klett-Cotta, 2002). See also ECtHR, *Lambert and others v France*, Grand Chamber, 5 June 2015.

[27] E Brown-Weiss, 'Our Rights and Obligations to Future Generations for the Environment' (1990) 84 *American Journal of International Law* 198. I have suggested that human dignity,

A similar point can be noted in relation to the concept of third generation rights for which effective constitutional mechanisms and human rights techniques have yet to be invented.[28]

Importantly as well in the transformation of human time is the realisation that human time is not just 'natural', but that it has become (to an increasing extent) man-made. More disturbingly, perhaps, is the awareness that human time can be—deliberately or accidentally—destroyed by men. This has a lot to do with (some) uses of (some) new technologies, for instance, with the genetic screening of *in vitro* embryos before their implantation in the womb and the destruction of those found to be 'defective'.[29] As is well known this is also related to men's unique ability to destroy the environment in which they live and which is ultimately necessary for their survival.[30]

Ultimately, realising the fragility of human time and that it can be made, and destroyed, by men has arguably led to a critical questioning of human rights, in terms of their definition and, above all perhaps, of their ability to protect human time and humanity. One response has been to narrow down the range of possibilities that medical development and liberal constructions of rights have opened up by, for instance, promoting a very conservative view on marriage and sexual relationships grounded on the argument that there is a 'natural' therefore a 'proper' way of doing things.[31]

Seen from this perspective, one has to consider the possibility that human dignity and human rights might have exhausted their ability to protect definitions and understandings of what humanity and human freedom are

understood as 'a new beginning', does not only apply to the post war and dictatorship contexts, but can also be extended to ensuring that future generations too can always begin afresh, ie that current generations must be mindful of leaving behind a legacy that makes this possible: Dupré, n 5 above, 204.

[28] HS Cho and OW Pedersen, 'Environmental Rights and Future Generations' in M Tushnet, T Fleiner and C Saunders (eds), *Routledge Handbook of Constitutional Law* (Oxford/ New York, Routledge, 2013) 401–12; and M Düwell, 'Human Dignity and Future Generations' in M Düwell, J Braarvig, R Brownsword and D Mieth (eds), *The Cambridge Handbook of Human Dignity* (Cambridge, Cambridge University Press, 2014) 551–58.

[29] This is also related to the memory of misuses of medical science and technology and the eugenics practices of the 1930s, culminating under the Nazi regime with its attempt to engineer a new human race. With its prohibition on human reproductive cloning and eugenic practices aiming at the selection of persons, Article 3 EU Charter partly echoes these concerns and attempts to prevent these practices from recurring.

[30] Hans Jonas proposed one of the first attempts to think and protect this time, through what has become known as the precautionary principle, *Prinzip Verantwortung* (Frankfurt am Main, Suhrkamp, 1989). More recently see LJ Kotzé, 'Human Rights and the Environment in the Anthropocene' (2014) 1 *The Anthropocene Review* 252.

[31] See, eg C Tollefsen, 'The Dignity of Marriage' in C McCrudden (ed), *Understanding Human Dignity* (Oxford, Oxford University Press, 2013) 483–500. The Hungarian Fundamental Law of 2011 can also be read from this perspective, in particular with regard to its dignity provision (Art II): 'Human dignity shall be inviolable. Every human being shall have the right to life and human dignity; *embryonic and foetal life shall be subject to protection from the moment of conception*' (emphasis added).

about.[32] The underlying assumption, as well as the hope, in this chapter is that, rather than having reached the end of the road, human rights still have a lot to offer as a privileged (if not exclusive) tool to accompany and protect the transformations of humanity and human time, and that the concept of human dignity has a crucial role to play in this.

B. Constitutional Time Without Direction

The flow of constitutional time also appears to be losing its sense of direction and the temporal boundaries constructed by European constitutionalism, and the ECtHR in particular,[33] seem to be crumbling away under the pressure of various factors, a process which the Euro crisis has made more visible, but which it is suggested has its roots earlier in the 1990s. The collapse of Communism in Central and Eastern Europe has arguably triggered a process of 'detemporalisation' (to refer to the work of Ost mentioned above) for European constitutionalism. In the 1990s, Europe reached a stage that had long been envisaged as only possible in a remote future. Liberal democracy was apparently triumphant and social peace was achieved, with levels of economic prosperity which were certainly higher than in the immediate post-war period, despite discrepancies between the former Western and Eastern parts of Europe. Deprived of a future that had driven the European construction since its foundation, European constitutionalism has been struggling to invent a new future and to keep constitutional time flowing within its foundational boundaries. In this respect, it is suggested that the EU mismanaged what Ost calls the plurality of social time and has been oblivious to the slow and sometimes erratic pace of democratisation. In other words, the Copenhagen criteria that candidate countries had to meet before being accepted into the EU disregarded the different rhythms of transition and uniqueness of each country involved.[34] Moreover, what the EU arguably did was to impose a much faster pace of democratisation on countries that had been dictatorships for the best part of 50 years than it had imposed on its (founding) Member States and on itself.

Combined with the Euro crisis, this imposition of an accelerated pace of change has upset the temporal boundaries which had structured European constitutional time into a past, a present and a future. The past, in its authoritarian and illiberal incarnations, is becoming increasingly attractive to a growing number of far right parties and may be seen as a future to

[32] G Frankenberg, 'Human Rights and the Belief in a Just World' (2014) 12 *International Journal of Constitutional Law* 35.

[33] See Chapter 3 for a more detailed discussion.

[34] C Dupré, 'After Reforms: Human Rights Protection in Post-Communist States' (2008) 5 *European Human Rights Law Review* 622.

aspire to for some governments. The future, which had largely been undetermined but driven by a spirit of emancipation and enhancement of human rights protection and democracy, is now increasingly being determined in a precise way through the imposition of economic and financial targets. These include the 3 per cent golden rule on allowed public deficit and the current objectives driving the management of draconian austerity packages, which arguably jeopardise the rights of future generations in an unprecedented way.[35] As a result of these measures, future generations will arguably not be free to shape their present on their own terms, but instead they will have to reimburse a crippling debt, which was not contracted by them and which, in many cases, was not even agreed by the democratically elected parliaments. As things currently stand, this would not only determine the quantity of money available for the public good, but it would also determine how this money is to be spent.[36] Finally, the present is also affected by the management of the Euro crisis, which is re-awakening (in some instances very deep) resentment, hatred and xenophobia[37] that the creation of the European Communities was meant to make a thing of the past, and that the EU and its Member States had more or less succeeded in achieving. This brief reflection on the temporal consequences of the Euro crisis management provides a good illustration of the significance, and fragility, of constitutional time for democracy.

Overall, the distinct temporalities of the constitutional past, present and future are being blurred. The specific financial targets set by the Euro group arguably depletes the future of its substance,—which is to remain unknown and undetermined, and function,—which is to move the present out of itself into the next temporal dimension. The positive role that human rights have had in shaping the present by making space within it for the future to unfold is being diminished by increasing criticism of a key actor in this process, namely, the ECtHR and its living instrument doctrine[38] and by the EU's

[35] This brings back to the fore the analysis of Peter Häberle on time and constitutionalism: he identified the public debt as one burden imposed on future generations and constraining their future (and putting it at risk), together with nuclear power. See 'Zeit und Verfassungskultur', above n 16, 665.

[36] See, eg D Adamski, 'Europe's (Misguided) Constitution of Economic Prosperity' (2013) 50 *Common Market Law Review* 47; and E Chiti and PG Teixeira, 'The Constitutional Implications of the European Responses to the Financial and Public Debt Crisis' (2013) 50 *Common Market Law Review* 683.

[37] The Greek and Hungarian situations are regularly reported in European media. This issue has regained actuality with the Euro crisis, but it has deeper and more complex roots: see for instance P Hockenos, *Free to Hate: The Rise of the Right in Post-Communist Eastern Europe* (New York/London, Routledge, 1993).

[38] K Lörcher, 'The Future of the European Court of Human Rights in the Light of the Brighton Declaration' in F Dorssemont, K Lörcher and I Schömann (eds), *The European Convention on Human Rights and the Employment Relation* (Oxford, Hart Publishing, 2013) 93.

refusal to follow this human rights logic[39] and to let the financial logic take precedence.[40]

As things stand therefore, the question 'what next?' is impossible to address, because 'next' and 'now' have been merged into one temporal dimension, with 'next' being a repetition and continuation of the 'now' rather than a change from the 'now'. Effectively asking the 'what next?' question requires a very different epistemological and political perspective on time, namely, to think that the present is no longer (and not only) the guaranteed smooth continuity taking us away from the past, but rather to consider the possibility of a return to the past and to the lack of democracy and humanity that this might entail. Moreover, the present has to be considered in its relation to the future, that is, as the time that prepares and protects the future, by (re)-opening a range of possible futures. While threats to the future (such as environmental destruction) may not be ignored by European constitutionalism, it is important for the future to remain undetermined. The purpose of constitutionalism is to make space for the future at the heart of the present, thus allowing for the possibility of change and rupture, while remaining aware of the possibility that the bad past may well come back, as time is not safely linear.[41]

As a result, the issue of a possible reversal of constitutional time, and with it of the decline of the constitutional *acquis* in terms of human rights protection and quality of democracy, has to be raised. As was very well understood by Thucydides,[42] democracy itself can never be achieved: it is therefore more helpful to think in terms of a constant, but not necessarily linear, process of democratisation.[43] This openness towards a plurality of undetermined futures, and wariness towards a single and predetermined future, are key characteristics of democracy.[44] As explained below, human dignity is one instrument that European constitutionalism could deploy in order to re-imagine constitutional and human time, ultimately providing constitutionalism with a direction and a meaning that are currently lacking.

[39] S Peers, 'The EU's Accession to the ECHR: The Dream Becomes a Nightmare' (2015) 16 *German Law Journal* 214.

[40] C-370/12 *Thomas Pringle v Government of Ireland and the Attorney General*, CJEU, 27 November 2012.

[41] This belief in the linearity of time may well be one reason why the Hungarian constitutional developments since 2010 are not taken more seriously by the EU.

[42] As referred to by C Castoriadis, *Domaines de l'homme: les carrefours du labyrinthe (2)* (Paris, Points Seuil, 1986).

[43] C Lefort, *L'Invention démocratique: les limites de la domination totalitaire* (Paris, Fayard, 1994) and in English: C Lefort, *Democracy and Political Theory* (D Mace (trans), Minneapolis, MN, University of Minnesota Press, 1988).

[44] K Popper, *The Open Society and its Enemy*, 5th edn (Princeton, NJ, Princeton University Press, 1966).

III. HUMAN DIGNITY AS HUMAN TIME

As will be recalled, the concept of human dignity is a privileged location of time in the framework of European constitutionalism, which carries the memory of the time of inhumanity and promises to prevent its return.[45] It is argued here that human dignity can be constructed as reflecting two further dimensions of time: first, by recognising humanity in its plural and new forms, it acknowledges the singularity of each of their temporal dimensions as time of one's own; secondly, human dignity, understood as *kairos*, is the concept that makes it possible to raise the question 'what next?' by introducing the possibility of a new beginning.

A. Human Dignity as Time of One's Own

This section argues that human dignity acknowledges that each human being lives in and constructs his or her own time, and that the time of one is not the time of all. This idea is expressed by human dignity defined as time of one's own, a term inspired by the work of Austrian sociologist of science,[46] Helga Nowotny, who referred to the term *Eigenzeit*, a term of physics used to distinguish between time (*Zeit*) and what was translated in English as 'proper time' (*Eigenzeit*) in the context of relativity theory.[47] In this scientific context, this term has a specific definition,[48] which is in its technical detail of little interest for our current argument. What was inspirational, however, was the realisation of time's plurality[49] and the idea that each human being has his or her own time, which is not necessarily the time of all, understood here as constitutional time. Human time is, of course, shaped by biology and genetics. However, in the same way as the constitutional definition of human beings does not reduce them to their mere humanity,[50] the constitutional construction of human time through human dignity as *Eigenzeit* does not reduce human time to its biological dimension (ie the fact that we

[45] See Chapter 3.

[46] Nowotny, above n 18.

[47] The idea of *Eigenzeit* is further elaborated by Ulrich Mückenberger, 'Time Abstraction, Temporal Policy and the Right to One's Own Time' (2011) 11 *Kronoscope* 66, 85–95, who draws from the work of Ost mentioned above.

[48] Nowotny, above n 18, 2.

[49] The idea of a plural time is not new: J Rifkin, *Time Wars: The Primary Conflict in Human History* (New York, Henry Holt and Company, 1987). Law (according to lawyers) is a primary locus for this plurality of times and solving the conflicts arising out of it, see S Kirste, 'The Temporality of Law and the Plurality of Social Times: The Problem of Synchronising Different Time Concepts through Law' in M Troper and A Verza (eds), 'Legal Philosophy: General Aspects (Concepts, Rights and Doctrines)' (2002) Beiheft 82 *Archiv für Rechts-und Sozialphilosophie* 23.

[50] See Chapters 2 and 3.

are born to die). Instead, it recognises that human beings have a unique ability to rise out of this biological time (while being, of course, bound by it and enjoying its 'natural' course) and to construct their own time. It is suggested that human dignity is the constitutional tool acknowledging this (making it possible), and defining it as *Eigenzeit* is therefore both a statement of fact and a (constitutional) claim to temporal self-determination, ie the freedom to construct one's own time. For this reason, I have chosen to translate '*Eigenzeit*' as time of one's own[51] (rather than 'proper time', which is the word chosen in the English translation of Nowotny's book). Human dignity as time of one's own is therefore the constitutional tool that creates and maintains a time in which humanity can flourish. This involves acknowledging the multiple dimensions of human time (eg individual, or as the time of mankind), as well as their location at the heart of a complex web of non-human temporalities, such as technological, planetary or financial times that exist outside the boundaries of human time. This further involves giving human beings the power, and freedom, to choose how to shape their own time individually, and collectively, the power to construct boundaries between human time and non-human time, perhaps as well as the duty to protect the time of mankind.

Eigen also means 'right', 'appropriate' or 'proper', and this dimension is also included in the phrase 'time of one's own', which has to be understood not only as temporal self-determination, but also as the time that is right for oneself, reflecting a particular set of needs and wishes for a person at a given point in her life. Everyone lives their life at different paces,[52] and what is right for one person at a given time may be wrong for another person at the same time or wrong for the same person at a different time of her life. The same chronological duration may therefore feel different and may have a different impact on different persons. Without formulating this quite in these terms, some judges have already acknowledged the unique time of human rights victims. It is arguably no coincidence that they have done this with reference to human dignity. For instance, the ECtHR has a very well-established practice (and hermeneutic policy) of being sensitive to a victim's temporal vulnerability in Article 3 cases (prohibition of torture and inhuman and degrading treatment or punishment). In particular, this time sensitivity became a key factor in an Article 3 case involving the police custody of a man (MS) who demonstrated clear signs of severe mental illness and distress. In that case, the ECtHR found that the time spent in police custody had been too long and generated a breach of Article 3 (inhuman and degrading treatment), despite the fact that the custody duration did not exceed

[51] By reference to V Woolf, *A Room of One's Own* (London, Penguin Classics, 2000) 53–54.

[52] On duration understood as being a polymorphic multitude of coincidences and discontinuities, see G Bachelard, *La dialectique de la durée*, 4th edn (Paris, Presses Universitaires de France, 2006).

the statutory limits, and the fact that police officers had actively attempted to attenuate the distressing conditions of their prisoner (and crucially did not take any positive steps to inflict inhuman and degrading treatment on him).[53]

A further illustration of the time of one's own is provided by the UK case of *McDonald* decided by the Supreme Court.[54] What was at stake was the provision of a care package for the applicant who, due to a range of medical problems, needed the help of a carer to use the toilet at night. The Court held that the support of a carer could lawfully be replaced by the compulsory use of incontinence pads, despite the important fact that the applicant was not incontinent. In the only dissenting opinion, Baroness Hale pointed out that the provision of pads did not meet the applicant's needs and she noted that they may even have a negative impact on the applicant's autonomy and speed up the deterioration of her condition.[55] This observation, apparently only made in passing in the judgment, however, points to a crucial time issue, in that it could be argued that the provision of pads was a breach of the applicant's human dignity as they prevented her from controlling the pace of her condition's (anticipated) deterioration, by making the carer's time prevail over her own time. In addition to this one-sided acknowledgement of time, what ultimately prevailed in this ruling was a financial assessment of time costed at an extra £22,000 a year (by the care provider) while the consequences of this ruling for the applicant's ability to shape her own time were ignored by the court.[56] This case arguably illustrates a fairly typical situation where human dignity as time of one's own is breached, thus further demonstrating the relevance, merits and difficulty of defining this concept in this time-sensitive manner in order to protect people in a whole range of care and medical situations.

While the *McDonald* case illustrates that (some) judges have a long way to go before they can fully grasp the necessity of protecting human time,

[53] *MS v United Kingdom*, Application no 24527/08, ECtHR, 3 August 2012, with a case note by D Bedford, 'MS v UK: Article 3 ECHR, Detention and Mental Health' (2013) 1 *European Human Rights Law Review* 72.

[54] *R (on the application of McDonald) (Appellant) v Royal Borough of Kensington and Chelsea (Respondent)*, 6 July 2011 [2011] UKSC 33. The applicant appealed to the ECtHR, which acknowledged that Art 8 (privacy) was engaged and duly noted the dignity issue at the heart of the dispute (at para 47). The ECtHR nevertheless held that the decision to withdraw the night-time carer was 'in accordance with the law' as the United Kingdom had not exceeded its margin of appreciation with regard to the 'allocation of limited state resources' (para 54) and the domestic courts had 'adequately balanced the applicant's personal interests against the more general interest ... towards the community at large' (para 57). *McDonald v United Kingdom*, Application no 4241/12, ECtHR, 20 May 2014.

[55] 'Such Department of Health Guidance as there is points the other way: that people should not be offered this form of assistance *prematurely*, in case they become unnecessarily dependent on it': Baroness Hale at para 75 (emphasis added).

[56] In a discussion of this ruling, Luke Clements argues that incontinence, in addition to generating anxiety and distress in those affected, has a clear financial cost: L Clements, 'Disability, Dignity, and Cri du Coeur' (2011) 6 *European Human Rights Law Review* 675, 683.

constitutional texts have started to acknowledge it as time of one's own in different ways. The EU Charter is used here as a representative text of reference, as it is the latest human rights instrument to come into force in the EU and it has also been drafted in consideration of developments in Member States, therefore reflecting some more general trends in this respect. Focusing on the explicit dignity references, it can be seen that the EU Charter acknowledges three types of human time.[57] First, and perhaps the most self-explanatory, is the time of the elderly, with the EU Charter making, for the first time,[58] an explicit connection between the elderly and their 'rights to lead a life of dignity and independence and to participate in social and cultural life' (Article 25).[59] This acknowledgement seems to be part of an increasing awareness (in legal scholarship and policy-making) that time takes on a particular quality for 'elderly people' and therefore requires particular attention on the part of (human rights) law. Tellingly, the EU Charter is cautious not to define the concept of 'elderly people' in terms of age under Article 25.[60] Seen from the prism of time and *Eigenzeit* this provision can be understood in two complementary ways. First, law (and society) must acknowledge the fact that human time evolves as we get older; the lack of a particular civil age's mention becomes very important as this signals the possibility of a nuanced approach to these changes and that some of us become 'elderly people' at different civil ages (depending on life-styles, work and working conditions and perhaps genetic make-up). Moreover, this acknowledges the fact that the common time of 'social and cultural life' has to allow for different temporalities and different rhythms, so as to include everyone; the time of all has to be set inclusively for everyone. This is particularly important considering that 'participation in social and cultural life' is understood as including participation in political life too.

[57] The EU Charter explicitly protects the rights of children under Art 24, but makes no reference to dignity in this provision.

[58] Neither the ECHR, nor the UN Universal Declaration of Human Rights acknowledges the elderly as a particularly vulnerable group of human beings, calling for specific protection. This may be partly due to demographic changes in the European population that have occurred since these two Conventions were adopted.

[59] C O'Cinneide, 'Article 25: The Rights of the Elderly' in S Peers, T Hervey, J Kenner and A Ward (eds), *The EU Charter of Fundamental Rights: A Commentary* (Oxford, CH Beck/Hart Publishing/Nomos, 2014) 693–707.

[60] Technically, the exact age definition of 'elderly' is disputed. This provision might have to be read as excluding from the 'elderly' category those under the age of 60 if it is read in the light of its source (Arts 24 and 25 of the Community Charter of the Fundamental Social Rights of Workers): see HD Jarass, *Charta der Grundrechte der Europäischen Union Kommentar* (Munich, Verlag/C H Beck, 2010) 256–57. This interpretation is however nuanced by those who read this provision as a re-affirmation of the general prohibition on discrimination under Art 21 EU Charter, with the specific application to elderly people; see P Lotito, 'Article 25: The Rights of the Elderly' in BT Mock and G Demuro (eds), *Human Rights in Europe: Commentary on the Charter of Fundamental Rights of the European Union* (Durham, NC, Carolina Academic Press, 2010) 158, 159. Generally see P De Hert and E Mantovani, 'Specific Rights for Older Persons?' (2011) 4 *European Human Rights Law Review* 398.

Secondly, the EU Charter arguably recognises workers' time under its Article 31.[61] The reference to 'dignity' is made in addition to the well-established (normatively, if not always in practice) protection of 'health and safety'. Moreover, although the explanatory notes identify the Social Charter and the Community Charter, namely, the protection against harassment, as a source of inspiration and possible meaning for 'dignity', this concept can arguably not be reduced to prohibition of harassment in the context of the workplace.[62] Rather, as will be recalled from the previous chapter, acknowledging human dignity at and through work carries a more ancient memory of struggles for working conditions that make it possible for workers to retain their human status (and not to be degraded to the level of a slave or animal, or turned into robots). It can be further understood as promoting the acknowledgment and protection of individual identities and human personalities. Following this logic, work could and should foster the 'pleasure of being oneself'.[63] This 'pleasure' has many dimensions, one of which is certainly the control over one's time. In other words, work time should fit with other times (such as personal time or civic time) and time at work should also be constructed with workers' input and in a way that preserves their individual *Eigenzeit*.[64] This is not a new problem and we need only recall Charlie Chaplin trying to keep up with the pace of the conveyor belt in *Modern Times*. As is well known too, according to some Marxist analysis, capitalism and industrialisation took a major step when workers' time became quantified and counted on a purely economic basis.[65] More recently, technology (perhaps particularly information technology) and globalisation have not always contributed to giving workers back some control over their time.[66] How Article 31 EU Charter is understood and developed into practice remains to be seen, but it is clear that workers' time and time at work are crucial issues of labour law that are not about to disappear from the human rights and constitutional agenda.[67]

[61] Workers' human dignity is discussed in greater detail in Chapter 5.

[62] A Giorgis, 'Article 31: Fair and Just Working Conditions' in BT Mock and G Demuro (eds), *Human Rights in Europe: Commentary on the Charter of Fundamental Rights of the European Union* (Durham, NC, Carolina Academic Press, 2010) 187–97; and A Bogg, 'Article 31: Fair and Just Working Conditions' in S Peers, T Hervey, J Kenner and A Ward (eds), *The EU Charter of Fundamental Rights: A Commentary* (Oxford, CH Beck/Hart Publishing/ Nomos, 2014) 833–68.

[63] A Cieslar, A Nayer and B Smeesters, *Le droit à l'épanouissement de l'être humain au travail: métamorphoses du droit social* (Brussels, Bruylant, 2007).

[64] See, eg MP Spencer, 'Producing Time and Space: Academic Work after Henri Lefebvre' (2013) 33 *Legal Studies* 478.

[65] EP Thompson, 'Time, Work-Discipline, and Industrial Capitalism' (1967) 38 *Past and Present* 56.

[66] H Rosa, *Accélération: une critique sociale du temps* (Paris, La Découverte, 2010).

[67] In particular see the work of Ulrich Mückenberger, above n 47.

The third type of human time acknowledged and protected by the EU Charter is the time of humanity. Although there is no single provision dedicated to it, identification of the time of humanity as a good worthy of human rights protection in the EU Charter can easily be reconstructed on the basis of a number of mentions. The Preamble acknowledges that the rights contained in the EU Charter have to be enjoyed 'with regard to ... future generations'. While this phrase is not repeated in the main body of the Charter and is not further qualified (in particular the EU Charter makes no mention of environmental protection), it clearly signals a new awareness of future generations' need for protection. Seen from a time perspective, this reference can be understood as acknowledging both that future generations have their own temporality, and, importantly, that current generations' time can contribute to shaping it. In addition, the EU Charter contains two new mentions that can be understood as indicating that protection of future generations' time starts with the ways in which current generations are being genetically shaped. This is expressed under Article 3 by 'the prohibition of eugenics practices, in particular those aiming at the selection of persons' (Article 3.2.b) and 'the prohibition of the reproductive cloning of human beings' (Article 3.2.d). These prohibitions can be understood as an attempt to control humanity's time by constructing normative boundaries in order to maintain a sort of temporal status quo. The EU Charter is not isolated in this approach and the Portuguese Constitution in its 1997 version can also be noted here for the connection it makes between the protection of human beings' 'genetic identity' and human dignity.[68] What is at stake in terms of substance is the protection of humanity's genetic make-up as it is, that is not interfering with it so as not to create a new type of human being who would be genetically engineered as identical to those created 'naturally'. Therefore, the protection of genetic identity is arguably related to the continuity of humanity, literally understood as the reproduction of its current genetic make-up. The question of why reproductive cloning of human beings should be prohibited has often been raised in terms of human dignity.[69] One answer may well be that, by interfering with the current genetic make-up of the human species, we break open the boundaries of humanity's time, without quite being able (as things currently stand) to control and predict where and how this new human time will flow.

[68] Article 26.3: 'The law shall guarantee the personal dignity and genetic identity of the human being, particularly in the creation, development and use of technology and scientific experimentation'. The Oviedo Convention prohibits discrimination against a person on grounds of his or her 'genetic heritage'.

[69] G Frankenberg, *Autorität und Integration: Zur Grammatik von Recht und Verfassung* (Frankfurt am Main, Suhrkamp, 2003) 283; generally see S Vöneky and R Wolfrum (eds), *Human Dignity and Human Cloning* (Leiden, Martinus Nijhoff Publishing, 2004).

B. *Kairos* of Human Rights

As seen in Chapter 3, one recurring feature of human dignity is its association with new beginning(s) and democracy's 'capacity to begin anew' by re-constructing dreams and projects.[70] This also implies that democracies are able to make space for what is not yet (to borrow from Ernst Bloch).[71] While this entertains important connections with utopia and the hope for a better world,[72] it is argued that human dignity is also a key instrument in facing the new and responding to deep changes.[73] To go back to François Ost's analysis of time, it is therefore crucial to make space for what he calls *kairos* at the heart of time, namely, for irregularities, hesitations, uncertainties and unforeseen events.[74] On this basis, it is suggested that human dignity encapsulates a particular constitutional construction of human time as the *kairos* of human rights.

Kairos is a Greek word related to time, which has a range of meanings. The simplest meaning flows from the distinction that Ancient Greeks made between continuous time (*chronos*) and the time of rupture and discontinuity (*kairos*). The importance of new starts and making space for the unpredictable at the heart of democracy was particularly eloquently highlighted by Cornelius Castoriadis, a great student of Athenian democracy.[75] In the context of constitutional law (and with no reference to Castoriadis), the idea of *kairos* was also developed by German scholar Stefan Kirste in an attempt to capture the unique moment and set of circumstances out of which a new constitution is made.[76]

On this basis, it is suggested that human dignity is a tool used by constitutions to make space for and to create a break in the continuous flow of time

[70] 'Human dignity needs a new guarantee which can be found only in a new political principle, in a new law on earth, whose validity this time must comprehend the whole of humanity while its power must remain strictly limited, rooted in and controlled by newly defined territorial entities': H Arendt, *The Origins of Totalitarianism* (New York, Harcourt, Brace, 1973) ix. See also A Kesby, *The Right to Have Rights: Citizenship, Humanity and International Law* (Oxford, Oxford Scholarship Online, 2012).

[71] E Bloch, *The Principle of Hope* (N Plaice, S Plaice and P Knight (trans), Cambridge, MA, Massachusetts Institute of Technology, 1986) and *Natural Law and Human Dignity* (DJ Smith (trans), Cambridge, MA, Massachusetts Institute of Technology, 1986).

[72] P Häberle, 'Demokratische Verfassungstheorie im Lichte des Möglichkeitsdenkens' (1977) 107 *Archiv für öffentliches Recht* 27.

[73] C Dupré, 'Dignity, Democracy, Civilisation' (2012) 33 *Liverpool Law Review* 319.

[74] Ost, above n 15, 27: 'Faire sa place au kairos, l'instant créateur, au sein du temps social, c'est reconnaître que le temps d'une société ouverte n'est pas régulier et uniforme; c'est admettre qu'il soit parcouru d'hésitations, traversé d'incertitudes, bousculé par des évênements imprévus'.

[75] Castoriadis, above n 42.

[76] Kirste, above n 20, 49. C Girard and S Hennette-Vauchez also referred to dignity as *kairos* of human rights with reference to attempts by some French commentators to re-found human rights in human dignity: *La dignité de la personne humaine: recherche sur un processus de juridicisation* (Paris, Presses Universitaires de France, 2004) 246–51.

(*chronos*), such as to terminate a dictatorial era and to mark the beginning of a new democratic time. Human dignity is the foundation of European constitutionalism not only with regard to the hope of a better world that it carries within itself, but also because it demarcates a line between the past and the present, as has been particularly well illustrated in post-1949 Germany and post-1989 Hungary.[77] However, human dignity is not just a special tool used to depart from Nazism (or fascism or communism); since the 2000s it has systematically been enshrined in constitutions as part of a significant constitutional overhaul, as illustrated by the Constitutions of Finland (1995 and 2000),[78] Hungary (2011)[79] and Iceland (2011 proposal).[80]

However, it is suggested here that the introduction of change does not only take place with the adoption of a new constitution at a special constitutional moment. Defining human dignity as the *kairos* of human rights is a way of acknowledging the fact that deep transformations can take place in between adoption of new constitutions and, conversely, that the time between two constitutional revisions is not purely smooth and linear, but that it is irregular, full of uncertainties and hesitations (to refer to François Ost's remarks above). In practice, human dignity's transformative function[81] arguably explains why it has been a key judicial instrument for departing from established case law and precedent, opening up a new path in an unchartered territory.[82] In order to make this possible, the abstract formulation of human dignity in constitutional texts, much criticised for its emptiness, becomes an essential component as it creates conceptual space for interpretations and constructions of human dignity that could not be anticipated at the time of drafting, making it therefore possible to respond to the unpredictable.

This transformative role of dignity in case law is arguably vital to the smooth functioning of democracy, which has to adjust constantly to changes, big and small, without amending the constitution each time. In judicial

[77] See Chapter 3.

[78] J Husa, *The Constitution of Finland: A Contextual Analysis* (Oxford, Hart Publishing, 2011).

[79] GA Tóth (ed), *Constitution for a Disunited Nation: Hungary's New Fundamental Law* (Budapest, Central European University Press, 2012); and I Pogany, 'The Crisis of Democracy in East Central Europe: The "New Constitutionalism" in Hungary' (2013) 19 *European Public Law* 341.

[80] Icelandic New Constitutional Bill of 29 July 2011, available at http://stjornarskrarfelagid.is/english/constitutional-bill/. See also AT Árnason, 'A Review of the Icelandic Constitution: Popular Sovereignty or Political Confusion' (2011) *Bij de Buren* 342, and H Landemore, 'Inclusive Constitution-Making: The Icelandic Experiment' (2014) *Journal of Political Philosophy* 1. Generally see J Skalski, *La révolution des casseroles; chronique d'une nouvelle constitution pour l'Islande* (Clamecy, La Contre Allée, 2012).

[81] S Hessel, *Indignez-vous!* (Montpellier, Indigène éditions, 2010). See also W Bonefeld and K Psychopedis (eds), *Human Dignity: Social Autonomy and the Critique of Capitalism* (Aldershot, Ashgate, 2005).

[82] C Dupré, 'Dignity, Democracy, Civilisation' (2013) 33 *Liverpool Law Review* 263, 271–72.

reasoning in particular human dignity has played a key hermeneutic role in responding to scientific changes and to changes in social expectations and practices. This is well illustrated, for instance, in relation to decisions on euthanasia or assisted suicide,[83] or the sensitive decision to let a brain-dead person die.[84] As discussed elsewhere, in these situations, human dignity's primary role is not to bring a ready-made answer, but to guide judges as they venture into new territories, to encourage them to consider the 'what if?' question raised by the applicants (eg what if Article 2 of the European Convention on Human Rights (ECHR) also meant the right to live in dignity until, and including, the very end of one's life, and not just the sanctity of life and right not to be arbitrarily killed by a state agent?).

Technically, in the context of human rights adjudication, reliance on human dignity makes discursive space to consider alternative and new ways of interpreting the law, and this concept has therefore provided judges with a key to unlock a difficult situation and to open up a new path in human rights protection. For instance, references to human dignity have played an instrumental role in extending the scope of Article 3 ECHR (the protection against inhuman and degrading treatment, ie severe forms of humiliation) to people who do not have the capacity to feel or perceive these treatments as humiliating or degrading due to mental illness.[85] This hermeneutic unlocking of Article 3 by bringing the argument of human dignity into the 'traditional' ways of thinking has therefore made it possible to protect people, who until then had been excluded from it. It has also led to a major transformation in the law, social attitudes and expectations in relation to the mentally ill or disabled, and to the recognition that their illness or disability can no longer be used as a shield to hide from the reality of their difference and their need to make a place for them in society.[86]

[83] *Pretty v United Kingdom*, Application no 2346/02, ECtHR, 29 April 2002, and *Lambert and others v France*, Application no 46043/14, ECtHR, 5 June 2015.

[84] The Irish High Court recently decided on the lawfulness of withdrawing life-support to a brain-dead woman whose foetus survived the accident that she did not. As Art 40.3.3 of the Irish Constitution 'acknowledges the right to life of the unborn ... with due regard of the equal right to life of the mother', this decision was particularly difficult and sensitive. The High Court gave the argument of human dignity its full consideration: 'This does not mean that the Court discounts or disregards the mother's right to retain in death her dignity [and] proper respect for her autonomy with due regard to the grief and sorrow of her loved ones and their wishes. *Such an approach has been the hallmark of civilised societies from the dawn of time. It is a deeply ingrained part of our humanity and may be seen as necessary both for those who have died and also for the sake of those who remain living and who must go on*. The Court therefore is unimpressed with any suggestion that considerations of the dignity of the mother are not engaged once she has passed away' (emphasis added): *PP v Health Service Executive*, No 10792P, 26 December 2014.

[85] *Keenan v United Kingdom*, Application no 27229/95, ECtHR, 3 April 2001 and *MS v United Kingdom*, Application no 24527/08, ECtHR, 3 August 2012.

[86] M Neal, '"Not Gods but Animals": Human Dignity and Vulnerable Subjecthood' (2012) 33 *Liverpool Law Review* 177.

Therefore, some substantive meanings of human dignity are, by definition, hard to pin down as they are to be found in movement and not in stability or in the smooth continuity and repetition of the constitutional *chronos*. In methodological terms, it becomes necessary to identify the pivot between the 'before' and the 'after' in order to understand human dignity: its substantive definition is arguably to be sought (and found) in the difference that the concept introduces to the law and in the impact that it has on a given situation. In this respect, defining human dignity as the *kairos* of human rights responds to recurring critiques of human dignity as a legal concept for which it is impossible to provide a complete substantive definition.[87] In other words, the concept of *kairos* emphasises that, in terms of substance, human dignity's definition neither lies in the sum of all specific definitions that might be found in (case) law, nor can it ever be equated with a mathematical formula or some other so-called scientific or objective definition of humanity. German scholarship has approached this apparent human dignity paradox with the concrete/abstract distinction: human dignity is an (*a priori*) abstract principle that can only be defined *a posteriori* as illustrated by a range of concrete examples, but never be exhausted in the sum of its parts.[88]

To conclude, incorporating time in the constitutional concept of human dignity makes it possible to bring to light a substantive definition for human dignity, while addressing a number of human dignity conundrums and providing new ways of understanding the existential crisis of constitutionalism and (hopefully) of overcoming it. The 'dignity time' discussed above is not a smooth, uniform and continuous time; it is a time full of gaps, irregularities and new beginnings. Human dignity's key constitutional role in relation to time is to ensure that human time can continue its flow, that in some cases a status quo is maintained (until we learn how to control and tame time better), or that in other cases a plurality of time can unfold at once. In all instances, protecting human dignity is seeking to guarantee that time can remain humane and human by allowing people to determine the precarious and constantly changing temporal equilibrium in which they live and to contribute to the wider decision-making process involving time that affects all.

IV. PROTECTING HUMAN TIME

Constructing human dignity as *kairos* and as time of one's own has highlighted the significance of time for understanding constitutionalism, as well

[87] C McCrudden, 'Human Dignity and Judicial Interpretation of Human Rights' (2008) 19 *European Journal of International Law* 655.

[88] For this reason, in methodological terms, trying to put together a substantive definition of human dignity by adding up all its concrete uses in case law (or constitutions) can only lead to scholarly frustration. See Chapter 4 for an alternative methodological approach.

as the polychrony of constitutional time. It is suggested that in this process human dignity could become a useful tool to synchronise the constitutional and human dimensions of time, and to make way for a new dynamic construction of time towards the possibility of a future.

A. Human Dignity as Synchrony

The concept of time of one's own and the realisation that time is plural raise the issue of law's role in managing this polychrony.[89] In particular, it is suggested that human dignity can play a key role in synchronising these various temporalities as it makes it possible to think of human rights in their connection to humanity as a whole.[90] For instance, human dignity has already been instrumental in jointly thinking the different generations of human rights, often artificially distinguished for ideological reasons, thus emphasising the principle of indivisibility of human rights.[91] Human dignity has been equally important in bringing together current generations and future generations, connecting the protection of one with the protection of the other.[92] Moreover, as discussed above, human dignity has been used to ensure that humanity's time is not jeopardised by individual time (eg the interference with genetic make-up under Article 3 EU Charter); conversely, individual time arguably has no continuity and therefore faces destruction if it cannot flow into the time of humanity. Finally, Article 25 EU Charter can be understood as a reminder that human life includes a time of elderliness, and must therefore be protected in the fullness of its continuity and change rather than by reference to an abstract and an everlasting youth.[93]

What is appearing, almost as a watermark, is a kind of temporal solidarity bringing together the various dimensions of human time in the constitutional concept of human dignity.[94] As a result, the concept of human dignity can neither be understood nor implemented in isolation from the wider human rights protection context. Human dignity, it is argued, can only be fully understood as part of an evolving constellation of rights. This has been perceptively argued by Susanne Baer, who put forward a triangular

[89] Kirste above n 49; see also Kirste, above n 20, 71.

[90] Dupré, n 5 above, 190, and Flick, above n 6, 39.

[91] See Chapter 5.

[92] A Lenze, 'Gleichheitssatz und Generationengerechtigkeit' (2007) 46 *Der Staat* 89; see also K Mathis (ed), *Efficiency, Sustainability, and Justice to Future Generations* (Dordrecht, Springer 2011).

[93] P Lotito emphasises the built-in equality under Art 25: above n 60, 158, 160.

[94] See also P Unruh, 'Kant—Menschenwürde—Sozialstaat' in R Grote *et al* (eds), *Die Ordnung der Freiheit: Festschrift f. Christian Starck zum 70. Geburtstag* (Tübingen, Mohr Siebeck, 2007) 133–50.

definition of human dignity, connecting it to liberty and equality.[95] In practice, judges have tended to interpret human dignity in connection with other rights, such as the right to life, equality, the fulfilment of personality or the prohibition of torture, inhuman or degrading treatment or punishment. From this point of view, the EU Charter's approach to a normative definition of human dignity is particularly interesting as it expressly constructs human dignity as part of a constellation of the core human rights protected by the EU under the first Title of the Charter.[96]

Therefore, human dignity's fuller sense only arises out of varying combinations and interactions, constantly adjusted to protect a particular dimension of human time, thus forming part of a wider process of making sense of constitutional time.[97] This is very well illustrated by some ECtHR rulings, where human dignity has been used, perhaps so far intuitively, as a way of delineating the boundaries between past, present and future. The first example is the marital rape ruling, where the construction of time, namely, of the past, was central to the dispute and to the reasoning of the Court.[98] On the one hand was the applicant's construction of (UK constitutional) time as an uninterrupted continuity since 1736,[99] as a result of which he claimed that the concept of rape between spouses did not exist and could not be punished by the law. On the other hand was the victim's reconstruction of time as endorsed and developed both by the UK House of Lords and the ECtHR, with a clear demarcation between the past and the present. Neither court denied the fact that there was a time when rape between spouses was not punished by the common law; both courts, however, re-directed this time by acknowledging the conceptual (and factual in the case) possibility of marital rape. While the UK House of Lords did this through a meticulous reconstruction of the common law, the ECtHR considered the issue through the prism of human dignity. This concept arguably made it possible

[95] S Baer, 'Dignity, Liberty, Equality: A Fundamental Rights Triangle of Constitutionalism' (2009) 59 *University of Toronto Law Journal* 417.

[96] See Chapter 3.

[97] Making sense of time not by reference to the grand narratives of totalitarianism (or of EU integration), but as understood by F Ost, 'Le temps, quatrième dimension des droits de l'homme' in M Borghi and P Meyer-Bisch (eds), *Société civile et indivisibilité des droits de l'homme* (Fribourg, Editions Universitaires de Fribourg, 2000) 109.

[98] *SW v United Kingdom*, Application no 20166/92, ECtHR, 22 November1995, discussed in Chapter 4.

[99] This refers to the date of a common law principle expressed by Sir Matthew Hale CJ in the following terms: 'But the husband cannot be guilty of rape committed by himself upon his lawful wife, for by their matrimonial consent and contract the wife hath given herself up in this kind unto her husband, which she cannot retract', quoted ibid para 7.

to move the common law out of its past and into the present of European constitutionalism.[100]

Human dignity can also serve to protect the present, its mere existence and duration. This is well illustrated in *D v United Kingdom*,[101] in which the ECtHR held that the applicant's prospective deportation to St Kitts would amount to inhuman treatment as he was in the advanced stages of AIDS and the quality of care he could be expected to receive in St Kitts would have 'the most dramatic consequences for him' (para 52). By attempting not to 'hasten his death' and 'further reduce his life expectancy' (para 52), the Court arguably protected the applicant's present, against a predictable acceleration of time into a very close future that meant the applicant's death. In this particular case, the Court did not refer to the term 'dignity', preferring the generic and formal phrase 'inhuman treatment'.[102] Nevertheless, it is argued that the concept of human dignity was at the core of this ruling, in the Court's emphasis on 'the compelling humanitarian considerations at stake' (para 54). Moreover, a similar attempt to protect an applicant's present by preventing the deterioration of her condition as long as possible, was made in the UK Supreme Court *McDonald* case discussed above and in which the judgment did include reference to human dignity.[103] When used in the context of care and serious illnesses, reliance on this concept by judges can be understood as an attempt to slow down the passage of time by preventing the deterioration of a medical condition (eg continuity of medical treatment) and the increasing loss of patients' autonomy and, in some cases, keeping death at bay as long as possible.

Last, human dignity has also been used to protect an applicant's future, ensuring that there is a future (rather than an ever-lasting present) and that the future can be a time to look forward to. This is nowhere better illustrated than in the lifelong sentence case law. The case of *Vinter and others v United Kingdom* is a key ruling of the ECtHR on this matter and it brings in the human dignity argument originally developed by the German Federal

[100] Reflecting on the importance of consent in the construction of democratic time, French political philosopher Pierre Manent observes that: 'c'est dans la création continuée du consentement que l'individu est vraiment un individu authentique, qu'il devient ce qu'il est précisément en exerçant toujours à nouveau activement, à chaque instant, sa liberté—en refusant de recevoir aucune obligation du passé, ce passé fût-il celui de nos propres choix … L'expression du consentement ouvre nécessairement un certain *avenir*': *Cours familier de philosophie politique* (Paris, Gallimard, 2011) 196.

[101] *D v United Kingdom*, Application no 146/1996/767/964, ECtHR, 21 April 1997.

[102] The absence of formal reference to the phrase 'human dignity' in this ruling can be explained by the fact that it does not appear in the text of the ECHR and, as a result its use by judges is far from systematic or consistent.

[103] *R (on application of McDonald) (Appellant) v Royal Borough of Kensington and Chelsea (Respondent)*, 6 July 2011 [2011] UKSC 33.

Constitutional Court.[104] In its general reflection on Article 3 and whole life orders, the ECtHR observed that:

> if such a prisoner is incarcerated without any prospect for release and without the possibility of having his life sentence reviewed, there is a risk that he can never atone for his offence: whatever the prisoner does in prison, however his progress towards rehabilitation, his punishment remains fixed and unreviewable. (para 112)

In relation to the specific case, the Court further noted that it is essential that the possibility of review and its timing should be known by the prisoner at the start of his sentence:

> it would be capricious to expect the prisoner to work towards his own rehabilitation without knowing whether, at an unspecified, future date, a mechanism might be introduced which would allow him, on the basis of that rehabilitation, to be considered for release. (para 122)

The argument of time, namely, that the prisoner can have a future and can work towards making his future better than his present, is so crucial that it is the main ground for finding that the absence of such possibility of review breaches Article 3. The ECtHR was, however, very cautious not to constrain the state to guarantee that this future will have a specific objective quality in the form of a possibility of release (para 131). What primarily mattered was that the applicant can have a future and imagine himself with a future, that is, a stage of his penalty that will be different from the present. The Court leaves this future open, encouraging the applicant's responsibility as autonomy to shape it. This ruling is arguably a very good example of how judges can make space at the heart of the present for the future to unfold. However, they do not predict, or predetermine the exact substance of the future.

Despite this openness, this ruling triggered considerable controversy in the United Kingdom and the Supreme Court held soon afterwards that the UK law complied with ECHR standards. Interestingly, Supreme Court judges noted the argument of hope and time made by the ECtHR, but found that 'the law of England and Wales therefore does provide to an offender "hope" or the "possibility" of exceptional circumstances which render the just punishment [whole life sentence] originally imposed no longer justifiable'.[105] Beyond the technical issues of the possibility of review and discretionary release of prisoners serving a life order, what is arguably at stake here is the freedom granted to prisoners to imagine their future as including the

[104] *Vinter and others v United Kingdom*, Applications nos 66069/09, 130/10 and 3896/10, ECtHR, Grand Chamber, 9 July 2013, with explicit references to German constitutional case law under para 113. This was followed by *Hutchinson v United Kingdom*, Application no 57592/08, ECtHR, 3 February 2015, discussed in Chapter 4.

[105] *R v Ian McLoughlin* and *R v Lee William Newell*, 18 February 2014, [2014] EWCA Crim 188, para 35.

possibility of release after a successful review of their sentence, or to be condemned to live in an eternal present, which can only be unlocked at the complete discretion of the Home Secretary and in exceptional circumstances or by the prisoner's death. This issue triggered a second ECtHR ruling in the case of *Hutchinson* soon afterwards, in which the ECtHR appeared to back down in that it reiterated the importance of human dignity under paragraph 19, but taking note of recent UK case law, found no violation of Article 3.[106]

This series of rulings has to be seen in a context of difficult relationships between the United Kingdom and ECtHR, characterised by increasingly vocal criticism of the ECtHR on the part of some members of the UK government and of some senior judges, and the *Hutchinson* ruling may therefore be understood as an attempt on the part of the ECtHR to soothe these tensions. With regard to the argument of time, however, two observations can be made. One is that life orders are as much a deprivation of freedom (by imprisonment) as a deprivation of one's future, or rather of the mere possibility of envisaging (and imagining) one's own future.[107] This comes out very clearly in the UK rulings, which acknowledge the possibility of reviewing the sentence, but only at the complete discretion of the Home Secretary. The second observation is the ECtHR's role (or rather attempt in this case) in synchronising prisoners' human time across Europe, as well as synchronising UK time with ECHR time. In this respect, and beyond a political or diplomatic reading of the *Hutchinson* case, it is clear that the ECtHR can only proceed in a very sensitive way, and that the joint pace of time can only be set through this process of judicial dialogue, in which human dignity arguably plays a key role in raising the issue of human time, as well as in setting the pace and direction in which constitutional time can evolve.

B. Human Dignity as a Compass Towards Modernity

It follows from the definition of human dignity as *kairos* of human rights that, epistemologically, this concept necessarily lies outside and before the (continuous) time of human rights (*chronos*) which is protected by constitutions and adjudication.[108] In terms of positive law, this is well illustrated by

[106] *Hutchinson v United Kingdom*, above n 104.

[107] This is such a severe punishment that some prisoners sentenced to life orders are asking for the death penalty to be re-instated so that they can executed instead of serving their sentence.

[108] This issue perhaps first arose in German scholarship: see G Dürig, 'Der Grundrechtssatz von der Menschenwürde. Entwurf eines praktikabeln Wertsystems der Grundrechte aus Artikel 1 Abs.I in Verbindung mit Artikel 19 Abs.II' (1956) 81 *Archiv für öffentliches Recht* 120. More generally see J Isensee, 'Menschenwürde: die säkuläre Gesellschaft auf der Suche nach dem Absoluten' (2006) 131 *Archiv für öffentliches Recht* 173.

the textual location of human dignity in codified constitutions and human rights instruments, where references to the concept are systematically to be found in three prime positions: in the Preamble,[109] under the very first Article,[110] or under the first Article of the Chapter on fundamental rights.[111] In each of these positions, human dignity is textually outside: outside the normatively binding part of the constitution (in the Preamble), or outside the list of positive rights enumerated in the constitution.

This position of externality is not one of alienation, in the sense of being void of normative meaning or being purely rhetorical. It has raised issues about the normative strength of human dignity when included only in the Preamble[112] and, more frequently and perhaps more controversially, about the legal nature of human dignity. These discussions started in Germany and were triggered by the constitutional location of human dignity under Article 1 and the phrasing '*the following basic rights* shall bind the legislature, the executive and the judiciary as directly applicable law' (emphasis added) under Article 1.3 of the German Basic Law. This has led to a consensus on the fact that human dignity does not quite have the same legal identity as the other enumerated rights and is a source of, or 'mother' of rights (*Muttergrundrecht*).[113] This well-rehearsed German discussion was transposed to the EU level in relation to the EU Charter, where human dignity occupies a similar position under Article 1 of the Charter. The drafters (among whom was the prominent German scholar, Roman Herzog, former president of the German Federal Constitutional Court), however, were quick to pre-empt another half-century of scholarly discussion and hesitations, and explicitly spelt out the dual nature that human dignity has under the Charter, ie both as a right and as a principle.[114]

It is suggested that human dignity's positioning outside human rights temporality makes it possible for judges to use this concept as a sort of 'compass

[109] For instance see the Constitutions of Ireland (1937), France (1946) and Hungary (2011).

[110] See, eg the1949 German Basic Law, the 1991 Romanian Constitution, the 2000 Constitution of Finland and EU Charter of Rights.

[111] See, eg Art 10 of the Spanish Constitution, Art 54 of the 1989 Hungarian Constitution and Art 30 of the 1997 Polish Constitution.

[112] Generally see: L Orgad, 'The Preamble in Constitutional Interpretation' (2010) 8 *International Journal of Constitutional Law* 714.

[113] Generally see A Barak, *Human Dignity: The Constitutional Value and the Constitutional Right* (Cambridge, Cambridge University Press, 2015) 156–69.

[114] 'The dignity of the human person is not only a fundamental right in itself but constitutes the real basis of fundamental rights': Text of the explanations relating to the complete text of the Charter as set out in CHARTE 4487/00 CONVENT 50, CHARTE 4473/00 (2000) 3. C Dupré, 'Article 1: Human Dignity' in S Peers, T Hervey, J Kenner and A Ward (eds), *The EU Charter of Fundamental Rights: A Commentary* (Oxford, CH Beck/Hart Publishing/Nomos, 2014) 3–24.

of interpretation'[115] in order to steer the development of human rights and of constitutionalism towards modernity.[116] Seen in this light, human dignity may be understood in three different and complementary ways which are explored here as three externality pairs interacting with each other. First, the externality of human dignity (as reflected by its positioning in constitutional texts) places this concept out of law's reach. This is one signification of the term 'inviolable', which often complements the reference to human dignity.[117] This adjective can be understood as the solemn promise to take all steps to ensure that human dignity is not breached, making it the axiomatic basis of European constitutionalism.[118] More to the point of my argument, human dignity's inviolability can also be understood in the sense that this concept can never be exhausted (namely, completely defined by the law) nor, importantly, corrupted by (positive) law. Therefore, human dignity's externality to human rights ensures that it remains untouched by the law and that, as such, it can always be a source for constitutional rights.

The second significant pair is externality-eternity. This was first explicitly formulated in the 1949 West German Basic Law under Article 79.3, nicknamed the 'eternity clause'.[119] Due to the specific phrasing and context of this provision, which determines the substantive requirement of future constitutional revisions (whereby the human dignity commitment should remain untouched by any constitutional reform), this eternity has generally been understood as being future-oriented.[120] Understanding human dignity as being located outside the temporality of human rights reveals, however, a different meaning for this concept's eternity. Namely, it does not refer to an everlasting present, but rather to the irrelevance of time: constitutional protection of human dignity does not depend on a particular constitutional text. It pre-

[115] G Rolla, 'Profili Costituzionali della Dignità Umana' in E Ceccherini (ed), *La Tutela della Dignità dell'Uomo* (Naples, Editoriale Scientifica, 2008) 57, 71: 'Infine, non va dimenticato che la dignità ... rappresenta, in un certo senso, la bussola che serve per interpretare il sistema costituzionale dei diritti'.

[116] This approach was explicitly adopted by the Hungarian Constitutional Court between 1990 and 1998, see C Dupré, *Importing the Law in Post-communist Transitions: The Hungarian Constitutional Court and the Right to Human Dignity* (Oxford, Hart Publishing, 2003) 89–92.

[117] For instance, see the German Basic Law, the Spanish Constitution, the Finnish Constitution and the EU Charter.

[118] C Dupré, 'Human Dignity: Rhetoric, Protection, and Instrumentalisation' in GA Tóth (ed), *Constitution for a Disunited Nation: On Hungary's 2011 Fundamental Law* (Budapest, Central European University Press, 2012) 149.

[119] Article 79.3 reads: 'Amendments to this Basic Law affecting the division of the Federation into Länder, their participation on principle in the legislative process, or the principles laid down in Articles 1 and 20 shall be inadmissible'. See UK Preuss, 'The Implications of "Eternity Clauses": The German Experience' (2011) 44 *Israel Law Review* 429.

[120] Generally see A Barak, 'Unconstitutional Constitutional Amendments' (2011) 44 *Israel Law Review* 321; and Y Roznai, 'Unconstitutional Constitutional Amendments: The Migration and Success of a Constitutional Idea' (2013) 61 *American Journal of Comparative Law* 657.

dates the constitution as the memory of recent and ancient times of indignity and inhumanity and it will continue to exist (even) after the constitutional text is amended or replaced. The full significance of the ECtHR's approach to human dignity becomes apparent: protecting dignity is not a question of time (namely, the absence of codification of this concept in 1950) but a question of 'essence'.[121] This ontological approach is also to be found in the positive law of a number of EU Member States, which have started protecting human dignity even in the absence of its specific temporal anchoring in a codified constitution (or bill of rights). As will be recalled from Chapter 4, this is the case in the United Kingdom where one of the very first uses of human dignity in case law presented it as 'an ancient value of the common law'.[122] It is also to be found in France where the constitutional protection of human dignity originates in a decision of the Constitutional Council despite the absence of an explicit dignity provision in the 1958 Constitution.[123] The European Union has arguably also endorsed the externality-eternity approach to human dignity with the Lisbon Treaty. Human dignity is enshrined in two (now familiar) positions: first, it is codified under the second Article of the Lisbon Treaty and the entire first Title of the EU Charter is dedicated to it. As the EU Charter has to be read in line with the ECHR under Article 52.3 EU Charter, the eternity of the EU human dignity concept is arguably also of an ontological nature, which drafters have felt would benefit from being spelt out under Articles 1 to 5 of the EU Charter.

The constitutional eternity of human dignity has sometimes been criticised (certainly in Germany) for the undemocratic nature of this choice, which binds for ever all subsequent drafters of constitutional amendments.[124] However, seen from the wider eternity-externality perspective, human dignity's eternity both points to and makes it possible to think of constitutional time (and the time of human rights) as '*temps long*',[125] as long-lasting time or eternal time: human time continues even after the time of the adoption (or revision) of a specific constitution. In other words, time is not confined to the temporal boundaries of a given constitution (between the time of its coming into force and the time of its revision). Therefore in this context, human dignity as the memory of the time past and as the promise and,—crucially,—imagination of the time yet to be,[126] arguably creates space at the heart of the constitution, that is crucial for democracy and particularly

[121] *SW v United Kingdom*, above n 98, para 44, discussed in Chapter 4.

[122] *R (On the application of A) v East Sussex CC (No 2)* [2003] EWHC 167; (2003) 6 CCLRep 194, para 57.

[123] Constitutional Council, 27 July 1994, Nos 94/343/344 DC, discussed in more detail in Chapter 4.

[124] C Möllers, 'Democracy and Human Dignity: Limits of a Moralized Conception of Rights in German Constitutional Law' (2009) 42 *Israel Law Review* 416.

[125] Ost, above n 15, 112.

[126] Bloch, above n 71.

important for overcoming crises, as it makes it possible to adopt a longer-term perspective and to start imagining and constructing the 'time after'.[127] Understood in this manner, 'eternal' human dignity may well be the ultimate guarantee of democracy as it is always possible to refer back to it, even during undemocratic times.

The third and last pair, externality-critique, is the logical consequence of the above pair. Human dignity's epistemological positioning outside the temporality (*chronos*) of human rights turns the concept into a powerful instrument of critique and assessment of constitutional developments and of human rights' interpretation. As Ost explained so well, human dignity as *kairos* is a questioning (*mise en question*)[128] of the *chronos* of constitution and human rights. Human dignity as *kairos* raises two complementary questions: 'is it right to retain the current *chronos*?' and if not, 'in which direction shall we steer the new *chronos*?' Answering these questions of course raises issues of uchronia and of utopia, that is about the kind of humanity that we want to construct by shaping time in a particular manner through the tools of constitutionalism that are at our disposal now.[129] The questions of uses and abuses of human dignity have often been discussed in the literature, with a semi-veiled critique that human dignity is a bad or weak concept because it is prone to judicial misuses, but without a clear discussion of what a 'right' use of the concept may be.[130] It is suggested that the external positioning of human dignity makes it possible to raise the question of the distinction between right and wrong uses of this concept. *A priori*, the externality-critique idea makes human dignity a compass for guiding decisions about constitutional developments, arguably thus explaining why judicial uses of human dignity have increased so much as a response to the various crises of European constitutionalism since the 1990s. *A posteriori*, the compass logic becomes a logic of critique to assess the quality of these developments and of human rights interpretation that have taken place.[131]

The epistemologically external positioning of human dignity discussed above must not be confused with a quasi-religious role for this concept.

[127] C Lefort, *L'Invention démocratique* (Paris, Fayard, 1994). Human dignity is reported by Horst Dreier to have been on the agenda of the German resistance to Nazism and included in the Kreisauer Memorandum: 'Artikel 1' in H Dreier *et al* (eds), *Grundgesetz Kommentar* (Tübingen, Mohr Siebeck, 2004) 153. On the darker past of dignity, see also Chapters 3 and 7.

[128] Ost, above n 15.

[129] P Häberle, 'Utopien als Literaturgattung des Verfassungsstaates' in P Häberle (ed), *Rechtsvergleichung im Kraftfeld des Verfassungsstaates: Methoden und Inhalte, Kleinstaaten und Entwicklungsländern* (Berlin, Duncker und Humblot, 1992) 695. On the concept of uchronia, see Nowotny, above n 18, 13 and last chapter.

[130] N Rao, 'On the Use and Abuse of Dignity in Constitutional Law' (2008) 14 *Columbia Journal of European Law* 201.

[131] J Habermas, 'Das utopische Gefälle: das Konzept der Menschenwürde und die realistische Utopie der Menschenrechte' (2010) 8 *Blätter für Deutsche und Internationale Politik* 43 and 'The Concept of Dignity and the Realistic Utopia of Human Rights' (2010) 41 *Metaphilosophy* 464.

As argued in the Introduction, human dignity as understood here is definitely a secular concept and its particular meanings can only be discovered and constructed through the mechanism of inclusive, transparent and democratic discussion, and through the procedural channels and fora of European constitutionalism, with (not surprisingly) courts playing a key role.[132] It is therefore important not to even try to fit human dignity into one of the existing legal boxes, exclusively defining it either as a right or as a value. Rather, as indicated at the outset, human dignity is more usefully understood as a heuristic mechanism for discussing and evaluating how best constitutional time should be constructed and human time protected. While the overall commitment to human dignity emanates from the people via the *pouvoir constituant* as reflected in human dignity's constitutional codification, the constant and gradual assessment of the direction and pace of constitutional time can be effectively undertaken by judges, who have to settle individual disputes over time by seeking to synchronise individual and constitutional time.

V. CONCLUSION

Human dignity, as argued in this chapter, is far more than a normative concept, focused on the interpretation of human rights. Its distinctive conceptual feature is that it operates through its close imbrication with constitutional and human time, constructing the present as a negative past and as a process of becoming, making space for a yet-to-be identified unknown for which constitutional provision must nevertheless be made. Ultimately, these temporal features of human dignity provide a mechanism, conceptual and political through case law, for synchronising different human and constitutional temporalities, making it possible for the future to unfold.

[132] As discussed in Chapters 4 and 7.

7

Re-Thinking European Constitutionalism: Dignity, Humanism, Democracy

I. INTRODUCTION

AS DISCUSSED IN the previous chapters, by providing a new foundation for human rights and democracy after the Second World War, human dignity has become one of the structuring principles of European constitutionalism, around which constitutional orders have been re-organised and which I have argued elsewhere has the same importance as the rule of law or as the separation of powers principles.[1] As will be recalled from Chapter 3, founding post-war constitutionalism in human dignity has inverted the relationship between the state and individuals,[2] putting the latter at the normative centre of constitutionalism and creating a special duty for the former to respect and protect individuals' humanity, and to consider the full dimensions of their unique human identity. While previous chapters have used the framework of European constitutionalism in order to understand the actual and potential uses of human dignity, this chapter adopts the converse approach and closes this study by reflecting on human dignity's wider theoretical significance for European constitutionalism. It is suggested that human dignity can shape theoretical understanding in two major ways.

First, the central role played by human dignity in positioning, defining and protecting humanity at the heart of European constitutionalism has arguably given the latter its distinctive identity and purpose as a form of humanism. From a theoretical point of view, human dignity-based constitutionalism in twenty-first century Europe, and specifically since 2009 with the coming into force of the Lisbon Treaty, is therefore no longer primarily and exclusively about defining boundaries of national and supranational sovereignty and rules on citizenship. Rather, it is about protecting

[1] See also C Dupré, 'Human Dignity in Europe: A Foundational Constitutional Principle' (2013) 19 *European Public Law* 319.

[2] L Weinrib, 'Human Dignity as Rights-Protecting Principle' (2004) 17 *National Journal of Constitutional Law* 325.

humanity in all its integrated and evolving dimensions, a purpose arguably best achieved by the complex and dynamic interplay of three types of constitutional orders, namely, the European Union, the European Convention on Human Rights (ECHR) and their common Member States. This particular practical purpose, it is further argued, also provides the theoretical justification for bringing these three constitutional orders together under the normative framework and doctrine of European constitutionalism.

Secondly, and as a result, it is suggested that human dignity-based European constitutionalism has given rise to a particular type of democracy, referred to here as dignity-democracy.[3] While retaining the core features of a liberal democracy, as broadly established before 1945, namely, the importance of elected parliaments as key institutions in the law-making process together with civil and political rights (with in particular the right to vote and key freedoms of thought and expression), dignity-democracy has arisen out of a particular experience and memory of times of inhumanity and of dictatorship. Dignity-democracy's acute awareness of its own vulnerability and propensity to fail and err arguably underpins a particular construction of constitutional time, which the concept of human dignity has been used to shape, distinguishing between the unwanted past, the present and an opening at the heart of the present for a plurality of futures to unfold. Technically, this has been translated by the prominence of a complex network of constitutional courts and human dignity's inviolability, a requirement that has arguably become so central to dignity-democracy that it now binds subsequent constitution-makers.

Ultimately this chapter identifies a number of key issues and features of European constitutionalism that can arguably help make fuller sense of its development. While the chapter does not aim to provide a comprehensive and polished theory, it underlines the emergence and importance of those features of European constitutionalism, thereby opening up new ways of thinking and understanding European constitutionalism, which can hopefully contribute to a better understanding of its complexities and potential for democracy in Europe.

II. CONSTITUTIONALISM AS HUMANISM

This study has brought to the fore the connection between human dignity and European constitutionalism, defining the latter as primarily being about protecting humanity.[4] This section reflects on this apparently simple

[3] For a first mention and exploration of dignity-democracy, see E Daly, *Dignity Rights: Courts, Constitutions and the Worth of the Human Person* (Philadelphia, PA, University of Pennsylvania Press, 2013).

[4] For a recent reflection on this, see Daly, ibid, 7 and 11–25; and A Barak, *Human Dignity: The Constitutional Value and the Constitutional Right* (Cambridge, Cambridge University

statement and argues that European constitutionalism can therefore be understood as a new form of humanism.[5] First of all, European constitutionalism is anchored in a very rich constitutional definition of humanity, including and going beyond its two classic components, namely, the right to life and the concept of citizenship. Moreover, human dignity has arguably given European constitutionalism its purpose and its evolving identity. Finally, thinking European constitutionalism through the prism of its humanism is not only about substance, but also this arguably sheds light on its specific structural make-up, thus providing a theoretical justification for including the ECHR (and with it the Council of Europe) in this normative and doctrinal framework.

A. Constitutional Humanity: More than Life and Citizenship

The first feature of European constitutionalism understood as a form of humanism is its particular definition of human beings, which while encompassing citizenship, is not reduced to this dimension, but includes two further human identities, namely, as man as individual human being and as worker. As discussed in previous chapters, a particularly important dimension of human dignity's role in shaping this definition has been to bring within the constitutional definition of human beings their identity as workers. Under European constitutionalism the protection of workers' human dignity does not flow from their citizenship (namely, the fact that they have the nationality of the state in which they work), but from their humanity as captured under Title I of the EU Charter and comprising a set of absolute rights, notably, not to be killed, not to be tortured, subjected to inhuman or degrading treatment or punishment, not to be held in slavery or forced labour, and not to be trafficked. As a result, what defines European constitutionalism as a humanism is not only this comprehensive set of rights which protects workers' humanity, but is also the absolute nature of these prohibitions, a breach of which may never be justified.

The second feature of European constitutionalism as a form of humanism is that its definition of humanity is anchored in an extremely strong protection of human life, originally derived from the principle of sanctity of life

Press, 2015) 124–37. See also D Feldman, 'Human Dignity as a Legal Value, Part I' (1999) *Public Law* 682, 684–85.

[5] Erin Daly in her book (above) notes the phrase '*democracia humanizada*' coined in Brazil to capture the impact of human dignity on the general understanding and practice of democracy (at 154–55). Peter Häberle is one of the first scholars to have connected constitutionalism with the construction of a particular 'image of man': *Das Menschenbild im Verfassungsstaat*, 4th edn (Berlin, Duncker und Humblot, 2008). I first reflected on this in C Dupré, 'Human Dignity in Europe: A Foundational Constitutional Principle' (2013) 19 *European Public Law* 319.

and technically protected under Article 2 ECHR combined with the two Additional Protocols abolishing the death penalty. As a result, European constitutionalism stands out in relation to other types of constitutionalism, such as the US model with which it has often been compared,[6] for its comprehensive and absolute prohibition on killing human beings, both as a form of criminal punishment as well as assisted suicide to terminally ill patients, as re-iterated by the European Court of Human Rights (ECtHR) in its *Pretty v United Kingdom* ruling in 2002.[7] The importance of the right to life and its connection with democracy were first elaborated by the ECtHR in its *McCann v United Kingdom* judgment,[8] delivered the same year as the ruling in *SW v United Kingdom*,[9] in which the ECtHR formulated its commitment to protecting human dignity as being the essence of the ECHR. Despite this resounding statement, the ECtHR has so far upheld sanctity of life rather than dignity of life in cases of assisted suicide, refusing to consider issues of quality of life under Article 2, and instead preferring to envisage them from the perspective of Article 8 on private life. However, formally and subsequently, it is suggested that the normative hierarchy between life and human dignity was apparently settled by the EU Charter, which enshrined human dignity under its Article 1, referring to its 'inviolability' to give it greater normative strength, above and beyond the right to life, the protection of which remains absolute, but which takes second place after the human dignity-commitment.

Combining these two absolutes has not proved an easy task, leading to much controversy and discussion. What has to be emphasised here is that the human dignity-based protection of human beings, while giving the right to life the fundamental importance discussed above, does not reduce human beings to their mere biological existence or 'bare life'.[10] Moreover, while it is now possible to define human beings in terms of their genetic make-up, European constitutionalism excludes a definition of humanity solely on

[6] See, eg G Nolte (ed), *European and US Constitutionalism* (Cambridge, Cambridge University Press, 2005).

[7] 'The Court is not persuaded that "the right to life" guaranteed in Article 2 can be interpreted as involving a negative aspect ... Article 2 of the Convention ... is unconcerned with issues to do with the quality of living or what a person chooses to do with his or her life ... Article 2 cannot, without a distortion of language, be interpreted as conferring the diametrically opposite right, namely a right to die; nor can it create a right to self-determination in the sense of conferring on an individual the entitlement to choose death rather than life': *Pretty v United Kingdom*, Application no 2346/02, ECtHR, 29 July 2002, at 39.

[8] *McCann and others v United Kingdom*, Application no 18984/91, ECtHR, 27 September 1995. See S Skinner, 'The Core of McCann: Lethal Force and Democracy under the ECHR' in C Ovey *et al* (eds), *The Right to Life: Twenty Years of Legal Developments since McCann v The United Kingdom, Publication in Honour of the Deputy Registrar of the European Court of Human Rights Michael O'Boyle* (2015, forthcoming).

[9] *SW v United Kingdom*, Application no 20166/92, ECtHR, 22 November 1995, discussed in more detail in Chapter 4.

[10] See the discussion on Homo Sacer in Chapter 3.

the basis of scientific and medical criteria.[11] In this respect, a key contribution of human dignity to European constitutionalism has been to position human beings in a relational context vis-à-vis the state and to protect their core constitutional expectation that they should never be reduced to mere instruments or objects at the discretion and service of the sovereign. This 'object formula', originally inspired by Kantian philosophy, has become a synonym of human dignity since the end of the Second World War and has been gradually developed in case law since then. This approach to human dignity has to be seen in the wider sense of a 'civilised' way of relating to each other in society, a term originally used by the ECtHR with reference to a 'civilised marriage' in its judgment on the lawfulness of imposing a criminal sanction in a case of marital rape. Seen from the perspective of constitutionalism as humanism, this emphasis on civilised relationships has brought to the fore the sense of the vulnerability and the fragility of humanity, thus emphasising the importance of human rights protection for the most vulnerable members of society.[12]

The last feature of European constitutionalism as a form of humanism is its ability to protect humanity that does not exist yet, to borrow the phrase from Ernst Bloch as discussed in Chapter 6. This includes human life *in utero* (and to a lesser extent life *in vitro*) through a combination of tight regulations on abortion in Member States and a set of positive obligations to protect the foetus, which, the ECtHR held, are binding on states without it being necessary to establish foetuses' subjective rights to life under Article 2 ECHR.[13] Importantly, the definition of humanity that is not in existence extends beyond human embryos and foetuses, and includes a dimension or form of humanity that cannot be defined and the existence of which may not even be certain. This is perhaps best illustrated by the concept of future generations,[14] which human dignity can help understand and protect, and

[11] Alain Supiot reminds us of the danger of a scientific definition of humanity as constructed and promoted by totalitarianism: 'The horrors of this period of unparalleled atrocities, from Verdun to Hiroshima via Auschwitz and the gulag, were not everywhere the same. But these horrors were variations on a single theme: man considered "scientifically", as "human material" (Nazi terminology) or "human capital" (Communist terminology), subjected to the same calculations of utility and to the same industrial methods as those used to exploit natural resources': A Supiot, *The Spirit of Philadelphia: Social Justice v the Total Market* (S Brown (trans), London, Verso, 2012) 2.

[12] M Neal, '"Not Gods but Animals": Human Dignity and Vulnerable Subjecthood' (2012) 33 *Liverpool Law Review* 177.

[13] *Vo v France*, Application no 53924/00, ECtHR, 8 July 2004.

[14] HS Cho and OW Pedersen, 'Environmental Rights and Future Generations' in M Tushnet, T Fleiner and C Saunders (eds), *Routledge Handbook of Constitutional Law* (London/New York, Routlege, 2013) 401–12; and M Düwell, 'Human Dignity and Future Generations' in M Düwell, J Braarvig, R Brownsword and D Mieth (eds), *The Cambridge Handbook of Human Dignity* (Cambridge, Cambridge University Press, 2014) 551–58. Generally see K Mathis (ed), *Efficiency, Sustainability, and Justice to Future Generations* (Dordrecht, Springer, 2011); and F Ekardt, 'Toward a New Approach in Discourse Theory of Justice and Law' (2012) *Archiv für Rechts-und Sozialphilosophie* 377.

for which European constitutionalism is gradually making normative space at its heart, through a range of provisions including environmental protection and prohibition of human reproductive cloning. This last dimension of humanity points to another core feature of European constitutionalism as a form of humanism, namely, its underpinning assumption that the constitutional definition of humanity is never closed and that it has to be understood as a project always under construction, a process which has driven the development of European constitutionalism and given it its particular identity and purpose.

B. Protecting Humanity: Identity and Purpose of European Constitutionalism

While the general purpose of constitutionalism has been associated with control over the exercise of political power, through its separation in branches and the establishment of a range of constitutionally recognised and protected rights, within the boundaries of a nation-state, it is argued here that the overall purpose of European constitutionalism is an attempt to construct the increasingly complex definition of humanity (sketched out above) in order to capture and protect the complexity of human identities and activities, against the various possible and evolving threats to them. This, as discussed below, is demonstrated by a reconstruction of the key stages of European constitutionalism's development as an endeavour to respond to changing and emerging threats to humanity.

Emblematic of the first stage in the construction of constitutionalism is the 1789 French Declaration of the Rights of Man and Citizen, which gave it its initial identity as a form of humanism. Crucial in this process was taking the source of political sovereignty away from God and placing it in human beings newly defined as citizens.[15] This severing of the constitutional ties with the divine authority arguably made it possible to lay the foundations of a sophisticated constitutional definition of humanity involving three components. The first one is biological, namely, man[16] as individual being born from a woman, with natural rights from birth. This definition implicitly rests on two principles, the principle of secularity, namely, man is no longer God's creature in the realm of constitutionalism; and the principle of equality.[17] The second dimension of human beings' constitutional identity

[15] See Chapter 2.

[16] In this context the term 'man' refers to the abstract constitutional definition of human beings as was originally used by the 1789 Declaration; it must not be read as denoting a bias towards male human beings.

[17] Generally see N Bobbio, *Eguaglianza e Libertà*, 2nd edn (Turin, Einaudi, 2009).

is civic, namely man as citizen, triggering a whole range of political rights, as well as a particular institutional organisation of power, within a constitutional framework. The third dimension of human beings' constitutional identity (developed roughly between 1793 and 1919) addressed the issue of economic activity and relationships, and can be summarised as man as worker, with the concept of human dignity giving the first justification for prohibiting slavery.[18]

The next major stage in the development of constitutionalism as a form of humanism was a response to Europeans' traumatic experience of inhumanity under the Nazi regime, the Holocaust and the Second World War. As a result, human dignity-based constitutionalism was further developed as a deliberate political commitment to erect a rampart against inhumanity, war and dictatorship. Drawing the lessons from the war and the Holocaust, the 1948 United Nations Universal Declaration of Human Rights endorsed and spelled out some key principles inherited from the Enlightenment, namely, fraternity, freedom and secularity. Biologically singular and unique, man was from then on explicitly defined as forming part of the human family and existing in a complex set of fraternal relationships with his fellow human beings. In Europe this particularly inclusive approach to humanity was to a large extent understood as a response to the segregation and extermination of those who, like Jews, homosexuals, Roma and the mentally disabled, had not been deemed human beings by the Nazis, who had relentlessly pursued their extermination. As a result, commitment to protect humanity against systematic destruction by a political regime gave European constitutionalism its distinctive post-war features, being anchored in the sacredness of humanity,—first expressed and codified as the inviolability of human dignity by the German Basic Law in 1949,—and strengthening the threefold definition of humanity as biological being, as citizen and as worker (with an increased protection under the International Labour Organization, reborn in 1944 under the motto that 'labour is not a commodity').[19] Technically, this led to the codification of constitutional rights with an enhanced degree of protection so as to require the absolute quality of those rights, which are particularly crucial for the existence and protection of humanity, exemplarily enshrined under Articles 2, 3 and 4 ECHR. As will be discussed below, but needs to be noted here, it is at that stage that constitutionalism became European and ceased to be mainly understood and implemented within the boundaries of the nation-state.

The subsequent stage in the development of European constitutionalism as a form of humanism particularly affected the EU and was arguably

[18] Discussed in Chapter 2 above.

[19] Article Ia of the Philadelphia Declaration adopted in 1944, see generally Supiot, above n 11. See Chapter 5.

captured in the EU's growing awareness of the importance of endorsing the constitutional definition of humanity developed by the ECHR and by Member States. This led to two key developments of constitutionalism in the early 1990s, which if they are not explicitly related, are arguably not purely coincidental either. The first was the creation of European citizenship by the 1992 Maastricht Treaty, perhaps in an attempt to improve the democratic legitimacy of its increasing competences and integration process, which was (and still is) not always popular or accepted across the EU.[20] The second development affecting European constitutionalism was the peaceful collapse of communist dictatorships in 1989 across Central and Eastern Europe. This brought to the fore the importance of civil and political rights and human beings' constitutional identity as citizens. Perhaps more importantly, this triggered on the part of the EU an awareness that human rights, the protection of which it had largely taken for granted (or happily left to its Member States and the ECHR), could no longer be ignored. This gave rise to the so-called Copenhagen criteria and the conditionality policy, according to which candidate countries had to meet a number of economic and financial criteria as well as human rights, including civil and political rights and protection of minorities. While this approach certainly was not without shortcomings,[21] its significance for the development of European constitutionalism may not be underestimated. In other words, this endeavour to protect human beings through the conditionality policy and the establishment of EU citizenship arguably brought EU constitutionalism closer to that of Member States and to the ECHR, paving the way towards an overarching commitment to democracy in 1996 with the Amsterdam Treaty. It is from this period that the EU definition of human beings started to evolve from a primarily *homo economicus* approach to humanity, to a fuller picture of human beings in all their dimensions and complexities.

2009, with the coming into force of the Lisbon Treaty and the EU Charter, marks the latest stage in the construction of European constitutionalism and can be seen as crowning the post-war developments mentioned above, inaugurating the age of dignity. On paper, the Treaty arguably fulfils the human dignity promise made in the immediate post-war era and offers the most complex definition of humanity so far, including its biological and genetic dimensions, civic identity, and the identity as workers; finally and importantly, this definition includes future generations (that may be understood

[20] N Reich, 'A European Constitution for Citizens: Reflections on the Rethinking of Union and Community Law' (1997) 3 *European Law Journal* 131. More recently, see W Maas, 'The Origins, Evolution, and Political Objectives of EU Citizenship' (2014) 15 *German Law Journal* 797 and A J Menéndez, 'Which Citizenship? Whose Europe? The Many Paradoxes of European Citizenship' (2014) 15 *German Law Journal* 907.

[21] A Williams, 'Enlargement of the EU and Human Rights Conditionality: A Policy of Distinction?' (2000) 25 *European Law Review* 610.

under the prohibition on human reproductive cloning and the commitment to a 'high level' of environmental quality as enshrined under Article 37 EU Charter).[22] In practice, this is translated by a uniquely broad range of rights protected under the EU Charter, and while the direct enforceability or justiciability of some of these provisions is still being discussed (and disputed by some), their inclusion in the same supranational bill of rights can be noted as closing the rift between types of rights that had split Europe during the Cold War. This arguably marks a significant development in European constitutionalism, which no longer has civil and political rights as its main (if not exclusive) focus, but also embraces social, economic and cultural rights.

This construction of European constitutionalism's primary aim as the protection of humanity does not, of course, exclude the economic dimension of the EU. What it does, however, is to set it in the longer-term development of constitutionalism in Europe and in the wider context of its interaction with Member States and with the ECHR. This contextualisation is crucial in highlighting the economic dimension as being just one dimension of European activities, and more precisely, as a dimension the purpose of which is not more integration per se. Rather, seen from the perspective of humanism, European economic integration arguably becomes a means to an end, namely, to sustain and develop the sophisticated definition of humanity and its protection, a process that can only enfold in a democratic framework, with due involvement of EU citizens and all those living and working in the EU, and due consideration of all the minorities (as discussed in the second part of this chapter).

C. The ECHR as Nexus of European Constitutionalism

The human dignity-commitment of the post-war era has led to the creation (or consolidation) of an international level of human rights protection, both in response to the experience that states could be the perpetrators of the worst human rights violations, and as an acknowledgement of the universal reach of human rights. As is well-known, in Europe this approach to human rights has led to the creation of the Council of Europe and the adoption of the ECHR with a unique system of protection centred on a specialist supranational court before which individuals can bring a petition against a High Contracting Party. The ECHR, which was originally set up as a separate and parallel order to that of the European Union (or EEC at first), has

[22] E Morgera and G Marín Durán, 'Article 37: Environmental Protection' in S Peers, T Hervey, J Kenner and A Ward (eds), *The EU Charter of Fundamental Rights: A Commentary* (Oxford, CH Beck/Hart Publishing, 2014) 983–1003. See also A Boyle, 'Human Rights and the Environment: Where Next?' (2012) 23 *European Journal of International Law* 613.

gradually been connected to the EU in two important stages: in the 1990s as a consequence of the conditionality policy, and in 2009 with the Lisbon Treaty providing for a possible EU accession to the ECHR and the requirement that the EU Charter rights should have the same meaning and scope as their counterparts in the ECHR. Understanding European constitutionalism as a form of humanism arguably sheds light on the theoretical significance of this development as a strategy to protect humanity and democracy, which is only possible in a fully European context.[23]

It is suggested that the constitutional definition of humanity at the heart of European constitutionalism has now reached such a level of sophistication that it can no longer be effectively protected by and within the sole boundaries of each constitutional order comprised in it. In other words, the sustained protection of humanity requires the continuous and balanced interplay among these different orders. In this respect, four factors are arguably determinant. The first factor is the externality of judicial scrutiny made possible by the ECtHR, which may sanction breaches of human rights as the case may be, as well as importantly promote judicial conversations, the only way that a more complete image of humanity can be shaped, that is one that captures a fuller range of its identities by drawing on comparative references and standards across Europe. In addition the ECtHR's externality places it in a pivotal position between Member States on the one hand, and between Member States and the EU (CJEU) on the other. In connecting constitutional orders, which are otherwise not formally always connected, the ECtHR provides a valuable channel of judicial communication and contributes to the consistency of human rights standards set by courts across the EU. The second factor is the ECtHR's specialism in the promotion of human rights and democracy, which has given it not only a unique expertise in this area, compared to domestic constitutional courts, and particularly to the CJEU which is a generalist court. Moreover and crucially, the ECHR adjudication is primarily focused on human rights considerations, rather than on economic considerations (as in the EU) or issues of national security or sensitivity (as may happen in Member States). It is not the case, of course, that the ECtHR is oblivious to these dimensions in its jurisprudence, but these issues are considered in the light of human rights, and not the other way round. In other words, with the ECHR protection of human rights is the rule and considerations of economic or national interest are the exception, a logic of interpretation which makes the whole difference to the

[23] The section focuses on the ECHR because the Lisbon Treaty explicitly refers to it. However, the overall argument made here could be extended to other Council of Europe institutions and in particular to the Venice Commission; see C Dupré, 'Unconstitutional Constitutions: A Timely Concept' in A von Bogdandy and P Sonnevend (eds), *Constitutional Crisis in the European Constitutional Area: Theory, Law, Politics in Hungary and Romania* (Oxford, Hart Publishing, 2015) 351, 362–63.

quality and outcome of judicial reasoning and construction of human rights. The third determinant factor in the sustained development of humanity's more sophisticated definition is arguably the possibility for individuals to bring their human rights claims before the ECtHR. As will be recalled, the sheer quantity of individual petitions, generating vast amounts of petitions and a caseload that is difficult to manage, have not been without problems for the ECtHR. What is often forgotten, however, is that this system has had the merit of bringing before the ECtHR a very wide range of applicants, each with her or his story, unique identity and (problematic) activity, leading the ECtHR constantly to fine-tune its case law to reflect the complexity of human experiences and vulnerability. It is suggested that it is only in this way—namely, without the mediation of preliminary rulings that would inevitably sanitise the complexity of human identities and needs—that the ECtHR has been able to develop its unique sensitivity for humanity at the heart of its protection of human dignity. The fourth and last factor is the ECtHR's particular role in shaping time by ensuring constitutional time's continuity across the EU, despite the discontinuities introduced by the many reforms of EC and EU Treaties and (substantial) revisions of constitutions or adoption of new constitutions. Against these changes, the ECHR has remained a constant and overarching point of reference since 1950, holding together European constitutionalism in its purpose to protect human rights and democracy. As will be recalled, the ECtHR's role in shaping constitutional time further involves a complex process of synchronising the various temporalities and rhythms across European constitutional orders. At the heart of this process is the living instrument method of interpretation deployed by the ECtHR and based on sensitive references to comparative law read in the light of the present day conditions. The pivotal position of the ECtHR discussed above gives this synchronisation process its (actual and potential) full European scope.

As a result, it is suggested that it is only by bringing the ECtHR into the theoretical framework of European constitutionalism that human beings can be considered in terms of the wide range of integrated dimensions of their complex identities, not just as petitioners but first and foremost as human beings, and not through the necessarily reductive prism of EU law. This points to the significance of an integrated European approach to protecting human beings, in the full and intertwined range of their identities, rather than from the dominant perspective of a single constitutional order, namely (and to put things a little crudely), primarily as *homo economicus* in the EU, as nationals in Member States or through the almost exclusive lens of their civil and political rights by the ECHR.

This is not to deny the growing importance of human rights protection for and in the EU, as discussed above particularly since the Lisbon Treaty. However, as will also be recalled, European constitutionalism is rooted in the experience that states cannot be trusted to protect humanity fully and effectively. As a result, in the same way that the constitutional protection of human rights available in Member States was not deemed to be a sufficient guarantee for their actual protection, the existing protection of human rights in the EU cannot be deemed sufficient in the absence of scrutiny by a specialist and external judicial body. This becomes particularly relevant since the failure of the EU accession process in December 2014,[24] which deprived the EU of a clearly structured institutional bridge with the ECHR in practice. The only bridge between the EU human rights developments and the ECHR left as a result is the requirement of interpretation under Article 52.3 EU Charter, the development of which arguably requires the conceptualisation of these connections in a more theoretical way in the framework of the tripartite and fully connected European constitutionalism outlined here.[25] Moreover, bringing together in the same theoretical framework of constitutionalism the EU, the ECHR and their shared Member States can shed light on the complex connections that have developed de facto over the years among these constitutional orders and, hopefully, can contribute to refining their construction.[26]

Overall, seen from the perspective of European constitutionalism as a form of humanism, the ECtHR becomes the theoretical nexus of European constitutionalism, without which the latter loses its distinctive identity and purpose, as well as the theoretical rationale for judicial interaction across its component constitutional orders. In fact, as is discussed below, this tripartite theoretical construction of European constitutionalism is so significant that it has given rise to a distinct type of democracy, referred to here as dignity-democracy.

III. DIGNITY-DEMOCRACY

Historically, the rise of human dignity could only take place after a liberal democratic framework had been established.[27] Moreover, it was the

[24] S Peers, 'The EU's Accession to the ECHR: The Dream Becomes a Nightmare' (2015) 16 *German Law Journal* 214.

[25] S Peers and S Prechal, 'Article 52: Scope and Interpretation of Rights and Principles' in S Peers, T Hervey, J Kenner and A Ward (eds), *The EU Charter of Fundamental Rights: A Commentary* (Oxford, CH Beck/Hart Publishing, 2014) 1455–1521; see also B Petkova, 'Three Levels of Dialogue in Precedent Formation at the CJEU and ECtHR' in K Dzehtsiarou, T Konstadinides, T Lock and N O'Meara (eds), *Human Rights Law in Europe: The Influence, Overlaps and Contradictions of the EU and ECHR* (London, Routledge, 2014) 73–91.

[26] K Dzehtsiarou, T Konstadinides, T Lock and N O'Meara (eds), *Human Rights Law in Europe: The Influence, Overlaps and Contradictions of the EU and ECHR* (London, Routledge, 2014).

[27] *A contrario* and as discussed in Chapter 2, the constitutional positioning of dignity in the sovereign has led to autocratic and imperial regimes, as under the Napoleonic rule. More generally, see RE Howard and J Donelly, 'Human Dignity, Human Rights and Political Regimes' (1986) 80 *American Political Science Review* 801.

realisation that human beings can take control over and shape their collective destiny that led to the creation both of the concepts of citizen and of democracy. The historical developments of human dignity have therefore largely followed the vicissitudes of democracy in Europe,[28] and the connection between dignity and democracy are now beyond doubt.[29] This section discusses three of the main distinctive features of this connection, namely, its particular construction of constitutional time, the key role played by the interaction of constitutional courts across Europe. Above all perhaps, its foundation in the human dignity-commitment, common to the ECHR, Member States and the EU since 2009, is not only tightly interlocked as a foundation of European constitutionalism: as a result, and arguably, it binds subsequent constitution-makers.

A. A Particular Construction of Time

Dignity-democracy is rooted in the acute and painful awareness that time is not necessarily mono-directional, and that if inhumanity happened once, it could very well happen again, albeit perhaps under a different guise.[30] Ultimately therefore, what is brought to light by the foundation of European constitutionalism in the 1949 human dignity commitment, which was endorsed and re-activated in 1989 and 2009, is the particular philosophy of history that has so far driven its construction and continues to drive it in the twenty-first century, namely, that democracy can never be achieved or guaranteed once and for all. As will be recalled from previous chapters, a key feature of European constitutionalism is its endeavour to set clear boundaries between the unwanted past kept at bay by the set of absolute prohibitions that now make up the normative core of human dignity under the EU Charter. The present, however, is not just understood and

[28] C Dupré, 'Dignity, Democracy, Civilisation' (2012) 33 *Liverpool Law Review* 263, 265.

[29] P Häberle, *L'État constitutionnel* (M Roffi (trans), C Grewe (rev and ed), Aix-en-Provence, Presses Universitaires d'Aix-Marseille, 2004) 159. P Häberle, *Europäische Verfassungslehre*, 6th edn (Baden-Baden, Nomos, 2009). More recently: '[democracy and human dignity] have an ontological relationship to one another: the recognition of human dignity enhances democratic praxis, and the democratic consolidation results in a more robust sense of human dignity': E Daly, *Dignity Rights: Courts, Constitutions, and the Worth of the Human Person* (Philadelphia, PA, University of Pennsylvania Press, 2013) 134. The connections between dignity and democracy have also been explored (so far in parallel) by some political scientists and theorists broadly as from the perspective of dignity defined as the antithesis to humiliation; see, eg A Margalit, *The Decent Society* (N Goldblum (trans), Cambridge, MA, Harvard University Press, 1996); and J Ober, 'Democracy's Dignity' (2012) 106 *American Political Science Review* 827.

[30] J Habermas, 'Learning by Disaster? A Diagnostic Look Back on the Short 20th Century' (1998) 3 *Constellations* 307; and K Günther, 'The Legacies of Injustice and Fear: A European Approach to Human Rights and their Effects on Political Culture' in P Alston (ed), *The EU and Human Rights* (Oxford, Oxford University Press, 1999) 117–44.

constructed as the rejection of a negative past, but rather it is considered and promoted as a constant process of democratisation, in which human beings can be active participants in the construction of constitutional time, making it therefore possible to protect a plurality of individual temporalities or (as discussed in Chapter 6) *Eigenzeit*, thus allowing them to unfold simultaneously and peacefully. In this process, human dignity has been a key tool used (primarily if not perhaps exclusively) by judges in order to synchronise these plural temporalities. Moreover, under the paradigm of European constitutionalism, the present is not just made of the smooth repetition of the same, but is instead a time which makes space for discontinuities and hesitations. Human dignity constructed as *kairos* (to borrow from François Ost as discussed in Chapter 6)[31] is what makes it possible to acknowledge these temporal hiccups and irregularities and, therefore, to overcome them by making space for the new and the unknown at the heart of the present.[32] While it is by definition unknown and kept open by European constitutionalism, the constitutional construction of the future is grounded in a spirit of emancipation, namely, in the fundamental hope that the future will be better than the present. In practice, this has given rise to a particular technique of judicial interpretation of human rights, epitomised by the living instrument doctrine of interpretation of the ECtHR, characterised by its future-facing dynamic (to contrast it with the past-facing approach of the originalist type of interpretation) towards an enhanced degree of human rights protection.[33]

Overall therefore, dignity-democracy is a type of democracy in which the fallibility of its institutions is acknowledged and addressed, typically but not exclusively, through regular elections and the possibility of amending constitutions and foundational treaties (at the supranational levels). Constitutional judges have been given a specific role in this process as expressed by Aharon Barak in his typically eloquent manner:

> Indeed, if we wish to preserve democracy, we cannot take its existence for granted. We must fight for it. This is certainly the case for new democracies, but it is also true of the old and well-established ones. The assumption that 'it cannot happen to us' can no longer be accepted. Anything can happen. If democracy was perverted and destroyed in the Germany of Kant, Beethoven and Goethe, it can happen anywhere. If we do not protect democracy, democracy will not protect us. I do not know whether the judges in Germany could have prevented Hitler from

[31] F Ost, *Le temps du droit* (Paris, Odile Jacob, 1999).

[32] C Dupré, 'Dignity, Democracy, Civilisation' (2012) 33 *Liverpool Law Review* 272: 'What reliance on dignity ... can achieve, however, is to flag up the novelty of a problem that cannot be expressed with the existing and more familiar tools and words of law, and to make space in judicial reasoning for discussing it'.

[33] Reliance on comparative law as part of the living instrument doctrine in the ECHR (as well as in similar approaches at the domestic level) is a key feature of European constitutionalism, which is also discussed below from the perspective of legitimacy of constitutional adjudication.

> coming to power in the 1930s. But I do know that a lesson of the Holocaust and of World War II is the need to enact democratic constitutions and to ensure that they are put into effect by judges whose main task is to protect democracy. It was this awareness that, in the post-World War II era, helped promote the idea of judicial review of legislative action and made human rights central.[34]

Seen in this light, the connection between the codification of human dignity and the rise of constitutional courts in Europe since the beginning of the post-war period assumes its full theoretical significance as being central to the institutional design of European constitutionalism, as well as to the legitimacy of human rights adjudication in dignity-democracy.

B. Constitutional Courts and their Democratic Legitimacy

Constitutional courts established since 1949 have been a novel and central institutional feature of European constitutionalism.[35] Their distinctive characteristic lies in the complex connections that bring them together with the two supranational courts (namely, the ECJ/CJEU and the ECtHR) in a sophisticated cross-European judicial network.[36] These courts' development has not been without criticism, largely based on their apparent competition (or rivalry) with each other or on the argument that they conflict with the historically central institutions of representative (or majority) democracy, namely, national parliaments and governments. In particular, recurring in the political and scholarly criticism has been the issue of constitutional courts' activism, which according to the critics has led courts to enter the territory of law-and-policy-making reserved for the elected parliament, and to impinge on the law-maker's democratic sovereignty.[37]

To be sure, constitutional courts and the two supranational courts are not devoid of design faults; nor are judges always right and their case law therefore certainly deserves sustained critical scrutiny by scholars and the

[34] A Barak, *The Judge in a Democracy* (Princeton, NJ, Princeton University, 2006) 20–21.

[35] See Chapter 3.

[36] M Claes, M de Visser, P Popelier and C Van de Heyning (eds), *Constitutional Conversations in Europe: Actors, Topics and Procedures* (Cambridge, Intersentia, 2012); see also J Komárek, 'National Constitutional Courts in the European Constitutional Democracy' (2014) 12 *International Journal of Constitutional Law* 525.

[37] Over recent years, criticism of the ECtHR has increased: K Lörcher, 'The Future of the European Court of Human Rights in the Light of the Brighton Declaration' in F Dorssemont, K Lörcher and I Schömann (eds), *The European Convention on Human Rights and the Employment Relation* (Oxford, Hart Publishing, 2013) 93–104. Criticism of the Constitutional Court has been particularly virulent in Hungary since the election of the Fidesz Prime Minister in 2010, culminating in a substantial reduction of the Constitutional Court's competences and number of judges through constitutional revision, see OW Lembcke and C Boulanger, 'Between Revolution and Constitution: The Roles of the Hungarian Constitutional Court' in GA Tóth (ed), *Constitution for a Disunited Nation: On Hungary's 2011 Fundamental Law* (Budapest, Central European University Press, 2012) 269–99.

political community alike. However, what the attacks against constitutional and supranational courts (perceived as a rival institutions to elected parliaments) arguably miss is the key role played by courts through human rights adjudication and in particular through their construction of human dignity in fostering the legitimacy of dignity-democracy. As Erin Daly perceptively observed, 'dignity rights may perhaps be the best justification for judicial activism rather than the worst illustration of it … the purpose and the effect of judicial interpolation are to enhance not the court's authority, but the people's'.[38]

In the context of European constitutionalism, this statement is particularly pertinent, as will be remembered from Chapter 4, as those who have benefitted from human dignity are what can be called here the voiceless minorities.[39] More precisely, they include the minorities understood numerically as a proportionally smaller group of people, such as homosexuals, transsexuals or foreigners. These minorities further include those who are in a situation of being dominated (by a majority), namely, those who are in a position of economic or other dependence on more powerful others, such as workers in relation to their employers and more generally what Alain Supiot calls the 'total market',[40] the poor, as well as women both in the domestic and work contexts.

The second feature of dignity-democracy is therefore the particular institutional design of its court system, which reflects the multi-layered imbrication of national and supranational levels of normativity. Much has been written about multi-layered constitutionalism,[41] with much of the discussion focusing on the thorny issue of the changing sovereignty of states as a result. Seen from the perspective of dignity-democracy these developments bring to

[38] Daly, above n 29, 145.

[39] By listening to them, judges have played a key role in giving the victims a voice. As such they form part of what K Günther calls 'complex universalism' which is 'procedural and deliberative. The procedural element consists in the inclusion of every single individual who raises his or her voice': 'The Legacies of Injustice and Fear: A European Approach to Human Rights and their Effects on Political Culture' in P Alston (ed), *The EU and Human Rights* (Oxford, Oxford University Press, 1999) 117, 120; see also J-P Costa, *La Cour Européenne des Droits de l'Homme: des juges pour la liberté* (Paris, Dalloz, 2013) 108–22.

[40] Supiot, above n 11. Due to the specialist nature of work-related disputes, generally settled by employment tribunals and courts, there is little constitutional case law on work and human dignity. As will be recalled from Chapter 4, the first dignity ruling of the Hungarian Constitutional Court in 1990 involved workers' right not to be automatically represented by trade unions. More recently, the ECtHR has delivered a number of rulings involving workers' rights, see V Mantouvalou, 'Labour Rights in the European Convention on Human Rights: An Intellectual Justification for an Integrated Approach to Interpretation' (2013) 13 *Human Rights Law Review* 529; and more generally R O'Connell, 'The Right to Work in the ECHR' (2012) 2 *European Human Rights Law Review* 176.

[41] See, eg I Pernice, 'Multilevel Constitutionalism in the European Union' (2002) 27 *European Law Review* 511; N Walker, 'The Idea of Constitutional Pluralism' (2002) 65 *Modern Law Review* 363 and JHH Weiler and M Wind (eds), *European Constitutionalism Beyond the State* (Cambridge, Cambridge University Press, 2003).

the fore the fact that the original reason for establishing those new levels of normativity and control over the exercise of state sovereignty, particularly in relation to human rights under the ECHR, is the (recent at the time) experience and evidence that sovereign states could no longer be trusted not to fail, and thereby not to destroy both humanity and democracy. The exact scope and boundaries of national and supranational sovereignty need further discussion and precision. However, what is perhaps more significant to note from the perspective of dignity-democracy is the constant interplay of these various levels of normativity, triggering a continuous dynamic process of mutual checks, ensuring that no one level of sovereignty may have the final say.[42] Seen in this light, the dignity-commitment of European constitutionalism enshrined at all normative levels establishes bridges and channels of communication among them, bringing them together in their shared endeavour towards protecting humanity. As has been discussed at length above, courts have played a key role in this dynamic process of gradual construction of human dignity, both through the existing channels of communication and remedies, as well as through the spontaneous deployment of comparative law in judicial reasoning.

Moreover, established as the guardians of their respective constitution and foundational treaty, and in order to protect human beings against human rights violations and abuse of power by the elected law-maker, these courts have played a key role in the constant testing and reactivation of constitution-drafters' foundational dignity-commitment. This points to the third and last institutional feature of dignity-democracy considered here, namely, the particular role of courts in protecting constitutional time, and in ensuring its smooth flow from a rejected past of inhumanity and anti-democracy towards an enhanced level of human rights protection and of democracy. This role was originally developed in a rather spontaneous and ad hoc manner through a particular type of interpretation known as teleological or purposive interpretation.[43] Within the framework of European constitutionalism and dignity-democracy, it is suggested that this type of interpretation has taken the form of a process (or endeavour) of synchronising the flow of constitutional time across the normative orders that make up European constitutionalism, in which reliance on comparative law, deployed as a core technique of interpretation by the ECtHR through the living instrument doctrine, has played a significant role. As will be recalled, with this doctrine the ECtHR has sought to interpret the ECHR rights in

[42] M Kumm, 'Who is the Final Arbiter of Constitutionality in Europe?: Three Conceptions of the Relationship between the German Federal Constitutional Court and the European Court of Justice' (1999) 36 *Common Market Law Review* 351; and A Pliakos and G Agnanostaras, 'Who is the Ultimate Arbiter? The Battle over Judicial Supremacy in EU Law' (2011) 36 *European Law Review* 109.

[43] A Barak, *The Judge in a Democracy* (Princeton, NJ, Princeton University, 2006) 20–21.

light of present day conditions, in a way that acknowledges that social, cultural and political expectations have changed since the adoption of the ECHR in 1950[44] and that protection of human rights must reflect these changes accordingly. Considering these expectations and human rights standards across the Council of Europe (as well as in the international community) therefore makes it possible for the ECtHR to determine the nature of these expectations. What the living instrument method of interpretation has further done is arguably to bring the respondent state's standards into line with common practice and degrees of protection, and thus to bring its past practice (incompatible with the ECHR) into a present characterised by its compatibility with human rights standards in Europe. This, it is further suggested, has led to a smooth flow of time by ensuring that no Member State remains stuck in a past characterised by human rights standards that are no longer acceptable, and that as a result human rights development follows a broadly similar pace across Europe. Former President of the ECtHR, Nicholas Bratza, eloquently described this synchronisation process in the following terms:

> The frequent anchoring of the Court's development of the case law to perceivable developments at national or international levels has been a further feature of the Court's case law *with a view to ensuring that legal developments keep pace with, but do not leap ahead of, societal changes within Europe.*[45] (emphasis added)

Seen in this light, the use of comparative law, on which the living instrument doctrine draws, arguably provides the ECtHR, and domestic constitutional courts in its wake, with much more than a source of inspiration.[46] Crucially, it legitimises the role of courts in synchronising the flow of constitutional time across Europe, by providing them with a clear direction towards an enhanced degree of human rights protection, together with clear boundaries by limiting the range of legitimate sources of inspiration from which they can draw. Reliance on comparative references outside these boundaries would arguably therefore be illegitimate if they led to the promotion of a lesser quality of human rights and democracy, reversing the course of time as constructed by European constitutionalism since the end of the Second World War. This points to a discussion of legitimate and illegitimate uses of comparative law by courts which is beginning to emerge, but which

[44] See Chapter 3.

[45] N Bratza, 'Living Instrument or Dead Letter: The Future of the European Convention on Human Rights' (2014) 2 *European Human Rights Law Review* 116, 124.

[46] Use of comparative law by courts has also been related to globalisation: G Frankenberg (ed), *Order from Transfer: Comparative Constitutional Design and Legal Culture* (Cheltenham, Edward Elgar, 2013); and E Mak, *Judicial Decision-Making in a Globalised World: A Comparative Analysis of the Changing Practices of Western Highest Courts* (Oxford, Hart Publishing, 2013).

falls outside the scope of this study.[47] As is discussed below, this particular construction of constitutional time is such a central feature of European constitutionalism that it binds the constitution-makers, both at the national level and at the supranational level, namely, the treaty-makers in the EU and Council of Europe.

C. Binding Constitution-Makers

As will be recalled, the dignity-commitment at the heart of European constitutionalism lies in its interlocked foundations and has been endorsed and reactivated by judges, who have woven it deeply into the fabric of constitutionalism.[48] In addition to these mechanisms to secure human dignity and protect this key feature of European constitutionalism, it is argued here that in the paradigm of dignity-democracy, treaty-and constitution-makers (at the national and supranational levels alike) are now bound by the dignity-commitment and that any revision of the constitutional text has to comply with it.[49]

De facto this feature largely results from well-established European practice, whereby constitution-makers have spontaneously endorsed the post-war dignity-commitment, sometimes making it an explicit requirement for constitutional revision of the constitution. In this respect, the so-called eternity clause of the 1949 German Basic Law has been particularly emblematic of this approach.[50] It has also opened a path toward the adoption of similar eternity clauses in other European constitutions.[51] De jure, constitution-makers' duty to commit to human dignity has also gradually been embedded in European constitutionalism, notably with the requirement imposed

[47] Generally see C Dupré, 'Globalisation and Judicial Reasoning: Building Blocks for a Method of Interpretation' in A Halpin and V Roeben (eds), *Theorising the Global Legal Order* (Oxford, Hart Publishing, 2009) 107–23; more recently and in a practical instance, see the problematic 'one-sided legal comparison' undertaken by the Hungarian Constitutional Court in its scrutiny of the constitutional amendment: G Halmai, 'Unconstitutional Constitutional Amendments: Constitutional Courts as Guardians of the Constitution?' (2012) 19 *Constellations* 182, 192–93.

[48] See Chapter 4.

[49] While academic discussion and political concerns have recently focused on problematic constitutional developments in Member States, it is important to note that revision of the EU Treaties is arguably also bound by the dignity-commitment under the paradigm of European constitutionalism proposed here. This raises a range of complex theoretical and practical issues that cannot be developed in this book.

[50] C Möllers, 'Democracy and Human Dignity: Limits of a Moralized Conception of Rights in German Constitutional Law' (2009) 42 *Israel Law Review* 416, and UK Preuss, 'The Implications of "Eternity Clauses": The German Experience' (2011) 44 *Israel Law Review* 429.

[51] Y Roznai, 'Unconstitutional Constitutional Amendments: The Migration and Success of a Constitutional Idea' (2013) 61 *American Journal of Comparative Law* 657, 685–90. The author notes the cases of Italy, Austria, the Czech Republic and Greece, with the Greek Constitution's explicit reference to human dignity as not being amendable (Art 110.1).

on candidate-countries to meet certain conditions, and in particular human rights standards, in order to join the EU after the collapse of Communism, which gave rise in the 1990s to what I have called 'conditionality constitutionalism'.[52] This commitment is now embedded at the highest supranational level, specifically under Articles 2, 6 and 7 of the Treaty on European Union.

From the theoretical perspective of European constitutionalism adopted here, this restriction on the sovereignty of constitution-makers flows from the inviolability of human dignity understood as being positioned outside constitutional time, namely, from its inviolability-eternity. As discussed in Chapter 6, in practice this distinctive temporal status places human dignity beyond the reach of constitution-makers. This 'untouchability' guarantees that human dignity can always remain a good shared by all—as a *res publica* at the heart of dignity-democracy—as it cannot be taken away by constitution-makers. Moreover and as a result, this temporal externality of human dignity guarantees that specific attacks against humanity can continue to be both identified and prohibited (and punished). Finally and crucially, the requirement to respect and protect human dignity arguably makes it possible for constitution-makers always to have a starting point and a new beginning. In other words, far from being an illegitimate restriction on the democratic sovereignty of constitution-makers and of 'the people', the dignity commitment provides them with what has been referred to as the *kairos* of human rights and of constitutionalism, namely, the possibility constantly to question and reinvent democracy,[53] as part of the smooth functioning of democracy, as well as in times of crisis.

In substance, two specific dimensions of human dignity are arguably binding on constitution-makers. The first is its normative core as codified under Title I EU Charter and comprising a set of absolute prohibitions from which the EU and its Member States may never derogate. The second dimension that is binding on constitution-makers is the dynamic and integrated process of judicial construction, which makes the human dignity-commitment real, thus ensuring its effectiveness through a constant re-activation and adjustment to the evolving threats to humanity and democracy. In terms of institutional design, this implies that constitutional courts and the two supranational courts retain their position within the complex judicial network that is characteristic of European constitutionalism, and that existing formal communication channels among them remain open. Moreover and in a theoretical sense, this requires that courts retain their role as guardians of constitutional time, and in particular that they retain their ability

[52] C Dupré, 'Unconstitutional Constitutions: A Timely Concept' in A von Bogdandy and P Sonnevend (eds), *Constitutional Crisis in the European Constitutional Area: Theory, Law, Politics in Hungary and Romania* (Oxford, Hart Publishing, 2015) 351, 355–56.
[53] See Chapter 6.

to synchronise the flow of time away from an inhuman past and toward a future characterised by an enhanced degree of protection of humanity and democracy, by reliance on the living instrument method of interpretation and similar uses of comparative references.

Overall, this affects the scope of constitutional change through formal constitutional revision, as well as the concept of 'constitution-makers' referred to above. To be more precise, under the paradigm of dignity-democracy it is suggested that the distinction between constituent power, namely, the historical '*pouvoir constituant*' (to refer to the 1789 context in which it was first invented and deployed in Europe), and the constituted power (namely, the '*pouvoir constitué*', or power to amend the constitution originally adopted by the '*pouvoir constituant*') has been blurred, with the latter now replacing the former in processes of formal constitutional revision.[54] Importantly, this makes it possible to discuss the quality of constitutional revision in terms of its constitutionality, namely its compatibility with European constitutionalism as constructed here.[55] Seen in this light, the multi-layered nature and integrated dynamic of this model of constitutionalism assumes its full significance as providing a set of criteria, the externality of which is crucial in rendering any assessment of a (contested) amendment's constitutionality possible and meaningful. With this in mind, the tripartite (or triangular) make-up of European constitutionalism envisaged here guarantees an increased level of scrutiny on constitutionality. While discussing the constitutionality of a national constitutional amendment in relation to the EU criteria is a necessary part of this process, and while the EU certainly has a key role and a duty to perform in terms of sanctioning eventual breaches of European constitutionalism,[56] it is suggested that the Council of Europe and its institutions also have a key role to play in this process, as is gradually emerging in practice.[57]

As things currently stand, one missing element in the framework of European constitutionalism is an effective mechanism to sanction serious and systematic breaches of constitutionalism. While the EU can impose a

[54] This distinction is discussed by Preuss, above n 50.

[55] The Hungarian situation prompted me to envisage this in a paper presented in January 2012 in Budapest: C Dupré, 'Unconstitutional Constitutions: A Timely Concept' in A von Bogdandy and P Sonnevend (eds), *Constitutional Crisis in the European Constitutional Area: Theory, Law, Politics in Hungary and Romania* (Oxford, Hart Publishing, 2015) 351–70; see also L Sólyom, 'Normenhierarchie in der Verfassung und verfassungswidrige Vefassungsänderungen' (2014) 55 *Jahrbuch für Ostrecht* 11; and G Halmai, 'Unconstitutional Constitutional Amendments: Constitutional Courts as Guardians of the Constitution?' (2012) 19 *Constellations* 182, 191–99.

[56] JW Müller, 'Should the EU Protect Democracy and the Rule of Law Inside Member States?' (2015) 21 *European Law Journal* 141.

[57] L Bode-Kirchhoff, 'Why the Road from Luxembourg to Strasbourg Leads Through to Venice: The Venice Commission as a Link Between the EU and the ECHR' in K Dzehtsiarou, T Konstadinides, T Lock and N O'Meara (eds), *Human Rights Law in Europe: The Influence, Overlaps and Contradictions of the EU and ECHR* (London, Routledge, 2014) 55–73.

number of sanctions of an economic and political nature under Article 7 TEU in particular, it is not certain that the EU or the ECHR could prevent a systematic turn away from dignity-democracy toward 'illiberal democracy' and eventually authoritarianism from happening in a Member State. In spite of this, European constitutionalism has a crucial role to play in fending off illiberal developments and systemic breaches of human rights. Human dignity's inviolability provides us with a key diagnostic tool in order to assess a given constitutional crisis by discussing the extent to which the substantive core of human dignity, the tripartite interplay of normative levels or the quality of judicial interpretation and construction of constitutional time are affected.

What human dignity further provides is the memory of inhumanity and of anti-democratic times, and the realisation that the constitutional codification of the phrase 'human dignity' on its own, namely understood outside the framework of European constitutionalism and without its particular core of absolute prohibitions, will not guarantee democracy, nor will it guarantee the full protection of humanity, as could be seen under the Franco[58] and Vichy[59] regimes. On that note, it is worth recalling that human dignity and constitutionalism have also a darker past in Europe, which needs further reflection in relation to this humanist and liberal analysis of dignity-democracy. The pre-war darker history of constitutionalism needs to be told and discussed in a fuller and more critical manner,[60] similarly the darker uses of human dignity in past constitutional contexts need to be more fully and more critically acknowledged and studied than they currently are. This, however, does not invalidate this principle's relevance in its current democratic context.[61] On the contrary, it is suggested that a closer and more

[58] The Statute Law of the Spanish People (Fuero de los Españoles) adopted by Franco in 1947 referred to dignity under Art 1: 'The Spanish State proclaims as *the ruling principle of its acts respect for the dignity*, integrity and the liberty of the human person, recognising man, the bearer of eternal values and the member of the national community, as the possessor of duties and rights, the exercise of which duties and rights guarantees in an orderly manner the common good' (emphasis added). L Sanchez Agesta, 'Die Entwicklung der spanischen Verfassung seit 1936' (1961) 10 *Jahrbuch des öffentlichen Rechts* 397. For further references, see H Dreier (ed), *Grundgesetzkommentar* (Tübingen, Mohr Siebeck, 2004) 153, n 66.

[59] The constitutional project drafted by Pétain enshrined human dignity as the foundation of the Vichy régime under its Art 1: 'Liberty and dignity of human persons are supreme values and intangible goods. Their protection demands order and justice from the state, and discipline from citizens'. While this constitutional statute was ultimately not adopted as a French constitution, it is not an inaccurate reflection of what the Vichy régime turned out to be in reality.

[60] C Joerges and NS Ghaleigh (eds), *The Darker Legacies of Law in Europe* (Oxford, Hart Publishing, 2003). Horst Dreier is one of the few constitutional commentators to point this problematic legacy out: H Dreier (ed), *Grundgesetzkommentar* (Tübingen, Mohr Siebeck, 2004) 152–53.

[61] See the Special Issue of the *German Law Journal* of 2005, in particular A Somek, 'Constitutional Erinnerungsarbeit: Ambivalence and Translation' (2006) 5 *German Law Journal* 357, and T Keiser, 'Europeanization as a Challenge to Legal History' (2006) 5 *German Law Journal* 473. See also C Joerges, 'Working Through "Bitter Experiences" Towards a Purified

critical engagement with these anti-democratic and illiberal uses of human dignity in constitutionalism can only help to understand the concept better, as well as to understand the limits and fragility of European constitutionalism in the face of increasing attacks.[62] While it is associated with moments of constitutional foundations, the memory function of human dignity is also essential in times of crisis as a powerful reminder of the disturbing continuities that can connect anti-democracy with democracy.[63]

IV. CONCLUSION

As this chapter has shown by drawing together the main elements of the arguments developed in this book, human dignity has been both a foundation and a key feature of European constitutionalism since the post-war era. Focused on humanity and humanism, and involving an essential theoretical and practical relationship with time, the model of dignity-democracy presented here serves both to explain and to understand the European development of human dignity in constitutional law and human rights, and to provide some new directions for thinking and imagining human rights protection. In this fragile period of the still young twenty-first century, the protective value and potential of European constitutionalism, and above all of dignity-democracy, are acutely important, as threats of human rights and liberal democracy increase in the teeth of crisis.

European Identity? A Critique of the Disregard for History in European Constitutional Theory and Practice' in E O Eriksen, C Joerges and F Rödl (eds), *Law, Democracy and Solidarity in a Post-national Union: The Unsettled Political Order of Europe* (Oxford, Routledge, 2008) 175–92. For a critique of dignity based on its usages in Nazi labour law, see JQ Whitman, 'On Nazi "Honour" and Dignity' in C Joerges and NS Ghaleigh (eds), *The Darker Legacies of Law in Europe* (Oxford, Hart Publishing, 2003) 243.

[62] P Blokker (ed), *New Democracies in Crisis? A Comparative Constitutional Study of the Czech Republic, Hungary, Poland, Romania and Slovakia* (New York, Routledge, 2013), and A von Bogdandy and P Sonnevend (eds), *Constitutional Crisis in the European Constitutional Area: Theory, Law, Politics in Hungary and Romania* (Oxford, Hart Publishing, 2015).

[63] S Skinner (ed), *Fascism and Criminal Law: History, Theory, Continuity* (Oxford, Hart Publishing, 2015); and S Skinner, 'Crimes Against the State and the Intersection of Fascism and Democracy in the 1920s–30s: Vilification, Seditious Libel and the Limits of Legality' (forthcoming, 2015).

8

Conclusion

Comment vivre sans inconnu devant soi?[1]

THE PURPOSE OF this book has been to explore the connections between the concept of human dignity and the rise of a particular type of constitutionalism in Europe since the Second World War. In this process the concept of human dignity has proved a very useful heuristic device for unlocking the equation of European constitutionalism and has brought to light the complex and evolving definition of humanity which lies at its heart, driving its evolution towards an enhanced quality of human rights protection and greater sophistication of constitutional mechanisms to do so. This book has also brought to light the connections between the protection of humanity and the quality of democracy, which in the European context have been such as to give rise to what I call dignity-democracy. It is understood here as a development of the majoritarian model of democracy, and is characterised by its particular construction of constitutional time and its acknowledgment of a richer definition of humanity, namely, one that is going beyond citizenship and the right to life, striving to embrace the complexity of evolving human identities. Moreover, human dignity has also proved to be a very useful tool for navigating across time and space, including the rich pre-war history of human dignity together with a fuller account of its developments since 1945, therefore considerably expanding the territory within which European constitutionalism is otherwise considered when reduced to its EU-Member States dimensions. It has also made it possible to join the dots between the three normative ensembles which make up European constitutionalism, namely, the European Convention on Human Rights (ECHR), the European Union and their Member States, and to propose a theoretical justification for bringing them together under the same normative and doctrinal framework.

Inevitably, as part of this process, I am aware of the gaps that remain in this account as I could not include all the Member States' constitutions

[1] M-C Char *et al* (eds), *Poèmes en archipel: anthologie de textes de René Char* (Paris, Gallimard, 2007) 203.

and had to focus on a selection instead. Similarly, I could not do justice to the richness of human dignity case law across Europe; quite possibly too, and despite my best efforts to be inclusive, some academic commentary might have escaped my attention. Some readers might find my focus too narrow or, on the contrary, my choice of perspective too broad and the distance between some of the more philosophical points and the reality too wide. Others may well find that I have put too much into the dignity bag. Nevertheless, I hope that I have provided in this book a solid enough basis for further reflection, and that I have awakened an interest in a concept that has not yet been much noticed in the EU by scholars, and certainly by some politicians, policy-makers and judges alike. I hope too that the theoretical framework that I have sketched out in this book can support further investigation into constitutionalism and human rights in Europe, and continue to shed light on their less well-known aspects, as well as on those we think we know so well. Above all, perhaps, I hope that I have managed to demonstrate that human dignity and human rights still have much to offer to democracy and humanity, and that European constitutionalism can be an effective framework within which to allow them to achieve their potential.

At the time of writing these lines, the crises of European constitutionalism hit the headlines almost on a daily basis and it has gradually become clear that the title of this book, *The Age of Dignity*, that I originally intended to be a reflection on a democratic and humanistic heritage and achievement, might also be understood as a sort of eulogy for a world gone by, as if it were only possible to understand what we have once we no longer have it. The Euro crisis, in particular, has brought close to the surface the deep fault-lines of democracy, the fragility of human rights as a human endeavour to keep inhumanity at bay and to safeguard our survival as a species and as a civilisation, and the ease with which fundamental human rights, such as the right to vote and the right to life, can be set aside in the governance of Europe. The tectonic plates of democracy and anti-democracy are rubbing against each other, and it is not sure which one will push the other into a new position.[2] Whether the logic of total capitalism (to refer to Alain Supiot's phrase and work used in this book) will triumph over the humanism that European constitutionalism has gradually developed has yet to be seen. Likewise, it is not sure that European constitutionalism will succeed in keeping constitutional time flowing within its established boundaries towards a higher level of human rights protection, giving humanity and democracy the future that they need to exist.

In this context of crisis and deep transformation, human dignity offers, I suggest, a unique resource on which to draw. First of all, as discussed in

[2] This metaphor is borrowed from WG Sebald: L Sharon Schwartz (ed), *The Emergence of Memory: Conversations with WG Sebald* (New York, Seven Stories Press, 2010) 56.

Chapters 6 and 7, its inviolability places human dignity out of reach of positive law, in the sense that its potential can never be exhausted, nor can it arguably be corrupted by positive law. It is therefore always possible to go back to the promise of human dignity, with its memory of inhuman times and aspirations for better futures, to assess the quality of transformation and change, and to orient them towards more justice and democracy. In this process, human dignity can arguably be effectively used to formulate questions and to face the unknown. Secondly, this foundational inviolability is complemented by a very strong normative substance both in terms of the type of rights—namely the right to life, the prohibition of torture, inhuman and degrading treatment and punishment, the prohibition of reproductive human cloning, and the prohibition of slavery, forced labour and human trafficking—and their absolute character explicitly enshrined under the EU Charter and the ECHR, as discussed in Chapter 3. Thirdly, the normative substance of human dignity reaches further and deeper into the fabric of European constitutionalism, giving rise to what I called by reference to the ECHR terminology a particular type of civilisation, within which people can expect to be treated in certain ways by the state and by fellow human beings. As discussed in Chapter 4, this civilising process is largely due to the gradual construction of human dignity by judges across Europe, a process characterised by a remarkable converging emphasis on self-determination and consent; welfare against destitution; the protection of humanity against genetic selection or manipulation and against commodification in a capitalist context; and finally and importantly, a minimum level of hospitality and respect for others, those who are different from the 'norm', such as those who have come from afar fleeing war and torture to seek asylum in the EU. In particular, as shown in Chapter 5, the concept of human dignity has made much more visible a crucial dimension of human identity at the heart of European constitutionalism, namely, that of workers. While in practice their protection through human rights still remains limited and contested, the centrality of this identity is beyond doubt both for the purpose of understanding and reconstructing the development of European constitutionalism, and for the purpose of assessing its democratic quality. This is because, as demonstrated in this book, the three identities of human beings, namely, as singular individuals in biological and genetic terms, as citizen and as worker, are brought together in a constitutional continuum, with the implication that breaching one negatively affects the others.

Does advocating human dignity as a compass for working our way out of the current crisis expect too much of this concept? Historically and as discussed in Chapters 2 and 3, human dignity has proved a very effective tool of constitutional transformation towards a greater quality of democracy and protection of humanity. Its codification in the immediate aftermath of the Second World War is exemplary of its use to deal with trauma and atrocities and to lay the foundations for a world in which human rights and international cooperation could ensure (as it was hoped at the time) that humanity and democracy could never be annihilated again. Human dignity, while occupying a central place within European constitutionalism, is, however, not the only resource that we can draw on in time of crisis. As a right it is complemented by a sophisticated set of other human rights codified at all normative levels (EU, ECHR and in most Member States). In particular, as argued by Susanne Baer, human dignity forms part of a dynamic and potent triangle of rights, together with equality and liberty,[3] driving the construction of human rights and strengthening the protection of human beings and, I suggest, increasing its resilience in the face of adversity. As a constitutional principle, it forms part of a whole cluster of principles that have structured the foundations and the development of constitutionalism in Europe, such as the principles of the rule of law, solidarity and democracy.[4]

Moreover, human dignity forms part of the wider political and normative framework of European constitutionalism, made of the three different types of constitutional order addressed here and consisting altogether of 30 legal systems, interlocked in a number of sophisticated ways and brought together by their shared commitment to human dignity and democracy, as discussed in Chapter 7. While strength does not always lie in numbers (as the majority can be wrong), it may be thought that the number of constitutional orders and their interconnections can serve as a safety mechanism against anti-democratic temptations and actual developments of an illiberal kind. Some reassurance might also be drawn from the corrective mechanisms available within European constitutionalism, in particular (but not exclusively) constitutional review within Member States, human rights adjudication by the ECtHR, as well as sanction proceedings at the EU level, including those under Article 7 TEU. Deployed under this wider constitutional framework, human dignity could certainly be an effective tool to work a way out of the current crisis.

A tool, however, is only effective if used in a proper manner. While this book has endeavoured to clarify and discuss the possible uses of human dignity, there is still scope for improvement in existing practices and procedures. In particular, enhancing the quality of judicial cooperation towards a more consistent interpretation and protection of human rights is likely to be especially important in the years to come, both with regard to the transparency of comparative law references (such as the 'living instrument' doctrine

[3] S Baer, 'Dignity, Liberty, Equality: A Fundamental Rights Triangle of Constitutionalism' (2009) 59 *University of Toronto Law Journal* 417.

[4] A von Bogdandy and J Bast (eds), *Principles of European Constitutional Law*, 2nd edn (Oxford, Hart Publishing, 2010); and A von Bogdandy, 'Common Principles for a Plurality of Orders: A Study on Public Authority in the European Legal Area' (2014) 12 *International Journal of Constitutional Law* 980. See also C Gearty, *Principles of Human Rights Adjudication* (Oxford, Oxford University Press, 2004).

by the ECtHR or the constitutional traditions common to the Member States by the CJEU) and to the creation or clarification of formal communication channels among courts across Europe. Moreover, with individual (alleged) victims of human dignity breaches being key actors, access to justice is another issue crucial to the development of European constitutionalism, in terms of the existence of effective remedies before courts and legal aid provision in order to reach them. What is really at stake in this respect, beyond the always contested issue of resource allocation, is courts' ability to continue their role as custodians of constitutional time, understood not as keeping time safely locked away in the box of the past but, as discussed in Chapters 6 and 7, as ensuring the flow of constitutional time away from a deliberately rejected past towards a future understood as open to a plurality of possibilities.

The stakes are certainly high, particularly considering Europe's darker past of anti-democratic regimes and nationalist antagonisms, which in time of crisis resurface with frightening ease and gain a disquietingly high level of popular support. This leaves neither space for complacency about achievements, nor for foolish idealism that, within the framework of European constitutionalism, democracy and humanity are safe. Nevertheless, it is argued here that the protection of human dignity in law, as analysed in this book, demonstrates both that it has been effectively used to enhance human rights protection in concrete ways, and that it has the potential, at the heart of European constitutionalism, to provide valuable parameters for ongoing advancement of human rights and democracy.

Bibliography

Achtsioglou, E and Doherty, M, 'There Must be Some Way Out of Here: The Crisis, Labour Rights and Member States in the Eye of the Storm' (2014) 20 *European Law Journal* 219

Ackermann, L, *Human Dignity: Lodestar for Equality in South Africa* (Cape Town, Juta & Co, 2012)

Ackermann, T, 'Case C-36/02 Omega Spielhallen-und Automatenaufstellungs-GmbH v Oberbürgermeisterin der Bundestadt Bonn' (2005) 42 *Common Market Law Review* 1107

Adamski, D, 'Europe's (Misguided) Constitution of Economic Prosperity' (2013) 50 *Common Market Law Review* 47

Agamben, G, *Homo Sacer, Sovereign Power and Bare Life* (D Heller-Roazen (trans), Stanford, CA, Stanford University Press, 1998)

Allen, R, Crasnow, R and Beale, A, *Employment Law and Human Rights*, 2nd edn (Oxford, Oxford University Press, 2006)

Allott, P, *Eunomia: New Order for a New World* (Oxford, Oxford University Press, 1990)

—— 'Kant or Won't: Theory and Moral Responsibility (The BISA Lecture, December 1995)' (1997) 23 *Review of International Studies* 339

Alston, P (ed), *The European Union and Human Rights* (Oxford, Oxford University Press, 1999)

—— *Labour Rights as Human Rights* (Oxford, Oxford University Press, 2005)

Andorno, R, 'Human Dignity and Human Rights as Common Ground for a Global Ethics' (2009) *Journal of Medicine and Philosophy* 1

—— 'International Policy and a Universal Conception of Human Dignity' in NJ Palpant and S Dilley (eds), *Human Dignity in Bioethics: From World Views to the Public Square* (Oxford/New York, Routledge, 2013) 127–41

Arendt, H, *The Origins of Totalitarianism* (New York, Harcourt, Brace, 1973)

Arlidge, A and Judge, I, *Magna Carta Uncovered* (Oxford, Hart Publishing, 2015)

Árnason, ÁT, 'A Review of the Icelandic Constitution: Popular Sovereignty or Political Confusion' (2011) *Bij de Buren* 342

Bachelard, G, *La dialectique de la durée*, 4th edn (Paris, Presses Universitaires de France, 2006)

Baer, S, 'Dignity, Liberty, Equality: A Fundamental Rights Triangle of Constitutionalism' (2009) 59 *University of Toronto Law Journal* 417

Bagaric, M and Allan, J, 'The Vacuous Concept of Dignity' (2006) 5 *Journal of Human Rights* 257

Barak, A, *The Judge in a Democracy* (Princeton, NJ, Princeton University, 2006)
—— 'Unconstitutional Constitutional Amendments' (2011) 44 *Israel Law Review* 321
—— 'Human Dignity: The Constitutional Value and the Constitutional Right' in C McCrudden (ed), *Understanding Human Dignity* (Oxford, Oxford University Press, 2013) 361–80
—— *Human Dignity: The Constitutional Value and the Constitutional Right* (Cambridge, Cambridge University Press, 2015)
Barroso, LR, 'Here, There and Everywhere: Human Dignity in Contemporary Law and in the Transnational Discourse' (2012) 35 *Boston College International and Comparative Law Review* 332
Bedford, D, 'MS v UK: Article 3 ECHR, Detention and Mental Health' (2013) 1 *European Human Rights Law Review* 72
—— *Constructing Human Dignity: An Investment Concept* (PhD thesis, University of Exeter School of Law, 2015, manuscript on file with the author)
Beiner, R (ed), *Hannah Arendt: Lectures on Kant's Political Philosophy* (Brighton, Harvester Press, 1982)
Bercusson, B, 'Episodes on the Path Towards the European Social Model: The EU Charter of Fundamental Rights and the Convention on the Future of Europe' in C Barnard, S Deakin and G Morris (eds), *The Future of Labour Law: Liber Amicorum Bob Hepple QC* (Oxford, Hart Publishing, 2004) 179–200
Bercusson, B (ed), *European Labour Law and the EU Charter of Fundamental Rights* (Baden-Baden, Nomos, 2006)
Besselink, LFM, 'The Parameters of Constitutional Conflict after Melloni' (2014) 39 *European Law Review* 531
Beyleveld, D and Brownsword, R, 'Human Dignity, Human Rights and Human Genetics' (1998) 61 *Modern Law Review* 661
—— *Human Dignity in Bioethics and Biolaw* (Oxford, Oxford University Press, 2001)
Bielefeldt, H, *Philosophie der Menschenrechte: Grundlagen eines weltweiten Freiheitsethos* (Darmstadt, Primus Verlag, 1992) 175–201
—— 'Die Menschenwürde als Fundament der Menschenrechte' in V Deile, FJ Hutter, S Kurtenbach and C Tessmer (eds), *Jahrbuch Menschenrechte 2005* (Frankfurt am Main, Suhrkamp, 2004) 143–54
Biggs, H, *Euthanasia, Death with Dignity and the Law* (Oxford, Hart Publishing, 2001)
Binchy, W, 'Dignity as a Constitutional Principle' in O Doyle and E Carolan (eds), *The Irish Constitution: Governance and Values* (Dublin, Thomson Round Hall, 2008) 307–26
Bioy, X, *Le concept de personne humaine en droit public* (Paris, Dalloz, 2003)

—— 'Le concept de dignité, rapport introductif' in L Burgogne-Larsen (ed), *La dignité saisie par les juges en Europe* (Brussels, Bruylant, 2010) 13–51

Bittner, C, 'Human Dignity as a Matter of Legislative Consistency in an Ideal World: The Fundamental Right to Guarantee a Subsistence Minimum in the German Federal Constitutional Court's Judgment of 9 February 2010' (2011) 12 *German Law Journal* 1941

Blackburn, R and Polakiewicz, J (eds), *Fundamental Rights in Europe: The European Convention on Human Rights and its Member States, 1950–2000* (Oxford, Oxford University Press, 2001)

Blanke, T, 'Fair and Just Working Conditions (Art.31)' in B Bercusson (ed), *European Labour Law and the EU Charter of Fundamental Rights* (Baden-Baden, Nomos, 2006) 357–78

Bloch, E, *The Principle of Hope* (N Plaice, S Plaice and P Knight (trans), Cambridge, MA, Massachusetts Institute of Technology Press, 1986)

—— *Natural Law and Human Dignity* (DJ Smith (trans), Cambridge, MA, Massachusetts Institute of Technology Press, 1986)

Blumenberg, H, *Work on Myth* (RM Wallace (trans), Cambridge, MA, Massachusetts Institute of Technology Press, 1990)

Böckenförde, EW, 'Abschied von den Verfassungsvätern: Die Neukommentierung von Art.1 des Grundgesetzes markiert einen Epochenbruch', *Frankfurter Allgemeine Zeitung*, 3 September 2003, 33

—— *Recht, Staat, Freiheit: Studien zur Rechtsphilosophie, Staatstheorie und Rechtssgeschichte* (Frankfurt am Main, Suhrkamp, 2006) 379

Bode-Kirchhoff, L, 'Why the Road from Luxembourg to Strasbourg Leads Through to Venice: The Venice Commission as a Link between the EU and the ECHR' in K Dzehtsiarou, T Konstadinides, T Lock and N O'Meara (eds), *Human Rights Law in Europe: The Influence, Overlaps and Contradictions of the EU and ECHR* (London, Routledge, 2014) 55–73

Bogdandy, A von, 'Common Principles for a Plurality of Orders: A Study on Public Authority in the European Legal Area' (2014) 12 *International Journal of Constitutional Law* 980

Bogdandy, A von and Bast, J (eds), *Principles of European Constitutional Law*, 2nd edn (Oxford, Hart Publishing, 2010)

Bogdandy, A von and Sonnevend, P (eds), *Constitutional Crisis in the European Constitutional Area: Theory, Law, Politics in Hungary and Romania* (Oxford, Hart Publishing, 2015)

Bogdandy, A von *et al*, 'Reverse So Lange: Protecting the Essence of Fundamental Rights Against EU Member States' (2012) 49 *Common Market Law Review* 489

Bogg, A, 'Article 31: Fair and Just Working Conditions' in S Peers, T Hervey, J Kenner and A Ward (eds), *The EU Charter of Fundamental Rights: A Commentary* (Oxford, Hart Publishing/Nomos, 2014) 833–68

Bognetti, G, 'The Concept of Human Dignity in European and US Constitutionalism' in G Nolte (ed), *European and US Constitutionalism* (Cambridge, Cambridge University Press, 2005) 85–107

Blokker, P (ed), *New Democracies in Crisis? A Comparative Constitutional Study of the Czech Republic, Hungary, Poland, Romania and Slovakia* (New York, Routledge, 2013)

Bobbio, N, *The Age of Rights* (A Cameron (trans), Cambridge, Polity Press, 2005)

—— *Eguaglianza e Libertà*, 2nd edn (Turin, Einaudi, 2009)

Bommarius, C, 'Germany's *Sozialstaat* Principle and the Founding Period' (2011) 12 *German Law Journal* 1879

Bon, P and Maus, D (eds), *Les grandes décisions des cours constitutionnelles Européennes* (Paris, Dalloz, 2008)

Bonefeld, W and Psychopedis, K (eds), *Human Dignity: Social Autonomy and the Critique of Capitalism* (Aldershot, Ashgate, 2005)

Borowsky, M, 'Würde des Menschen' in J Meyer (ed), *Kommentar zur Charta der Grundrechte der Europäischen Union,* 3rd edn (Baden-Baden, Nomos, 2011) 94–120

—— 'Würde des Menschen' in MJ Meyer (ed), *Kommentar zur Charta der Grundrechte der Europäischen Union*, 4th edn (Baden-Baden, Nomos Verlag, 2014) 1–124

Boulanger, C, *Hüten, Richten, Gründen: Rollen der Verfassungsgerichte in der Demokratisierung Deutschlands und Ungarns* (Berlin, Epubli, 2013)

Boyle, A, 'Human Rights and the Environment: Where Next?' (2012) 23(3) *European Journal of International Law* 613

Bratza, N, 'Living Instrument or Dead Letter: The Future of the ECHR' (2014) 2 *European Human Rights Law Review* 116

Brown-Weiss, E, 'Our Rights and Obligations to Future Generations for the Environment' (1990) 84 *American Journal of International Law* 198

Brownsword, R, 'Human Dignity, Human Rights and Simply Trying to Do the Right Thing' in C McCrudden (ed), *Understanding Human Dignity* (Oxford, Oxford University Press, 2013) 345–58

Buckley, J, 'NS v Secretary of State for the Home Department (C-411/10)' (2012) 2 *European Human Rights Law Review* 205

Bundesverfassungsgericht (ed), *Nachschlagewerk des Bundesverfassungsgerichts* (Karlsruhe, R v Decker's Verlag/CF Müller, 2004)

Burger, K, *Das Verfassungsprinzip der Menschenwürde in Österreich* (Frankfurt am Main, Peter Lang, 2002)

Burgogne-Larsen, L, 'La dignité dans la jurisprudence de la CEDH' in L Burgogne-Larsen (ed), *La dignité saisie par les juges* (Brussels, Bruylant, 2010) 64–67

Burgogne-Larsen, L (ed), *La dignité saisie par les juges* (Brussels, Bruylant, 2010)

Cappelletti, M (ed), *Access to Justice and the Welfare State* (Alphen aan den Rijn/Stuttgart, Brussels/Florence, Sijthoff/Klett-Cotta/Bruylant/Le Monnier, 1981)
Capps, P, *Human Dignity and the Foundation of International Law* (Oxford, Hart Publishing, 2009)
Carozza, PG, 'Human Dignity and Judicial Interpretation of Human Rights: A Reply' (2008) 19 *European Journal of International Law* 931
Carusi, D, 'Laicità del Diritto e Pari Dignità delle Persone' (2009) 1 *Politica del Diritto* 93
Cassese, A, 'Can the Notion of Inhuman and Degrading Treatment be Applied to Socio-Economic Conditions?' (1994) 2 *European Journal of International Law* 141
Cassirer, E, 'Giovanni Pico della Mirandola: A Study in the History of Renaissance Ideas' (1942) 2 *Journal of History of Ideas* 123
—— *The Philosophy of the Enlightenment* (Princeton, NJ, Princeton University Press, 1951)
Castoriadis, C, *Domaines de l'homme: les carrefours du labyrinthe (2)* (Paris, Points Seuil, 1999)
Ceccherini, E (ed), *La Tutela della Dignità dell'Uomo* (Naples, Editoriale Scientifica, 2008)
Celan, P, 'Corona' in B Wiedemann (ed), *Die Gedichte: Kommentierte Gesamtausgabe* (Frankfurt am Main, Suhrkamp, 2005) 39
Celotto, A, 'Articolo 3' in R Bifulco, A Celotto and M Olivetti (eds), *Commentario alla Costituzione, volume primo* (Milanofiori Assago, UTET Giuridica, 2006) 65–87
Champeil-Desplats, V and Slama, S, 'Qu'elle protège ou qu'elle punisse, la dignité n'est pas la même pour tous' (2014) *Revue des Droits de l'Homme, Actualités Droits-Libertés*
Char, M-C *et al* (eds), *Poèmes en archipel: anthologie de textes de René Char* (Paris, Gallimard, 2007)
Chiti, E and Teixeira, PG, 'The Constitutional Implications of the European Responses to the Financial and Public Debt Crisis' (2013) 50 *Common Market Law Review* 683
Cho, SH and Petersen, OW, 'Environmental Rights and Future Generations' in M Tushnet, T Fleiner and C Saunders (eds), *Routledge Handbook of Constitutional Law* (London and New York, Routledge, 2013) 401–12
Christodoulidis, E and Veitch, S (eds), *Lethe's Law: Justice, Law and Ethics in Reconciliation* (Oxford, Hart Publishing, 2001)
Cieslar, A, Nayer, A and Smeesters, B, *Le droit à l'épanouissement de l'être humain au travail: métamorphoses du droit social* (Brussels, Bruylant, 2007)
Claes, M, de Visser, M, Popelier, P and Van de Heyning, C (eds), *Constitutional Conversations in Europe: Actors, Topics and Procedures* (Cambridge, Intersentia, 2012)

Clements, L, 'Disability, Dignity and Cri du Coeur' (2011) 6 *European Human Rights Law Review* 675

Collste, G, 'Human Dignity, Immigration and Refugees' M Düwell, J Braarvig, R Brownsword and D Mieth (eds), *The Cambridge Handbook of Human Dignity* (Cambridge, Cambridge University Press, 2014) 461–68

Conolly, WE, *Theory Out of Bounds* (Minneapolis, MN, University of Minnesota Press, 2002)

Cornell, D *et al* (eds), *The Dignity Jurisprudence of the Constitutional Court of South Africa: Cases and Materials* (New York, Fordham University Press, 2013)

Costa, J-P, *La Cour Européenne des Droits de l'Homme: des juges pour la liberté* (Paris, Dalloz, 2013)

—— 'Human Dignity in the Jurisprudence of the European Court of Human Rights' in C McCrudden (ed), *Understanding Human Dignity* (Oxford, Oxford University Press, 2013) 393–402

Cotter, J, 'The German Federal Constitutional Court and Welfare Benefits for Asylum Seekers: Consequences for the Direct Provision and Dispersal Scheme in Ireland? Part II' (2013) 2 *Irish Law Times* 23

Coughlin, J, 'Pope John Paul II and the Dignity of the Human Being' (2003) 27 *Harvard Journal of Law and Public Policy* 65

Cuocolo, L, *Tempo e Potere nel Diritto Costituzionale* (Milan, Giuffrè Editore, 2009)

Daly, E, *Dignity Rights: Courts, Constitutions and the Worth of the Human Person* (Philadelphia, PA, University of Pennsylvania Press, 2013)

Davezies, P, 'Évolution des organisations du travail et atteintes à la santé. Contribution au séminaire interdisciplinaire "Les Nouvelles Organisations du Travail"' (1999) 3 *Travailler* 87

De Hert, P and Mantovani, E, 'Specific Rights for Older Persons?' (2011) 4 *European Human Rights Law Review* 398

De Schutter, O, 'Human Rights in Employment Relationships: Contracts as Power' in F Dorssemont, K Lörcher and I Schömann (eds), *The European Convention on Human Rights and the Employment Relation* (Oxford, Hart Publishing, 2013) 105–39

De Visser, M, *Constitutional Review in Europe: A Comparative Analysis* (Oxford, Hart Publishing, 2014)

Deleuze, G and Guattari, F, *What is Philosophy?* (H Tomlinson and G Burchill (trans), London, Verso, 1994)

Di Ciommo, M, *Dignità Umana e Stato Costituzionale* (Florence, Passigli Editori, 2010)

Dolso, GP, 'Articolo 3' in S Bartole and R Bin (eds), *Commentario Breve alla Costituzione* (Padova, CEDAM, 2008) 14–37

Dorssemont, F, Lörcher, K and Schömann, I (eds), *The European Convention on Human Rights and the Employment Relation* (Oxford, Hart Publishing, 2013)

Douglas-Scott, S, 'A Tale of Two Courts: Luxembourg, Strasbourg and the Growing European Human Rights *Acquis*' (2006) 43 *Common Market Law Review* 629
—— 'The European Union and Human Rights after the Treaty of Lisbon' (2011) 11 *Human Rights Law Review* 645
Dreier, H, 'Artikel 1' in H Dreier *et al* (eds), *Grundgesetz Kommentar* (Tübingen, Mohr Siebeck, 2004) 139–231
—— 'Human Dignity in German Law' in M Düwell, J Braarvig, R Brownsword and D Mieth (eds), *The Cambridge Handbook of Human Dignity* (Cambridge, Cambridge University Press, 2014) 375–85
Dreier, H *et al* (eds), *Grundgesetz Kommentar* (Tübingen, Mohr Siebeck, 2004)
Dubout, E, 'La dignité dans la jurisprudence de la Cour de Justice des Communautés' in L Burgogne-Larsen (ed), *La dignité saisie par les juges* (Brussels, Bruylant, 2010) 56–79
Dupré, C, *Importing the Law in Post-communist Transitions: The Hungarian Constitutional Court and the Right to Human Dignity* (Oxford, Hart Publishing, 2003)
—— 'Dignité dans l'Europe constitutionnelle: entre inflation et contradictions' in J Ziller (ed), *L'Européanisation des droits constitutionnels à la lumière de la Constitution pour l'Europe* (Paris, L'Harmattan, 2003) 121–35
—— 'Human Dignity and the Withdrawal of Medical Treatment: A Missed Opportunity?' (2006) 6 *European Human Rights Law Review* 687
—— 'After Reforms: Human Rights Protection in Post-Communist States' (2008) 5 *European Human Rights Law Review* 622
—— 'Unlocking Human Dignity: Towards a Theory for the 21st Century' (2009) 2 *European Human Rights Law Review* 190
—— 'Globalisation and Judicial Reasoning: Building Blocks for a Method of Interpretation' in A Halpin and V Roeben (eds), *Theorising the Global Legal Order* (Oxford, Hart Publishing, 2009) 107–23
—— 'Human Dignity: Rhetoric, Protection, and Instrumentalisation' in GA Tóth (ed), *Constitution for a Disunited Nation: On Hungary's 2011 Fundamental Law* (Budapest, Central European University Press, 2012) 143–70
—— 'Dignity, Democracy, Civilisation' (2013) 33 *Liverpool Law Review* 263
—— 'Human Dignity in Europe: A Foundational Constitutional Principle' (2013) 19 *European Public Law* 319
—— 'Article 1: Human Dignity' in S Peers, T Hervey, J Kenner and A Ward (eds), *The EU Charter of Fundamental Rights: A Commentary* (Oxford, CH Beck/Hart Publishing/Nomos, 2014) 3–24
—— 'Unconstitutional Constitutions: A Timely Concept' in A von Bogdandy and P Sonnevend (eds), *Constitutional Crisis in the European Constitutional Area: Theory, Law, Politics in Hungary and Romania* (Oxford, Hart Publishing, 2015) 351–70

Dupré, C, 'Constructing the Meaning of Human Dignity: Four Questions' in C McCrudden (ed), *Understanding Human Dignity* (Oxford, Oxford University Press, 2013) 113–22

Dupré, C and Yeh, J-r, 'Constitutions and Legitimacy over Time' in M Tushnet, T Fleiner and C Saunders (eds), *Routledge Handbook of Constitutional Law* (Oxford/New York, Routledge, 2013) 45–56

Dürig, G, 'Der Grundrechtssatz von der Menschenwürde: Entwurf eines praktikabeln Wertsystems der Grundrechte aus Art.1 Abs.I in Verbindung mit Art.19 Abs.II des Grundgesetzes' (1956) 81 *Archiv für öffentliches Recht* 117

Düwell, M, Braarvig, J, Brownsword, R and Mieth, D (eds), *The Cambridge Handbook of Human Dignity* (Cambridge, Cambridge University Press, 2014)

—— 'On the Border of Life and Death: Human Dignity and Bioethics' in M Düwell, J Braarvig, R Brownsword and D Mieth (eds), *The Cambridge Handbook of Human Dignity* (Cambridge, Cambridge University Press, 2014) 526–34

—— 'Human Dignity and Future Generations' in M Düwell, J Braarvig, R Brownsword and D Mieth (eds), *The Cambridge Handbook of Human Dignity* (Cambridge, Cambridge University Press, 2014) 551–58

Dworkin, R, *Justice for Hedgehogs* (Cambridge, MA, Belknap Press, 2011)

—— 'What is Democracy?' in GA Tóth (ed), *Constitution for a Disunited Nation: On Hungary's 2011 Fundamental Law* (Budapest, Central European University Press, 2012) 25–34

Dzehtsiarou, K, Konstadinides, T, Lock, T and O'Meara, N (eds), *Human Rights Law in Europe: The Influence, Overlaps and Contradictions of the EU and ECHR* (London, Routledge, 2014)

Eberle, EJ (ed), *Dignity and Liberty: Constitutional Visions in Germany and the United States* (Westport, CT, Praeger, 2002)

—— 'Observations on the Development of Human Dignity and Personality in German Constitutional Law: An Overview' (2013) 33 *Liverpool Law Review* 203

Edelman, B, *La personne en danger* (Paris, Presses Universitaires de France, 1999)

Ekardt, F, 'Toward a New Approach in Discourse Theory of Justice and Law' (2012) *Archiv für Rechts-und Sozialphilosophie* 377

Elster, J, Offe, C and Preuß, UK, *Institutional Design in Post-communist Societies: Rebuilding the Ship at Sea* (Cambridge, Cambridge University Press, 1998)

Feldman, D, 'Human Dignity as a Legal Value, Part I' (1999) *Public Law* 682

—— 'Human Dignity as a Legal Value, Part II' (2000) *Public Law* 61

Fenwick, C and Novitz, T (eds), *Human Rights at Work: Perspectives on Law and Regulation* (Oxford, Hart Publishing, 2010)

Ferrara, G, 'La Pari Dignità Sociale' in *Studi in Onore di Giuseppe Chiarelli, Tomo Secondo* (Milan, Giuffrè, 1974) 1087–105

Finer, SE *et al* (ed), *Comparing Constitutions* (Oxford, Clarendon Press, 1995)

Fletcher, GP, 'Human Dignity as a Constitutional Value' (1984) 22 *University of Western Ontario Law Review* 171

—— 'In God's Image: The Religious Imperative of Equality under the Law' (1999) 99 *Columbia Law Review* 1608

Flick, GM, 'Dignità Umana e Tutela dei Soggetti Deboli: Una Riflessione Problematica' in E Ceccherini (ed), *La Tutela della Dignità dell'Uomo* (Naples, Editoriale Scientifica, 2008) 39–56

Flora, P and Heidenheimer, AJ (eds), *The Development of Welfare States in Europe and America* (New Brunswick, Transaction Books, 1987)

Foster, C, *Human Dignity in Bioethics and Law* (Oxford, Hart Publishing, 2011)

Frahm, K and Gebauer, J, 'Patent auf Leben? Der Luxemburger Gerichtshof und die Biopatent-Richtlinie' (2002) 1 *Europa Recht* 78

Frankenberg, G, *Autorität und Integration: Zur Grammatik von Recht und Verfassung* (Frankfurt am Main, Suhrkamp, 2003)

—— 'Torture and Taboo: An Essay Comparing Paradigms of Organised Cruelty' (2008) 56 *American Journal of Comparative Law* 403

—— 'Human Rights and the Belief in a Just World' (2014) 12 *International Journal of Constitutional Law* 35

Frankenberg, G (ed), *Order from Transfer: Comparative Constitutional Design and Legal Culture* (Cheltenham, Edward Elgar, 2013)

Fraser, D, *Law after Auschwitz: Towards a Jurisprudence of the Holocaust* (Durham, NC, North Carolina Academic Press, 2005)

Fredman, S, *Human Rights Transformed: Positive Rights and Positive Duties* (Oxford, Oxford University Press, 2008)

—— 'Positive Duties and Socio-economic Disadvantage: Bringing Disadvantage onto the Equality Agenda' (2010) 3 *European Human Rights Law Review* 290

Freeman, M, 'The Problem of Secularism in Human Rights Theory' (2004) 26 *Human Rights Quarterly* 475

Frohwerk, A, *Soziale Not in der Rechtssprechung der EGMR* (Tübingen, Mohr Siebeck, 2012)

Frydman, P, 'L'atteinte à la dignité de la personne humaine et les pouvoirs de police municipale' (1995) 6 *Revue Française de Droit Administratif* 1204

Gadamer, HG, *Wer bin Ich und wer bist Du: Kommentar zu Celans 'Atemkristall'* (Frankfurt am Main, Suhrkamp, 1986)

—— *Au commencement de la philosophie: pour une lecture des Présocratiques* (Paris, Seuil, 2001)

Gauchet, M, *La révolution des droits de l'Homme* (Paris, Gallimard, 1989)

Gearty, C, *Principles of Human Rights Adjudication* (Oxford, Oxford University Press, 2004)

—— 'Socio-economic Rights, Basic Needs, and Human Dignity: A Perspective from Law's Front Line' in C McCrudden (ed), *Understanding Human Dignity* (Oxford, Oxford University Press, 2013) 155–72

Gerstenberg, O, 'Expanding the Constitution Beyond the Court: The Case of Euro-Constitutionalism' (2002) 8 *European Law Journal* 172

Ghanea, N, Stephens, A and Walden, R (eds), *Does God Believe in Human Rights? Essays on Religion and Human Rights* (Leiden, Martinus Nijhoff Publishers, 2007)

Giampierretti, M, 'Articolo 41' in S Bartole and R Bin (eds), *Commentario Breve alla Costituzione* (Padova, CEDAM, 2008) 403–19

Giese, B, *Das Würde-Konzept: Eine normfunktionale Explikation des Begriffes Würde in Art.1 Abs 1 GG* (Berlin, Duncker und Humblot, 1975)

Ginsburg, T and Dixon, R (eds), *Comparative Constitutional Law* (Cheltenham, Edward Elgar, 2011)

Giorgis, A, 'Article 31: Fair and Just Working Conditions' in BT Mock and G Demuro (eds), *Human Rights in Europe: Commentary on the Charter of Fundamental Rights of the European Union* (Durham, NC, Carolina Academic Press, 2010) 187–97

Girard, C and Hennette-Vauchez, S (eds), *La dignité de la personne humaine: recherche sur un processus de juridicisation* (Paris, Presses Universitaires de France, 2004)

Glendon, MA, *Rights Talk: The Impoverishment of Political Discourse* (New York, Free Press, 1991)

—— *A World Made New: Eleanor Roosevelt and the Universal Declaration of Human Rights* (New York, Random House, 2002)

Glensy, RD, 'The Right to Dignity' (2011) 66 *Columbia Human Rights Law Review* 65

Godechot, J (ed), *Les Constitutions de la France depuis 1789* (Paris, Garnier Flammarion, 1979

Goos, C, *Innere Freiheit: Eine Rekonstruktion des grundgesetzlichen Würdebegriffs* (Bonn, Bonn University Press, 2011)

—— 'Würde des Menschen: Restoring Human Dignity in Post-Nazi Germany' in C McCrudden (ed), *Understanding Human Dignity* (Oxford, Oxford University Press, 2013) 79–94

Gorz, A, *Métamorphoses du travail: critique de la raison économique* (Paris, Gallimard, 1988)

Grabenwarter, C, *European Convention on Human Rights: A Commentary* (Munich/Oxford, Verlag CH Beck/Hart Publishing, 2014)

Gragl, P, *Accession of the EU to the European Convention on Human Rights* (Oxford, Hart Publishing, 2013)

Graumann, S, 'Human Dignity and People with Disabilities' in M Düwell, J Braarvig, R Brownsword and D Mieth (eds), *The Cambridge Handbook of Human Dignity* (Cambridge, Cambridge University Press, 2014) 484–91

Griller, S and Ziller, J (eds), *The Lisbon Treaty: EU Constitutionalism Without a Constitutional Treaty?* (Vienna, Springer, 2008)

Grimm, D, 'Dignity in a Legal Context: Dignity as an Absolute Right' in C McCrudden (ed), *Understanding Human Dignity* (Oxford, Oxford University Press, 2013) 381–93

Groppi, T and Ponthoreau, MC (eds), *The Use of Foreign Precedents by Constitutional Judges* (Oxford, Hart Publishing, 2013)

Grossi, P, 'Dignità Umana e Libertà nella Carta dei Diritti Fondamentali dell' Unione Europea' in M Siclari (ed), *Contributi allo Studio della Carta dei Diritti Fondamentali dell' Unione Europea* (Turin, Giappichelli, 2003) 41–60

—— 'La Dignità nella Costituzione Italiana' in E Ceccherini (ed), *La Tutela della Dignità dell'Uomo* (Naples, Editoriale Scientifica, 2008) 79–111

Grote, R *et al* (eds), *Die Ordnung der Freiheit: Festschrift f. Christian Starck zum 70. Geburtstag* (Tübingen, Mohr Siebeck, 2007)

Grover, S, 'A Response to Bagaric and Allan's "Vacuous Concept of Dignity"' (2009) 13 *International Journal of Human Rights* 615

Gukosvkj, MA, 'Giovanni Pico della Mirandola: Uomo del Medioevo o del Rinascimento?' in *L'Opera e il Pensiero di Giovanni Pico della Mirandola nella Storia dell'Umanesimo* (Conference Proceedings) (Florence, Istituto di Studi sul Rinascimento, 1965)

Günther, K, 'The Legacies of Injustice and Fear: A European Approach to Human Rights and their Effects on Political Culture' in P Alston (ed), *The European Union and Human Rights* (Oxford, Oxford University Press, 1999) 117–44

Gutiérrez-Gutiérrez, I, 'Die Menschenwürde als europäischer Verfassungsbegriff—Rechtsvergleichender und verfassungsrechtlicher Beitrag zur deutschen Debatte um die Menschenwürde' (2006) 89 *Kritische Vierteljahreschrift für Gesetzgebung und Gesellschaft* 384

Häberle, P, 'Zeit und Verfassung' (1974) 21 *Zeitschrift für Politik* 111

—— 'Demokratische Verfassungstheorie im Lichte des Möglichkeitsdenkens' (1977) 107 *Archiv für öffentliches Recht* 27

—— '"Gott" im Verfassungsstaat?' in P Häberle (ed), *Rechtsvergleichung im Kraftfeld des Verfassungsstaates: Methoden und Inhalte, Kleinstaaten und Entwicklungsländer* (Berlin, Duncker und Humblot, 1992) 212–25

—— 'Zeit und Verfassungskultur' in P Häberle (ed), *Rechtsvergleichung im Kraftfeld des Verfassungsstaates: Methoden und Inhalte, Kleinstaaten und Entwicklungsländer* (Berlin, Duncker und Humblot, 1992) 627–72

—— '1789 als Teil der Geschichte, Gegenwart und Zukunft des Verfassungsstaates' in P Häberle (ed), *Rechtsvergleichung im Kraftfeld des Verfassungsstaates: Methoden und Inhalte, Kleinstaaten und Entwicklungsländer* (Berlin, Duncker und Humblot, 1992) 685–720

—— 'Aspekte einer Verfassungslehre der Arbeit' in P Häberle (ed), *Rechtsvergleichung im Kraftfeld des Verfassungsstaates: Methoden und Inhalte, Kleinstaaten und Entwicklungsländer* (Berlin, Duncker und Humblot, 1992) 524–51

—— 'Utopien als Literaturgattung des Verfassungsstaates' in P Häberle (ed), *Rechtsvergleichung im Kraftfeld des Verfassungsstaates: Methoden und Inhalte, Kleinstaaten und Entwicklungsländer* (Berlin, Duncker und Humblot, 1992) 673–783

—— *L'État constitutionnel* (M Roffi (trans), C Grewe (ed), Aix-en-Provence, Presses Universitaires d'Aix-Marseille, 2004)

—— *Das Menschenbild im Verfassungsstaat*, 4th edn (Berlin, Duncker und Humblot, 2008)

—— *Europäische Verfassungslehre*, 6th edn (Baden-Baden, Nomos, 2009)

—— 'Un jurista universal nacido en Europa: Interview with F Balaguer Callejón' (2010) 13 *Revista de Derecho Costitucional Español*, available at www.ugr.es/<redece/REDCE13/articulos/12Entrevista.htm

Häberle, P (ed), *Rechtsvergleichung im Kraftfeld des Verfassungsstaates: Methoden und Inhalte, Kleinstaaten und Entwicklungsländer* (Berlin, Duncker und Humblot, 1992)

Habermas, J, 'Learning by Disaster? A Diagnostic Look Back on the Short 20th Century' (1998) 5 *Constellations* 307

—— 'Das utopische Gefälle, das Konzept der Menschenwürde und die realistische Utopie der Menschenrechte' (2010) 8 *Blätter für Deutsche und Internationale Politik* 43

—— 'The Concept of Dignity and the Realistic Utopia of Human Rights' (2010) 41 *Metaphilosophy* 464

Halmai, G, 'Unconstitutional Constitutional Amendments: Constitutional Courts as Guardians of the Constitution?' (2012) 19 *Constellations* 182

Harmon, SHE, Laurie, G and Courtney, A, 'Dignity, Plurality and Patentability: The Unfinished Story of *Brüstle v Greenpeance*' (2013) 38 *European Law Review* 92

Hasebe, Y and Pinelli, C, 'Constitutions' in M Tushnet, T Fleiner and C Saunders (eds), *Routledge Handbook of Constitutional Law* (Oxford/New York, Routledge, 2013) 9–20

Héas, F, 'Observations sur le concept de dignité appliqué aux relations de travail' (2010) 746 *Le Droit Ouvrier* 1

Hennette-Vauchez, S, 'A Human Dignitas? Remnants of the Ancient Legal Concept in Contemporary Dignity Jurisprudence' (2011) 9 *International Journal of Constitutional Law* 32

Hepple, B (ed), *The Making of Labour Law in Europe: A Comparative Study of Nine Countries Up to 1945* (London, Mansell Publishing, 1986)
Herdegen, M, 'Artikel 1' in T Maunz and G Dürig (eds), *Grundgesetz Kommentar*, looseleaf edn (Munich, CH Beck Verlag, 2003) 1–58
—— 'Artikel 1' in T Maunz and G Dürig (eds), *Grundgesetz Kommentar*, looseleaf edn (Munich, CH Beck Verlag, 2005) 1–68
Hervey, T and Kenner, J (eds), *Economic and Social Rights under the EU Charter of Fundamental Rights* (Oxford, Hart Publishing, 2003)
Herzfeld Olsson, P, 'The ILO Acquis and EU Labour Law' in M Rönnman (ed), *Labour Law, Fundamental Rights and Social Europe* (Oxford, Hart Publishing, 2011) 27–55
Hessel, S, *Indignez-vous!* (Montpellier, Indigène éditions, 2010)
Hill, TE, *Dignity and Practical Reason in Kant's Moral Theory* (Ithaca, NY, Cornell University Press, 1992)
—— 'Kantian Perspectives on the Rational Basis of Human Dignity' in M Düwell, J Braarvig, R Brownsword and D Mieth (eds), *The Cambridge Handbook of Human Dignity* (Cambridge, Cambridge University Press, 2014) 215–21
Hirschl, R, *Towards Juristocracy: The Origins and Consequences of the New Constitutionalism* (Cambridge, MA, Harvard University Press, 2004)
—— *Constitutional Theocracy* (Cambridge, MA, Harvard University Press, 2010)
Hockenos, P, *Free to Hate: The Rise of the Right in Post-Communist Eastern Europe* (London, Routledge, 1993)
Hofmann, H, 'Die versprochene Menschenwürde' (1993) 118 *Archiv für öffentliches Recht* 357
Holló, A and Erdei, Á (eds), *Selected Decisions of the Constitutional Court of Hungary (1998–2001)* (Budapest, Akadémiai Kiadó, 2005)
Honderich, T, *The Oxford Companion to Philosophy*, 2nd edn (Oxford, Oxford University Press, 2005)
Howard, RE and Donelly, J, 'Human Dignity, Human Rights and Political Regimes' (1986) 80 *American Political Science Review* 801
Hughes, G, 'The Concept of Dignity in the Universal Declaration of Human Rights' (2011) 39 *Journal of Religious Ethics* 1
Hunt, L, *Inventing Human Rights: A History* (NewYork/London, WW Norton & Company, 2008)
Husa, J, *The Constitution of Finland: A Contextual Analysis* (Oxford, Hart Publishing, 2011)
Hutchings, K, *Time and World Politics, Thinking the Present* (Manchester/New York, Manchester University Press, 2008)
Iglesias, T, 'The Dignity of the Individual in the Irish Constitution: The Importance of the Preamble' (2000) 89 *Studies* 19

International Federation of the Red Cross and Red Crescent Societies, *Think Differently: Humanitarian Impacts of the Economic Crisis in Europe* (Geneva, IFRC, 2013)

Ippolito, F and Velluti, S, 'The Relationship Between the CJEU and the ECtHR: The Case of Asylum' in K Dzehtsiarou, T Konstadinides, T Lock and N O'Meara (eds), *Human Rights Law in Europe: The Influence, Overlaps and Contradictions of the EU and ECHR* (London, Routledge, 2014) 156–87

Isaac, JC, 'A New Guarantee on Earth: Hannah Arendt on Human Dignity and the Politics of Human Rights' (1996) 90 *American Political Science Review* 61

Isensee, J, 'Menschenwürde: Die säkuläre Gesellschaft auf der Suche nach dem Absoluten' (2006) 131 *Archiv des öffentlichen Rechts* 173

Ishay, MR, *The History of Human Rights: From Ancien Times to the Globalization Era* (Berkeley, CA, University of California Press, 2004)

Ishay, MR (ed), *The Human Rights Reader: Major Political Essays, Speeches, and Documents from Ancient Times to the Present* (New York, Routledge, 2007)

Jaber, D, *Über den mehrfachen Sinn von Menschenwürde-Garantien: Mit besonderer Berücksichtigung von Art.1 Abs. 1 Grundgesetz* (Frankfurt, Ontos Verlag, 2003)

Jackson, VC, 'Constitutional Dialogue and Human Dignity: States and Transnational Constitutional Discourse' (2004) 65 *Montana Law Review* 15

Jacobs, F, 'Judicial Dialogue and the Cross-Fertilization of Legal Systems: The European Court of Justice' (2003) 38 *Texas International Law Journal* 547

Jarass, H (ed), *Charta der Grundrechte der Europäischen Union unter Einbeziehung der vom EUGH entwickelten Grundrechte und der Grundrechtsregelungen der Verträge: Kommentar* (Munich, CH Beck, 2010)

Jaspers, APCM and Betten, L (eds), *25 Years European Social Charter* (Deventer, Kluwer Law and Taxation Publishers, 1988)

Jeannin, L, 'Le principe de dignité dans l'espace de la Convention Européenne des Droits de l'Homme' in C Girard and S Hennette-Vauchez (eds), *La dignité de la personne humaine: recherche sur un processus de juridicisation* (Paris, Presses Universitaires de France, 2005) 176–88

Jenks, CW, *Human Rights and International Labour Standards* (London, Stevens & Sons Ltd, 1960)

Joerges, C, 'Working Through "Bitter Experiences" Towards a Purified European Identity? A Critique of the Disregard for History in European Constitutional Theory and Practice' in EO Eriksen, C Joerges and F Rödl (eds), *Law, Democracy and Solidarity in a Post-national Union: The Unsettled Political Order of Europe* (Oxford, Routledge, 2008) 173–91

—— 'Europe's Economic Constitution in Crisis and the Emergence of a New Constitutional Constellation' (2014) 15 *German Law Journal* 985
Joerges, C and Ghaleigh, NS (eds), *The Darker Legacies of Law in Europe* (Oxford, Hart Publishing, 2003)
Joerges, C and Rödl, F, 'Informal Politics, Formalised Law and the "Social Deficit" of European Integration' (2009) 15 *European Law Journal* 1
Jonas, H, *Prinzip Verantwortung* (Frankfurt am Main, Suhrkamp, 1989)
Jones, J, '"Common Constitutional Traditions": Can the Meaning of Human Dignity under German Law Guide the European Court of Justice?' (2004) *Public Law* 167
—— 'Human Dignity in the EU Charter of Fundamental Rights and Before the European Court of Justice' (2012) 33 *Liverpool Law Review* 281
Kahn-Freud, O, *Labour Law and Politics in the Weimar Republic* (R Lewis and J Clark (eds), Oxford, Basic Blackwell, 1981)
Kant, I, *Groundwork of the Metaphysics of Morals* (M Gregor (trans and ed), Cambridge, Cambridge University Press, 1991)
—— *The Metaphysics of Morals* (M Gregor (trans and ed), Cambridge, Cambridge University Press, 2009)
Kateb, G, *Human Dignity* (Cambridge, MA, Belknap Press of Harvard University Press, 2011)
Katrougalos, G and O'Connell, P, 'Fundamental Social Rights' in M Tushnet, T Fleiner and C Saunders (eds), *Routledge Handbook of Constitutional Law* (Oxford/New York, Routledge, 2013) 375–86
Keiser, T, 'Europeanization as a Challenge to Legal History' (2006) 5 *German Law Journal* 473
Kemmerer, A, 'Dignified Disciplinarity: Towards a Transdisciplinary Understanding of Human Dignity' in C McCrudden (ed), *Understanding Human Dignity* (Oxford, Oxford University Press, 2013) 649–58
Kenner, J, 'New Frontiers in EU Labour Law: From Flexicurity to Flex-Security' in M Dougan and S Currie (eds), *50 Years of European Treaties: Looking Forward and Thinking Back* (Oxford, Hart Publishing, 2009) 279–310
Kenny, J, 'European Convention and Social Welfare' (2010) 5 *European Human Rights Law Review* 495
Kertész, I, *Être sans destin* (N and C Zaremba (trans), Paris, Actes Sud, 1998)
—— *Fateless* (N and C Zaremba (trans), London, Vintage, 2006)
Kesby, A, *The Right to Have Rights: Citizenship, Humanity and International Law* (Oxford, Oxford Scholarship Online, 2012)
Khaitan, T, 'Dignity as an Expressive Norm: Neither Vacuous Nor a Panacea' (2012) 32 *Oxford Journal of Legal Studies* 1

Kirste, S, 'The Temporality of Law and the Plurality of Social Times: The Problem of Synchronising Different Time Concepts Through Law' in M Troper and A Verza (eds), *Legal Philosophy: General Aspects (Concepts, Rights and Doctrines)* (2002) Beiheft 82 *Archiv für Rechts- und Sozialphilosophie* 23
—— 'Die Zeit der Verfassung' (2008) 56 *Jahrbuch des öffentlichen Rechts der Gegenwart* 35
Klein, A, *La Dignità dell'Uomo nel Pensiero del Rinascimento* (Turin, Giappichelli, 1976)
Klein Goldewijk, B, Contreras Baspineiro, A and Carbonari, PC (eds), *Dignity and Human Rights: The Implementation of Economic, Social and Cultural Rights* (Antwerp, Intersentia, 2002)
Knoepffler, N and O'Malley, M, 'Human Dignity: Regulative Principle and Absolute Value' (2010) 21 *Journal International de Bioéthique* 63
Kochenov, D, 'The Right to Have What Right? EU Citizenship in Need of Clarification' (2013) 19 *European Law Journal* 502
Kohen, A, *In Defense of Human Rights: A Non-religious Grounding in a Pluralistic World* (Oxford, Routledge, 2007)
Kolnai, A, 'Dignity' (1976) 51 *Philosophy* 251
Komárek, J, 'National Constitutional Courts in the European Constitutional Democracy' (2014) 12 *International Journal of Constitutional Law* 525
Kommers, DP, *The Constitutional Jurisprudence of the Federal Republic of Germany* (Durham, NC, Duke University Press, 1997)
—— 'Autonomy, Dignity, Abortion' in T Ginsburg and R Dixon (eds), *Comparative Constitutional Law* (Cheltenham, Edward Elgar, 2011) 441–58
Kondylis, P, 'Würde' in O Brunner, W Conze and R Koselleck (eds), *Geschichtliche Grundbegriffe: Historisches Lexikon zur politisch-sozialen Sprache in Deutschland* (Stuttgart, Klett-Cotta, 1992) vol 7, 645–77
Könemann, B, *Der verfassungsunmittelbare Anspruch auf das Existenzminimum* (Hamburg, Verlag Dr Kovač, 2005)
Kotzé, LJ, 'Human Rights and the Environment in the Anthropocene' (2014) 1 *The Anthropocene Review* 252
Kotzur, M, 'Peter Häberle zum 80. Geburtstag' (2014) 139 *Archiv des öffentlichen Rechts* 287
Kraynak, RP and G Tinder (eds), *In Defense of Human Dignity: Essays for Our Times* (Notre Dame, IN, University of Notre Dame Press, 2003)
Kretzmer, D and Klein, E (eds), *The Concept of Human Dignity in Human Rights Discourse* (The Hague, Kluwer Law International, 2002)
Kumm, M, 'Who is the Final Arbiter of Constitutionality in Europe?: Three Conceptions of the Relationship Between the German Federal Constitutional Court and the European Court of Justice' (1999) 36 *Common Market Law Review* 351

Landemore, H, 'Inclusive Constitution-Making: The Icelandic Experiment' (2014) *Journal of Political Philosophy* 1

Leader, S, 'Inflating Consent, Inflating Function, and Inserting Human Rights' in J Dine and A Fagan (eds), *Human Rights and Capitalism: A Multidisciplinary Perspective on Globalisation* (Cheltenham, Edward Elgar, 2006) 28–47

Lefort, C, *Democracy and Political Theory* (D Mace (trans), Minneapolis, MN, University of Minnesota Press, 1988)

—— *L'Invention démocratique: les limites de la domination totalitaire* (Paris, Fayard, 1994)

Leigh, I and Ahdhar, R, 'Post-Secularism and the European Court of Human Rights: or How God Never Really Went Away' (2012) 75 *Modern Law Review* 1064

Leijten, I, 'The German Right to an *Existenzminimum*, Human Dignity and the Possibility of a Minimum Core Socioeconomic Rights Protection' (2015) 16 *German Law Journal* 23

Leisner, WG, *Existenzsicherung im öffentlichen Recht, Minimum, Grundlagen, Förderung* (Tübingen, Mohr Siebeck, 2007)

Lembcke, OW and Boulanger, C, 'Between Revolution and Constitution: The Roles of the Hungarian Constitutional Court' in GA Tóth (ed), *Constitution for a Disunited Nation: On Hungary's 2011 Fundamental Law* (Budapest, Central European University Press, 2012) 269–99

Lenaerts, K, 'Interlocking Legal Orders in the European Union and Comparative Law' (2003) 52 *International and Comparative Law Quarterly* 873

Lendvai, P, *Hungary Between Democracy and Authoritarianism* (London, Hurst & Company, 2012)

Lenze, A, 'Gleichheitssatz und Generationengerechtigkeit' (2007) 46 *Der Staat* 89

Letsas, G, *A Theory of Interpretation of the European Convention on Human Rights* (Oxford, Oxford University Press, 2007)

—— 'Strasbourg's Interpretive Ethic: Lessons for the International Lawyer' (2010) 21 *European Journal of International Law* 527

Lohmann, G, 'Human Dignity and Socialism' in M Düwell, J Braarvig, R Brownsword and D Mieth (eds), *The Cambridge Handbook of Human Dignity* (Cambridge, Cambridge University Press, 2014) 126–34

Lörcher, K, 'The New Social Dimension in the Jurisprudence of the European Court of Human Rights (ECtHR): The *Demir and Baykara* Judgment: its Methodology and Follow-up' in F Dorssemont, K Lörcher and I Schömann (eds), *The European Convention on Human Rights and the Employment Relation* (Oxford, Hart Publishing, 2013) 4–46

—— 'The Future of the European Court of Human Rights in the Light of the Brighton Declaration' in F Dorssemont, K Lörcher and I Schömann (eds), *The European Convention on Human Rights and the Employment Relation* (Oxford, Hart Publishing, 2013) 93–104

Lotito, P, 'Art. 25: The Rights of the Elderly' in BT Mock and G Demuro (eds), *Human Rights in Europe: Commentary on the Charter of Fundamental Rights of the European Union* (Durham, NC, Carolina Academic Press, 2010) 158–64

Maas, W, 'The Origins, Evolution, and Political Objectives of EU Citizenship' (2014) 15 *German Law Journal* 797

Macklin, R, 'Human Dignity is a Useless Concept: It Means No More than Respect for Persons or their Autonomy' (2003) 327 *British Medical Journal* 1419

Mahlmann, M, *Elemente einer ethischen Grundrechtstheorie* (Baden-Baden, Nomos Verlag, 2008)

—— 'The Basic Law at 60: Human Dignity and the Culture of Republicanism' (2010) 11 *German Law Journal* 9

—— 'Six Antidotes to Dignity Fatigue in Ethics and Law' in C McCrudden (ed), *Understanding Dignity* (Oxford, Oxford University Press, 2013) 593–614

Maillard, S, *L'émergence de la citoyenneté sociale Européenne* (Aix en Provence, Presses Universitaires de Aix-Marseille, 2008)

—— 'L'émergence de la citoyenneté sociale Européenne' (2009) *Droit Social* 88

Mak, E, *Judicial Decision-Making in a Globalised World: A Comparative Analysis of the Changing Practices of Western Highest Courts* (Oxford, Hart Publishing, 2013)

Manent, P, *Cours familier de philosophie politique* (Paris, Gallimard, 2011)

Mantouvalou, V, 'Labour Rights in the European Convention on Human Rights: An Intellectual Justification for an Integrated Approach to Interpretation' (2013) 13 *Human Rights Law Review* 529

—— 'The Prohibition of Slavery, Servitude and Forced Labour and Compulsory Labour under Article 4 ECHR' in F Dorssemont, K Lörcher and I Schömann (eds), *The European Convention on Human Rights and the Employment Relation* (Oxford, Hart Publishing, 2013) 143–58

—— 'Workers Without Rights as Citizens at the Margins' (2013) 16 *Critical Review of International Social and Political Philosophy* 366

Marcus Helmons, S (ed), *Dignité humaine et hiérarchie des valeurs: les limites irréductibles* (Brussels, Bruylant, 1999)

Margalit, A, *The Decent Society* (N Goldblum (trans), Cambridge, MA, Harvard University Press, 1996

Marhaun, T, *Menschenwürde und Völkerrecht* (Tübingen, Köhler-Druck, 2001)

Markesinis, B and Fedtke, J (eds), 'The Judge as a Comparatist', Special Issue (2005) 80 *Tulane Law Review* 11

Marks, Susan, 'The European Convention on Human Rights and its "Democratic Society"' (1996) 66 *British Yearbook of International Law* 209

Marks, Stephen P, 'Poverty' in D Moeckli, S Shah and S Sivakumara (eds), *International Human Rights Law*, 2nd edn (Oxford, Oxford University Press, 2014) 567–89

Marshall, TH, *Citizenship and Social Class and Other Essays* (Cambridge, Cambridge University Press, 1950)

Martens, Ph, 'Encore la dignité humaine: réflexion d'un juge sur la promotion par les juges d'une norme suspecte' in *Mélanges en Hommage à P Lambert* (Brussels, Bruylant, 1999) 561

Mathieu, B, 'Bioéthique: un juge constitutionnel réservé face aux défis de la science' (1994) *Revue Française de Droit Administratif* 1019

—— 'Pour une reconnaissance de "principes matriciels" en matière de protection constitutionnelle des droits de l'Homme (1)' (1995) *Recueil Dalloz Sirey (Chronique)* 211

Mathis, K (ed), *Efficiency, Sustainability, and Justice to Future Generations* (Dordrecht, Springer, 2011)

Mattioni, A, 'Profili Costituzionali della Dignità Umana' (2008) 2–3 *Rivista di Scienze Giuridiche* 251

Maurer, B, *Le principe du respect de la dignité humaine dans la Convention Européenne des Droits de l'Homme* (Paris, La Documentation Française, 1999)

McCann, D, 'Decent Working Hours as a Human Right: Intersections in the Regulation of Working Time' in C Fenwick and T Novitz (eds), *Human Rights at Work: Perspectives on Law and Regulation* (Oxford, Hart Publishing, 2010) 509–28

McCrudden, C, 'Human Dignity and Judicial Interpretation of Human Rights' (2008) 19 *European Journal of International Law* 655

McCrudden, C (ed), *Understanding Dignity* (Oxford, Oxford University Press, 2013)

Menéndez, AJ, 'A Pious Europe? Why Europe Should Not Define Itself as Christian' (2005) 30 *European Law Review* 133

—— 'The Existential Crisis of the European Union' (2013) 14 *German Law Journal* 454

—— 'Which Citizenship? Whose Europe: The Many Paradoxes of European Citizenship' (2014) 15 *German Law Journal* 907

Menéndez, AJ and Eriksen, EO (eds), *Arguing Fundamental Rights* (Vienna, Springer, 2006)

Menke, C, 'Dignity as the Right to Have Rights: Human Dignity in Hannah Arendt' in M Düwell, J Braarvig, R Brownsword and D Mieth (eds), *The Cambridge Handbook of Human Dignity* (Cambridge, Cambridge University Press, 2014) 332–42

Meyer, J (ed), *Kommentar zur Charta der Grundrechte der Europäischen Union*, 4th edn (Baden-Baden, Nomos Verlag, 2014)

Meyer, MJ, 'Kant's Concept of Dignity and Modern Political Thought' (1987) 8 *History of Political Ideas* 319

Miccù, R and Pernice, I (eds), *The European Constitution in the Making* (Baden-Baden, Nomos, 2004)

Michalowski, S, 'Art.3: The Right to Integrity of the Person' in S Peers, T Hervey, J Kenner and A Ward (eds), *The EU Charter of Fundamental Rights: A Commentary* (Oxford, CH Beck/Hart Publishing/Nomos, 2014) 39–60

Mikołajczyk, B, 'Is the ECHR Ready for Global Ageing?' (2013) 17 *International Journal of Human Rights* 511

Mock, BT and Demuro, G (eds), *Human Rights in Europe: Commentary on the Charter of Fundamental Rights of the European Union* (Durham, NC, Carolina Academic Press, 2010)

Moller, K, 'On Treating Persons as Ends: The German Aviation Security Act, Human Dignity, and the German Federal Constitutional Court' (2006) *Public Law* 457

Möllers, C, 'Democracy and Human Dignity: Limits of a Moralized Conception of Rights in German Constitutional Law' (2009) 42 *Israel Law Review* 416

Moltmann, J, *On Human Dignity: Political Theology and Ethics* (Minneapolis, MN, Fortress Press, 2007)

Morange, J, *La Déclaration des Droits de l'Homme et du Citoyen (26 août 1789)* (Paris, Presses Universitaires de France, 1989)

—— 'La dignité humaine en tant que composante de l'ordre public: l'inattendu retour en droit administratif Français d'un concept controversé' (2008) 5 *Revue Française de Droit Administratif* 979

Morgera, E and Marín Durán, G, 'Article 37: Environmental Protection' in S Peers, T Hervey, J Kenner and A Ward (eds), *The EU Charter of Fundamental Rights: A Commentary* (Oxford, CH Beck/Hart Publishing, 2014) 983–1003

Morijn, J, 'Balancing Fundamental Rights and Common Market Freedoms in Union Law: *Schmidberger* and *Omega* in the Light of the European Constitution' (2006) 12 *European Law Journal* 15

Morsink, J, *The Universal Declaration of Human Rights: Origins, Drafting and Intent* (Philadelphia, PA, University of Pennsylvania Press, 1999)

Mowbray, A, 'The Creativity of the European Court of Human Rights' (2005) 5 *Human Rights Law Review* 57

Moyn, S, 'The Secret History of Constitutional Dignity' in C McCrudden (ed), *Understanding Human Dignity* (Oxford, Oxford University Press, 2013) 95–113

Mückenberger, U, 'Time Abstraction, Temporal Policy and the Right to One's Own Time' (2011) 11 *Kronoscope* 66

Müller, JW, 'Should the EU Protect Democracy and the Rule of Law Inside Member States?' (2015) 21 *European Law Journal* 141

Munby, J, 'Dignity, Happiness and Human Rights' (2011) *Elder Law Journal* 32

—— 'What Price Dignity?' (2012) 15 *Community Care Law Report* 5

Neal, M, '"Not Gods but Animals": Human Dignity and Vulnerable Subjecthood' (2012) 33 *Liverpool Law Review* 177

Nicol, D, *The Constitutional Protection of Capitalism* (Oxford, Hart Publishing, 2010)

Nipperdey, HC (ed), *Die Grundrechte und Grundpflichten der Reichsverfassung: Kommentar zum zweiten Teil der Reichsverfassung, Dritter Band* (Kronberg, Scriptor Verlag, 1930)

Nira, R, 'Articolo 41' in R Bifulco, A Celotto and M Olivetti (eds), *Commentario alla Costituzione* (Turin, UTET, 2006) 846–63

Nolte, G (ed), *European and US Constitutionalism* (Cambridge, Cambridge University Press, 2005)

Nowak, M and Charbord, A, 'Article 4: Prohibition of Torture and Inhuman or Degrading Treatment or Punishment' in S Peers, T Hervey, J Kenner and A Ward (eds), *The EU Charter of Fundamental Rights: A Commentary* (Oxford, CH Beck/Hart Publishing/Nomos, 2014) 61–100

Nowotny, H, *Eigenzeit, Enstehung und Strukturierung eines Zeitgefühles* (Frankfurt am Main, Suhrkamp, 1989)

—— *Time, The Modern and Postmodern Experience* (N Plaice (trans), Cambridge, Polity Press, 1994)

Ober, J, 'Democracy's Dignity' (2012) 106 *American Political Science Review* 827

O'Cinneide, C, 'A Modest Proposal: Destitution, State Responsibility and the European Convention on Human Rights' (2008) 8 *European Human Rights Law Review* 583

—— 'Article 25: The Rights of the Elderly' in S Peers, T Hervey, J Kenner and A Ward (eds), *The EU Charter of Fundamental Rights: A Commentary* (Oxford, CH Beck/Hart Publishing/Nomos, 2014) 693–707

O'Connell, R, 'The Right to Work in the ECHR' (2012) 2 *European Human Rights Law Review* 176

O'Dowd, TJ, 'Dignity and Personhood in Irish Constitutional Law' in G Quinn, A Tingram and S Livingstone (eds), *Justice and Legal Theory in Ireland* (Dublin, Oak Tree Press, 1995) 163–83

Offe, C, 'Europe Entrapped: Does the EU have the Political Capacity to Overcome its Current Crisis?' (2013) 19 *European Law Journal* 595

Olivetti, M, 'Article 1: Human Dignity' in BT Mockand G Demuro (eds), *Human Rights in Europe: Commentary on the Charter of Fundamental Rights of the European Union* (Durham, NC, North Carolina University Press, 2010) 3–11

O'Mahony, C, 'There is No Such Thing as a Right to Human Dignity' (2012) 10 *International Journal of Constitutional Law* 551

O'Neill, O, *Constructions of Reason: Explorations of Kant's Practical Philosophy* (Cambridge, Cambridge University Press, 1989)

Orgad, L, 'The Preamble in Constitutional Interpretation' (2010) 8 *International Journal of Constitutional Law* 714

Ost, F, *Le temps du droit* (Paris, Odile Jacob, 1999)

—— 'Le temps, quatrième dimension des droits de l'Homme' in M Borghi and P Meyer-Bisch (eds), *Société civile et indivisibilité des droits de l'Homme* (Fribourg, Editions Universitaires de Fribourg, 2000) 109–30

Ost, F and Van Hoecke, M (eds), *Time and Law: Is it the Nature of Law to Last?* (Brussels, Bruylant, 1998)

Palonen, K, Pulkkinen, T and Rosales, JM (eds), *The Ashgate Research Companion to the Politics of Democratization in Europe* (Farnham, Ashgate, 2008)

Pavia, ML and Revet, T (eds), *La dignité de la personne humaine* (Paris, Economica, 1999)

Peers, S, 'The EU's Accession to the ECHR: The Dream Becomes a Nightmare' (2015) 16 *German Law Journal* 214

Peers, S, Hervey, T, Kenner, J and Ward, A (eds), *The EU Charter of Fundamental Rights: A Commentary* (Oxford, CH Beck/Hart Publishing/Nomos, 2014)

Peers, S and Prechal, S, 'Article 52: Scope and Interpretation of Rights and Principles' in S Peers, T Hervey, J Kenner and A Ward (eds), *The EU Charter of Fundamental Rights: A Commentary* (Oxford, CH Beck/Hart Publishing, 2014) 1455–1521

Peers, S and Ward, A (eds), *The European Union Charter of Fundamental Rights* (Oxford, Hart Publishing, 2004)

Pernice, I, 'Multilevel Constitutionalism in the European Union' (2002) 27 *European Law Review* 511

Pernice, I *et al* (eds), *Konstitutionalisierung jenseits des Staates: Zur Verfassung der Weltgemeinschaft und den Gründungsverträgen internationaler Organisationen* (Baden-Baden, Nomos Verlag, 2002)

Perry, MJ, *Toward a Theory of Human Rights: Religion, Law, Courts* (Cambridge, Cambridge University Press, 2007)

Petkova, B, 'Three Levels of Dialogue in Precedent Formation at the CJEU and ECtHR' in K Dzehtsiarou, T Konstadinides, T Lock and N O'Meara (eds), *Human Rights Law in Europe: The Influence, Overlaps and Contradictions of the EU and ECHR* (London, Routledge, 2014) 73–91

Picker, E, *Menschenwürde und Menschenleben: Das Auseinderdriften zweier fundamentaler Werte als Ausdruck der wachsenden Relativierung des Menschen* (Stuttgart, Klett-Cotta, 2002)
Pignagnoli, FS (ed), *Giovanni Pico della Mirandola: La Dignità dell'Uomo* (Bologna, Edizioni Scolastiche Pàtron, 1969)
Pliakos, A and Agnanostaras, G, 'Who is the Ultimate Arbiter? The Battle over Judicial Supremacy in EU Law' (2011) 36 *European Law Review* 109
Pogany, I, *Righting Wrongs in Eastern Europe* (Manchester, Manchester University Press, 1997)
—— 'The Crisis of Democracy in East Central Europe: The "New Constitutionalism" in Hungary' (2013) 19 *European Public Law* 341
Polanyi, K, *The Great Transformation: The Political and Economic Origins of Our Time*, 2nd edn (Boston, NJ, Beacon Press, 1951)
Popper, K, *The Open Society and its Enemy*, 5th edn (Princeton, NJ, Princeton University Press, 1966)
Preuss, UK, 'The Implications of "Eternity Clauses": The German Experience' (2011) 44 *Israel Law Review* 429
Radnóti, S, 'A Sacred Symbol in a Secular Country: The Holy Crown' in GA Tóth (ed), *Constitution for a Disunited Nation: On Hungary's 2011 Fundamental Law* (Budapest, Central European University Press, 2012) 85–110
Ramm, T, 'Epilogue: The New Ordering of Labour Law 1918–45' in B Hepple (ed), *The Making of Labour Law in Europe: A Comparative Study of Nine Countries Up to 1945* (London, Mansell Publishing, 1986) 277–300
Rao, N, 'On the Use and Abuse of Dignity in Constitutional Law' (2008) 14 *Columbia Journal of European Law* 201
—— 'Three Concepts of Dignity in Constitutional Law' (2011) 86 *Notre Dame Law Review* 18
Rau, M and Schorkopf, F, 'Der EuGH und die Menschenwürde' (2002) 34 *Neue Juristische Wochenschrift* 2448
Réaume, D, 'Dignity, Choice and Circumstances' in C McCrudden (ed), *Understanding Human Dignity* (Oxford, Oxford University Press, 2013) 539–58
Reich, N, 'A European Constitution for Citizens: Reflections on the Rethinking of Union and Community Law' (1997) 3 *European Law Journal* 13
—— 'Union Citizenship: Metaphor or Source of Rights' (2000) 7 *European Law Journal* 4
Revenga Sánchez, M, 'La dignité dans la jurisprudence constitutionnelle Espagnole' in L Burgogne-Larsen (ed), *La dignité saisie par les juges en Europe* (Brussels, Bruylant, 2010) 199–216

Rials, S (ed), *La Déclaration des Droits de l'Homme et du Citoyen* (Paris, Hachette, 1988)
Rifkin, J, *Time Wars: The Primary Conflict in Human History* (New York, Henry Holt and Company, 1987)
Riley, S, 'Human Dignity: Comparative and Conceptual Debates' (2010) 6 *International Journal of Law in Context* 117
—— 'The Function of Human Dignity' (2013) 5 *Amsterdam Law Forum* 90
Rodgers, G, Lee, E, Swepston, L and Van Daele, J, *The ILO and the Quest for Social Justice, 1919–2009* (Geneva, International Labour Organization, 2009)
Rödl, F, 'Constitutional Integration of Labour Constitutions' in EO Eriksen, C Joerges and F Rödl (eds), *Law, Democracy and Solidarity in a Post-national Union: The Unsettled Political Order of Europe* (Oxford, Routledge, 2008) 152–71
Roermund, B van, 'The Embryo and its Rights: Technology and Teleology' (2013) 14 *German Law Journal* 1939
Rolla, G, 'Profili Costituzionali della Dignità Umana' in E Ceccherini (ed), *La Tutela della Dignità dell'Uomo* (Naples, Editoriale Scientifica, 2008) 57–78
Roman, D, *Le droit public face à la pauvreté* (Paris, Librairie Générale de Droit et de Jurisprudence, 2002)
—— 'Le principe de dignité dans la doctrine de droit social' in C Girard and S Hennette-Vauchez (eds), *La dignité de la personne humaine: recherche sur un processus de juridicisation* (Paris, Presses Universitaires de France, 2004) 70–87
Rönnman, M (ed), *Labour Law, Fundamental Rights and Social Europe* (Oxford, Hart Publishing, 2011)
Rosa, H, *Accélération, une critique sociale du temps* (Paris, La Découverte, 2010)
Rosanvallon, P, *Le sacre du citoyen: histoire du suffrage universel en France* (Paris, Gallimard, 1992)
—— *La crise de l'État providence* (Paris, Seuil, 1992)
Rosen, M, *Dignity: Its History and Meaning* (Cambridge, MA, Harvard University Press, 2012)
Rozakis, CL, 'The European Judge as a Comparatist' (2005) 80 *Tulane Law Review* 257
Roznai, Y, 'Unconstitutional Constitutional Amendments: The Migration and Success of a Constitutional Idea' (2013) 61 *American Journal of Comparative Law* 657
Ruggeri, A, 'Appunti per uno Studio sulla Dignità dell'Uomo, Secondo Diritto Costituzionale' (2011) 1 *Rivista Telematica dell'Associazione Italiana dei Costituzionalisti* 1
Sadurski, W, *Constitutionalism and the Enlargement of Europe* (Oxford, Oxford University Press, 2012)

Sajó, A, 'How the Rule of Law Killed Hungarian Welfare Reform' (1996) 5 *East European Constitutional Review* 31

—— *Limiting Government: An Introduction to Constitutionalism* (Budapest, Central University Press, 1999)

Samuel, L, *Fundamental Social Rights: Case Law of the European Social Charter* (Strasbourg, Council of Europe Publishing, 1997)

Sanchez Agesta, L, 'Die Entwicklung der spanischen Verfassung seit 1936' (1961) 10 *Jahrbuch des öffentlichen Rechts* 397

Sandkühler, HJ (ed), *Menschenwürde: philosophische, theologische und juristische Analysen* (Frankfurt am Main, Peter Lang, 2007)

Scheinin, M (ed), *The Welfare State and Constitutionalism: Nordic Perspectives* (Århus, Phønix -Trykkeriet A/S, 2001)

Schiemann, K, 'A Response to *The Judge as a Comparatist*' (2005) 80 *Tulane Law Review* 281

Schnapper, D, *La démocratie providentielle: essai sur l'égalité contemporaine* (Paris, Gallimard, 2002)

Schwartz, H, *The Struggle for Constitutional Justice in Post Communist Europe* (Chicago, IL, Chicago University Press, 2000)

Schwarzburg, K, *Die Menschenwürde im Recht der europäischen Union* (Baden-Baden, Nomos, 2012)

Scott, RJ, 'Dignité/Dignidade: Organizing Against Threats to Dignity in Societies after Slavery' in C McCrudden (ed), *Understanding Human Dignity* (Oxford, Oxford University Press, 2013) 61–77

Sensen, O, *Kant on Human Dignity* (Berlin, De Gruyter, 2011)

Sharon Schwartz, L (ed), *The Emergence of Memory: Conversations with WG Sebald* (NewYork, Seven Stories Press, 2010)

Siegel, R, 'Dignity and Sexuality: Claims on Dignity in Transnational Debates over Abortion and Same-sex Marriage' (2012) 10 *International Journal of Constitutional Law* 355

Simonin, A 'La dignité de la personne humaine n'est pas une idée révolutionnaire' in C Girard and S Hennette-Vauchez (eds), *La dignité de la personne humaine: recherche sur un processus de juridicisation* (Paris, Presses Universitaires de France, 2004) 309–13

Skalski, J, *La révolution des casseroles: chronique d'une nouvelle constitution pour l'Islande* (Clamecy, La Contre Allée, 2012)

Skinner, S, 'The Core of *McCann:* Lethal Force and Democracy under the ECHR' in C Ovey *et al* (eds), *The Right to Life: Twenty Years of Legal Developments since McCann v The United Kingdom, Publication in Honour of the Deputy Registrar of the European Court of Human Rights Michael O'Boyle* (2015, forthcoming)

—— 'Crimes against the State and the Intersection of Fascism and Democracy in the 1920s–30s: Vilification, Seditious Libel and the Limits of Legality'(forthcoming, 2015)

Skinner, S (ed), *Fascism and Criminal Law: History, Theory, Continuity* (Oxford, Hart Publishing, 2015)

Smith, CT and Fetzer, T, 'The Uncertain Limits of the European Court of Justice's Authority: Economic Freedom versus Human Dignity' (2004) 10 *Columbia Journal of European Law* 445

Sólyom, L, 'Normenhierarchie in der Verfassung und verfassungswidrige Vefassungsänderungen' (2014) 55 *Jahrbuch für Ostrecht* 11

Sólyom, L and Brunner G (eds), *Verfassungsgerichtsbarkeit in Ungarn: Analysen und Enscheidungssammlung, 1990–1993* (Baden-Baden, Nomos, 1995)

—— *Constitutional Judiciary in a New Democracy: The Hungarian Constitutional Court* (Ann Arbor, MI, University of Michigan Press, 2000)

Somek, A, 'Constitutional Erinnerungsarbeit: Ambivalence and Translation' (2006) 5 *German Law Journal* 357

Soskice, J, 'Human Dignity and the Image of God' in C McCrudden (ed), *Understanding Human Dignity* (Oxford, Oxford University Press, 2013) 229–43

Spencer, MP, 'Producing Time and Space: Academic Work after Henri Lefebvre' (2013) 33 *Legal Studies* 478

Spranger, TM, 'Case Note' (2002) 39 *Common Market Law Review* 1147

Steenbakkers, P, 'Human Dignity in Renaissance Humanism' in M Düwell, J Braarvig, R Brownsword and D Mieth (eds), *The Cambridge Handbook of Human Dignity* (Cambridge, Cambridge University Press, 2014) 85–94

Steigleder, K, 'Human Dignity and Social Welfare' in M Düwell, J Braarvig, R Brownsword and D Mieth (eds), *The Cambridge Handbook of Human Dignity* (Cambridge, Cambridge University Press, 2014) 472–76

Stolz, J, *Hongrie: apprentie sorcière du nationalisme* (Paris, Éditions du Cygne, 2012)

Stone, A, *The Birth of Judicial Politics in France* (Oxford, Oxford University Press, 1992)

Stuckler, D and Basu, B, *The Body Economic: Why Austerity Kills* (New York, Basic Books, 2013)

Supiot, A, *The Spirit of Philadelphia: Social Justice v the Total Market* (S Brown (trans), London, Verso, 2012)

Teitel, R, *Transitional Justice* (Oxford, Oxford University Press, 2010)

Testard, J 'Repenser la procréation médicalement assistée', *Le Monde Diplomatique*, April 2014, 28

—— *Faire des enfants demain* (Paris, Seuil, 2014)

Thompson, EP, 'Time, Work-Discipline, and Industrial Capitalism' (1967) 38 *Past and Present* 56

Tiedemann, P, *Menschenwürde als Rechtsbegriff: eine philosophische Klärung* (Berlin, Berliner Wissenschafts-Verlag, 2007)

Tissot, O, 'Pour une analyse juridique du concept de "dignité" du salarié' (1995) *Droit Social* 972

Tollefsen, C, 'The Dignity of Marriage' in C McCrudden (ed), *Understanding Human Dignity* (Oxford, Oxford University Press, 2013) 483–500

Torres Perez, A, 'Melloni in Three Acts: From Dialogue to Monologue' (2014) *European Constitutional Law Review* 308

Tóth, GA (ed), *Constitution for a Disunited Nation: Hungary's New Fundamental Law* (Budapest, Central European University Press, 2012)

Triska JF (ed), *Constitutions of the Communist Party-States* (Stanford, CA, Hoover Institution Publications, 1968)

Tushnet, M, Fleiner, T and Saunders, C (eds), *Routledge Handbook of Constitutional Law* (Oxford/New York, Routledge, 2013)

—— *Advanced Introduction to Comparative Constitutional Law* (Cheltenham, Edward Elgar, 2014)

Unruh, P, *Die Herrschaft der Vernunft: zur Staatsphilosophie Immanuel Kants* (Baden-Baden, Nomos, 1993)

—— *Weimar Staatslehre und Grundgesetz: ein verfassungstheoretischer Vergleich* (Berlin, Duncker und Humblot, 2004)

—— 'Kant—Menschenwürde—Sozialstaat' in R Grote *et al* (eds), *Die Ordnung der Freiheit: Festschriftf. Christian Starck zum 70. Geburtstag* (Tübingen, Mohr Siebeck, 2007) 133–50

Valadier, P, 'Jacques Maritain's Personalist Conception of Human Dignity' in M Düwell, J Braarvig, R Brownsword and D Mieth (eds), *The Cambridge Handbook of Human Dignity* (Cambridge, Cambridge University Press, 2014) 260–68

Varjú, M, *European Union Human Rights Law: The Dynamics of Interpretation and Context* (Cheltenham, Edward Elgar, 2014)

Veil, S, *Redécouvrir le préambule de la Constitution: Rapport au Président de la République* (Paris, La Documentation Française, 2008)

Veneziani, B, 'La Costituzione Europea, il Diritto del Lavoro e le Icone della Solidarietà' in B Bercusson, U Carabelli, B Trentin, C Vigneau and L Zoppoli (eds), *Costituzione Europea: Quale Futuro?* (Rome, Ediesse, 2006) 9–92

Verdrussen, M (ed), *La justice constitutionnelle en Europe centrale* (Brussels, Bruylant, 1997)

Vergottini, G de (ed), *Giustizia Costituzionale e Sviluppo Democratico nei Paesi dell'Europa Centro-Orientale* (Turin, G Giappichelli, 2000)

Vincenti, U, *Diritti e Dignità Umana* (Rome, Editori Laterza, 2009)

Vincze, A and Varjú, M, 'Hungary: The New Basic Law' (2012) 18 *European Public Law* 437

Virilio, P, *Le Futurisme de l'Instant* (Paris, Galilée, 2009)

Vöncky, S and Wolfrum, R (eds), *Human Dignity and Human Cloning* (Leiden, Martinus Nijhoff Publishing, 2004)

Waldron, J, *Dignity, Rank and Rights* (Oxford, Oxford University Press, 2012)
—— 'How Law Protects Dignity' (2012) 71 *Cambridge Law Journal* 200
—— 'Citizenship and Dignity' in C McCrudden (ed), *Understanding Dignity* (Oxford, Oxford University Press, 2013) 327–43
Walker, N, 'The Idea of Constitutional Pluralism in the European Union' (2002) 65 *Modern Law Review* 365
Weiler, J and Wind, M (eds), *European Constitutionalism Beyond the State* (Cambridge, Cambridge University Press, 2003)
Weinrib, L, 'Human Dignity as Rights-Protecting Principle' (2004) 17 *National Journal of Constitutional Law* 325
Weiß, W, 'Human Rights in the EU: Rethinking the Role of the European Convention on Human Rights after Lisbon' (2011) 7 *European Constitutional Law Review* 64
Wetz, FJ, 'Die Würde des Menschen—Ein Phantom?' (2001) 87 *Archiv für Rechts-und Sozialphilosophie* 315
Wetz, FJ (ed), *Texte zur Menschenwürde* (Stuttgart, Reclam, 2011)
White, R, 'Article 34: Social Security and Social Assistance' in S Peers, T Hervey, J Kenner and A Ward (eds), *The EU Charter of Fundamental Rights: A Commentary* (Oxford, CH Beck/Hart Publishing/Nomos, 2014) 927–49
Whitman, JQ, 'The European Transformation of Harassment Law: Discrimination versus Dignity' (2003) 9 *Columbia Journal of European Law* 241
—— 'On Nazi "Honour" and Dignity' in C Joerges and NS Ghaleigh (eds), *The Darker Legacies of Law in Europe* (Oxford, Hart Publishing, 2003) 243–66
Wicks, E, 'The Meaning of "Life": Dignity and the Right to Life in International Human Rights Treaties' (2012) 12 *Human Rights Law Review* 199
Will, R, 'Die Menschenwürde: Zwischen Versprechen und Überforderung' in F Roggan (ed), *Mit Recht für Menschenwürde und Verfassungsstaat: Festgabe für Dr Burkhart Hirsch* (Berlin, Berlin Wissenschaftsverlag, 2006) 29–46
Williams, A, 'Enlargement of the EU and Human Rights Conditionality: A Policy of Distinction?' (2000) 25 *European Law Review* 610
Wilsher, D, 'Law and the Financial Crisis: Searching for Europe's New Gold Standard' (2014) 20 *European Law Journal* 241
Winkler, IT and Mahler, C, 'Interpreting the Right to a Dignified Minimum Existence: A New Era in German Socio-Economic Rights Jurisprudence?' (2013) 13 *Human Rights Law Review* 199

Wolfram, K, 'Die Rolle der Menschenwürde in der EU-Verfassungsdebatte' in M Fisher (ed), *Der Begriff der Menschenwürde: Definition, Belastbarkeit und Grenzen* (Frankfurt am Main, Peter Lang, 2005) 27–46
Wolin, S, 'What Time is It?' (1997) 1 *Theory & Event* 1
Woolf, V, *A Room of One's Own* (London, Penguin Books, 1928, reprinted 2000)
Youngs, R, 'Germany: Shooting Down Aircraft and Analyzing Computer Data' (2008) 6 *International Journal of Constitutional Law* 331

Index

www.ingramcontent.com/pod-product-compliance
Ingram Content Group UK Ltd.
Pitfield, Milton Keynes, MK11 3LW, UK
UKHW020138290926
15471UKWH00003B/564